Civil Procedure in Bulgaria

Civil Procedure in Bulgaria

Valentina Popova

This book was originally published as a monograph in the International Encyclopaedia of Laws/Civil Procedure.

Founding Editor: Roger Blanpain
General Editor: Frank Hendrickx
Volume Editor: Wannes Vandenbussche

Wolters Kluwer

Published by:
Kluwer Law International B.V.
PO Box 316
2400 AH Alphen aan den Rijn
The Netherlands
E-mail: lrs-sales@wolterskluwer.com
Website: www.wolterskluwer.com/en/solutions/kluwerlawinternational

Sold and distributed by:
Wolters Kluwer Legal & Regulatory U.S.
7201 McKinney Circle
Frederick, MD 21704
United States of America
E-mail: customer.service@wolterskluwer.com

ISBN 978-94-035-4925-5

e-Book: ISBN 978-94-035-4545-5
web-PDF: ISBN 978-94-035-4555-4

The Author

Valentina Popova was born on 7 September 1957 in the town of Blagoevgrad, Bulgaria. In 1981 she graduated summa cum laude from the Faculty of Law of Sofia University (Bulgaria) 'Saint Kliment Ohridski'.

During 1981–1982, she was an apprentice at law in the District Court of Blagoevgrad. In 1982, she worked as a jurisconsult in Blagoevgrad. During 1982–1985, she was a junior judge in the District Court of Blagoevgrad, and, under an Ordinance of the Ministry of Justice, she also worked as a judge at Blagoevgrad Regional Court.

Since 1986 she has been working at the Faculty of Law of Sofia University 'Saint Kliment Ohridski' where she is currently Professor of Civil Procedure Law. She is holding the same position at the Southwest University in Blagoevgrad, Bulgaria. Popova has served two terms as the Chair of the Control Board of the Sofia University 'Saint Kliment Ohridski'. Currently, she is the ombudsman of Sofia University 'Saint Kliment Ohridski'.

In 2001, she received her PhD in Law defending a PhD thesis on 'The Defence Against Withholding in Adversary Proceedings'. Her professorial thesis was on the European Civil Procedure and Part Seven of the Bulgarian Civil Procedure Code.

She is a member of the Union of Lawyers and the Union of Research Associates in Bulgaria. Since 1994 she has also been working as an attorney. She is an arbitrator at both the Commercial Arbitration Court of the National Foundation of Lawyers and the Arbitration Court of the Association of Microenterprises and a member of its Presidential Council.

During 1992–1993, she specialized in Germany and France on the topic 'The Court as a Justice Administering Body' under NATO's programme 'Democratic Institutions'. In 1993, she specialized in bankruptcy at the University of Geneva. In 2011 and 2012, she specialized in Insolvency in Bulgarian and German Law at the Law Faculty, University of Saarland, Saarbruecken, Germany. She was a participant in the XIII World Congress of Procedural Law, Salvador de Bahia, Brazil; in the XIV World Congress on Procedural Justice, Heidelberg, Germany, 25–30 July 2011; in the XVI World Congress on Procedural Justice in Japan; and in many other international scientific forums.

She has worked as an expert in the working groups on bankruptcy. She takes part in the legislative activity by giving expert opinion about bills regarding amendments to the old and new Civil Procedure Code and the new Bank Bankruptcy Act. She participates as a lecturer in seminars on bankruptcy, civil procedure matters (enforcement procedure, inclusive) and on European civil procedure matters for practising lawyers.

Prof. Popova has authored the following monographs: 'Withholding. Substantive Law Issues', Sofia, 1993, 1st edition; 2002, 2nd edition; 'The Defence Against Withholding in Adversary Proceedings', Sofia, 2002; 'Comments on the Commercial Code'. Part IV 'Bankruptcy', vol. I, Sofia, 1996; §21–24, §26–28 of Chapter VII 'Bankruptcy' in 'New Provisions of Commercial Law', Sofia, 2000; §1, §2, §10, §11 of 'Commercial Bankruptcy', Sofia, 2004; 'National Centre for legal education' publishers, 'European Civil Procedure and Part Seven of the Bulgarian Civil Procedure Code', Ciela publishers, 2011, as well as more than 100 studies and articles dealing with the matters of bankruptcy and civil procedure, six of them being published abroad. In 2010, Ciela Publishers issued her collected works in three volumes (V. Popova. Selected works in three volumes).

Table of Contents

Table of Contents

List of Abbreviations

AA	Act on Amendments (to another Act)
AB	Act on the Bar
AC	Arbitration Court
ACE	The Attorney's Code of Ethics
ACI	Act of Credit Institution
AICA	Act on the International Commercial Arbitration
ALSMD	Act on the Liability of the State and Municipalities on Damages
ANNA	Act on Notaries and Notarial Activity
ANA	Act on Normative Acts
APA	Administrative Procedure Act
APD	Act on Protection from Discrimination
Art.	Article
ASC	Attorneys' Supreme Council
ASF	Act on State Fees
ASO	Act for the State Official
ASP	Act on Suing People
BBA	Bank Bankruptcy Act
BCCI	Bulgarian Chamber of Commerce and Industry
BGN	Bulgarian Lev
BIA	Bulgarian Industrial Association
BNB	Bulgarian National Bank
C	Constitution
CA	Court of Appellation
CAP	Code of Administrative Procedure
CC	Constitutional Court
C. Code	Commercial Code
CCA	Constitutional Court Act
C. Ch.	Civil Chamber
CCN	Code of Commercial Navigation

List of Abbreviations

CCP	Code of Civil Procedure
CD	Constitutional Decision
CECBM	Code of Ethical Conduct of Bulgarian Magistrates
CEEO	Certificate for EEO
CM	Council of Ministers
CLPA	Civil Legal Procedure Act
COMECON	Council for Mutual Economic Assistance
CPA	Consumer Protection Act
CPrC	Consumer Protection Commission
ChPA	Child Protection Act
CPC	Criminal Procedure Code
CRA	Civil Registration Act
CRRA	Copyright and Related Rights Act
CSA	Court System Act
DC	District Court
DP	Decree of the Plenum
ECPHRFF	European Convention for the Protection of Human Rights and Fundamental Freedoms
EDETSA	Electronic document and Electronic trust services Act
EEA	Agreement on the European Economic Area
EEC	Treaty establishing the European Community (EEC Treaty)
EPEJ	Electronic portal for e-Justice
EU	European Union
FC	Family Code
GMCC	General Meeting of the Civil College
GMCom.C.	General Meeting of the Commercial College
GMCC and the Com.C. of the SCC	General Meeting of the Civil College and the Commercial College of the SCC
GNP	Gross National Product
IA	Inheritance Act
ICAA	International Commercial Arbitration Act
ID	Interpretative Decision
JAR	Judicial Administration Rules
LAA	Legal Aid Act
LC	Labour Code
LFRB	Law on Foreigners in the Republic of Bulgaria
MPA	Minors Protection Act
MTEA	Medical Treatment Facilities Act

NA	National Assembly
'Norma' ELS	'Norma' Electronic Legal System
NATO	North Atlantic Treaty Organization
NBLA	National Bureau for Legal Assistance
NFL	National Foundation of Lawyers
NIJ	National Institute of Justice
NOLA	National Office of Legal Assistance
NUJ	National Union of Jurisconsults
OCA	Obligations and Contracts Act
OD	Ordinance-Decree
Ord. No. 30	Ordinance No. 30
PA	Property Act
para.	Paragraph
PBA	Private Bailiffs Act
PB	Private Bailiff
PC	Penal Code
PFA	Persons and Family Act
PILC	Private International Law Code
PRB	People's Republic of Bulgaria
RASSA	Rules on the Application of the Social Support Law
RB	Republic of Bulgaria
RC	Regional Court
RCA	Regulations for court administrating
RPA	Registered Pledges Act
SA	State Arbitration
SAA	State Arbitration Act
SAC	Supreme Administrative Court
SB	State Bailiff
SBC	Supreme Barristers' Council
SC	Supreme Court
SCA	Structure of the Courts Act
SCC	Supreme Court of Cassation
SG	State Gazette
SJC	Supreme Judicial Council
SPA	State Protection Act
TCP	Transitional and Concluding Provisions
TFEU	Treaty on the Functioning of the European Union
TSPC	Tax and Social Procedure code
TTJA	Travelling Trial Judges Act

List of Abbreviations

URM	Unified Register of Mediators
WIE	Writ of immediate execution
ZPO	*Zivilprozessordnung* – Civil Procedure Code in Germany and Austria

Preface

The book is dedicated to the Bulgarian Code of Civil Procedure. It presents an analysis of civil procedure law in Bulgaria. The achievements of the Bulgarian procedure science and practice have been taken into account. It aims at taking an accurate and clear picture of the civil procedure in Bulgaria. The monograph may be used by readers who are interested in civil procedure in our country, as well as by lawyers who deal with comparative legal analysis in the field of civil procedure.

General Introduction

§1. General Background (Information on the Political and Legal System of the Country)

1. Bulgaria is a republic with a parliamentary form of government (Article 1(1) C)). It is a unitary State with local self-government; autonomous territorial formations are not admitted (Article 1(2)C). On 10 November 1989, a gradual transition towards market economy and political system of bourgeois – democratic type started. In 1991, the Great General Assembly adopted the new Constitution via which the Constitution of 1971 was repealed. In the *new* State Constitution of 1991 (Article 11(1)) the multiple-party system of government was established. The Constitution lays down the principles of separation of powers (Article 8 C), political pluralism (Article 8 C), public and private property, inviolability of private property (Article 17 C), free-market economy and equal rights of all individuals and legal bodies (Article 19 C) and the right of legal defence of all citizens when their rights are violated (Article 56 C). The National Assembly (NA) is proclaimed the only body of legislative power (Article 72 C). The establishment of the Constitutional Court (CC) provided an interpretation of the Constitution and controlled the compatibility of the laws enacted by the NA (Article 149 C) with the Constitution. The establishment of the Supreme Administrative Court (SAC) provided control of the compatibility with the law of the acts of the Council of Ministers and the ministers themselves. It realizes supreme control for the accurate and equal application of the law in the administrative jurisdiction (Article 125 C).

In 2003 the Republic of Bulgaria became a full member of NATO. Since 1 January 2007 it has been a member of European Union (EU).

2. With respect to the national Bulgarian legislation, the acts regulating the economic and market relations should be noticed.

One of the most important legislative instruments in regulating market relations is the Commercial Act passed in 1991.

In parallel with the political changes, large-scale privatization was conducted. Regarding privatization, the Privatization and Post-Privatization Control Act of 2002 which repealed the Act on Transformation and Privatization of State and Municipal Enterprises of 1 January 1992 is currently in effect.

Regarding the bank system, the current operative act is the *Act on Credit Institutions* (ACI). The bank bankruptcy is regulated in a special Bank Bankruptcy Act (BBA) and in the Law on Bank Deposit Guarantee.

3. A new CCP was adopted (entered into force on 1 March 2008, SG, No. 59 of 2007).

There was also new legislation in the social sphere. In 2000 a Child Protection Act (ChPA) was adopted. In 2009, a new Family Code (FC) was passed which replaced the Family Code from 1985. The new FC sets up three different regimes of property community between the spouses: legal matrimonial regime of community in respect of the assets acquired during the marriage as a result of the mutual contribution and the real property rights, acquired before the marriage, as well as those, acquired during the marriage by way of inheritance and donation; legal regime of division; contractual regime. The Consumer Protection Act (CPA) was adopted (2006).

4. Most of the acts passed after 1989 and after the adoption of the 1991 Constitution are in strict conformity with European law. However, the recent legislation has a negative tendency – very frequent changes made not only to the previous statutes but also to those passed after 10 November 1989 impair one of the most valuable qualities of the law as a public relations regulator: its stability.

§2. Delimitation of the Subject Matter

I. Definition of the Term 'Civil Procedure'

5. Civil proceedings provide a remedy-sanction[1] in the event of wrongful development of substantive civil law relationships[2] that can have its expression in legal dispute, non-execution of executable arrears or another pretence and danger of impeding the forthcoming remedy provided by adversary proceedings or enforcement. In order to provide the proper remedy in civil legal relationships, the CCP regulates three different but related proceedings: adversary, enforcement and security proceedings.

6. Adversary proceedings are used in the consideration of civil law disputes and the determination by res judicata.[3] The remedy-sanction of these proceedings is based on this force. Res judicata denotes both an obligation of the parties, their heirs and successors to adjust their conduct to the legal relationship ascertained by the court (Article 298(1) and (2) CCP) and a preclusion of relitigation of the same legal dispute (Article 299 CCP). All State bodies (including courts, State institutions and municipalities in the Republic of Bulgaria) are obliged to comply with the decision that has taken effect if an issue is put to them, and the civil legal relationship is prejudicial for this issue (Article 297 CCP). These proceedings consist of general adversary proceedings in which all civil cases are heard, and particular adversary proceedings regarding the civil rights explicitly specified in the CCP (matrimonial

1. The content of the remedy determines the sanction imposed.
2. Legal relations governed by the equality before the law of the parties (in rem, security, family, inheritance, commercial, etc.).
3. In accordance with Bulgarian law, adversary proceedings are court and arbitration proceedings.

proceedings, juridical partition, proceedings in commercial disputes, proceedings in class actions, summary proceedings, etc.).

7. Enforcement proceedings are employed for compulsory satisfaction of executable unsatisfied pretences. The enforcement proceedings consist of separate means of compulsory execution depending on the content of the satisfied pretence. There are common rules regarding the grounds for compulsory execution; order for payment proceedings; the issuance of a writ of execution and its challenge; the challenge of the arrear under the writ of execution; the commencement, suspension and completion of enforcement proceedings; the remedy to the debtor, claimant and third persons by appeal against the actions and omissions of the bailiff; and the remedy through a claim to third persons affected by the enforcement.

8. Security proceedings are employed where there is a danger of impeding the forthcoming remedy provided by the adversary or enforcement proceedings. Security proceedings are court proceedings, including those where arbitration for considering a civil law dispute was agreed. They are conducted in two stages: admission of security and imposition of security.

9. Insolvency of the merchant is a particular form of a wrongful development of commercial legal relationships (Articles 607a(1), 608 C. Code), including over-indebtedness regarding limited liability companies, joint-stock companies and public partnerships limited by shares (Articles 607a(2), 742(1) C. Code). Part IV 'Bankruptcy' of the C. Code regulated the bankruptcy proceedings as a collective procedure comprising: recuperation proceedings; in the event of impossibility of recuperation – converting the debtor's assets into cash and distributing the sums received; upon exhaustion of the bankruptcy estate – compulsory court liquidation.

10. Civil proceedings are regarded as a procedure – a dynamic content, consisting of a chain of subsequently performed procedural actions by parties and the legal defence body. These actions bring about the final act of the legal defence body, that gives rise to the above-mentioned defence and sanction consequences. The civil proceedings are also regarded a legal relationship. It is a chain of elementary legal relationships, arising in progression and realized and acquitted between the judicial body and each of the parties, which is finalized by rendering a legal act and its coming into force.

11. Apart from civil proceedings as a remedy-sanction, judicial interference in civil legal relationships can also take the form of assistance in their rightful development (Article 2 CCP). This is the so-called indisputable judicial administration of civil legal relationships exercised by security proceedings (e.g., adoption, divorce on the grounds of mutual consent). Its particularity is existence of no dispute between two opposing parties.

The theory places the so-called disputable judicial administration beyond the scope of civil proceedings. However, this administration is not regulated under the

CCP, but by the norms contained in the substantive laws and the particular provisions in the CCP. What is typical of this regulation is that the court makes a judgment about the expedience of the exercise of joint rights and obligations (e.g., the way of exercising the parent's rights and obligations in case of a parent's dispute), while the adversary proceedings determine disputes over the existence or non-existence of civil relationships and the court cannot make a determination for expedience. The decisions rendered have the same level of stability. On the grounds of Article 439(2) CCP, a new claim concerning a particular legal relationship can be brought only on the grounds that new facts came into existence, and the same goes for the disputable judicial administration. New proceedings regarding the dispute of the way joint rights exercising are admissible only if newly occurred facts that have come into existence are alleged.

II. Distinction with Other Types of Procedure (Administrative, Criminal)

12. The courts in the Bulgarian court system are not divided into civil and criminal courts. Both civil and criminal cases are heard according to different procedures. According to the CCP and the CPC civil and criminal proceedings have the following relations:

- The persons who suffered damages resulting from the crime are entitled to bring a civil claim for damages in criminal proceedings and become civil claimants (Article 84(1) CPC) This is inadmissible if the civil claim is already brought according to the procedure CCP (Article 84(2) CPC). The civil claim brought in criminal proceedings is handled under the rules of the CPC, and insofar certain rules are missing, the CCP applies (Article 88(1) CPC). Also, the civil claim in criminal proceedings can be brought against the defendant as well as against other persons bearing the responsibility for the damages resulting from the crime (Article 86 CPC). These persons have the status of civil defendants (respondent) (Article 89 CPC). This is within the scope required for defence of the civil claim that the civil claimant has the following rights: take part in court proceedings; demand security for the civil claim; examine the case-file and obtain excerpts that he/she needs; produce evidence; make requests, comments and raise objections, as well as to file appeal against acts of the court which infringe upon his/her rights and legal interests (Article 87(1) CPC). Within the scope required for defence against the civil claim the civil defendant has the following rights and legal interests provided in Article 90(1) CPC.
- The sentence that takes effect is binding on the court considering the civil consequences, with respect to the following: whether the act was committed, its wrongfulness and the culpability of the perpetrator (Article 300 CCP; Article 413(1) CPC). All elements of the *corpus delicti* are necessarily established. If it is of the category of resultant crimes, determination of the amount of damages is also necessary. The ascertainment of the contribution of the injured person in causing damages, specified in the sentence, is not binding on the court considering the civil consequences of the acts unless this contribution constitutes an element of the *corpus delicti*.

- The criminal court is obliged to comply with the decision if it is enforced (Article 297 CCP) and its subject matter is a civil relationship prejudicial for the criminal responsibility (for instance, stealing a chattel), if the decision is rendered in a case involving the defendant and the injured person (Article 298(1) and (2) CCP).
- According to Article 124(5) CCP, the claim for ascertaining the circumstance of a crime, important for a particular civil legal relationship or for reversing a judgment that has taken effect, is only admissible when the criminal prosecution has not commenced or is terminated for any of the reasons specified in Article 24(1), items 2–5 CPC or is suspended for any of the reasons specified in Article 25, item 2 CPC and Article 26 CPC or the perpetrator remained unknown. These facts could not be established in civil proceedings where they are relevant to the disputed civil legal relationship. If, during the course of civil proceedings, are revealed circumstances on which the outcome of the proceedings depends, the court is obliged to suspend the proceedings (Article 229(1), item 5 CCP). The civil case must be suspended, if a court considers a criminal case where the sentence has bearing on the civil case (Article 229(1), item 4 CCP).

13. Civil proceedings are in a particular relation with administrative proceedings. The res judicata effect of a decision, rendered in civil proceedings, has to be complied with in prejudicial matters in administrative proceedings (Article 297(1) CCP). The civil case court must comply with the decision that has taken effect and was rendered in administrative proceedings grounded on a complaint against an administrative act. It is enacted on an administrative legal relationship prejudicial for the civil law dispute (Article 302 CCP). According to Article 17(2) CCP the court pronounces on the validity of administrative acts as an incidental question regardless of whether the said acts are subject to judicial review. *The court may not pronounce on the legal conformity of administrative acts as an incidental question, save as where any such act is opposed to a party to the case who did not participate in the administrative proceeding for the issuing and appellate review of the said act.*

14. Civil proceedings also have particular relations with constitutional proceedings. If the Supreme Court of Cassation (SCC) and SAC establish an inconsistency between a law and the Constitution, they suspend proceedings in the case and refer the matter to the CC (Article 150(2) C, Article 16 CCA, Article 15 APC). The regional, the district and the appellate courts are not authorized to make such a request but are however obliged to notify the SCC if it deems the governing law to be contrary to the Constitution (Article 15 CSA). The civil action should be also suspended in the event that, at the request of the authorized bodies and persons there is already an action before the CC and the CC has accepted the hearing of a claim which challenges the constitutionality of an act applicable to the case (Article 229(1), item 6 CCP).

III. Are There Separate Court Systems and Rules of Procedure?

15. There are no separate court systems and rules of procedure for treating civil and commercial cases in Bulgarian civil procedure.

§3. Sources of Civil Procedure Law (Including a Brief Historical Perspective)

16. There was a procedure for administering justice as early as the Bulgarian State (a State of the early-feudal type, established in 681). Krum's Laws from the beginning of the ninth century are the oldest monument of Bulgarian legislation. The first written Bulgarian law after adopting Christianity was the Act on Suing People (ASP), created at the end of the ninth century. This act regulated the status of the judge as a State body of power, appointed by the central authority. It also regulated the participation of the '*poslouhi*' (the old justice administrators of the Slavs who were not public officials) in the justice administering body in certain categories of cases. This body was headed either by a specialized judge (a public official) or by the district governor. The procedural rules regarding evidence show that the State justice administering procedure was highly developed at the time, although there was no distinction between civil and criminal procedure.

From 1018 to 1185, when the Bulgarian people lived under the Byzantine yoke, Byzantine law applied. During the Second Bulgarian State, the Kórmchaia book was in effect. It is presumed that the Eclogue and ASP from the First Bulgarian State remained in force.

The Turks ruled Bulgaria from 1396 to 1878. The applicable law was Ottoman law. The Bulgarians, however, retained the nature of their common-law norms of matrimonial, contract and succession law.

17. After the liberation, in 1880, the Structure of the Courts Act (SCA) was adopted. It provided a court system consisting of trial courts, district courts, appellate courts and an SCC.[4] The trial courts consisted of a single judge, while the other courts sat in panels. The participation of jurors was provided only in several categories of criminal actions. In 1899, a new SCA was adopted, setting out higher requirements for the judges regarding their educational qualification. In 1892, the Civil Legal Procedure Act (CLPA) was adopted based on the Russian CLPA of 1864. The CLPA underwent several changes borrowed from the German and Austrian legislation. Proceedings were based on the adversary system and on the principle of the so-called formal truth. The assertory oath and the confession made by the party were binding on the court. Proceedings were three-instance. The intermediate appellate instance decided on the case merits without limitation on presentation of new evidence. The SCC acted as a cassation instance. The grounds for cassation of a decision were explicitly and thoroughly set out in the law and the

4. Matrimonial actions fell under the competence of the church courts. Administrative jurisdictions, such as the Supreme Court of Auditors and the Supreme Administrative Court, were set up for hearing administrative disputes. The district courts had their bailiffs, and later bailiffs.

SCC was bound by the grounds stated in the appeal. It did not have the right to decide on the merits of the case except where the grounds for cassation violated substantive law.

After World War I considerable changes were made in the judicial system, some of which concerned civil procedure. With the Travelling Trial Judges Act (TTJA) the advocate's defence in trial courts was banned (Article 3 TTJA) and so was the obligation of the court to give instructions to the parties in performing their procedural actions (Article 6 TTJA). With the Act on Rural Municipal Courts each rural municipality set up its rural municipal court with competence over personal claims to the amount of up to BGN 1,000. The judges had a two-year term of office and were directly elected by the population. The procedure in these courts was rather simplified. The statement of a claim could be filed either in writing or orally (Article 13), the parties acted in person and the advocate's defence was inadmissible (Article 17). The court was obliged to try to reconcile the parties (Article 15), and, should this turn out to be impossible, was obliged to hear the case in one sitting (Article 16). The decisions (except for claims of up to BGN 100) were subject to appeal to the trial judge (Article 27).

On 19 May 1934, a military coup d'etat took place and an authoritarian regime was established. The Ordinance-Decree (OD) on municipal courts provided that, each municipality had to have municipal courts and the mayors perform its jurisdictional functions. These courts had jurisdiction over claims whose amount did not exceed BGN 100 (Article 14), the appeals under Article 26 CLPA if the value of the estate did not exceed BGN 5,000, as well as the claims for partition of succession provided that the value of succession did not exceed BGN 10,000.

18. On 9 September 1944, the socialist system was established. On 4 December 1947, a new Constitution was adopted. Basic principles were laid down concerning judicial activities: lawfulness (Article 56(1)), independence of the judges and their sole subjection to the law (Article 56(2)), equality of citizens before the law (Article 71(1)) and setting up of specialized courts was only possible by law (Article 59(1)).[5] The following are provided for: the court's panels, participation of jurors (Article 57) and selectivity of judges and jurors (Article 58).

Changes were made in the CLPA. The most important were the two-instance hearing of cases and the obligation of the court to remind the parties that they did not provide evidence regarding certain circumstances. The SCA of 1948 provided that the following courts were general jurisdiction courts: the people's courts (regional courts at present), district courts and the Supreme Court. Under the PFA of 1949, matrimonial actions fell under the jurisdiction of State general courts. The

5. They should be classified as courts. The legal doctrine of that time used the term 'special jurisdiction' instead of the term 'special courts', as a synonym. A body independent of the parties could be seen in the SA, Burlaw courts and the Labour Disputes Commission. However, the legislator assigned jurisdictional functions to the administrative bodies. Art. 79(2) CCP (repealed in 1992) set out that the disputes regarding money receivables between State-owned enterprises, institutions and cooperatives (excluding cooperative farms) not exceeding BGN 200 were decided administratively by the body superior to the debtor. Following §120 of the Rules on Railways the Minister of Transport decided the disputes over fees wrongfully taken by the Bulgarian State railways.

SA at the CM was set up for hearing and deciding civil law disputes between socialist organizations (State institutions and enterprises and not-for-profit social organizations) in 1950.

The Constitution of 1971 and the SCA of 1976 (SG, No. 23/1976) set out that in the PRB justice is administered by the courts (Article 125(1) C) (Supreme Court, district courts, regional courts and courts-martial – Article 126(2) C, Article 3(1) SCA) and that extraordinary courts were inadmissible (Article 126(3) C, Article 3(3) SCA). However, Articles 126(2) C and 12 SCA provided that in certain types of cases other bodies for administering justice could also be set up by the law. Thus, constitutional grounds were created for setting up bodies outside the court system for administering justice. The participation of jurors was laid down, except in cases where the law provided otherwise (Article 127 C, Article 7 SCA). The jurors had the same rights as the judges. Moreover, following this Constitution, the judges were elected (Article 128 C, Article 6 SCA). It also laid down the obligation of the courts to apply the laws precisely and equally to all individuals and legal entities (Article 130 C). However, a number of the norms provided grounds for establishing legal privileges in favour of the State and its legal entities (Articles 14, 15, 16, 21 C).

The CCP was adopted in 1952. Most texts of the Code were adopted from the German one – Zivilprozessordnung (ZPO). As to certain aspects however the Code was modelled on the CCP of the RSFSR and borrowed its basic and procedural institutes, e.g., the two-instance hearing of cases. The judicial review could only start on the request of the Chief Prosecutor or the chairman of the SC, the active participation of the prosecutor in civil proceedings, the obligation of the court to render support to the parties in their performance of procedural acts and to point out that no evidence was provided regarding certain circumstances and the right of the court to collect evidence.

The legal infrastructure thus outlined also has other characteristic features. Article 9 of the revoked CCP (am. SG, No. 55/1992) provided that the parties were forbidden to make agreements according to which cases under the jurisdiction of the people's courts should be heard by foreign courts or by Conciliation Boards, except for disputes between socialist organizations and foreign enterprises. The confession of a party was not binding in court (Article 127 CCP). The active participation of the court in clarifying the case was also expressed in the non-commitment of the second-instance court to the grounds stated in the appeal (the second-instance proceeding was a controlling and overruling proceeding) and its capacity to overrule the decision, including the non-appealed parts and the parts regarding the joint parties that did not appeal, provided the grounds for overruling concern them as well (Article 206 CCP). Various procedural preferences were introduced in favour of State institutions and enterprises, cooperatives and social organizations: subject-matter jurisdiction of district courts over disputes between district courts and individuals (Article 80), ex officio notification by the court regarding cases it could enter into (Article 122, repealed, SG, No. 124/1997), non-judicial enforcement occasions (Article 237, item c), inadmissibility of securing a claim for money receivables against State institutions and enterprises (Article 312), inadmissibility of enforcement of decisions against State institutions (Article 399 CCP), preferential satisfaction of arrears of banks, State enterprises and cooperatives (Article 136(1), items 7 and 8 OCA – repealed, SG, No. 12/1993); consecutiveness of enforcement of decisions against socialist organizations and exclusion of many of their estates (Articles 400 and 402, repealed, SG, No. 124/1997), enforcement against amounts in the accounts of socialist organizations (Articles 405–413 CCP – repealed, SG, No. 124/1997), with State banks being the enforcement bodies; and participation of the Ministry of Finance as a control party in cases involving fixed assets managed by State enterprises (Article 19 CCP).

19. The norms set in the Constitution of 1991 regulating judicial power (including the structure and competence of courts) as well as the principles regarding procedure – Chapter VI; basic principles (Chapter I), basic rights and obligations of citizens (Chapter II) are sources of civil procedure law.

Substantial amendments to the old CCP were made in 1997: the court's duty to instruct the parties to the case on the burden of proof and that evidence should be provided for the facts alleged by them was dropped off; the controlling nature of the second-instance proceedings was annulled and the intermediate appellate proceedings as a full appeal, with the possibility for the parties to state facts and to point out and submit evidence that they could claim, respectively indicate and submit to the first instance was set; the supervisory review was revoked as an extraordinary way to appeal to enforced decisions before the SC and the cassation appeal institute before the SCC was established as a regular third instance.

20. The Court System Act (CSA) is of great importance for the civil procedure. The main basic principles of the judicial power are: in adopting their acts judges are based on the law and the evidence gathered in the case (Article 3 CSA) and impartially discharge their functions (Article 4); they are obliged to ensure openness, accessibility and transparency in their actions in pursuance of the CSA and in pursuance of the procedural laws; judges must be politically neutral in carrying out their duties (Article 6 CSA); everyone is entitled to a fair and open trial within reasonable time before an independent and impartial court. Citizens and legal entities are entitled to judicial protection that cannot be denied to them. Subject to the terms and procedure specified by law citizens may obtain legal aid, which is financed by the State (Article 7 CSA); cases and files are distributed electronically inside judicial bodies on the basis of the random selection principle (Article 9 CSA); judicial proceedings in civil cases are conducted before three instances – the first, the intermediate appellate and the cassation ones, unless otherwise is provided by law (Article 10(1) CSA); judicial acts that have entered into force could only be repealed in cases provided for by a law (Article 10(3) CSA); one judge may not take part in examining the same case at different court instances (Article 11(2) CSA); the time limits specified by procedural laws are obligatory to the judges (Article 12(2) CSA).

21. The CCP which was adopted in 2007 and came into force on 1 March 2008[6] is a basic source of the Bulgarian Civil procedure law. It consists of the rules about: standard action procedure, enforcement proceedings, security and non-adversary proceedings. Besides, regarding the EU regulations in respect to the civil proceedings Part VII – Special Rules Regarding the Procedure on Lawsuits under the Effect of European Union Law – was added to the CCP.

22. The arbitration proceedings are regulated with the Act on International Commercial Arbitration (AICA). On the grounds of Article 1 and §3 AICA, this act is applicable both to international commercial arbitration, when the place of the arbitration proceedings is on the territory of the Republic of Bulgaria and when the arbitration proceedings are between parties with domiciles or seats in the Republic of Bulgaria (internal arbitration awards).

With respect to the bankruptcy proceedings, the following provisions are applicable: common bankruptcy proceedings – Part IV of the Commercial Act (CA) Bankruptcy; Bank Bankruptcy – the BBA; an insurer's bankruptcy – Chapter VII of the Insurance Code (IC).

The provisions of great importance regarding the enforcement procedure are: Chapter XXXIV of the Tax Social Procedure Code (TSPC), regulating the connection and the interrelation between the TSPC proceedings in reference to collecting public arrears on the one hand and the enforcement proceedings established by the CCP on the other hand as well as the bankruptcy proceedings; the Private Bailiffs Act (PBA) from 2005; Article 37 ASP.

Nowadays these legal issues are regulated in Part II of the Private International Law Code (PILC).

In 2004 the Mediation Act was adopted. It underwent several amendments (*see* paragraphs 479–484).

There are also procedural norms in the substantive laws, such as those providing rebuttable presumptions (Article 45(2) Obligations and Contracts Act (OCA)) or rules on admissibility of certain means of evidence (Article 205(2) OCA).

23. Acts of binding interpretation are specific sources of civil procedure law: the decisions of the CC on interpreting the Constitution (Article 149, item 1 C), the acts of authoritative interpretation provided by the body issuing the act, e.g., the NA regarding the laws it issued, the interpretative decisions of the General Meeting of the Civil College (GMCC) and the General meeting of the Commercial college (GMCom.C.) of the SCC (Article 130(2) CSA).

24. In connection to the great reforms and the rapid change in legislation the effect of the procedural norms in reference to time is of major importance. The established understanding is that the new procedural law not only applied in newly instituted proceedings, but also in pending proceedings. In that case, the procedural actions performed, while the previous procedural law was effective, retain their

---

6. The new CCP has undergone many modifications, almost every year, and sometimes several in a year. That affects the core value of the law – its stability and leads to enforcement difficulties. The last amendments are in effect as of 30 Jun. 2021.

legal consequences, but the consequences, provided in the new procedural law, are attached to the last procedural action. At times, the legislator adopts explicit norms concerning the effect of procedural law regarding the pending proceedings at the time it takes effect.

25. EC Regulations are important international sources of the civil procedure with an international (cross-border) element within the EU. *Applicable are both EC regulations adopted after 1 January 2007 as well as those adopted prior to that date* (Article 2 Treaty Concerning the Accession of the Republic of Bulgaria and Romania to the European Union).

26. The international conventions[7] and other multilateral treaties or bilateral agreements[8] ratified duly and containing norms concerning the civil procedure are

7. *Vienna Convention on Civil Responsibility for Nuclear Damage*; *Vienna Convention on Diplomatic Relations; European Convention on Foreign Trade Arbitration*; *European Convention on Interstate Exchange of Legal Information*; *European Agreement on Referral of Requests for Legal Assistance*; *Convention on Delivery Abroad of Court and Out-of-Court Documents Related to Civil or Commercial Actions*; *Convention on Protection of Children and Cooperation in the Field of International Adoption*; *Convention on Protection of Human Rights and Basic Freedoms*; *Convention on International Access to Jurisdiction*; *Convention on Eliminating the Requirement for Legalization of Foreign Public Acts*; *Rules on the Arbitration of the United Nations Commission on International Trade Law (UNCITRAL)*; *Convention on Settling through an Arbitration Procedure of Disputes Ensuing from Relations of Economic and Scientific and Technical Collaboration*; *The Hague Convention on collecting evidence abroad in connection with civil and commercial actions; The Hague* Convent*ion of 19 Oct. 1996 on Jurisdiction, Applicable Law, Recognition, Enforcement and Co-operation in Respect of Parental Responsibility and Measures for the Protection of Children; The Hague Convention of 2007 on international recovery of child support and other forms of family maintenance and the Protocol on the law applicable to maintenance obligations (the Hague Protocol of 2007) International Convention on Aligning Certain Rules Regarding International Air Transport signed in Warsaw on 12 Oct. 1929; The Hague Convention of 2015 on Choice of Court Agreements* (effective 1 Oct. 2015).
8. *Albania* – Treaty on legal assistance in civil actions; *Algeria* – Treaty on judicial and legal assistance in civil, commercial, matrimonial and criminal actions; *Armenia* – Treaty on legal assistance in civil actions (a party to HC No.12, 28, 29, 33, 34, 37); *Austria* – Treaty for legal assistance in civil actions and documents (The Treaty is not denunciated but is used only in the part which not regulated by the EC regulations on the civil matter and the HC No. 12, 28, 29, 33, 34, 37) under the conditions of those acts; *Azerbaijan* – Treaty on legal assistance in civil actions; *Belarus* – Treaty on legal assistance in civil actions; *Belgium* – Convention between Bulgaria and Belgium on some judicial matters; *China* – Treaty on legal assistance in civil actions (A party to the HC No. 12, 14, 20, 28, 33); *Cuba* – Treaty on legal assistance in civil, matrimonial and criminal actions (A party to the HC No. 33); *Cyprus* – Treaty on legal assistance in civil and criminal actions (The Treaty is not denunciated but is used only in the part which is not regulated by the EC regulations on the civil matter and the HC No. 12, 14, 20, 28, 29, 33, 34, 37); *Czech Republic* – As an assignee to the Treaty between the People's Republic of Bulgaria and the Czechoslovak Socialist Republic on legal assistance and regulation of the relations regarding civil, matrimonial and criminal actions; *France* – Treaty on mutual legal assistance in civil actions (The Treaty is not denunciated but is used only in the part which is not regulated by the EC regulations on the civil matter and the HC No. 12, 14, 20, 28, 29, 33, 34, 37 under the conditions of those acts); *Georgia* – Treaty on legal assistance in civil actions (A party to the HC No. 12, 28, 33); *Greece* – Treaty on legal assistance in civil and criminal actions (The Treaty is not denunciated but is used only in the part which is not regulated by the EC regulations on the civil matter and the HC No. 12, 14, 20, 28, 29, 33, 34, 37 under the conditions of those acts); *Hungary* – Treaty on legal assistance in civil, matrimonial and criminal action (The Treaty is not denunciated but is used only in the part which is not regulated by the EC regulations

sources of the international civil procedure law. According to Article 5(4) C any international instruments ratified by the constitutionally established procedure, promulgated and taken effect with respect to the Republic of Bulgaria, are considered part of the domestic legislation of the country. They supersede any domestic legislation stipulating otherwise.

---

on the civil matter and the HC No. 12, 14, 20, 28, 29, 33, 34, 37 under the conditions of those acts); *Italy* – Treaty on legal assistance and enforcement of judgments on civil actions (The Treaty is not denunciated but is used only in the part which is not regulated by the EC regulations on the civil matter and the HC No. 12, 14, 20, 28, 29, 33, 34, 37 under the conditions of those acts); *Korea* – Treaty on rendering mutual legal assistance in civil, matrimonial and criminal action; *Kuwait* – Treaty on legal and judicial assistance in civil and criminal actions (A party to the HC No. 14, 20); *Libya* – Treaty on legal collaboration; *Macedonia* – Treaty on legal assistance in civil actions (A party to the HC No. 12, 14, 28, 29, 33); *Mongolia* – Treaty on rendering mutual legal assistance in civil, matrimonial and criminal actions, (A party to the HC No. 12, 33); *Poland* – Treaty on legal assistance and judicial relations in the field of civil, matrimonial and criminal actions (The Treaty is not denunciated but is used only in the part which is not regulated by the EC regulations on the civil matter and the HC No. 12, 14, 20, 28, 29, 33, 34, 37 under the conditions of those acts); *Romania* – Treaty on legal assistance in civil, matrimonial and criminal action (The Treaty is not denunciated but is used only in the part which is not regulated by the EC regulations on the civil matter and the HC No. 12, 14, 20, 28, 29, 33, 34, 37 under the conditions of those acts); *Russian Federation* (A party to the HC No. 12, 14, 20, 33); *Kyrgyzstan* (A party to the HC No. 12); *Turkmenistan* (A party to the HC No. 28); *Tajikistan* which are assignees to the USSR to the Treaty on legal assistance in civil, matrimonial and criminal action; *Slovakia* – as an assignee to the Treaty between the People's Republic of Bulgaria and the Czech Socialist Republic on legal assistance and on regulating the relations regarding civil, matrimonial and criminal actions; *Syria* – Treaty on legal assistance in matrimonial, civil and criminal actions; *Tunisia* –Treaty on legal assistance in civil and criminal actions; *Turkey* –Treaty on legal assistance in civil and criminal actions (A party to the HC No. 12, 14, 20, 29, 33); *Ukraine* –Treaty on rendering mutual legal assistance in civil actions; *Uzbekistan* –Treaty on rendering mutual legal assistance in civil actions (A party to the HC No. 28); *Vietnam* – Treaty on legal assistance in civil, matrimonial and criminal actions (A party to the HC No. 28); *Yemen* – Treaty on legal assistance in civil and criminal action (The Treaty is not denunciated but is used only in the part which is not regulated by the EC regulations on the civil matter and the HC No. 12, 14, 20, 28, 29, 33, 34, 37 under the conditions of those acts); as assignees to *Yugoslavia* to the Treaty on mutual legal assistance: *Slovenia* (Only in the part which is not regulated by the EC regulations on the civil matter and the HC No. 12, 14, 20, 28, 29); *Bosnia and Herzegovina* (A party to the HC No. 12, 14, 20, 28, 29); *Croatia* (A party to the HC No. 12, 14, 20, 28, 29, 34); *Monte Negro* A party to the HC No. 12, 20, 28, 29, 34); *Serbia* (A party to the HC No. 12, 14, 20, 28, 29). Bilateral legal assistance treaties with EU Member States were concluded prior Bulgaria's accession. They apply only to matters not covered by an EC regulation and under the conditions laid down in the relevant act. The treaties with non-EU countries are applicable to cases to which the relevant international conventions are not applicable as well as when the states are not parties to these conventions or under relevant international treaties when they observe the international agreements which have already been concluded by the parties thereto.

§4. General Features of the Administration of Justice in Civil Matters

I. Characteristics of the Procedure: Adversary and/or Inquisitorial Procedure, Role of the Judge and of the Parties, Oral and/or Written Procedure

27. Bulgarian adversary proceedings are based on the immediacy and orality principles (Article 11 CCP). Allegations and challenges are made before the court considering and determining the case. The court also rules upon the admissibility of the evidence. In first-instance proceedings the panels consist of only one judge, who also acts as the rapporteur. As for the intermediate appellate court and the cassation court instance, where the panel is composed of three judges, one of the members of the panel reports on the case. The procedural actions of the parties are performed in a court session before the whole panel of the court and not just before the judge who reports on the case.

The cases are heard within court sessions. The Bulgarian procedural legislation distinguishes: an open to the public court session (the parties are subpoenaed and the public may be present), open sessions in camera (the parties are subpoenaed and no public is present) and a closed session (the parties are not subpoenaed and public is not allowed).

Procedural actions are generally conducted orally in an open court session and recorded in the minutes (Article 100, Article 150 CCP). Where the procedural action is taken outside a court session (e.g., the filing of the claim and the response of the defendant), a copy for the opposing party must be provided (Article 100 in connection with Article 8(3) CCP). The parties can conduct procedural actions in an electronic form (Article 102b – in effect from 30 June 2021). They must comply with the requirements of Regulation (EU) No.910/2014 and with the Electronic document and Electronic trust services Act (EDETSA).[9]

The parties can conduct procedural actions in electronic form (Article 102b in connection with Article 102e in force from 30.06.2021),[10] for which the law requires written form (statement of claim, response to a statement of claim, appeal, cassation appeal, request for issuance of an enforcement order under Article 410) (*see* paragraphs 163, 182) or can be conducted in written form (e.g. written defences – Article 149(3)). They must conform to the requirements of Regulation (EC) No. 910/2014 and Electronic document and Electronic trust services Act (Article 102b(2)).[11] They can be submitted via email (arg. Article 360d, item 3 Structure of the Courts Act and Ordinance No. 6 on the procedure for performing procedural

9. They must be signed with a qualified electronic signature, when the law requires a handwritten signature.
10. Under Bulgarian law, the term 'procedural actions of the parties' covers their procedural actions addressed to the court, with which they exercise their procedural rights.
11. They must be signed with a qualified electronic signature, when the law requires a handwritten signature.

actions and certifying statements in electronic form of the Supreme Judicial Council), as well as through the EPEJ's system.[12]

The development of e-justice was launched and developed. An information system has been created and is to be completed and improved, approved by the SJC plenum in coordination with the Minister of Justice and the Chairman of the State Agency for Electronic Government (https://portal.justice.bg). EPEJ aims to facilitate and speed up: the exercise of the above-mentioned procedural actions by the parties (*see* footnote No. 5); serving of notices and papers, access of the parties to the case materials in an electronic folder.[13]

The oral hearing (Articles 143–150 CCP) is preceded by: (a) the so-called exchange of papers between the parties (bringing the claim to the court, the court's obligation to send to the defendant a copy of it and the evidence attached to it, the defendant's ability to respond to the claim and the duty of the court to send the claimant a copy of it and the evidence attached to it); (b) the first hearing for the preparation of the case is closed (Article 140 CCP). An open court hearing is then scheduled (Article 140 (3) CCP).

The testimony of the witnesses is obtained by questioning the witnesses in a court session (Articles 170–171 CCP). No written testimony is admissible. The conclusion of the expert is produced in writing (Article 199 CCP) and the expert is heard in the court session to which the parties are subpoenaed and may question him/her in order for the conclusion to be clear (Article 200 CCP). Article 156a (SG, No. 98 of 2020) lays down the conditions under which it is admissible for a witness to be questioned (*see* paragraph 316), for a party to give explanations (*see* paragraph 327), and for an expert to be heard via videoconference, combining the requirement of immediacy with current needs and modern technical possibilities. It is inadmissible for the court to render its judgment on the grounds of evidence gathered in another case. The only exception is provided for in Article 232 CCP (*see* paragraph 257).

Deviations from the principle of immediacy can be seen in several directions: (a) there is no principle of irremovability of the starting panel of judges, which has begun reviewing the case. The decision is rendered by the panel that finalized the hearing of the case (Article 235(1) CCP); (b) if some pieces of evidence do not fall

---

12. The first method is still used more in practice, because EPEJ is still in the process of construction and improvement (*see* footnote No. 13). The system for secure electronic service https://edelivery.egov.bg/ of the State Agency for Electronic Government is also used – for the State institutions that are registered in the system (not all of them have registered), and for those legal entities and individuals, who have registered and indicated it as a method of service under Arts 38 and 38a CCP.
13. Unfortunately, it is evident from the information on the current state of the portal /https://portal.justice.bg/Home/AboutTheSystem/ that at present not all courts have joined the EPEJ. In addition, the functions of the EPEJ for the performance of procedural actions of the parties for which the law requires a written form (statement of claim, response to the statement of claim, appeal, etc.) have not yet been established or may be established or may be performed in writing form (e.g. written defence). The system for sending papers and summons is still not functioning properly, although the method of service is provided for in the CCP. It is expected to start working after the entry into force of Art. 50a (SG, issue 110 of 2020, which will be in force from 30.06.2022) of the Bar Act, which stipulates that the obligation for lawyers to register and maintain a profile in the EPEJ and in the information system for secure electronic service under Art. 20, item 1, letter 'a' of the Electronic Government Act, but it is not certain what will happen.

under the jurisdiction of the court, the court is entitled to delegate the collecting to the local regional judge; (c) the inspection can be carried out by the whole panel, by a delegated member or by another delegated court (Article 204(2) CCP); (d) if persons are examined, the court may not be present in person at the examination entitling experts to do so (Article 206 CCP); (e) if documents are attached to the file, they can be submitted in the form of copies certified by the parties. However, the party is obliged to submit the original of the document or a certified copy if this is requested (Article 183 CCP); (f) the intermediate appellate court makes its conclusions on the grounds of the evidence collected both in intermediate appellate and in first-instance proceedings; (g) the parties may submit written defences instead of oral pleadings (Article 149(3) CCP). There is a deviation from the principle in the particular proceedings in commercial disputes (*see* paragraph 369).

28. The principle of disposition is in the grounds of Bulgarian civil procedure. The court proceedings begin upon the request of the person concerned. If the public interest requires the right to be protected regardless of its holder, the legislator establishes legal means providing this protection through the legitimization of the prosecutor in the cases specified explicitly by the law (Article 6(1), Article 26(1) CCP). When the public interest requires such protection, in the cases explicitly listed under the law, the court has the duty to examine and adjudicate the respective civil law issues ex officio including: e.g., the obligation of the court to render its decision on alimony, matrimonial home and exercise of parental rights regarding minors born in the marriage along with its decision on dissolution of the marriage due to divorce or invalidation, even though the parties to the case did not demand it (Article 322(2) CCP). Only the person seeking protection is entitled to make a change in the subject matter of the case (Articles 214, 398 and 426(2), sentence II CCP). At any stage of the adversary proceedings, the parties are entitled to make an agreement (Articles 149(1), 234 CCP). The court can be set aside by withdrawing (Article 232 CCP) or waiving the claim (Article 233 CCP). The court is also obliged to suspend the proceedings if a request is made by both parties (Article 229(1), item 1 CCP). The bailiff suspends the enforcement proceedings (Article 432, item 2 CCP) or terminates them (Article 433(1), item 2 CCP) on request of the claimant. The appeal can be filed against the decision as a whole or against separate parts (Article 258(2) CCP). With respect to the correctness of the appellate judgment, the decision of the SCC concerns only the merits stated in the cassation appeal (Article 290(2) CCP), except in cases of invalidity, inadmissibility of the decision and contradiction with an imperative substantive law norm. The intermediate appellate proceedings or the cassation proceedings are suspended, if the appeal is withdrawn and the appealed decision takes effect (Article 264(1) CCP; Article 296, item 2 CCP).

The dispositive principle is also manifested in the admission of the claim by the defendant. Article 237 CCP proclaims that where the defendant admits the claim, the court acting on a motion by the claimant terminates the trial and renders decision conforming to the admission (*see* paragraph 148).

II. Fundamental Guarantees (Constitution, Human Rights Treaties, General Principles of the Law): Establishment of Courts by Law, Independence and Impartiality, Reasons, Publicity, Fair Trial, Reasonable Time, Appeal, Etc.

29. In the Republic of Bulgaria, justice in civil cases is administered by the SCC, SAC, appellate courts, district courts, courts-martial and regional courts (Article 119(1) C). Specialized courts can be set up by way of a law (Article 119(2) C). Until now, no specialized court under Bulgarian law for hearing civil disputes have been created. No extraordinary courts are allowed to be set up (Article 119(3) C).

30. In performing their functions, the judges are independent and obey only the law (Article 117(2) C). The judges have to perform their actions and render their acts on the grounds of the law and the evidence in the case, which is assessed in accordance with their conscience and free inner conviction (Article 3 CSA, Articles 12 and 235(2) CCP). The decision is rendered after a closed meeting of the panel of judges that take the decision for terminating the case (Articles 21(1) and (5) and 235(1) CCP).

Judges enjoy the so-called functional immunity, concerning only the actions carried out in the performance of the judge's duties. *In the course of exercising the judicial power, the judges bear no criminal or civil responsibility for their official actions or for the adopted acts, with the exception of those cases in which an intentional crime was committed* (Article *132(1) C).* The conditions and order for imposing disciplinary penalties are provided in the CSA (*see* paragraph 53). A guarantee of the judges' independence is their irremovability (*see* paragraph 51). The judge should be impartial. Article 22 CCP provides on the imperative grounds banning the judge to hear a case and render a decision (*see* paragraphs 49–50). The judge is obliged to make an exception and suspend his duties himself where the grounds exist, otherwise each of the parties may claim the striking off of the judge (Article 23 CCP). Judges are neither entitled to give any prior opinion regarding the cases assigned, nor are they entitled to give any opinions regarding cases that were assigned (Article 212 CSA).

The norms are in accordance with Article 6 ECHR and Article 47 CFHREU of 2000.

31. The principle of lawfulness is explicitly set forth in the Constitution (Article 4(1), Article 117(1) C) as well as in Article 5 CCP.

In civil procedure, the lawfulness principle comprises the observance of procedural and substantive law. The procedural actions of the court and the parties should comply with the requirements of the procedural law. It is provided in Articles 7(1), 101(1), 129(1) and (2), 262(1) and (2), Article 286(1) and (2), etc. CCP that the court, acting ex officio, observes the due performance of procedural steps and when it is necessary grants the party a period of time for correcting its actions if they do not comply with the procedural law. Non-observance of the procedural law by the court constitutes grounds for appeal against its rulings barring the proceedings or those explicitly stated in the law (Article 274, CCP) or its decision (Article 270(3),

Article 281, items 1–3 CCP). In certain cases, this non-observance is grounds for revocation of decisions that have already taken effect (Article 303(1), items '5', '6' CCP).

In rendering its decision, the court applies the substantive law precisely (Articles 4, 117(2) C; Articles 5 and 235(2) CCP). If the decision is inconsistent with the substantive law the intermediate appellate court repeals it and renders a new decision upon the merits (Article 271(1) CCP). The breach of substantive law constitutes grounds for cassation of the decision of the intermediate appellate court (Article 281, item 3 CCP).

The principle of lawfulness also applies to security proceedings, it is guaranteed by the possibility of appeal against the ruling admitting the security and the ordinance for imposing it (Article 396 CCP).

The obligation to observe the principle of lawfulness is also valid in performing the enforcement actions that consists of the opportunity of appealing against the actions or omissions of the State or private enforcement magistrate in breach of the procedural law (Article 435 CCP) or the claims for remedy to third parties affected by the enforcement (Article 440 CCP). The guarantee for observance of the law also comprises the remedy to the debtor if he/she challenges the receivable subject to the enforcement (Articles 439, 420, 438 CCP), respectively subject to the order for payment proceedings (Articles 414, 415, 420 CCP – *see* paragraphs 378–398), bailiff's liability (Articles 441, 442a CCP).

32. Ensuring compliance with the principle of lawfulness and the principle of truth, as laid down in the Constitution and the CCP, as well as the requirement for a fair trial, are the so-called in Bulgarian legislation, doctrine and practice, ex officio grounds, proclaimed in Article 7 CCP. It establishes three ways of operation of the ex officio principle: ex officio course of proceedings; the obligation of the court to observe the admissibility and the due performance of the procedural actions by the parties and instruct the party as to the nature of the non-conformity of the procedural step performed thereby and to the term for curing the non-conformity (Article 101 CCP); the court is obliged to facilitate the parties in clarifying the factual and legal aspects of the case. Pursuant to Article 7(3) CCP the court monitors ex officio for unfair terms in a contract, concluded with a consumer and provides an opportunity for the parties to express a position on these questions.

The court is obliged to make a written report on the case (Article 146 CCP) (*see* paragraph 173). It should rule over the burden of proof (Article 146(1), item 5 CCP) as well as instruct the parties as to the circumstances that need not be proved (Article 146(2) CCP) and provide the parties with the possibility to undertake the procedural steps (Article 146(3) CCP). Besides, with respect to the active court's participation in clarifying the case, it must be noted its duty to pose questions to the parties for clarification of the facts (Article 145(1) CCP). Another important obligation of the court is instructing the parties to particularize their allegations and removing any contradictions therein (Article 145(2) CCP). According to Article 195(1) CCP, an expert witness is appointed on a motion by a party or ex officio where special knowledge is required in the field of science, art, skilled crafts, etc.

According to Article 7(2) CCP the court should serve upon the parties a duplicate copy of those acts which are subject to a separate appellate review. Another ex officio principle is in the declaring of nullity and inadmissibility of the appealable judgment even where there has not been any request in this respect (*see* paragraph 230) as well as the reversion of an incorrect judgment with respect to the necessary co-parties of the appellant who have not appealed (Article 271(3) CCP – *see* paragraph 222).

33. The legal proceedings assert the truth (Article 121(2) C). The principle is explicitly proclaimed in Article 10 CCP and stipulates: 'the court should afford the parties an opportunity and should facilitate the parties in establishing the facts relevant to adjudication of the case'.

There is no doubt that the court's active participation in clarifying the disputed facts is an important contribution in ascertaining the truth. The adversary principle is also of great importance in this relationship since the parties themselves are best acquainted with the actual relationships. A guarantee for the application of the principle of assertion of the truth is also: the requirement for the court and the court's official to be impartial and the grounds for recusal in the cases stipulated by the Code (Article 22 and Article 24 CCP); the publicity and immediacy principle set in Article 11 CCP (*see* paragraph 35).

The *principle of assertion of the truth* is also developed through the opportunity to reverse effective judgments on the grounds of Article 303(1), items 1, 2, 5, 6 CCP (*see* paragraphs 243–249). On the contrary, however, the manifestation of this principle is strongly limited within the, widely known in the doctrine and practice, *concentration principle* (*see* paragraph 36).

34. In the Constitution, *the adversary principle* is established together with *the equality of the parties principle* (Article 121(1) C). Article 8 CCP 'Adversary Principle' stipulates explicitly this fundamental principle, while Article 9 CCP stipulates *the equality of the parties principle*. The party's right to participation principle, the equality of the parties' principle and the adversary principle are basic rules related very closely. According to Article 122(1) C, individuals and legal entities are entitled to defence at all stages of the proceedings. According to Article 9 CCP, the court affords the parties an equal opportunity to exercise the rights conferred thereon. The court applies the law equally in respect of all.

Each party has the right to be heard by the court before rendering an act relevant to the rights and interests of the said party (Article 8(1) CCP). Under the conditions of Article 156a CCP it can be heard via videoconference (*see* paragraph 27 and paragraph 327). According to Article 8(2) CCP the parties must indicate the facts underlying their demands and should present evidence supporting the said facts. But the party bears the burden of proof. It is obliged to allege the facts if he/she wants them to be taken into consideration in the course of the case proceedings, respectively to submit evidence if he/she wishes the evidence to be collected (Article 129, Article 131 CCP). Article 8(3) stipulates that the court gives the parties an opportunity to familiarize themselves with the demands and arguments of the opposite party, with the subject matter of the case and the progress thereof, as well as to express a position on the said demands, arguments and subject matter.

Regarding the equality of parties and the respondent's right to defence there are some relevant rights provided. The plaintiff may not withdraw the statement of action without the consent of the respondent if he/she wants to do this after the end of the first hearing of the case (Article 232 CCP). The grounds of the action are admissible only if that will not hamper the respondent's defence (Article 214(1) CCP).

35. According to Article 121(3) C, cases in all courts are heard in court sessions which are open to the *public*, unless the law states otherwise. Article 132(1) and (2) CSA stipulate that courts examine cases in public hearings and the publicity of trial may only be limited by law. The principle of publicity of the civil procedure is proclaimed in Article 11 CCP.

The court, acting either ex officio or on a motion by any of the parties, may decree that the case be examined or only some steps be performed behind closed doors where: the public interest so necessitates; the protection of the privacy of the parties, of the family, or of the persons under curatorship so necessitates; the case involves a trade, industrial, inventor's or tax secret and the public disclosure would impair any defensible interests; other valid reasons apply (Article 136(1) CCP).

The principle of publicity of the adversary proceedings is a serious guarantee for ensuring the impartiality of the court. The witnesses find it hard to commit perjury and the experts find it harder to give false conclusions when they are in the courtroom.

A deviation from the principle of publicity is allowed for in Article 376 CCP concerning the particular proceedings in commercial disputes (*see also* paragraph 169).

The principle of publicity also applies to the pronouncement of the court's judgment. According to Article 235(5), sentence II the judgment must be published in the register of judgments of courts, which is public. According to Article 64(1) CSA the court acts are published on the web page of the respective court.

There is an exception to the principle of publicity in security proceedings as well. They are conducted in a closed court session and the parties do not participate (*see* paragraph 206).

36. Article 13 CCP in compliance with Article 6(1) European Convention for the Protection of Human Rights and Fundamental Freedoms (ECPHRFF) proclaims that the court examines and adjudicates the cases within a reasonable period of time. The principle applies both to hearing and determining the cases. Article 235(5) CCP provides that the court should publish its judgment together with its motives within one month after the hearing of the case was completed.

The case's examination within a reasonable time limit depends not only on well-organized procedural steps of the court but also on the diligent exercise of the procedural rights of the parties as it is stipulated in Article 3 CCP. To avoid fraud protracting of the cases, the so-called concentration rule or principle of concentrating the evidence was introduced into the new CCP. The principle is not specified explicitly in Part I, chapter II CCP, named 'Basic principles' of the CC. Reasonably, in the legal doctrine and practice this principle is deduced from a number of norms which introduce preclusions and secure the concentration of the evidential material (Articles 127, 131, 140 (1), 143(1) and (2), 142(1), 260, item 5, 263(2), 266(1) and (2) CCP).

37. In compliance with Article 6(1) ECPHRFF and Article 47 Charter of Fundamental Rights, Article 7 CSA stipulates that everyone is entitled to a fair and open trial within a reasonable time before an independent and impartial court; subject to the terms and procedure specified by law citizens may obtain legal aid, which are financed by the State. Legal aid consists of providing free legal defence (Article 94 CCP). The terms and conditions are regulated in Chapter X CCP, the Law on Legal Aid and the BBA (*see* paragraph 300). In the Bulgarian civil procedure, there is no rule of mandatory advocacy. The parties may exercise their procedural rights personally.

38. The interested party may request the annulment of an enforceable judgment when the European Court of Human Rights has found a violation of the ECHR by a final decision and the new examination of the case is necessary to remedy the consequences of the violation (Article 303(1), item '6' CCP).

Part I. Judicial Organization

Chapter 1. The Courts and Their Members

§1. Courts

I. Structure of the Court System

39. Justice in the Republic of Bulgaria is administered by the courts. According to the Bulgarian Constitution, setting up neither so-called special jurisdictions,[14] nor extraordinary chambers are admissible (*see* paragraph 29). The courts specified in the Constitution are: the SCC, SAC, appellate courts, district courts, courts-martial and regional courts (Article 119(1) C). The courts-martial are specialized courts, which hear cases involving crimes committed by either military men or persons employed by the armed forces but they apply the PC and the CPC, which are also applied by the courts of general jurisdiction. According to the Constitution, there is no division of the courts into civil, criminal and administrative courts. The only exception is the SAC, which is the final instance in administrative cases, and that competent instance which considers complaints against the acts issued by the Council of Ministers (CM) or a minister. According to Article 6 CPC the criminal cases are determined only by the courts specified in the Constitution.

The courts specified in the Constitution are also constitutionally guaranteed. They cannot be revoked by law. Only specialized courts, such as administrative courts (Article 61(1) CSA; *see* paragraph 44), can be set up by law (Article 119(2) C). There are no specialized courts for hearing certain categories of civil cases, however some civil disputes are already within the competence of administrative courts (*see* paragraph 70). Extraordinary courts are inadmissible (Article 119(3) C).

The structure, organization and activity of the courts as well as the statute of the judges are regulated by the CSA. Article 61(1) CSA proclaims that the courts in the Republic of Bulgaria are regional, district, administrative, military, appellate ones,

14. I must point out, however, that in recent years some State bodies, which are out-of-court system, have been given judicial functions in administrative disputes (cf. e.g., CD No. 6/11.11.2008 on const. case No. 5/2008 for the Commission for protection of Competition, in which it was accepted that it is sufficient for the act to be subject to appeal in court in order to comply with Art. 119 C). These bodies are called in doctrine and practice administrative jurisdictions. I support the opinion that Art. 119(2) C allows specialized courts to be established by law, as part of the judicial system, guaranteeing the independence and impartiality of judges, but not special jurisdictions outside the judicial system (*see* the reservation on the cited const. decision). This opinion is shared in the civil procedure doctrine and is followed in the legislation regulating the civil process.

the SCC and SAC, specialized criminal courts[15] and specialized appellate criminal courts. Those specialized courts that were set up by law on the grounds of Article 119(2), can also be abolished by law, in the same way they were set up.

Article 119 C is in compliance with Article 6 Human Rights Protection and Basic Freedoms Convention, Article 43 European Convention on Human Rights, Article 14(1) International Covenant on Civil and Political Rights, Article 10 General Declaration on Human Rights, assuring a competent, independent and unbiased court.

40. The regional court is the basic first-instance court.[16] It has jurisdiction over all cases except those that fall under the jurisdiction of another court by virtue of law (Article 76 CSA, Article 103 CCP). The regional court consists of judges and is chaired by a chair (Article 77(1) CSA). Divisions may be set up at the regional court (Article 77(2) CSA). According to Article 78 CSA, the regional court hears cases in panels of one judge, unless the law provides otherwise.

Regional courts also have competence over a number of security proceedings: establishment of a fact of legal significance, certifiable by a document duly drawn up if such a document was not drawn up before or the document drawn up was destroyed or it is impossible for such a document to be restored (Articles 542 et seq. CCP), declaring the absence or death of a missing person (Articles 549 et seq. CCP), probate proceedings like sealing and inventorying the heritage (Articles 553 et seq. CCP), invalidation of securities (Articles 560 et seq. CCP), permission for disposal of property and drawing sums from a deposit of a minor or a person under interdiction (Article 130(3), Article 165(4) FC), etc.

41. District courts[17] are first-instance courts in civil cases provided for by Article 104 CCP (*see* paragraph 90) in a panel of one judge and second-instance courts in appeals from the regional courts in a panel of three judges unless otherwise provided for by law (Article 82(1), item 2, Article 83(1) CSA, Article 20 CCP). The district court hears complaints against the refusal of a regional court to issue the security instrument (Article 538 CCP); disputes over subservience of civil cases between the regional courts within its district also fall within the competence of the district court (Article 122) CCP); the appeals against the refusal of the bailiff to perform an enforcement action (Article 436(1) in connection with Article 435 CCP).

The district court consists of judges and junior judges (*see* paragraph 47) and is headed by a chairperson (Article 84(1) CSA). According to Article 84(2) CSA divisions depending on the amount and type of cases and the number of judges may be set up based on a resolution of the general assembly of district court judges.

42. The appellate court[18] only has second-instance competence (Article 101(1) CSA) over appeals against decisions and rulings of the district courts within its

15. Under the jurisdiction of such courts are the special criminal cases (Art. 63(1) and (5) CSA; Arts 411a – 411f CPC.
16. There are 113 regional courts in the Republic of Bulgaria.
17. There are twenty-eight district courts in the Republic of Bulgaria. The Sofia city court has the status of a district court.
18. There are five appellate courts in the Republic of Bulgaria, situated in Sofia, Varna, Burgas, Veliko Tarnovo, Plovdiv.

venue rendered in their capacity of first-instance courts (Article 101(1) CSA, Article 258(1), Article 274(2) CCP). The appellate court also hears disputes between the district courts regarding subservience (Article 122 CCP); complaints against refusals of the district courts regarding entry proceedings (Article 606 CCP). The appellate court consists of judges and is headed by a chairperson (Article 102(1) CSA). Civil, commercial and criminal divisions may be set up by a resolution of the judges general meeting (Article 103 CSA). The appellate court sits in a panel of three judges, unless otherwise provided for by law (Article 105 CSA, Article 20 CCP).

43. The SCC is the Supreme Court instance in criminal and civil cases (Article 108(1) CSA). It is the third regular cassation instance in civil cases. Under Article 47 ICAA, the claims for the revocation of arbitration decisions are under the jurisdiction of the SCC (*see* paragraph 91). The SCC consists of a civil, commercial and criminal colleges. There are departments in the colleges (Article 109(4) CSA). The SCC sits in panels of three judges, unless otherwise provided for by law; as a general assembly of the respective college when examining a request for the adoption of an interpretative decision. In cases of contradictory or erroneous jurisprudence on the interpretation or application of the law, interpretative decisions are adopted by the general meeting of the respective college of the SCC (Article 124(1) CSA). The interpretative decisions are binding on the bodies of judicial and executive power, on local government bodies, as well as on all bodies issuing administrative acts (Article 130(2) CSA).

The Plenum of the SCC consists of all judges of the SCC. It is held if at least two-thirds of the total number of judges is present and it should adopt resolutions by a majority of more than half of the judges present (Article 111(1) and (6) CSA). It specifies the composition of colleges and the number and composition of divisions.

44. According to Article 119(2) C and Article 61(1) CSA (*see* paragraph 70) specialized administrative courts consider administrative cases (Article 89(1) CSA).[19] The seats and judicial venues of the administrative courts coincide with those of the district courts (*see* paragraph 41). The administrative court hears administrative cases in a panel of one judge, unless otherwise provided for by law. In proceedings before the administrative court a prosecutor with the administrative department of the respective district prosecution office takes part, in cases provided for by law (Article 90 CSA). The administrative court consists of judges and is headed by a chairperson. By a resolution of the general assembly of judges at the administrative court, divisions specialized by subject matter may be set up (Article 91 CSA).

The SAC is the final judicial instance in administrative jurisdiction. The SAC is a cassation instance for all judicial acts of all administrative courts regarding the lawfulness of administrative instruments (Article 208 CAP). Under Article 217(1) CAP a case is examined by a three-judge panel of the SAC, where the judgment has been rendered by an administrative court, and by a five-judge panel, where the judgment has been rendered by a three-judge panel of the SAC. The SAC rules on disputes over the lawfulness of the instruments of the CM and the ministers, as well as

19. Though several types of civil cases are within their competence (*see* para. 70 regarding jurisdiction).

over the lawfulness of any other instruments specified by law as subject to appeal only to the SAC (Article 165 AP). The sub-legal acts are appealed before the respective court which considers the case in a panel of three judges (Article 191(1) CAP). The SAC consists of judges and is headed by a chairperson. In SAC there are colleges, composed of departments (Article 117(1) and (2) CSA). In cases of discrepancy or incorrect judicial practice of the SCC and the SAC joint interpretative decrees can be issued, and are adopted at the common meetings of the respective colleges of the two courts (Article 124(2) CSA).

Some civil law disputes are also included in the competence of administrative courts (*see* paragraph 70; Article 128(1), items 6, 7, 8 CAP, Article 1 ALSMD), which are reviewed following the order of the CAP.

II. Administration of the Court

45. The SJC has an important role in the organization of the judiciary (Articles 129, 130, 131, 132a C, Articles 16–39 CSA). The adopted by the SJC Regulations for courts administrating (RCA),[20] Rules on Administration of the SCC; Rules of Administration of the SAC, set the administration units, their functional characteristics, the organization of the work in the courts, the official timetable, the types of job description of the clerks, the procedure for conducting a competition, the conditions for incompatibility for the court clerk and the authorities responsible for their appointment.

The SJC has an Inspectorate (Chapter III CSA), which inspects the organization of the courts' and bodies' administration, the organization of the court cases' setting and development, as well as the finalization of the cases within the set deadlines; analyses and summarizes cases that have been closed by an enforceable judicial act; in the case of violations, it notifies the administrative head of the relevant body of the judiciary and the relevant SJC college; makes proposals to impose disciplinary sanctions on judges, prosecutors, investigators and administrative heads of the judiciary; performs audits of integrity and conflicts of interest of judges, their property declarations, as well as establishes actions that undermine the prestige of the judiciary and those related to violation of the independence of judges, prosecutors and investigators; examines claims for breaching the right the case to be examined and resolved within a reasonable term.

III. Bench and 'Ministère Public'/Public Prosecutor (If Any)

46. In Bulgarian law, the term 'magistrates' is also used (Article 28(2); Article 50(3); Article 123(6) CSA; Article 20, Article 160(1) RCA). The Code of Ethical

20. The administration of the courts is general and specialized (Art. 14 RCA). The general administration assists the activities of the administrative head of the court, the court administrator or the administrative secretary and the specialized administration. The specialized administration assists and ensures the implementation of the judicial activity (Art. 16(1) RCA). Both administrations consist of employees of RCA assigned departments.

Conduct of Bulgarian Magistrates (CECBM) adopted by the SJC states that this code is applicable to all judges, prosecutors and investigators, members of the SJC, inspectors in the Inspectorate of the SJC called 'magistrates' for the purposes of this code.

Of these persons, only judges are members of the court. As I pointed out (*see* paragraph 41) the junior judges also possess the quality of judges and are part of the district court. The judicial assistants (Articles 244–248 CSA), do not have the quality of judges or magistrates. They must meet the requirements of Article 162 CSA and have passed a competition for a judicial employee. They have the powers under Article 246a CSA, with which they assist judges and administrative heads in their work.

In Bulgarian law, the prosecutor is not a member of the court and is not a member of its panel. The structure of the prosecution and the powers of the prosecutors are defined in Article 126 and 127 C and Chapter VI CSA. According to Article 127, item 6 and Article 26(2) CCP, the public prosecutor is entitled to participate in the proceedings only when it is particularly provided in the law.[21] Then he/she participates in the proceedings with the rights of a party (Article 26(3) CCP).

IV. Appointment of Judges (Public Prosecutors and of Members of the 'Ministère Public')

47. Judicial positions are: Judge at the Supreme Court of Cassation, Supreme Administrative Court, Appellate Court, District Court, Administrative Courts, Jury Judge (Article 163 CSA). Only a Bulgarian citizen may be appointed for a judge. He/she should meet the following requirements: to have a university major in law; to have passed the length of service required by the CSA and has acquired legal capacity; not to be sentenced to imprisonment for a deliberate crime, despite rehabilitation; to possess the necessary moral and professional qualities corresponding to the CECBM; not to suffer from a mental illness (Article 162 CSA). The appointment is made after competitions held by the SJC[22] by five-member selection committees, determined according to the competitions' materials. The members of the selection committee consist of one senior law scholar holding an academic position

21. According to Art. 336(1) CCP, he/she is entitled to bring an action for the interdiction of one person. According to Art. 336(2) CCP participation of the prosecutor is mandatory when the claim for disability of one person is filed by one of the legitimate according to Art. 336(1) CCP persons (spouse, close relatives). The prosecutor may bring actions: to revoke the security issued when it was ordered in violation of the law (Art. 537(3) CCP); to revoke or amend the decision to declare the absence or death of a person if it is established that the absent person is alive or that the exact date of his death is different from that declared by the court (Art. 552(1) CCP); for the inadmissibility or nullity of the entry, as well as the non-existence of a recorded circumstance in the respective public register (Art. 604 CCP); for the dissolvent of marriage in the cases of Art. 7(1), items 1, 2 and 3 FC, as well as in the cases of Art. 7(2) FC (Art. 47(1), items 3 and 4 FC); to dispose of the company for invalidity due to reasons provided for in Art. 70,(1) CCP (Art. 70(2) C. Code); for the dissolution of the company when its activity contradicts the law (Art. 155(2) C. Code).
22. Ordinance No. 1/9 Feb. 2017 contains detailed regulations on the competitions for magistrates and election of administrative leaders of the court system bodies.

as associate professor or professor, as well as four members having the status of an acting judge, prosecutor or inspector (Article 189(5) CSA).

A person who has at least three years of service (Article 164(1) CSA) can be appointed as a judge at a district court. A person who has at least eight years of service (Article 164(2) and (4) CSA) can be appointed as a judge at a district and administrative court. A judge in an appellate court shall be a person who has at least ten years of service (Article 164(4) CSA). A person who has at least twelve years of service (Article 164(5) CSA) is appointed as a judge at the Supreme Court of Cassation and the Supreme Administrative Court. The junior judge has also the capacities of a judge (Article 163(5) CSA) (For a junior judge, a person can be appointed who meets the requirements of Article 162 CSA. Under Article 240 CSA, he/she is appointed for a term of two years). This period may be extended for a further six months by decision of the SJC. A junior judge with more than one year of service may be seconded to a vacant post in a district court in the same judicial district. According to Article 243 CSA, the junior judge appointed under Article 240 CSA is appointed as a judge in a district court without holding a competition. If such a vacancy does not exist in the respective district court, the person is offered a position in another court district.

A centralized contest for a jury position is held for the following: junior judges and initial appointment in a regional, district and administrative courts (Article 176(1) CSA). For junior judges, it is held once a year. The initial placement competition is held at least once a year. The SJC determines the number of vacant positions in the court through a competition for initial appointment (Article 178(1) CSA). The positions for junior judges and the vacant positions for initial recruitment as well as the competition for them are announced by the SJC through promulgation in the State Gazette, publication in a central daily newspaper and on the website of the SJC on the Internet (Articles 179–180 CSA).

A person who meets the requirements of Article 162 CSA may participate in the junior judge competition. The contest for initial appointment may be participated by a person who meets the requirements under Article 162 CSA and has passed an internship under Article 164 CSA connected with the position for which the competition was opened (Article 181 CSA).

The competition includes a written and oral examination. The written test is anonymous and includes knowledge verification by case studies in the relevant legal field and a test in EU law and human rights law (Article 184(2) CSA). Candidates who passed the written exam with a score at least 'Very good (4.50)' in all sections are admitted to an oral examination. Candidates who passed the oral exam with a score of no less than 'Good (4)' take part in the ranking. The competition committee ranks the candidates for each position according to the results of their performance, the score of each candidate being a sum of the marks from the written and oral examination.

The administrative heads notify the respective college of the SJC on the number of positions which are expected to be vacated during the next year, until 30 September of the previous year. The SJC determines the number of vacant positions as of the date of announcing of the competition for each individual organ of the judiciary, prosecutor's office and investigating authorities for their occupation by promotion. The promotion is done through a special contest. The vacant positions are announced by the SJC Judge's College following the order of Article 179 CSA for each body of the judiciary and are held after a competition. Competitions for higher-ranking judiciary bodies are announced by decision and are held prior to the announcement of competitions for lower-level bodies. An applicant for a position through a promotion competition may be a judge who has experience under Article 164 CSA for the vacancy announced. The selection board rank the candidates for the transferring to another position according to the results of the last evaluation and checks by the higher judiciary bodies and the Inspectorate to the SJC, the data of their career file and the assessment of the cases examined and completed which the selection board selected and submitted by the candidates, on the basis of which an overall assessment of the professional qualities of the candidates is made. The Competition Commission prepares a protocol for the ranking of the candidates with a motivated opinion and sends the results of the ranking with the entire competition documentation to the SJC Judge's College, which decides on the sequence of the ranking by the positions filling in.

Decisions of the SJC on the appointment of a judge, both after a competition through an examination and after a competition through appraisal, are subject to appeal to the SAC within seven days of their issuance. A three-member panel of the SAC examines the appeal and its decision is final.

§2. Members of the Judiciary

48. The legal status of the judge is regulated in Chapter VI 'Judicial power' of the Constitution and in Chapter IX 'Statute of judges, public prosecutors and investigators' of the CSA issued on the grounds of Article 133 C, and accordingly, the status of judges, the conditions and procedure for appointing and discharging them, as well as their responsibility are regulated by law (*see* paragraph 47).

It is typical of modern Bulgarian civil proceedings that the panel in civil proceedings does not include jurors, but only professional judges. The established opinion is that civil law disputes require to be heard and determined by professional judges of high morality and high professional qualification in law.

I. Incompatibilities

49. While in office, the judge cannot: be a Member of Parliament, a mayor or a municipal councillor; holds a position in State bodies, municipal bodies or institutions of the European Union, except for a European Delegated Prosecutor; exercises commercial activity in any form, including personally, through an affiliated person and/or with a prominent and/or hidden agent or as a partner, manager, or to participate in supervisory boards, boards or boards of directors or control bodies of commercial companies, cooperatives or non-profit-making legal entities which carry out business activities, with the exception of those professional associations in which they are members;[23] receives remuneration for performing a contract or other legal relationship with a State, municipal or public organization,[24] a trading company, a cooperative, a non-profit legal person, a natural person or a sole trader, and to exercise a liberal profession or other paid professional activity; is a member of political parties or coalitions, organizations with political ends, performs political activity, or is a member of an organization or performs activities that affect its independence; is a member of a trade union outside the system of the judiciary (Article 195(1) CSA).

Judges, prosecutors and investigators may not be members of election commissions for election of members of parliament, members of the European Parliament from the Republic of Bulgaria, presidents and vice presidents of the republic and municipal councillors and mayors (Article 195(3) CSA).

50. Participation in the panel of judges in a particular case is barred for any person who is a party to the case, or together with any of the parties to the case is subject to disputed or connected legal relationship or is a spouse or a relative of a party or a relative of a party's ward. A 'relative' here meaning a person related in a direct line, or in a collateral line – within the fourth degree, or by affinity – within the third degree, or is in the same relationship with the representative of the party, lives in factual marriage with a party to the case or with their representative, a person that has been a representative or proxy of a party to the case; who has taken part in the deciding of the case in another court instance or has been a witness or expert in the proceedings, or with regard to such a person exist other circumstances which give rise to reasonable doubts about his/her impartiality (Article 22(1) CCP).

II. End of Functions

51. The judges become irremovable by a decision of the Supreme Judicial Council, after acquiring five years' experience and after undergoing a professional assessment, when the assessment's grade is a positive one (Article 129(3) C; Article 209(1) CSA). They are discharged from office only upon reaching the age of 65, resignation, enactment of a sentence of imprisonment for an intended crime, in the event of permanent incapacity for performing his/her duties for more than a year, in case of serious breach or regular non-performance of their duties or actions injuring the reputation of the judiciary and where it is found that they perform actions are not allowed or hold positions they are not allowed to hold under Article 195(1) CSA (Article 129(3) C, Article 165(1) CSA).

23. Judges are free to form and be members of organizations that protect their independence and professional interests and support their professional qualifications (Art. 217(1) CSA). Such a professional organization is the Union of Judges.
24. The judge may, when taking up his/her post, also receive remuneration for: scientific research and teaching activities or the exercise of copyright; participation in European and international programmes and projects; participation in the elaboration of drafts of normative acts, which are assigned by the National Assembly, the Supreme Judicial Council or by bodies of the executive power (Art. 195(2) CSA).

III. Discipline

52. In performing their functions, the judges are independent and obey only the law (Article 117(2) C) and are bound to observe it and apply it correctly. They are bound to observe the determined procedural terms for the exercise of their powers (Article 212(2) CSA). Judges cannot express a preliminary position on their assigned cases as well as a position on cases, which are not assigned to them (Article 212 CSA). The judges are obliged to keep the meeting secret regarding the outcome of the case (Articles 155 and 212 CSA). This is a guarantee of the independence of the court.

53. A guarantee of the judges' independence under Article 132 C is that they do not bear not only criminal but also civil liability for damages caused in the course of performance of their duties, unless they have committed a general crime. Judges bear disciplinary liability for faulty non-performance of their official duties, regular violations of the terms specified in the procedure laws, carrying out actions or omitting to carry out actions which bring about an unjustified delay in the proceedings, and violation of the rules of the Code of Ethics of the Judiciary; action or omission that ruins the prestige of the judiciary; failure to execute other professional duties (Article 307, paragraphs 1–3 CSA). The disciplinary liability is effective regardless of the civil, criminal or administrative penal liability, if such is provided for (Article 307(5) CSA).

The disciplinary punishments, provided for in Article 308(1), items 3, 4 and 6 CSA, are imposed on the judges by a decision of the respective college of the SJC (Article 311, item 2, Article 316 CSA). The decisions of the SJC are subject to appeal to the SAC (Article 323 CSA). The suction under item 1 is imposed by the administrative chair of the court and is approved or reversed by the SJC.

Chapter 2. The Bar

§1. Exercise of the Legal Profession

I. Conditions for Admission

54. According to Article 134(1) C *the bar is free, independent, and self-governing*. The attorney offers legal assistance and defence of the freedoms, rights and legal interests of individuals and legal entities (Article 2(1) AB) *before the bodies of judicial power as well*. The organization of the bar and its activity, the procedure for acquisition and revocation of attorney's rights and his legal status are regulated by AB.

55. Any Bulgarian citizen or a citizen of the European Economic Area (EEA) and Switzerland possessing legal capacity can become an attorney, provided that he/she meets the following requirements: to be a higher-education graduate in law, to have acquired the legal capacity of a lawyer, to have two years of experience in practising law, to have passed the examination specified in the AB (except when having experience more than five years or has a PhD in Law) and to possess the required moral and professional qualities (Article 4(1) AB).

According to Article 5 AB an attorney cannot be: a person sentenced to imprisonment for an intended indictable offence, a person placed under interdiction or suffering from a mental illness, a trader, a civil servant, a person who works under an employment relationship, except for an academic position in a university or scientific organization, a person who is discharged from the office of judge, prosecutor or investigator under the conditions of Article 129(3), item 5 C or is dismissed for disciplinary reasons from the office of registry judge, or State bailiff, legal counsel or inquirer, a person who is deprived of the legal capacity of a notary or a bailiff, etc.

56. The attorneys who have taken an oath and the attorneys whose names are entered in the list of the bar college are the prerequisites for the acquisition of attorney's rights (Article 3(2) AB). Although the colleges are regional, the entry in the list of the bar college does not limit the attorney's practice only to the region of that college. He/she is free to practice throughout the country, to appear before any regional, district or appellate court in the Republic of Bulgaria, and also before the SCC and the SAC. According to Article 24(2) AB, the parties can be represented and defended before the SCC and the SAC by an attorney who has at least five years' juridical duration of service.

Junior attorneys are also entitled to work in the bar. According to Article 20(1) AB, a lawyer with less than two years of juridical duration of service who meets the requirements of Article 4(1), items 1, 2, 4 and 5 AB can be entered as a junior attorney on the grounds of a decision of the Bar Council provided that no obstacles under Article 5 AB are present. The junior attorney has the rights and obligations of an attorney with the restrictions specified in the AB. According to Article 20(9) AB, the junior attorney acquires the rights of an attorney after a period of two years, unless the obstacles specified in Article 5 AB are present.

The attorney's defence is not obligatory in Bulgarian civil proceedings. In civil proceedings the procedural representatives per procuration can be legal advisers or other employees of juridical education working in institutions, enterprises, cooperatives and other public organizations and legal entities and the sole proprietor (Article 32, item 3 CCP) and other persons provided for in the laws (Article 32, item 4 CCP).

57. According to Article 10(1) AB, a citizen of a foreign country who acquired the legal capacity of an attorney in accordance with the legislation of his/her country is entitled to act before the judiciary bodies in the Republic of Bulgaria as a defender or attorney of a citizen of his/her country, together with a Bulgarian attorney, if a treaty between the Bulgarian State and the foreign State provides this, or on the grounds of reciprocity he/she made a request for it to the chair of the SBC. The chair of the SBC renders a motivated decision within seven days following the filing of the request. The decision refusing the admission of the foreign attorney as a defender before a judiciary body can be appealed to the SCC within fourteen days following its announcement.

58. According to Article 11 AB, a citizen of a Member State of the EU a party to EEA and Switzerland who has acquired legal capacity as an attorney in accordance with the legislation of his/her country, is entitled to exercise the profession of an attorney under his/her professional title of origin on the territory of the Republic of Bulgaria. Such an attorney is called, though not quite correctly, an attorney from the EU. Where there is a requirement for minimum experience in order to be a procedural representative before the court, the attorney from the EU should certify his/her experience. While practising in the Republic of Bulgaria the foreign attorney has the rights and obligations of a Bulgarian attorney (Article 14 AB). The attorney from the EU is liable for any damages in all events of faulty non-performance of his/her obligations under the AB (Article 15 AB).

When the attorney exercises his/her profession temporary on the territory of the Republic of Bulgaria prior to the first act, he/she is obliged to notify in writing the respective Bar Council and to present a document certifying his/her legal capacity in the country where it was acquired, proof of insurance, identity document, as well as the written consent of a lawyer from the relevant Bar Association who will accompany the applicant in case of litigation. The chairman or a member of the Bar Council appointed therefore immediately issues the attorney from the EU lawyer a certificate of notification. The refusal to issue a certificate under Article 14(3) AB is subject to appeal to the Chairperson of the SBC, which pronounces immediately.

According to Article 16 AB, the attorney from the EU is entitled to settle permanently in the territory of the Republic of Bulgaria and can work as an attorney under his/her professional title in the country in which he/she acquired the legal capacity of an attorney. The SAC makes the entry of the bar college (firm) in the State of origin, which member the foreign attorney is. The SBC gives a notification to the competent body of the country in which the legal capacity of an attorney was acquired, notifying it of the entry of the foreign attorney into the Single Register of foreign attorneys.

According to Article 17 AB, after three years of effective and uninterrupted exercise of the profession of an attorney under his/her professional title in the country where the legal capacity of an attorney was acquired or *after successfully passing the examination, the attorney from the EU is entitled* to seek entry into a bar college in the Republic of Bulgaria. The entry into a bar college provides the foreign attorney with the rights of a Bulgarian attorney.

At present the Bulgarian legislator has executed its engagements towards the EU with regard to the implementation into the internal law of the rules of Council Directive 77/249/EEC (*see* paragraph 55) and of Directive 98/5/EC.

II. Rights and Duties

59. According to Article 29(1) AB, the attorney is equal to a judge in the respect and assistance due to him/her by the courts, the bodies of pretrial proceedings, as well as by the administrative and other bodies.

The attorney has free access to the files and can search them and make copies of the papers and he/she also has priority in receiving information from the court, the bodies of pretrial proceedings and the administrative bodies within the country (Article 31 AB). The papers and dossiers of the attorney, as well as his/her electronic documents, computer and other information carriers, are inviolable and are not subject to examination or seizure. The correspondence between the attorney and his/her client is inviolable too and is not subject to examination and cannot be used as a means of evidence (Article 33(1) and (2) AB).

The attorney is obliged to practise his/her profession conscientiously and his/her conduct should make him worthy of trust and respect in the society: to be governed by the rules of law and to protect the rights and legal interests of their clients in the best possible way; to accurately inform their clients of their rights and obligations to keep his/her integrity and independence in the discharge of his/her professional duties (Article 40(1) AB).

The attorney has the right to transfer his/her powers to another attorney, which he/she was entrusted with under a client's letter of attorney, only with the consent of the client (Article 25(4) AB). He/she neither have the right to represent or defend both parties to the case at the same time, nor does he/she have the right to take up a case for one of the parties and subsequently for the other one, unless the interests of the parties are contradictory ones, and the parties have given their consent (Article 43(3)). Attorneys who are partners do not have the right to represent opposing parties (Article 43(4)).

According to Article 44 AB, an attorney who is entered in the National Register for legal assistance is obligated to provide legal assistance in accordance with the Legal Aid Act (LAA) whenever he/she is nominated to do so. The attorney is obligated to provide legal assistance in the proceedings just as though the client authorizes him.

The Attorney's Code of Ethics (ACE) of the SBC lays down the rules of attorneys' ethics.

III. Discipline

60. The attorney is liable for any damages in all events of faulty non-performance of his/her obligations under the AB or the ordinances of the SBC if the rights and legal interests of the client are injured because of this non-performance (Article 51 AB). The attorney and the junior attorney bear disciplinary responsibility for non-performance of obligations (Articles 131 and 132 AB). In such cases under Article 129(1) AB the competence is of the disciplinary court of the college in which the lawyer is registered, the Supreme Disciplinary Court, respectively. The decision of the Disciplinary Court is subject to appeal before the Supreme Disciplinary Court.

§2. (Public) Institutions and (Private) Organizations

61. The attorneys are organized in bar colleges on the territorial principle. The regions, number and seats of the bar colleges, the setting up of new colleges and the closing down of existing ones is determined by the SBC (Article 78(3) AB). No more than one bar college can be established in the seat of a district court (Article 78(4) AB). Currently the number of bar colleges and the regions thereof are the same as the number and regions of the district courts. The bar college is a legal entity, and it consists of the attorneys whose names are entered in its list (Article 78(2) AB). The bodies of the bar college are the General Assembly, the Barristers' Council (including the chair), the Control Council and the Disciplinary Court (Article 79 AB).

62. The bar also has its nationwide organization. The General Meeting of the attorneys from all over the country hears and approves the report of the SBC, the Supreme Control Council and the Supreme Disciplinary Council, and elects the SBC and its chair, the Supreme Control Council and the Supreme Disciplinary Council and its chair (Article 113 AB).

The SBC issues the ordinances assigned to it by the AB and adopts the Attorney's Ethical Code, convenes and holds the general meeting of the attorneys from all over the country, implements its decisions and reports, keeps the Single Registers of attorneys, junior attorneys and the associations of attorneys, the Single Register of foreign attorneys who have the right to appear as defenders before a Bulgarian court, organizes a centre for training of attorneys and determines the conditions and training programmes for improving the qualification, gives its opinion about projects for statutory instruments and makes proposals for improvements in the operative legislation, makes proposals to the chair of the SCC for rendering rulings and interpretative decisions and gives its opinion, etc.

The Supreme Control Council controls the activity of the control councils of the bar colleges and reports in the general meeting of the country's attorneys (Article 127 AB).

The Supreme Disciplinary Court as the first-instance court has jurisdiction over disciplinary cases instituted against members of Barristers' councils, control councils or disciplinary courts of the colleges, the SBC, the Supreme Control Council and the Supreme Disciplinary Court.

63. According to Article 3(1) AB, the attorneys are free to work on their own or through the associations provided for in the AB:

(a) The association of attorneys, in which attorneys, attorneys from the EU whose names are entered in the Single Register of the foreign attorneys and attorneys' firms unite their activities under a contract of association. The rules of Articles 357–364 OCA apply to these associations. The contract also specifies the bounds of common activities (Article 52 AB). According to Bulgarian law, the unincorporated partnership is not a legal entity. The procedural representation in civil cases is made by an attorney, who is required to have the necessary authorization; he/she must appear in person (Article 32, item 1 CCP). He/she is not a representative of an attorneys' partnership, but a representative of the client, who is a party to the case.

(b) According to Article 57(1) AB, one or more attorneys, as well as the foreign attorneys who are permanently settled on the territory of the Republic of Bulgaria or temporarily exercising their profession are entitled to set up attorneys' firms. The attorneys' firm is a legal entity. An attorney cannot be a member of more than one attorney's firms. The seat of the attorneys' firm is entered in the register of the district court. According to Article 64 AB, the attorney's membership in an attorneys' firm does not limit his/her capacity to exercise the profession of attorney on his/her own, unless otherwise provided in the contract. As for the defence and representation before the court, the bodies of pre-court proceedings, the administrative bodies and services, individuals and legal entities, the client authorizes the attorneys' firm. The manager of the attorneys' firm reauthorizes one or several partners. The client is entitled to choose an attorney and to authorize him/her as a procedural representative, though the contract is concluded with the attorneys' firm (Article 71 AB). Article 72 provides that each partner bears personal responsibility for any damages inflicted to the client. The attorneys' firm bears joint responsibility with the attorney up to the amount of the instalments made.

(c) The third form of joint exercise of the profession of an attorney under the AB is the conclusion of cooperation contracts between attorneys and attorneys' firms (Article 76 AB) for the performance of certain legal work or the joint assumption of work in proceedings.

64. In connection with the *Directive 98/5/EC of the European Parliament and of the Council* to facilitate practice of the profession of lawyer on a permanent basis in a Member State other than that in which the qualification was obtained, Article 77a AB provides that the attorneys from the EU enlisted in the Single Register of the foreign attorneys are eligible of practising their profession together with other foreign attorneys whose names are entered in the Single Register of the foreign attorneys as well as with other attorneys whose names are entered in the respective attorney register under the forms of joint practising the attorney profession specified in Chapter Ten, sections I–III AB.

Besides, one or more attorneys from the EU are eligible for practising the attorney profession on the territory of the Republic of Bulgaria in a branch of their group established in another EU Member State. The partners might also be attorneys under Article 4(1) AB. The registration and the activity of the branch are performed according to the procedure under Articles 57–58, 60–75 AB. The limit concerning the number of attorneys under Article 58, sentence I AB is not applicable.

Chapter 3. The Bailiffs

§1. Exercise of the Profession

65. There are two types of bailiffs in Bulgaria: a State bailiff (SB) and private bailiff (PB). SB under Bulgarian law has a common executive competence for all executive methods. He/she may only be a person who has a degree in law and passed the required training JSA and has acquired legal capacity and meets the additional requirements under Article 267 in connection with Article 162 CSA; Article 5 PBA. These requirements are a guarantee for conducting a lawful enforcement process. Both types of bailiffs are appointed by the Minister of Justice (MJ) after competitions conducted by the Ministry of Justice separately for the SB and the PB.

Both types of bailiffs carry out the enforcement under the CPC and are obliged to perform their functions lawfully. The same actions and inactions are subject to appeal (Article 435 CCP) and the order of appeal.

If necessary for the execution, bailiff may order to open the buildings of the debtor and to search his belongings, dwelling and other premises. State offices, municipalities, organizations and citizens are required to assist the bailiff. Upon request, the police authorities are required to assist the bailiff in performing his/her functions. In relation to enforcement, the bailiff has the right of access to information in the judicial and administrative services, including NRA, NSSI, ESGRAON, the Central Depository, the persons keeping a register of government securities, the Traffic Police, the Register of Bank Accounts and Safes with the BNB, etc. In cases where the debtor's personal presence is necessary and he/she does not appear, the bailiff may order the police authorities to fetch him/her.

66. According to Article 264(2) CSA, SBs execute private enforcement.[25] Article 264(2) CSA provides that each district court has an SB. SBs do not have the capacity of judges and cannot resolve legal disputes. Each SB operates in a region that coincides with the region of the regional court.[26] There is a judicial enforcement service in judicial regions with two or more SBs, one of whom being appointed as the head of the office by the Minister of Justice for a term of five years with the right to reappointment. The SB is obliged to exercise his/her powers lawfully. For disciplinary reasons, he/she has disciplinary responsibility, may be removed from office by the Minister of Justice in the case of serious or systematic violations (Article 271 CSA). For damages caused by his/her unlawful actions, the property liability lies with the Ministry of Justice on the ground. Article 441 CCP in connection with Article 49 OCA, which has the right of recourse against SB up to a maximum amount of his/her monthly remuneration (Article 278 in connection with Article 206 LC), unless the offence is committed.

---

25. SBs may be also entrusted with the collection of receivables of the judiciary.
26. When the position is not occupied, or the appointed SB is prevented from performing it and cannot be replaced by another SB from the same court, the chairman of the respective district court or the MJ may second a SB from another judicial district in his place (Art. 274 CSA).

67. Unlike SB, who is a State body, PB is a private person to whom the State has assigned a public function, and the law enforcement and the enforcement of civil rights in the broad sense of the word. It is stipulated in Article 2(1) PBA that PB is a person delegated by the State to enforce private claims.[27] According to Article 2(4) PBA, his/her region is the same as that of the respective district court.[28] The obligation of the PB is to form the enforcement case when duly addressed by a request is the same as the SB (Article 19(1) PBA, Article 435(1) CCP). For damages caused by his illegal actions and inactions, PB has property liability (Article 441 CPC).

§2. (Public) Institutions and (Private) Organizations

68. There is an Inspectorate with the Minister of Justice. It controls the activities of SBs and PBs, including the activity on the formation, movement and finalization of enforcement cases, and summarizes and analyses the practice in these cases (Article 372(1) CSA).

Disciplinary punishment of the DUI is imposed by the Minister of Justice with a motivated order. A proposal to impose a disciplinary punishment on SB may be made by the President of the regional or district court concerned and by the Chief Inspector of the Inspectorate to the Minister of Justice. Prior to imposing the penalty, the Minister of Justice hears the person or gives him/her the opportunity to submit written explanations or objections to the proposal made within seven days. The disciplinary punishment is deemed to have been enforced as of the date of notifying the SB of the order of the Minister of Justice. The order of the Minister of Justice may be appealed to the SAC by SB to whom disciplinary punishment has been imposed in person and by the petitioner. The appeal does not suspend the enforcement unless the SAC decides otherwise. The decision of the three-member panel of the SAC is subject to a cassation appeal before a five-member panel of the SAC.

SBs have their own independent, voluntary, professional organization – the Association of State Bailiffs that aims to protect their professional, intellectual, cultural, social and material interests; to promote the establishment of the profession of SB and to enhance its prestige vis-à-vis the State and society.

69. The Chamber of Private Bailiffs is a legal entity with headquarters in Sofia. All PBs are its members by right. The bodies of the Chamber are the General

27. According to Art. 2(2) and (3) PBA, the State and the bodies competent to establish public receivables may assign to the PBA the collection of public receivables.
28. According to Art. 40(1) PBA, a PB may be replaced by another PB from the same or neighbouring region. The relations between them are regulated by an agreement. The substitute is obliged to notify the Council of the Chamber of PB of his deputy within seven days. The replacement may not last more than three months continuously and more than six months in one calendar year (Art. 40(3) PBA. When the PB is absent or unable to perform its functions and there is no one to replace him, he is obliged to notify the Council of the Chamber, which appoints the PB to take over his replacement during this time. The replacement may not last more than one month continuously and more than three months in one calendar year (Art. 41 PBA).

Assembly, the Council of the Chamber, the Control Council and the Disciplinary Committee (Article 3 PBA). The Chamber creates and keeps a register of PBs.

The activity of the PB is reviewed and controlled by the Inspectorate with the Minister of Justice and the Council of the Chamber. PB has disciplinary liability for guilty failure to fulfil his/her obligations under the law and the statute of the Chamber and a panel of the Disciplinary Committee[29] of the Chamber of Private Bailiffs may be subject to disciplinary punishment as provided in Article 68 PBA. Disciplinary proceedings are instituted at the request of the Minister of Justice or by a decision of the Chamber Council.[30] The session is held in camera, inviting PB, a representative of the Chamber Council and a representative of the Minister of Justice. The decision of the Disciplinary Board may be appealed before the SAC by the PB, the Chamber of the Council and the Minister of Justice.

29. There is a quota of the Chamber of PB and quota of the Ministry of Justice.
30. The PB can provide explanations within seven days of notification.

Part II. Jurisdiction

Chapter 1. Domestic Jurisdiction

§1. Subservience: Disputes over subservience – Resolution of Subservience Conflicts: Special Procedures –Effects of a Ruling on the Subservience Issue

70. The term 'subservience' is typical for Bulgarian civil procedure. In principle, all civil cases fall within the jurisdiction of the ordinary courts. As has been pointed out (*see* paragraph 29), there are no specialized courts in Bulgaria for dealing with certain types of civil cases. However, Article 128(1), items 6, 7, 8 APC provides for the jurisdiction of the administrative courts for claims for damages[31] caused by unlawful acts, actions and omissions of administrative bodies and officials; as well as for damages caused by judicial activity of administrative courts and the SAC; damages for the enforcement damages, which is performed by the public executors with the National Revenue Agency (NRA) for the collection of public receivables under the procedure of the TSPC, as well as for declaring of invalidity or revocation of decisions of administrative courts. These claims are considered under the procedure of Chapter XI of the APC 'Compensation proceedings', which are referenced by Article 1 (2) ALSMD. Additionally, according to Article 203(3) APC claims for damages caused by a sufficiently significant violation of EU law are considered under this chapter, and the standards of non-contractual liability of the State for violation of EU law for property liability and for admissibility of the claim apply. In Article 128 APC the legislator uses the term 'subservience'. Administrative courts are specialized courts founded on the grounds of Article 119(2) C, which specialization refers both to administrative and civil law disputes due to the legal connection of ancillary claims for damages with the unlawful nature of the acts and actions of the provided organs.

Claims for damages, caused to citizens by law enforcement bodies (investigative bodies, the prosecution or the court), specified in Article 2 ALSMD and the Commission for Counter-Corruption and Unlawfully Acquired Assets Forfeiture, as well as for damages caused by these bodies due to violation of EU law, are under the subservience of the general courts and are considered under the CCP (Article 2, Article 2a and Article 2b ALSMD).

31. Under Art. 1(1) ALSMD the State and the municipalities are liable for those damages.

Claims for damages caused by PBs are under the subservience of the general courts, and the Ministry of Justice is responsible for them (Article 441 CCP in connection with Article 49 OCA).

71. In the cases when the damages have been caused to citizens by illegal acts, actions or omissions of State bodies and officials the claim for indemnification should be laid by the order of the ALSMD (Article 74(2) APD), i.e., before the administrative courts and it is considered under the order of the CAP (Article 1(2) ALSMD). Even when no proceedings have been conducted before the Commission for Protection Against Discrimination under Section I of APD, item 4 of the Interpretative Order of 19 May 2015 of the Civil College of the Supreme Court of Cassation and Second Board of the Supreme SAC, Case No. 2/2014). Besides every person whose rights have been affected by an administrative act issued in violation of this or other laws, settling equality of treatment may appeal it in the administrative court by the order of the CAP (Article 73 APD). In the progress of these proceedings, it is possible a claim on indemnity for damages to be lodged along with the underlying claim (Article 204(2) CAP).

According to Article 74(1) APD in the cases under Section I any person who has suffered damages from violation of rights under this or other laws, governing equality of treatment, may file a claim for compensation under the general procedure against the persons and/or bodies that have caused the damages. This claim is considered by the general courts following the procedure of the CCP.

72. The court is obliged to monitor the subservience ex officio. Under Article 15(1) CCP the question whether a case that is initiated must be heard by the courts can be raised by the parties and by the court ex officio *at any stage of the case* unless a normative act provides a time period for that.

The ruling of the court regarding subservience can be appealed by a private appeal (Article 15(2) CCP). The ruling of the second instance is subject to cassation appeal to the SCC, if it bars further development of proceedings, i.e., when the court considered that the case is not subservient to it (Article 274(3), item 1 CCP; item 9 of ID No. 1-2013-GMCC and the Com.C. of the SCC).[32]

In Interpretative Decree No. 1 of 29.09.2016 under ID No. 1-2015-GMCC and the Com.C. of the SCC and the General Assembly of the judges of the I and II board of the SAC it was accepted that a judicial act issued by a court that is not competent under the rules of subservience, distributing cases between civil and administrative courts, is inadmissible. This view is also shared in legal doctrine.[33]

32. In this ID it was accepted that the ruling by the appellate court, which affirms a ruling of the first-instance court, which has disregarded the recusal for non-subservience is not subject to cassation appeal, as it is not of the category of rulings, which block the development of the proceedings, provided in Art. 274(3), item 1 and 2 CCP.

33. *See* Popova, V. Subservience and disputes on subservience under the new CCP and APC; Published in: 'V. Popova, Selected works', item III 'Selected works', Ciela publishing, 2010, pp. 78–101; electronic issue 'Ciela Norma' – 10 March 2010, available at http://www.ciela.net; Mingova, A. in Stalev, J., Mingova, A., Popova, V., Stamboliev, O., Ivanova, R. Bulgarian civil procedure law, S., 2020, p. 500; pp. 556–557; Ivanova, R. In Stalev, J., Mingova, A., Popova, V., Stamboliev, O., Ivanova, R., p. 119.

73. Article 16 CCP, entitled *Dispute on the scope of jurisdiction,* stipulates that if the court and the other institutions have refused to hear the lawsuit as not belonging to their scope of subservience, the claimant may initiate a dispute on the scope of subservience before the SCC.[34] There is a duplication of procedure that protects the legal interest if the court refused to hear the case because of its non-subservience – under Article 15(2) and Article 274 CCP, the claimant is entitled to appeal against the ruling of the court regarding subservience with a preclusive term (Article 275 CCP – *see also* paragraph 78). The legislator did not provide a term regarding the initiation of the dispute over subservience before the SCC. Article 16 CCP does not stipulate an opportunity for an appealing of the SCC's ruling on the dispute initiated by the claimant referring the subservience issue. There is not a provided procedure for the SCC referring to the examination of the disputes over subservience.

74. The rules for distribution of cases between the general and administrative courts are contained in Article 128 APC (*see* paragraph 70), entitled 'Subservience'. The APC is not consistent in its use of the term 'subservience'. The title of Article 128 APC is 'Subservience'. It defines the competence of the administrative courts and states: 'All cases on requests for: ... are subservient to the administrative courts' and lists the cases under the subservience of the administrative courts (*see* paragraph 70). In Article 135(5) APC, however, disputes over jurisdiction between general and administrative courts are called jurisdictional disputes. In Article 135(5) APC it is provided: 'The disputes on jurisdiction between the general and the administrative courts are decided by a chamber of three representatives of the SCC and two representatives of the SAC". As a result of the provided inconsistency there is also an inconsistency in Interpretative Decree No. 1 of 29.09.2016 under ID No. 1/2015-GMCC and the Com. C. of the SCC and the General Assembly of the judges of the I and II boards of the SAC (*see* paragraph 72). The dispositive part mentions subservience, while the motives mention jurisdiction.

In case law the case is transmitted to the administrative court, when the ruling under Article 15(2) CCP enters into effect. This ruling is not binding on the administrative court. Under Article 135(6) CAP if the court, to which the case has been sent, finds that it is not within its jurisdiction, it must send it to the court under

34. However, according to the Constitution (*see* para. 29), it is inadmissible to grant a justice administering power to an institution that is not a court and the texts of Arts 14–17 CCP are copied from the old CCP. A dispute over subservience between a court of general jurisdiction established under Art. 119(1) C, to which civil cases are subservient according to Art. 14 CCP, and a court belonging to the system of specialized administrative courts is regulated by Art. 135 APC. Under the current legal system, a dispute over subservience may arise between the court and the administrative body when arguing about the type of case, e.g., in connection with the distinction between State and municipal receivables and public and private ones (Art. 162 TIPCC). The public receivables are established by the order and by the body, determined in the respective law (Art. 166(1) TIPCC). The act for establishing a public receivable is subject to appeal before the respective administrative court. Taxes unduly paid are refundable (Art. 129 TIPCC). The act for establishing the public receivable and the refusals for partial or complete refunding of the paid money is appealed by the order of appeal of the revision act (Arts 131 and 168 TPSC), what in accordance with Art. 120(1) C also includes the court appeal (Arts 131, 156 TIPCC in connection with Art. 131 TIPCC).

Article 135(3), respectively, under Article 135(4) or (5) CCP, to determine the jurisdiction.[35] So, if there is a dispute between ordinary and administrative courts, the court to which the case has been sent will seize the SCC, respectively the SAC (depending on the fact if the court is a part of the ordinary courts' system or the administrative courts' system) and the relevant mixed chamber (panel) will be formed under paragraph 5 of Article 135 consisting of three representatives of the SCC and two representatives of the SAC. This chamber of judges from the SCC and SAC is not bound by the entered into force ruling under Article 15(2) CCP. It can decide that the case is subservient to the general courts, including when under the procedure for cassation appeal of the ruling it has reached the SCC (Article 274(3), item 1 CCP; item 9 ID No. 1-2013-GMCC and the Com.C. of the SCC) and the three-member panel of the SCC has decided that the case is subservient to the general courts.

§2. Subject-Matter jurisdiction: Disputes over Subject-Matter Jurisdiction – Resolution of Subject-Matter Jurisdiction Conflicts: Special Procedures – Effects of a Ruling on the Subject-Matter Jurisdiction Issue

I. Factors to Be Taken into Account (E.g., the Value of the Claim, Other Factors): Overview of the Jurisdiction of Different Courts

75. Subject-matter jurisdiction under Bulgarian civil procedure law is a system of rules according to which the civil cases within the jurisdiction of the general courts are distributed among the regional and district courts as first-instance courts. The subject matter of the case is the criterion used by the legislator in distributing the cases by the rules of subject-matter jurisdiction. The regional court is the basic first-instance court. It has jurisdiction over all civil cases except those that fall under the jurisdiction of the district courts by virtue of law (Article 103 CCP, Article 76 CSA).

76. Under Article 104 CCP the district court, as a first-instance court, has jurisdiction over claims for establishing or disputing the origin, revocation of adoption, putting under a restraint order or repealing it; any actions for ownership and other rights in rem to an immovable property with a cost of the action exceeding BGN 50,000; claims regarding civil and commercial cases, the amount exceeding BGN 25,000, except for the claims for alimony, for labour disputes and for receivables under deficit deeds;[36] claims for establishing inadmissibility or invalidity or non-existence of circumstances entered in the register of the district court where so provided for in a law, and claims that fall within the district court's jurisdiction under other laws. These are the following claims: recognition and enforcement of decisions of foreign courts (Article 118(2) and Article 119(1) PILC), protection of both

35. Pursuant to Art. 135(8) APC the rulings under disputes for subservience are not subject to appeal.
36. Regardless of the amount of the claim, the regional court has jurisdiction over ownership claims (Art. 356 CCP) and claims for juridical partition (Art. 341 CCP).

membership in commercial companies and certain membership rights (Article 71 C. Code), revocation of decisions of the general meeting of a commercial company (Article 74 C. Code), winding up of a commercial company (Articles 95, 155, 252 C. Code), rendering a commercial company illegitimate (Article 70 C. Code), and claims under Articles 645, 646 and 647 C. Code, as well as those under Article 135 OCA relating to bankruptcy proceedings (Article 649 C. Code) and the class actions (Article 381 CCP, *see* paragraph 372).

II. Main Claims and Ancillary Claims

77. Both practice and doctrine assume that a case can fall within the jurisdiction of the district court if two cases are mutually related and the principal claim is under the jurisdiction of the district court, while the ancillary claim is under the jurisdiction of the regional court, e.g., where a claim for establishing fatherhood is joined with an alimony claim. The legislator accepted this notion with the explicit provision of Article 104, item 6 CCP.

III. Legal Significance: Disputes over Subject-Matter Jurisdiction – Resolution of Jurisdiction Conflicts (Special Procedures: Effects of Ruling on the Jurisdiction Issue, Etc.)

78. Subject-matter jurisdiction has the nature of an absolute procedural prerequisite, and the court is obliged to observe it ex officio. However, this does not revoke the right of the parties to a challenge on the grounds of an absence of subject-matter jurisdiction. Article 119(1) CCP states that an objection to the subject-matter jurisdiction of the case may be lodged prior to the close of the proceeding in the Court of Second Instance and may furthermore be raised ex officio by the court. The subject-matter jurisdiction established by law cannot be changed on the grounds of an agreement of the parties to the case (Article 117 CCP).

Where the court finds that a case does not fall within its subject-matter jurisdiction, it is obliged to discontinue the proceedings and to send the case to the competent court (Article 118(2), sentence I CCP). The proceedings are regarded as pending from the day the statement of claim was filed with the incompetent court (Article 118(2), sentence II CCP). The ruling is subject to appeal by a private appeal to the superior court (Article 121 CCP). The rulings of the intermediate appellate courts that dismiss a private appeal against the ruling are subject to cassation appeal before the SCC (Article 274(3) CCP; ID No. 1-2013-GMCC and the Com.C. of the SCC[37]). The entry into force of the ruling on subject-matter jurisdiction is a prerequisite for sending the case to the other court.

37. The ruling of the appellate court, which confirms the ruling of the first-instance court, which disregarded the objection on subject-matter jurisdiction, is not subject to cassation appeal, as it is not in the category of acts provided for in Art. 274(3), item 1 and item 2 CCP, item 9 ID No.1/2013 on ID No.1/2013 GMCC and the Com. C. of the SCC.

The court where the case is sent has the right to raise a dispute over jurisdiction. The dispute over subject-matter jurisdiction between a regional and district court is subject to determination by the appellate court (Article 122 CCP). The ruling under Article 122 CCP, issued under a dispute over jurisdiction between the courts is not subject to appeal as it does not fall within the acts, provided in Article 274(3), item 1 and 2 CCP (item 9 ID No. 1-2013 on ID No. 1/2013-GMCC and the Com.C. of the SCC).

There are now two procedures under Bulgarian law for considering a dispute over subject-matter jurisdiction. One is following a complaint of a party. The other is in a dispute raised by the court to which the case was sent. The practice in the cases is contradictory: when the issue of subject-matter jurisdiction is resolved under the procedure of Article 122 CCP, whether the appellate court is bound by this ruling or can redecide it; when the ruling under Article 121 CCP has been appealed and the appeal has been disregarded, whether the jurisdiction is stabilized or when appealing the decision rendered in the case, the appellate court may decide something else.

If a case under the jurisdiction of the district court was considered and determined by a regional court, that decision is inadmissible. The district court, in its capacity of an intermediate appellate court, is obliged to invalidate the decision of the regional court and to determine the case as a first-instance court (Article 270(3) CCP). According to Article 270(4) CCP, the decision of the district court cannot be reversed for the reason that the case is under the jurisdiction of the regional court.

§3. Venue (Territorial Jurisdiction): Disputes over Venue Jurisdiction – Resolution of Jurisdiction Conflicts: Special Procedures – Effects of a Ruling on the Venue Jurisdiction Issue

I. Factors to Be Taken into Account: Overview of the Different Rules

79. Venue jurisdiction is a system of rules according to which the civil cases falling under the subject-matter jurisdiction of regional courts, or district courts, as the first instance, are distributed among the courts of the same level (regional or district) in accordance with the venue of the court. The relationship between the case and the venue of the court determines the venue jurisdiction.

80. General venue jurisdiction is determined by the relationship between the defendant and the venue of the court.

Where the defendant is an individual, the general venue jurisdiction is determined by the permanent address of the defendant (Article 105 CCP). A person's permanent address is that address in the settlement which the person has indicated for entry in the population registers (Article 93 Civil Status Law). The notion of permanent address differs from the notion of habitual residence which is used in Article 4(1), item 1 PILC (with its legal definition under Article 48(7) PILC).

The Bulgarian legislator stressed on the registration of the individuals in the civil status register when the definition of the inner local jurisdiction was made there the difference between the jurisdiction and the international subservience is. It refers both – to the permanent and the current address.

Claims against minors or persons under interdiction are lodged in the place of residence of their legal representatives (Article 106 CCP).

Under Article 107 CCP, the claim against a person of unknown residence is lodged in the place of the permanent address of his/her proxy or representative, and if the person of unknown residence has no proxy or representative, the claim is lodged in the permanent address of the claimant. The same rules apply to those cases where the defendant does not reside at the permanent address within the territory of the Republic of Bulgaria. If the claimant does not have a permanent address in the Republic of Bulgaria, the claim is lodged with the court in Sofia.

The general venue jurisdiction is determined by the place of management or the seat of the defendant if the defendant is a legal entity (Article 108(1) CCP).[38] As for disputes arising from direct relations with legal entities' departments or branches, the claims can also be lodged by the location of the department or branch (Article 108(1), sentence II CCP, Article 20 C. Code). This jurisdiction is elective. The claimant is entitled to choose between this and the jurisdiction by the legal entity's seat. In these cases, only the venue jurisdiction is specified. It is the legal entity that is a party to the case, and not the branch or department, because they are not legal entities.

Except for cases under Articles 109 and 110 CCP, claims against the State and State establishments and their branches are lodged with the court within the venue where the legal relationship forming the subject matter of the dispute arose. If it was established abroad, the claim is lodged with the courts in Sofia (Article 108(2) CCP).

81. At the discretion of the claimant, the alimony claim can be lodged in the permanent address of the defendant (Article 112 CCP). Only the claimant has the right to choose between the two possibilities specified above. The right regarding the choice of jurisdiction only applies to a claimant seeking alimony and on the grounds of Article 150 FC in a case of a supplement to an adjudicated alimony but not to the claimant who lodged a claim under Article 150 FC for lowering the amount of alimony. The objective is to alleviate the situation of the persons seeking alimony.

A consumer may bring an action, alternatively, before the court exercising jurisdiction over the current or permanent address of the said consumer (Article 113 CCP).[39] Labour claims may be brought by the worker against his employer and at the place where he normally works (Article 114 CCP).

82. According to Article 109 CCP, the claims for property rights over a real estate, partition of a jointly owned real estate, borders and protection in cases of impaired possession of a real estate are lodged in the real estate's location. It is also this location where the following claims are lodged: claims for concluding a final contract for establishing and transferring property rights over a real estate, and

38. The headquarters of the legal entity is the same as the office of its management (Art. 132 CRA, Art. 12(2) C. Code).
39. Under Art. 94 CRA the present address is the address where the person is staying. In accordance with Art. 96(1) CRA one's present address is declared personally by filling in an address card with the municipal administration.

claims for denouncing and invalidating contracts for property rights over a real estate. Here the capacity of the defendant is not important; the defendant can be an individual, a legal entity or the State (Article 108(2) CCP, *see* paragraph 80). If the real estate is situated in several venues, the claim under Article 109 CCP is lodged with the court of any of these venues, at the discretion of the claimant (Article 116 CCP).

The venue of the real estate can be challenged by the parties or by the court ex officio prior to the conclusion of the trial in the first-instance court (Article 119(2) CCP). This jurisdiction determines the distribution of cases between Bulgarian and foreign courts and surpasses even the judicial immunity under Article 18(1), item 5 CCP in connection with Article 12 CIPL (*see* paragraph 94).

83. Claims for inheritance, invalidation of testaments, partition of inheritance or invalidation of a voluntary partition are lodged where inventory of the inheritance was taken (Article 110(1) CCP). According to Article 1 Inheritance Law, this is the last place of residence of the testator. If this was a Bulgarian citizen and upon his/her death his place of residence was not the Republic of Bulgaria, the above claims can be lodged in his/her last permanent address or with the court within whose venue his/her estates are located (Article 110(2) CCP).

84. The claim for damages from a tort is lodged where the act was committed or in the permanent address of the defendant (Article 115 CCP). Compensation claims under the Insurer's Insurance Code against the Insurer, the Guarantee Fund and the National Bureau of Bulgarian Motor Insurers shall be brought before a court in whose area at the time of the occurrence of the insured event the present or permanent address of the plaintiff is located or its registered office; on the occurrence of the insured event or at the place where the insured event occurred (Article 115(2) CPC).

85. According to Article 111 CCP, claims for pecuniary receivables on contractual grounds may also be brought, alternatively, before the court exercising jurisdiction over the current address of the respondent. This jurisdiction is also elective.

86. The claim against defendants from different venues is lodged with the court of any of those venues (Article 116 CCP), but only if he/she has joined the claims against the defendants.

II. Main Claims and Ancillary Claims

87. The following claims are lodged with the court where the first claim was lodged: the counterclaim of the defendant against the claimant (Article 211 CCP), the cross-claim of the principal party against a co-party (Article 219(3) CCP) and the Principal Intervention claim under Article 225 CCP. If these claims are lodged in separate cases, they fall within the jurisdiction of another court in accordance with the rules of venue jurisdiction.

Also, if certain parties joined their claims and their cases are mutually connected, the venue jurisdiction of the principal claim determines the venue jurisdiction of the ensuing claim, and if the claim is lodged in other proceedings, it falls under the jurisdiction of another court according to the rules of venue jurisdiction (for instance, a claim for denouncing a contract and a claim for returning the receipts, a revindication claim and a claim for damages caused to a chattel).

III. Contract for Venue (Territorial) Jurisdiction

88. By a contract concluded in writing, the parties can specify that a certain dispute over property is determined by a court different from the one under whose jurisdiction the case falls according to the rules of venue jurisdiction (Article 117(2) CCP). This provision does not apply to jurisdiction under Article 109 CCP. An agreement on choice of court under consumers' actions and under labour disputes should take effect only if concluded after the dispute has arisen (Article 117(3) CCP). The court does not examine contractual jurisdiction ex officio. A challenge on the grounds of a contract for venue jurisdiction can only be made by the defendant, no later than within the time limit for an answer to the statement of action (Article 119(3) CCP).

IV. Legal Significance of Territorial (Venue) Jurisdiction: Disputes over Territorial (Venue) Jurisdiction – Resolution of Venue Jurisdiction Conflicts: Special Procedures – Effects of a Ruling on the Jurisdiction Issue

89. Venue jurisdiction (except the jurisdiction under Article *109 CCP) is a relative procedural prerequisite.* The court does not examine it ex officio. The jurisdiction of the case can only be challenged by the defendant, no later than within the term for replying to the statement of action (Article 119(3) CCP). A challenge to the jurisdiction of the case on the grounds of the real estate's location (jurisdiction under Article 109 CCP) can be made either by a party or by the court ex officio prior to the close of the proceeding in the Court of First Instance. Any changes in the factual circumstances, justifying the venue jurisdiction, which have occurred after the submission of the statement of action, should be no grounds for transmittal of the case (Article 120 CCP).

If the court finds the case is not under its own jurisdiction, it sends it to the competent court. In that event, the case is regarded as pending before that court from the day the statement of claim was filed with the incompetent court, and the actions performed by or before that court remain in force (Article 118(2) CCP). Thus, both the pendency of the case and the substantive law consequences of lodging the claim are preserved, and the claimant is protected from the risk of expiration of the limitation or preclusive terms.

The interested party can appeal the ruling on venue jurisdiction (Article 121 CCP). The ruling of the appellate court, which disregards the private appeal against it, is subject to cassation appeal before the SCC (Article 274(3) CCP; ID No.

1-2013-GMCC and the Com.C. of the SCC[40]). The entry into force of the ruling for venue jurisdiction is a prerequisite for sending the case to the other court.

The court to which the case is sent can raise a dispute for venue jurisdiction. The court superior to all determines the disputes between the courts concerning venue jurisdiction. If the courts are situated in regions of different superior courts, the dispute is determined by the superior court where it was the last to accept or refuse to hear the case. The ruling under Article 122 CCP, issued under a dispute over jurisdiction between the courts is not subject to appeal as it does not fall within the category of acts, provided in Article 274(3), item 1 and 2 CCP, item 9 ID No. 1-2013 on ID No. 1-2013-GMCC and the Com.C. of the SCC.

There are two procedures under Bulgarian law for considering a dispute over subject-matter jurisdiction. One is following a complaint of a party. The other is in a dispute raised by the court to which the case was sent. The practice in the cases is contradictory: when the issue of subject-matter jurisdiction is resolved under the procedure of Article 122 CCP, whether the appellate court is bound by this ruling or can decide it; when the ruling under Article 121 CCP has been appealed and the appeal has been disregarded, whether the jurisdiction is stabilized or when appealing the decision rendered in the case, the appellate court may decide something else.

The party concerned is entitled to appeal against the ruling regarding the jurisdiction (Article 121 CCP).

§4. Functional Jurisdiction

90. Functional jurisdiction is a system of rules by which the juridical functions related to civil cases are distributed among the courts of different levels: the courts of first, second and third instance. According to Bulgarian civil procedure, regional courts are first-instance courts (Article 76 CSA, Article 103 CCP – *see* paragraph 40). District courts act as first instance in the cases specified in Article 104 CCP (*see* paragraphs 41 and 76), and as second instance (intermediate appellate instance) in the other cases (Article 83 CSA, Article 258(1) CCP – *see* paragraphs 41, 207). Appellate courts are second-instance courts (intermediate appellate courts) in the cases which, according to the rules of subject-matter jurisdiction, fall under the jurisdiction of district courts as first instance (Article 101(1) CSA; Article 258(1) CCP – *see* paragraphs 42, 207). The SCC is the regular third instance (Article 108(1) CSA, Article 280(1) CCP – *see* paragraphs 43, 228) for cassation of adversary judgments. The possibility for cassation is restricted considerably in the new CCP (*see* paragraph 228).

91. There are certain particularities regarding the functional jurisdiction and competency of the SCC as far as the claims for reversal of an arbitration award are concerned. According to the amendments to Article 47 ICAA of 2002, these claims are under the jurisdiction of the SCC as first instance. In this case, the SCC is the first and only instance (*see* paragraphs 43, 475).

---

40. The ruling of the appellate court, by which the appeal is upheld, is not subject to cassation appeal before the Supreme Court of Cassation (ID No. 1-2013-GMCC of the SCC).

Chapter 2. International Jurisdiction: Jurisdiction over International (Transborder) Cases Within the EU

§1. Rules Applicable in the Absence of a Treaty

92. The rules of PILC and CCP specify the international competence of Bulgarian courts when the international element involves an EU Member State (*see* paragraphs 92–100) and there are no particular norms in the international contracts and conventions, bilateral treaties between the countries, as well as for cases whose international element is related to an EU Member State but are beyond the scope of EU regulations, respectively.

93. Pursuant to Article 4(1), item 1 PILC, legal defence before the Bulgarian courts can be sought against a defendant whose habitual residence or whose seat according to the statutes of organization is in the Republic of Bulgaria. According to Article 4(2) PILC, where the dispute has arisen in the course of direct relations with a branch of a legal entity, this branch being registered in the Republic of Bulgaria. The term 'habitual residence' (Article 94 CRA),[41] differs from the meaning of the term 'permanent address' (Article 93 CRA). Those addresses should be registered in the respective civil registration office (Article 22(1) CRA). According to Article 48(7) PILC, the term 'habitual residence' of an individual denotes the place in which he/she has settled down and lives, without this being necessarily connected with a registration or a permit for stay. In order for this place to be determined, certain facts of a personal and a professional aspect should be considered, these facts either ensuing from the permanent connections of the person with the said place, or ensuing from the person's intentions to create such connections.

For the defence of Bulgarian citizens and legal entities through the jurisdiction of Bulgarian courts, Article 4(1), item 1 PILC specifies that it can be sought when the claimant or plaintiff is a Bulgarian citizen or legal entity registered in the Republic of Bulgaria, while Articles 32, 33 and 34 of the provided for the possibility of subpoenaing persons whose address is abroad. This provision might run against the conflict norms of other States, and so the recognition and enforcement of a judgment rendered by a Bulgarian court could turn out to be problematic in the respective foreign State.

94. The international competence of Bulgarian courts and other bodies is exclusive only in those cases where this is explicitly provided for in law (Article 22 PILC). According to Article 12(1) PILC, the cases under Article 109 CCP relating

41. According to Art. 3(1) CRA all Bulgarian citizens; foreigners who have: been granted a long-term or permanent residence permit in the Republic of Bulgaria; who have been granted refugee status or humanitarian status or who have been granted asylum in the Republic of Bulgaria are entered into the Population Register. The term 'residence address' is used in the Law for Residence and Departure from the Republic of Bulgaria for the Citizens of the EU who are not Bulgarian Citizens and the Members of their Families, which is valid for citizens of an EU Member State who are not Bulgarian nationals and their family members, the citizens of the countries of the European Economic Area and Switzerland and their family members who are not EU citizens are eligible for entry into force (Art. 20a CRA).

to immovable property situated in the Republic of Bulgaria, and the cases relating to enforcement against such property or security for it, as well as the cases relating to the transfer or ascertainment of property rights over such property are within the exclusive competence of Bulgarian courts. According to Article 19 PILC, if the legal entity is registered in the Republic of Bulgaria, the Bulgarian courts have exclusive competence over the claims under Article 104, item 5 CCP when the legal entity has been registered in the Republic of Bulgaria. This rule applies to the claims for invalidity or dissolution of a company or another legal entity, and the claims for reversal of acts of the company's bodies, or protection of membership, or challenging the transformation of a commercial company, or money equalization upon transformation, all these concerning the cases in which the company or the other legal entity has been registered in the Republic of Bulgaria. As far as the claims regarding rights over objects of industrial property are concerned, the Bulgarian courts have exclusive competence in those cases where the patent has been issued in the Republic of Bulgaria or the registration thereof has been made in the Republic of Bulgaria (Article 13 PILC).

95. It is laid down in Article 110(2) CCP, that if the testator was a Bulgarian citizen but his/her heritage has been found abroad, the claims for inheritance, invalidation of testaments, partition of inheritance or invalidation of a voluntary partition may be lodged either by his/her last place of residence or with the court within the venue of which his/her estates are located. Article 14 PILC provides for the competence of Bulgarian courts in those cases whereas at the time of his/her death the testator was habitually residing in the Republic of Bulgaria or was a Bulgarian citizen, as well as where a part of his/her property is located in the Republic of Bulgaria.

96. According to Article 25(1) Code of Commercial Navigation (CCN) in those cases where a dispute arises ensuing from relationships connected with commercial navigation and one of the parties has its legal address in another State or is a citizen of another State, the two parties may submit the dispute to a court or an arbitration in either of the two States or in a third State, provided that both parties have agreed thereto. Should there be no such agreement, the competent court is the one of the States in which the legal address of the vessel's owner is (Article 25(2) CCN).

97. In view of the importance of the matrimonial actions for the civil State of the persons, Article 7 PILC sets forth that the matrimonial actions fall within the jurisdiction of Bulgarian courts if one of the spouses is a Bulgarian citizen or has his/her habitual residence in the Republic of Bulgaria. According to Article 8 PILC, in those cases where the conditions specified in Article 7 PILC are present, the Bulgarian courts also have competence over the cases regarding personal and property relations between the spouses.

The origin-related cases under Article 9(1) PILC are concerned, it is laid down that the Bulgarian courts and other bodies have competence over the proceedings regarding the establishing and challenging of origin, with the exception of the cases under Article 4 PILC, and where the child or the parent who is a party to the proceedings is a Bulgarian citizen or has his/her habitual residence in the Republic of

Bulgaria. In those cases where the conditions are present, this competence is also valid for the cases relating to personal or property relations between parents and children (Article 9(2) PILC).

The Bulgarian courts and other bodies have competence over the cases regarding the admission of adoption, its invalidation or termination, with the exception of the cases under Article 4 of the PILC (this Article regulating the general competence), and those cases where the adoptive parent, or the adopted person, or a parent of the adopted person is a Bulgarian citizen, or has his/her habitual residence in the Republic of Bulgaria (Article 10(1) PILC). The Bulgarian courts have competence over those cases which concern property relations between an adoptive parent and an adopted person if the adoptive parent or the adopted person is a Bulgarian citizen, or has his/her habitual residence in the Republic of Bulgaria, as well as in the cases under Article 4 PILC (Article 10(2) PILC).

The Bulgarian courts have competence over the claims for maintenance, with the exception of the cases under Article 4(1) PILC and those cases in which the person seeking maintenance has his/her habitual residence in the Republic of Bulgaria (Article 11 PILC).

According to Article 12(2) PILC, the Bulgarian courts have competence over the claims regarding property rights on movable property with the exception of the cases under Article 4 PILC, and those cases in which the property is located in the Republic of Bulgaria.

The Bulgarian courts also have competence over claims relating to copyright and rights similar thereto, provided that the defence is sought on the territory of the Republic of Bulgaria (Article 13(1) PILC).

The Bulgarian courts have competence over the claims concerning contractual relations with the exception of the cases under Article 4 PILC and when the place of performance of the obligation is within the Republic of Bulgaria or the defendant has his/her main place of business in the Republic of Bulgaria (Article 15 PILC).

The Bulgarian courts have competence over consumers' claims with the exception of the cases under Article 4 PILC and those cases in which the consumer has his/her habitual residence in the Republic of Bulgaria, and the conditions specified in Article 95(2) PILC are present (Article 16(1) PILC). As for an agreement regarding the choosing of the court in such cases, it is admissible only where the said agreement has been made after the dispute arose (Article 16(2) PILC).

The Bulgarian courts have jurisdiction over cases related to labour disputes where the employee habitually does his/her job in the Republic of Bulgaria, as well as in the cases under Article 4 PILC (Article 17(1) PILC). An agreement regarding the choosing of court is admissible only where the said agreement has been made after the dispute arose (Article 17(2) PILC).

The Bulgarian courts have competence over claims regarding damages from tort, with the exception of the cases under Article 4 PILC, and also where the act resulting in damages has been done in the Republic of Bulgaria, or the damages or part thereof has occurred in the Republic of Bulgaria (Article 18(1) PILC). This competence is also present in the cases of a direct claim brought in by the injured person against the insurer or the person whose responsibility is sought (Article 18(2) PILC).

The Bulgarian courts are also competent to secure a claim for the consideration of which they have no international competence, provided that the object of the security measure is situated in the Republic of Bulgaria and it is possible for the decision of the foreign court to be acknowledged and enforced in the Republic of Bulgaria (Article 25 PILC).

The Bulgarian enforcement bodies (State and private bailiffs) have exclusive competence over the performance of actions of enforcement in those cases where the obligation forming the subject matter of these actions has to be performed by a person having his/her habitual residence in the Republic of Bulgaria, or the object of the said actions is situated in the Republic of Bulgaria (Article 26 PILC).

In those cases where the grounds for the international competence existed at the time the proceedings were instituted, the said competence is preserved even where these grounds drop off in the course of proceedings (Article 27(1) PILC). If no international competence was existing at the time the proceedings were instituted, the said competence is set up in those cases where the grounds for this competence have occurred in the course of proceedings (Article 27(2) PILC).

International competence is examined ex officio. The determination regarding its presence or absence of international competence is subject to being appealed against in accordance with the procedure laid down for intermediate appeal and cassation appeal (Article 28 PILC).

98. The foreign states and persons enjoying juridical immunity are excluded from the jurisdiction of the Bulgarian court. According to Article 18(1) CCP the Bulgarian court is competent to examine actions where to a foreign State, as well as a person enjoying judicial immunity, is a party in the following cases: (i) where judicial immunity is waived; (ii) under actions based on contractual relations, where the obligation is performed in the Republic of Bulgaria; (iii) under actions for damages sustained as a result of a tort or delict where the harmful act was committed in the Republic of Bulgaria; (iv) under actions regarding rights to succession property and vacant succession in the Republic of Bulgaria; (v) under cases which are under the exclusive jurisdiction of the Bulgarian courts.

The provisions of Article 18(1), items 2, 3 and 4 CCP do not apply to any legal transactions and moves performed in execution of official functions of the persons or, respectively, in connection with the exercise of sovereign rights of the foreign State.

Article 18(1) and (2) CCP is in compliance with Article 31 Vienna Convention on Diplomatic Relations and the United Nations Convention on Jurisdictional Immunities of States and Their Property.

99. Pursuant to Article 23(1) PILC, where the subject matter of an action consists in a property right and the dispute is not within the exclusive competence of the Bulgarian courts, it is possible for the action to be assigned to a foreign court, provided that the parties agree thereto in writing. It is under the same conditions that an action which falls within the jurisdiction of a foreign court may be heard by a Bulgarian court. This does not refer to maintenance claims. Unless the agreement between the parties provides otherwise, it is assumed that it assigns to Bulgarian or foreign courts the exclusive competence over the dispute regarding which it has been made.

In those cases where it is impossible for the competence of the Bulgarian courts to be agreed by way of an agreement under Article 23(1) PILC, the said competence may be agreed without such an agreement, provided that, prior to the closure of the first session in the case, the defendant agrees to it either explicitly or tacitly, through his/her actions regarding the subject matter of the dispute (Article 24 PILC).

100. The Bulgarian court suspends ex officio the proceedings which have been instituted before it in those cases where there is a pending action before a foreign court between the same parties, and on the same grounds, and on the same claim and it is expected that, within reasonable time, the said pending action will end with a final decision, which might be recognized and enforced in Bulgaria (Article 37 PILC). The Bulgarian court gives its opinion about legal relationships which condition the outcome of the legal dispute, even in those cases where the disputes do not fall within their jurisdiction (Article 38(1) PILC). In those cases where there exist pending proceedings abroad connected with the conditioning legal relationship, the Bulgarian court is entitled to suspend the proceedings which have been instituted before it if it is reasonably expected that the decision of the foreign court will be recognized in the Republic of Bulgaria (Article 38(2) PILC).

§2. International Treaties

101. The United Nations Convention on Jurisdictional Immunities of the States and their Property of 2004; Vienna Convention on Diplomatic Relations (in force since 1968), Vienna Convention on Consular Relations (in force since 1969); United Nations Convention on Special Missions (regarding the Immunity of Special Missions and Representations (in force in Bulgaria since 1987) are of significant importance for the international jurisdiction of the Bulgarian courts concerning the scope of juridical immunity.

102. The Vienna Convention on civil responsibility for nuclear damage provides for special international subservience of the claims for damages caused by nuclear accidents provided for in Article II of the Convention.

103. As for international subservience, the Warsaw Convention of the year 1929 is also of great importance for international subservience and for the harmonization of certain rules regarding international air traffic. (Article 28, items 1, 2; Articles 29, 32, sentence II of this Convention).

The Convention on the Contract for the International Carriage of Goods by Road (CMR) is also important for the competence of the court (Articles 31(1), 33, 37, 38, 39(2) of this Convention).

104. The Lugano Convention on Jurisdiction and the Enforcement of Judgments in Civil and Commercial Matters of 2007 (Chapter III) applies to the international jurisdiction of the Bulgarian courts, where the case is on legal relationships involving entities domiciled or having their registered office in an EU Member State Switzerland, Iceland and Norway.

Other conventions and agreements concluded between the EU and non-EU countries should apply to the international jurisdiction of the Bulgarian courts.

105. As for the international subservience regarding civil actions that form part of security proceedings, it is important to consider the Convention on Protection of Children and Collaboration in the Field of International Adoption (Articles 4, 5, 6, 14, 15, 17 of this Convention). Currently the matters of international adoption are regulated in Article 10 and Article 84 PILC. Chapter Eight, section V Special Rules for International Adoption of the FC, Part Six: Non-contentious Proceedings CCP, and some other Ordinances issued by the Ministry of Justice.

The Hague Convention on Jurisdiction, Applicable Law, Recognition, Enforcement and Cooperation in Respect of Parental Responsibility and Measures for Children Protect is applicable to civil matters in connection with the 1980 Hague Convention on the Civil Law Aspects of International Child Abduction.

106. The Hague Convention on Choice-of-Court Agreements (effective 1 October 2015) is applied to the international competence of Bulgarian courts.

As for the derogation of the international subservience of State courts, it is important to consider the European Convention on Foreign Trade Arbitration.

Article 19(1) and (2) CCP (*see* paragraph 150), and the Bulgarian International Commercial Arbitration Act (*see* paragraph 460) are in compliance with this Convention.

107. Concerning the international competence of Bulgarian courts: there are also a number of bilateral treaties (*see* paragraph 26) on legal assistance in civil cases concluded by the Republic of Bulgaria with other non-EU countries, such as Albania, Algeria, Libyan Arab Jamahiriya, Belarus, Vietnam, China, Cuba, Mongolia, Syria, Tunisia, Turkey, Yemen, Kuwait, China. China, Syria, Uzbekistan, etc. (*see* paragraph 26). The treaties with the relevant EU Member States apply only to matters not covered by a regulation or a Directive. The contracts with non-EU countries party to the relevant Hague Convention or other Convention apply only to matters not governed by the Convention.

§3. Competence in Civil and Commercial Matters with a Transborder Element in an EU Member State

108. The respective EC regulations[42] are applied to the jurisdiction on cases with an international (transborder) element in another Member State.

42. *See* V. Popova, Current issues of the European Civil Procedure and Part VII of the CCP, Ciela, 2011.

Council Regulation (EC) No. 1215/2012 on jurisdiction and the recognition and enforcement of judgments in civil and commercial matters which replaced Council Regulation (EC) No. 44/2001 is the main regulation whose norms distribute the jurisdiction over civil and commercial matters with international (transborder) element inside the EC between the courts of the EC Member States, with the exception of the cases specified in Article 1(1), sentence II and Article 2 of Regulation (EC) No. 1215/2012. The latter defines the competence of the courts on securing the claim (Article 35 Regulation (EC) No. 1215/2012).[43]

The general competence is distributed in Article 4 Regulation (EC) No. 1215/2012, corresponding to Article 2(1) Regulation (EC) No. 44/2001. The claims against the persons domiciled in a Member State, *whatever their nationality*, are sued in the courts of that Member State. Persons who are not nationals of the Member State in which they are domiciled are governed by the rules of jurisdiction applicable to nationals of that State. Persons domiciled in a Member State may be sued in the courts of another Member State only by virtue of the rules set out in sections 2–7 of Chapter II, Article 5(1) Regulation (EC) No. 1215/2012, corresponding to Article 3(1) of Regulation (EC) No. 44/2001. The notion 'domicile' is defined in Article 62 of Regulation (EC) No. 1215/2012 is applicable to natural persons, while Article 63 of Regulation (EC) No. 1215/2012 is applicable to legal entities.

According to Article 62 of Regulation (EC) No. 1215/2012, corresponding to Article 59 of Regulation (EC) No. 44/2001, in order to determine whether a party (a natural person) is domiciled in the Member State whose courts are seized of a matter, the court applies its internal law. There is no legal definition of the place of residence or domicile in Bulgarian domestic law. The definition of the term 'habitual residence' of a natural person is in Article 48(7) PILC. In relation to the jurisdiction over the cases in which the defendant is a natural person, there are two normative acts in the Bulgarian law – the PILC for cases with an international element and the CCP in connection with the CRA. According to Article 93 CRA a person's permanent address is that address in the settlement which the person has indicated for entry in the population registers. A person may only have one permanent address. Bulgarian citizens residing primarily abroad who are not recorded in the population registers and cannot indicate a permanent address in the Republic of Bulgaria are entered officially in the population registers of the region of Sredets in Sofia. The permanent address is formal and does not always reflect the actual permanent or usual place of residence of the person. According to Article 94 CRA the current address is the address where the person lives. Citizens are required to enter their permanent and current address in the registers. The current address of the Bulgarian citizens whose place of residence is abroad is reflected in the population register only under the name of the State in which they live (Article 94(3) CRA). Therefore when Regulation (EC) No. 44/2001 was valid via Ruling No. 886 of 9 November 2011 on Com. Case No. 130/2011 of the Second College of the SCC it was accepted that when the Bulgarian citizen has no current address in the Republic

43. *See* Popova, V. Über einige Besonderheiten des bulgarischen Sicherungsverfahrens und der Verordnung Nr. 1215/2012 über die gerichtliche Zuständigkeit und die Anerkennung und Vollstreckung von Entscheidungen in Zivil- und Handelssachen. Civil Procedure Review, Sept., 2017, ISSN 2191-1339, www.civilprocedurereview.com

of Bulgaria (Article 94(3) CRA) the permanent residence in another Member State should be entered in the population registers as a current address (in the case of Greece – certified by an appropriate document), in line with Article 59(1) of Regulation (EC) No. 44/2001 that the present address is the one that matters and the case against this defendant is not within the jurisdiction of the Bulgarian court.

According to Article 4(1), item 1 PILC, the Bulgarian courts and other authorities have international jurisdiction where: the defendant has a habitual residence, statutory seat or principal place of business in the Republic of Bulgaria. Article 48(7) PILC contains a legal definition of the notion 'habitual residence' of a natural person in the sense of the PILC – the place where he/she resides predominantly without the need for a registration or residence or establishment permit. The determination of the place should be in accordance with the personal or professional circumstances arising from the person's lasting ties to that place or his/her intention to establish such relationships. The PILC was adopted prior to Bulgaria's joining the EU under the aegis of harmonizing Bulgarian with the European law when Regulation (EC) No. 44/2001 was effective. Then the legislator understood the synchronization as copying the regulations into Bulgarian law. The concept under Article 48(7) PILC corresponds to Article 2(1) of Regulation (EC) No. 44/2001 (repealed) and of Article 4 (1) of the current Regulation No. 1215/2012. In the practice of the SCC during the operation of Regulation (EC) No. 44/2001 (Ruling No. 9 of 13 January 2010, on Com. Case No. 435/2009 of the Second College of SCC) and during the operation of Regulation (EC) 1215/2012 (Ruling No. 543 of 16 June 2016 with C. Case No. 1754/2016) and the constant practice of the SCC quoted therein, that in the connection with Article 62 (1) of Regulation (EC) No. 1215/2012 and Article 4(1) of Regulation (EC) No. 1215/2012 applies Article 48(7) PILC concerning the habitual residence of the natural person and the habitual residence criteria provided therein. However, it is established in Annex I of Regulation (EC) No. 44/2001 which norms of the internal law should not be applied.

The entire provisions of Article 4(1) PILC are specified for the Republic of Bulgaria in this annex. Nowadays' situation is the same: under Article 5(2) of Regulation (EC) No. 1215/2012 in accordance with Article 76(1), item 'a' of Regulation No. (EC) 1215/2012 List No. 1 'The Rules of Competence' referred to in Article 5(2) of Regulation (EC) No. 1215/2012[44] (Official Journal of the European Union, C 390 of 24 November 2015). Article 4(1) of Regulation (EC) No. 1215/2012, however, consists of two items. In my opinion there are grounds for excluding the application of Article 4(1), item 2 PILC. Those provisions are in contradiction with Regulation (EC) No. 1215/2012 because they establish that the Bulgarian courts have international jurisdiction of where: the claimant or applicant is a Bulgarian national or is a legal entity registered in the Republic of Bulgaria. As far as Article 4(1), item 1 PILC is concern I find that it is not in contradiction with Regulation (EC) No. 44/2001, but in agreement with Article 3(1) of Regulation (EC) No. 1215/2012 which uses the criterion of defendant's habitual residence, regardless of his/her nationality. List No. 1 'The Rules of Competence' in Article 5(2) of Regulation

44. The information was notified by the Republic of Bulgaria.

(EC) No. 1215/ 2012 should be explicitly amended limiting the inapplicability to Article 4(1), item 2 PILC that cannot be done without the active participation of the Republic of Bulgaria.[45]

According to Article 63(1) of Regulation (EC) No. 1215/2012 for the purposes of this regulation, a company or other legal person or association of natural or legal persons is domiciled at the place where it has its: (a) statutory seat, or (b) central administration, or (c) principal place of business. Several types of special jurisdiction are foreseen in Chapter II of Regulation (EC) No. 1215/2012.

Section 3 of Regulation (EC) No. 1215/2012 foresees special jurisdiction in matters relating to insurance. Regarding the consumer protection there are provisions for special jurisdiction over matters related to consumer contracts are determined by section 4. Section 5 sets out jurisdiction over matters relating to individual contracts of employment, jurisdiction. Section 6 of Regulation (EC) No. 1215/2012 regulates the exclusive jurisdiction regarding the cases listed in Article 24 of Regulation (EC) No. 1215/2012.

According to Article 27 of Regulation (EC) No. 1215/2012 where a court of a Member State is seized of a claim which is principally concerned with a matter over which the courts of another Member State have exclusive jurisdiction by virtue of Article 24 of Regulation (EC) No. 1215/2012, it declares of its own motion that it has no jurisdiction.

The terms on prorogation of jurisdiction of the courts in the Member States are set out in section 7 of Regulation (EC) No. 1215/2012. The prorogation jurisdiction under Article 24 of Regulation (EC) No. 1215/2012 is exclusive. Agreements or provisions of a trust instrument, customer, employee or officer conferring have exclusive jurisdiction. The agreement should have been concluded after the arising of the dispute.

Section 8 of Regulation (EC) No. 1215/2012 has special rules for jurisdiction examination according to its distribution.

109. Regulation (EC) No. 2201/2003 concerning jurisdiction and the recognition and enforcement of decisions in matrimonial matters and the matter of parental responsibility provides over two types of proceedings:

(1) For the proceedings on divorce, marriage annulment and legal separation of the spouses[46] the legislator has foreseen a number of alternatives. Article 6 Regulation (EC) No. 2201/2003 aims at preventing the attempts to use the jurisdiction of a Member State whose national procedure and substantive law on matrimonial proceedings and the relations between the spouses and between parents and children may be used in favour of one of the parties to the case to the detriment of the other party.

45. *See* V. Popova, Actual problems … , pp. 20–21 about the situation under Regulation (EC) No. 44/2001.

46. The institution of lawful separation does not exist in Bulgarian family law.

(2) When determining the criteria for jurisdiction over the proceedings on matters of parental responsibility,[47] personal relationships between parents and children, and return of a child the European legislator has viewed the idea for adequate protection of the children's rights. That is why the State of the jurisdiction is the one of habitual residence of the child[48] but in some cases of a change in the child's residence under the agreement between the holders of the parental responsibility (Article 8 and item 12 of the motives of Regulation (EC) No. 2201/2003). To avoid fraud movement of the child aimed at acquiring jurisdiction beneficial for the respective parent Article 9 of Regulation (EC) No. 2201/2003 continuing jurisdiction of the child's former habitual residence. It is applied when there is a decision on parental responsibility and an amendment of the provisions are requested due to a change in the circumstances relevant to the parental responsibility. According to Article 10 of Regulation (EC) No. 2201/2003 the jurisdiction in cases of wrongful removal or retention of the child, the courts of the Member State where the child was habitually resident immediately before the wrongful removal or retention retains their jurisdiction until the child has acquired a habitual residence in another Member State.

In the cases when the habitual residence of the child is in a third non-Member State not a contracting party to the Hague Convention (e.g., Russia and the Arab countries are not on the list http://www.hcch.net/index_en.php?act=conventions.status&cid=70) the jurisdiction is regulated to guarantee the defence of the child. Then the jurisdiction is deemed to be in the child's best interest, in particular, if it is found impossible to hold proceedings in the third State in question (Article 12(4) of Regulation (EC) No. 2201/2003).

Article 13 Regulation (EC) No. 2201/2003 provides that where a child's habitual residence cannot be established and jurisdiction cannot be determined on the basis of Article 12 of Regulation (EC) No. 2201/2003, the courts of the Member State where the child is present have jurisdiction. The rule also applies to refugee children or children internationally displaced because of disturbances occurring in their country.

Article 14 Regulation (EC) No. 2201/2003 provides for cases where no court of a Member State has jurisdiction pursuant to Articles 8–13 of Regulation (EC) No. 2201/2003, jurisdiction is determined, in each Member State, by the laws of that State.

110. Regulation (EC) No. 4/2009 has special rules on jurisdiction on maintenance obligations under Article 1(1) of this Regulation arising from a family relationship, parentage, marriage or affinity.

Article 3 Regulation (EC) No. 4/2009 foresees several competences on such cases. The jurisdiction conferred by agreement is admissible. Its parameters are set

47. Therefore, the notion has a meaning autonomous for Regulation (EC) No. 2201/2003 which legal definition is in Art. 2(7) of Regulation (EC) No. 2201/2003.
48. The notion 'habitual residence of the child' is autonomous for the application of Regulation (EC) No. 2201/2003. The ECJ has already had to pronounce on the matter e.g., the case C-523/07).

for in Article 4 Regulation (EC) No. 4/2009. There are two hypothesizes according to which the courts of a Member State have jurisdiction over a dispute on maintenance: (a) Where no court of a Member State has jurisdiction pursuant to Articles 3, 4 and 5 of Regulation (EC) No. 4/2009, and no court of a State party to the Lugano Convention which is not a Member State has jurisdiction pursuant to the provisions of that Convention, the courts of the Member State of the common nationality of the parties have jurisdiction (Article 6 Regulation (EC) No. 4/2009); (b) where no court of a Member State has jurisdiction pursuant to Articles 3, 4, 5 and 6 Regulation (EC) No. 4/2009), the courts of a Member State may, on an exceptional basis, hear the case if proceedings cannot reasonably be brought or conducted or would be impossible in a third State with which the dispute is closely connected (Article 7 Regulation (EC) No. 4/2009 – Forum necessitates).

111. Regulation (EC) No. 861/2007 establishing a European small claims procedure is also applicable in Bulgaria.[49] It applies where at least one of the parties is domiciled or habitually resident in a Member State other than the Member State of the court or tribunal seized or of a court or tribunal within the meaning of Article 3 of Regulation (EC) No. 861/2007. It is applicable to all types of civil and commercial cases, with the exception of those specified in Article 2(1) sentence II and Article 2(2). In view of the division of jurisdiction among the courts of the individual Member States, the rules of Regulation No. 1215/2102 should apply (*see* the instruction in item 4 of Form A).

112. Regulation (EC) No. 1896/2006 creating a European order for payment procedure (EOPP) regulates the procedure autonomous of the European Civil Procedure for creating legal enforcement grounds (by the national court of the Member States) for a money receivable (regardless of its amount) arising from contract grounds,[50] in civil and commercial cases with a transborder element within the meaning of Article 3 of Regulation (EC) No. 1896/2006. The competence is defined in Article 6(1) of Regulation (EC) No. 1896/2006, referring to the rules of Regulation (EC) No. 1215/2012, respectively, due to the close link between the EOPP and the adversary proceedings if the debtor contests the claim.

113. The competence in cross-border jurisdiction is specified in Chapter III of Regulation (EC) No. 650/2012. It provides on jurisdiction, applicable law, recognition and enforcement of decisions and the recognition and enforcement of authentic acts in the field of succession and on the creation of a European Certificate of Succession is relevant for jurisdiction in cross-border cases. It applies to inheritance in case of death, except for the matters under Article 1(1), item 1 and Article 1(2) 2 of Regulation (EC) No. 650/2012.

---

49. It is a standard and unified procedure for dealing with these cases, which is an alternative to the possibility of bringing a claim under Regulation No. 1215/2012.
50. The regulation is not applied to receivables arising from non-contractual obligations, unless they have been the subject of an agreement between the parties or there has been an admission of debt, or they relate to liquidated debts arising from joint ownership of property. (Art. 2(2), item 'd' Regulation (EC) No. 1896/2006.

Part III. Actions and Claims

Chapter 1. Actions

§1. Definition

114. Civil actions denote adversary proceedings regulated by civil procedure norms, the subject matter of the said proceedings being civil legal relationships in the broad sense of the term, i.e., substantive civil law relationships regulated by the method of equality of the parties thereto, regardless of the civil law branch that regulates them: civil law, property law, contractual law, family law, inheritance law, labour law, commercial law, etc.

115. The proceedings in commercial disputes were differentiated in Chapter 32 of the new CCP 'Proceedings in Commercial Disputes' as particular adversary proceedings (*see* paragraph 117). In the legal definition of the notion of **proceedings in commercial disputes** (Article 365 CCP) the legislator used the subject matter of the case specified in Article 365 CCP as criteria but only when the case falls in the jurisdiction of the district court (*see* paragraph 41). According to Article 104, item 4 CCP claims on civil and commercial disputes amounting BNG 25,000 are under the jurisdiction of the district court. Thus, cases which subject matter is specified in Article 365 CCP but amount less than BGN 25,000 are considered by the regional court following the general adversary proceedings, although they are also called commercial cases in Article 280(3), item 1 CCP. According to Article 280(3), item 1 CCP, appellate decisions on civil claims BGN 5,000 and 20,000 – on commercial claims are not subject to cassation appeal.

116. According to Prof. J. Stalev the subject matter of a case is the substantive law right at issue – the subject matter of the claim. He defines it as the right which is claimed or disclaimed by the claimant, and whose legal nature directly follows from the grounds and the petition of the claim on the basis of the legal norm, and simultaneously, he *underlines* that the defendant's defence, and the defendant's counter rights forming the subject matter of his/her defence do not form part of the subject matter of the case.[51] In my opinion the subject matter of the case is the disputed substantive law right at issue which forms the subject matter of the claim, and the counter rights of the defendant forming the subject matter of his/her defence in those cases where the law provides for the opportunity of their being introduced in

51. *See* J. Stalev, A. Mingova, V. Popova, R. Ivanova, *Balgarsko ...* , *supra*, pp. 199–201.

the case through defence. Such is the defence against set-off and also the defence with the right of retention. According to Article 298(4) CCP the decision rendered thereupon has the force of res judicata. The subject matter of the defence against set-off is the counter receivable of the defendant and the compensation right, while the subject matter of the defence with the right of retention is the receivable for improvements and the right of retention. What is concerned here is the counter rights of the defendant, which are enforceable against the right claimed by the claimant. The defence aims at rejecting the claim or putting the judgment under the condition of a simultaneous performance of the counter receivable of the defendant. Article 298(4) CCP, extends the force of res judicata of the judgment over rights, that the legislator has allowed for them to be claimed through defence and to become part of the subject matter of the case. What is special about the subject matter introduced through defence is its relation with the subject matter of the claim and its subordination to this subject matter.[52]

The prejudicial legal relationships not forming part of the subject matter of the case is beyond doubt in doctrine and practice. These relationships may form the subject matter of the case if the claimant in the first court session at the first instance or defendant in reply to the statement of claim claims an incidental ascertainment claim under Article 212 CCP.

117. Owing to the nature of the adversary procedure and the defensive function thereof – consideration and determination of a civil legal dispute through the force of res judicata – it is a general type adversary procedure, regulated under Part II CCP 'Adversary Proceedings', this being the procedure for all civil cases. In view of the specificity of certain rights or the extreme importance of the legal relationship at issue, Part III CCP regulates the respective special adversary proceedings: Summary Proceedings (Chapter 25); Matrimonial Proceedings (Chapter 26); Civil Status Proceedings (Chapter 27); Putting under a Restraint Order (Chapter 28); Juridical Partition (Chapter 29); Protection and Restoration of Ownership (Chapter 30); Proceedings for the Conclusion of a Final Contract (Chapter 31); Proceedings in Commercial Disputes (Chapter 32); Proceedings in Class Actions (Chapter 33).

§2. Admissibility

118. In the Bulgarian procedural doctrine and practice, the requirements for admissibility of the action, including the parties' legitimization, are always regarded as requirements for admissibility of the claim and are called procedural prerequisites (*see* paragraphs. 122–125).

52. *See* V. Popova In: Stalev, A. Mingova, V. Popova, O. Staboliev, R. Ivanova, *Balgarsko ..., supra*, pp. 422–429.

§3. Vexatious Litigation

119. Pursuant to Article 3 CCP, under fear of liability for damages, the parties to the proceedings are bound to exercise their afforded procedural rights in good faith.[53]

A judgment, which has taken effect, cannot be disputed by the party as delivered under fictitious proceedings (Article 299(3) CCP; *see also* paragraph 189).

53. Regarding the liability of the party, which unduly causes the delay in the proceedings *see* para. 162.

Chapter 2. Claims and Defences

§1. Definition: Claim – Right to Claim: Procedural Prerequisites

120. The claim is a procedural action, a statement of will of the claimant, addressed to the court, and requesting that the latter consider the civil legal dispute in accordance with the procedure for adversary proceedings, with the participation of the parties, and settle it through the force of res judicata.

On the one hand, it is a statement of knowledge, as it contains the statement of the claimant regarding the substantive law relationship between himself/herself and the defendant. On the other hand, it is an expression of will, addressed to the court, aiming at giving rise to the desired legal consequences – the consideration and determination of the civil legal dispute through the force of res judicata. Being an expression of will, it may be admissible or inadmissible; being a statement it may be well-grounded or ungrounded.

In legislation the term 'claim' has two meanings. In some texts it is used in the meaning outlined in the theory of procedure (Article 17(1) OCA – a claim for declaring the simultaneousness of transactions; Article 134(2) OCA – the creditor's claim for property rights where his/her debtor fails to take actions). The term is typically used in this meaning in constitutive claims for potestative rights that are exercised through the court (Article 19(3) OCA – a claim for the conclusion of a final contract; Article 34(1) PA – a claim for juridical partition; Article 32(3) OCA – a claim for invalidation of the transaction). In some substantive laws the term 'claim' is used to denote the substantive law civil subjective right (Article 54(1) OCA – the regressive claim of a person bearing responsibility for damages that have been faultily caused by another; Article 59(2) OCA – the receivable ensuing from an unjust enrichment; Article 127(2) OCA – the receivable due to a joint debtor (the latter having paid the creditor) by the other co-debtors for the said debtor's part, in view of the debtors' internal relationships).

Sometimes (where the subject matter of the case is a property right claim, e.g., a revindication claim, negatory claim or a potestative right forming the subject matter of a constitutive claim) the term 'claim' in doctrine and practice denotes both the claim lodged with the court and the right forming the subject matter of the claim.

The claim is important as: (a) it sets the beginning of the adversary proceedings; (b) it specifies the subject matter of the case and the due parties thereto; (c) it shows the type of defence sought; (d) it predetermines the defence of the defendant; (e) it maintains the pendency of the proceedings; it determines the subject matter of the judgment.

121. The right to claim is a subjective public procedural right addressed to the court. The right to claim is always connected with the obligation of the court corresponding to this right. Article 2 CCP provides that the court is obliged to consider and determine all requests for defence and collaboration lodged therewith. When denoting the right to claim, the literature uses the above term as well as the terms 'right to jurisdiction according to the procedure for adversary proceedings'; 'right to justice according to the procedure for adversary proceedings'; 'right to legal defence according to the procedure for adversary proceedings'; 'right to adversary proceedings defence'.

As the adversary proceedings involve a dispute between two parties and aim at providing a remedy-sanction in the presence of a legal dispute, both parties (the claimant and the defendant) are entitled to the right to claim regarded as a right to request that the dispute be considered in accordance with the procedure for adversary proceedings and be determined through the force of res judicata. The defendant, in spite of becoming a party to the proceedings against his/her will, also has the right to claim in the proceedings. He/she is a bearer of this right, so that he/she be able to defend his/her legal sphere injured by the legal dispute. In the proceedings that have been instituted against the defendant by the claimant, the defendant exercises his/her right to claim (right to justice) with respect to the same legal dispute. [54] As for the right to legal defence of the defendant, the provision of Article 232, sentence I CCP is indicative. If the claim is withdrawn after the closure of the first court session, the proceedings cannot be terminated without the defendant's consent.

The right to claim accrues when the legal dispute between the parties arises, prior to commencing the proceedings. Just like the adversary proceedings, which have a dynamic factual content – a sequence of actions specified by the procedure law – the right to claim is a dynamic right, composed of separate powers, the content, ways and sequence of exercise thereof being regulated under the procedure law – the CCP. The judgment that has taken effect extinguishes the right to claim as the latter has already been exercised, has been consumed and has accomplished its objective.

122. The procedural prerequisites are the conditions on which the due exercise of the right to claim depends on. The procedural prerequisites determine the admissibility of both the claim and the proceedings.

Depending on whether the court has the obligation to examine them ex officio, or has the right to check them in those cases where the defendant has made an objection, they into absolute and relative ones. The fact that the court has the obligation to examine ex officio the absolute procedural prerequisites does not revoke the right of the parties to the case to invoke the presence, or the absence thereof, respectively. This is valid for all absolute procedural prerequisites.

According to Bulgarian procedure law the court renders its judgment on the procedural prerequisites by a ruling. (arg. Article 252 CCP). According to Article 254 CCP the ruling should be motivated. The requirement for motivating is a guarantee of the serious work of the court and of the lawfulness of the said act. The rulings, which do not terminate the proceedings, may be changed or overruled by the same court following a change in the circumstances, an error or an omission (Article 253 CCP). According to Article 274(1) CCP, private appeals may be lodged against the

54. If one of the parties has lodged a claim, then the party against which the claim has been lodged is not allowed to lodge the same claim (arg. Art. 126(1) CCP). In the proceedings instituted by the claimant against the defendant the latter exercises his/her rights regarding the said legal dispute to be considered and determined with a res judicata effect.

ruling of the court: (a) where the ruling bars the further development of proceedings, and (b) in the cases explicitly provided for in the law.[55]

123. Procedural prerequisites for the existence of the right to claim:

a. The positive procedural prerequisites for the existence of the right to claim are:
   - Presence of a legal dispute regarding a civil substantive law relationship.
   - Procedural legal personality (legal capacity) of the parties.

   Procedurally licensed is the one who is qualified under substantive law (Art. 27(1) CCP). The claim by a claimant who is not a legal entity in the material right is inadmissible. An action against a defendant who is not a party to substantive law is also inadmissible. The procedural legal capacity is an absolute procedural prerequisite for the emergence of the right to a claim (item 2 of ID No. 1 of 09.07.2019 on ID No. 1-2017-GMCC and the Com.C. of the SCC). In this ID it was accepted that adversary proceedings, where the defendant designated in the statement of claim has passed away before the submission of the claim, are inadmissible and subject to termination due to initial absence of a party having legal capacity, with which a valid procedural relationship can be established. The branch of the legal entity (of a commercial company, inclusive) does not have a legal capacity, so there is no legal procedural capacity. The provision in Art. 108(1), sentence II CCP, means the particular local jurisdiction of the branch does not make it a legal entity and the action must be brought against the legal entity whose branch it is. The court sees to the ex officio for the procedural capacity of the parties.
   - Procedural legitimization.

   The legal interest of the parties in resolving the legal dispute (Art. 124(1) CCP) determines their procedural legitimization. Procedural legitimization is defined as the appurtenance of the right to claim in favour of a certain person.[56] It is this interest in settling the dispute itself which determines the appurtenance of the right to claim to a certain person, and also determines the procedural legitimization. As the adversary proceedings involve a dispute between two parties, the examination regarding procedural legitimization should comprise both an examination of the legal interest of the claimant in lodging the claim and an examination of his/her interest in lodging the claim against the specific defendant. Thus, an examination is made of both the legitimization of the claimant and the legitimization of the defendant in this quality of his/hers. The legal interest in the determination of the legal dispute is present where the legal sphere of the legal entities is directly affected by the said dispute. That is

55. The ruling of the court regarding subservience may be appealed against by way of a private appeal both where the proceedings are terminated therewith, and where the court has accepted the case for consideration (Art. 15(2) CCP).
56. *See* J. Stalev, A. Mingova, V. Popova, R. Ivanova, *Balgarsko ...* , *supra*, pp. 144–145; *compare* V. Popova, *Civil Procedure ...* , *supra*, para. 121, sub-para. A, item 3.

why it is primarily the parties to the civil legal relationship that have legal interest in the determination of the dispute, and they are legitimized to be parties to the case, respectively. The lodging of a claim for the defence of somebody else's right is admissible only in the cases explicitly provided for in the law (Art. 26(2) CCP). In these cases the bearer of the right at issue is necessarily constituted as a party to the case (Art. 26(4) CCP). As for ascertainment claims, the legal interest could be present both for the parties to the legal relationship at issue, and for a third party to the said legal relationship, the legal sphere of the third party being directly affected by this legal relationship. These are mostly ascertainment claims challenging somebody else's legal relationship (Art. 464 CCP; Art. 17 OCA) when defendants to the claim are two subjects in competing legal relationship.[57] The situation regarding the claims for annulment under Art. 135 OCA and Art. 647 C. Code is similar. These are claims which the Bulgarian procedure doctrine treats as constitutive ones, but they are very similar to the ascertainment claims, because what is claimed is that the debtor's actions or transactions concluded with third parties be declared relatively invalid regarding the creditor (Art. 135 OCA), or regarding the creditors, respectively (Art. 647 C. Code) and that the said claims be lodged against the debtor and the third party. In ID No. 1-20.12.2019 on ID No. 1-2019, the GMCom.C. of the SCC provided that in proceedings regarding claims under Art. 59(3) and (5) BBA for declaring set-offs as relatively invalid, the competent parties are the trustee in bankruptcy of the bank which has declared bankruptcy and the creditor who has conducted the set-off, but not the bank in its procedural role as defendant under the claim, although it is a separate legal entity. This ID is difficult to share but represents mandatory legal practice. The court monitors ex officio for the procedural legitimization, resp. for the legal interest.

- Procedural prerequisite for the existence of the right to claim is subservience (*see* paragraphs 69–73). The court has the obligation to examine the subservience ex officio (Art. 15(1) CCP).

b. Negative procedural prerequisites (also called procedural obstacles) for the existence of the right to claim:
   - The force of res judicata is an absolute negative procedural prerequisite. According to Art. 299(1) CCP a dispute determined through a judgment that has taken effect cannot be determined anew, except for the cases where the law provides otherwise.
   - In the literature an opinion is presented according to which the limitation results in the extinguishment of the right to claim, therefore, it is treated as a negative procedural prerequisite regarding the existence of the right to claim. Thus, according to this opinion, if the limitation term has expired, the court should disallow claim as inadmissible prior

57. Regardless of the absence of doubt in doctrine, ID No. 7-2020-GMCC and the Com.C. of the SCC for issuance of an interpretative decision was formed on the question: 'In proceedings under a claim by a third party for the invalidity of the agreement, are the parties to the agreement indispensable or facultative parties'.

to considering the merits of the case, and should decide by a ruling, and not a decision.[58] In my opinion the expiry of the limitation term does not result in the extinguishment of the right to claim (the right to request that the dispute be determined through the force of res judicata). That expiry gives rise to a substantive law defence in favour of the debtor – the substantive law subjective right to refuse to fulfil the required obligation.[59] If the debtor exercises this right of his/hers, invoking it through a defence, then it is the right to enforcement that is extinguished, and not the right to claim. And because of that I support the practice of Bulgarian courts lasting for several decades which disallows the claim for this right by a decision on the merits of the case if the limitation term has expired. Where an objection regarding limitation has been lodged, first is to consider whether the claimant's right has accrued and does exist and to collect evidence regarding the matters relevant thereto. These concern the merits of the case and the substantive law dispute. This construction complies with the provision of Art. 118 OCA, according to which the execution of a receivable extinguished through limitation is not unduly paid as the judgment disallowing the condemnation claim because of the expiry of its limitation term disallows the right to enforcement and not the receivable. Furthermore, the said judgment establishes both the existence of the receivable and the extinguishment by limitation. And this is so because the condemnation claim requesting sentencing of the defendant is disallowed.

The same notion should apply regarding the newly introduced by the Bulgarian legislator institute of absolute prescription, for monetary receivables against physical persons (Art. 112 OCA). The rule in Art. 118 OCA also applies to it (arg. Art. 112, last sentence OCA).

– The preclusive term brings about the extinguishment of the right to claim. The expiry of this term is a negative procedural prerequisite, i.e., it is a procedural obstacle to the existence of the right to claim. The preclusive terms are established for the exercise of certain potestative rights exercised through a constitutive claim (for example the preclusive term under Art. 31 FC regarding the lodging of a claim for the greatest part of the matrimonial property on the grounds of Art. 29 FC and the claim under Art. 30 FC for a share of the private property of the spouse; the preclusive term under Art. 33(2) OCA regarding the lodging of a claim for invalidation of a contract). As the preclusive terms are laid down through imperative legal norms, the court has the obligation to examine them ex officio.

---

58. *See* J. Stalev, A. Mingova, V. Popova, O. Staboliev, R. Ivanova, *Balgarsko …* , *supra*, p. 168.
59. In this sense *see also* P. Goleva, S. Chernev 'Za haraktera na pogasitelnata davnost', *Byuletin na Saiuza na yuristite v Balgaria* ('The Nature of Limitation', *Bulletin of the Union of Bulgarian Lawyers*), No. 6, 1986, pp. 18–24; V. Popova, Prihvashtane. Materialnopravni problemi, II izd. (Withholding. Substantial Law Matters, 2nd edition) (Sofia: Feneya Publishing House, 2002), pp. 185–186; V. Popova, Vazrajenieto … , (Sofia, Feneya Publishing House, 2002), pp. 243–244.

124. The CCP also provides for the procedural prerequisites for the due exercise of the right to claim.

A. Positive Prerequisites:

- The procedural legal capacity of the party.
- The presence of power of representation in those cases where the claim is lodged by a representative of the party.

At any stage of the proceedings the court has the obligation to consider ex officio the presence of procedural legal capacity, the legal power of representation, the parent's or guardian's consent for lodging the claim, or the absence thereof (Article 101 in connection with Articles 28, 29, 30 CCP). The court specifies the term for curing the defects therein. Upon the expiry of this term if the defects have not been cured, the procedural steps are deemed non-performed. (Article 101(3) CCP) and if the defect concerns the very bringing in of the statement of claim, it is returned (Article 129(3) CCP) and if the case has been already constituted, the proceedings are terminated (Article 129(4) CCP):

- The observance of the requirements set forth in Articles 127 and 128 CCP regarding the form and content of the statement of claim and the enclosures thereto about which the court has the obligation to consider ex officio.
- Generic jurisdiction and local jurisdiction are also positive procedural prerequisites for the due exercise of the right to claim. Generic jurisdiction is an absolute procedural prerequisite. (Article 119(1) CCP). *Venue is a relative procedural prerequisite.* According to Article 119(4) CCP, the generic jurisdiction of the case can be challenged only by the defendant, and not later than in the reply to the statement of claim, outside the cases under Article 119(2) and (3). This term is preclusive. The local jurisdiction under the location of the property (Article 119 (2) CCP), as well as the jurisdiction under Article 108(2), Article 113, and Article 115(2) (Article 119(3) CCP) is an absolute procedural prerequisite, for which the court is bound to monitor ex officio.

B. Negative procedural prerequisites for excising duly the right to claim:

- The presence of a pending action between the same parties on the same civil law dispute is an absolute negative procedural prerequisite for the due exercise of the right to claim. According to Article 126(1) CCP, where, either before the same court or before different courts, there are two pending actions between the same parties, and on the same grounds, and on the same claim, the action which was commenced later is terminated by the court ex officio, except for the cases for awarding an initially unclaimed part of the receivable, subject to a case under an already pending partial claim (item 3 of ID No. 3-22.04.2019 on ID No. 3/2016-GMCC and the Com.C. of the SCC).
- The court is obliged to suspend the case where: there is a pending trial between the same parties on another dispute, which is preliminary to the still incomplete

process (Article 229(1), item. 4 CCP); there is a pending criminal case which is a prerequisite for civil proceedings, or when criminal proceedings reveal criminal circumstances from which the outcome of the case (Article 229(1), items 4 and 5 in the connection with Article 300 CCP and 124(5) CCP). In ID No. 1-09.07.2019 on ID No. 1/2017, the GMCC and the Com.C. of the SCC accepted that an appellate decision, rendered in the presence of circumstances for suspension under Article 229(1), item 4 CCP (regardless of when the circumstances have arisen – before the first-instance court or the appellate court), is inadmissible.

125. Submitting the civil dispute to an arbitration court is specific (Article 19 CCP) (*see* paragraph 459). In the literature it is treated as a negative procedural prerequisite for the due exercise of the right to claim, since the arbitration clause does not bring about derogation of the subservience of the courts.[60] I find it should be one of the negative procedural prerequisites for the existence of the right to claim. It is true that it does not bring about derogation of the subservience of the courts. That is due to the fact that the law has regulated it as a relative procedural prerequisite, i.e., as a procedural prerequisite that has to be examined by the court ex officio. According to Article 8(1) ICAA the court with which a claim has been lodged regarding a dispute that is the subject of an arbitration agreement is obliged to terminate the proceedings if the party invokes the said agreement within the term for submitting a reply to the statement of claim. The term is a preclusive one. This shows, where the arbitration clause constitutes grounds for the right to claim before the respective arbitration court the latter will bring about derogation of the subservience of the State court only if the party invokes the arbitration clause within the said preclusive term.

§2. Types of Claims: Distinctions

126. Depending on the type of defence sought, in the Bulgarian procedure literature the claims are divided in three types: ascertainment claims, condemnation claims and constitutive claims (Article 124 CCP). The subject matter of the claim is also of major importance for this division.

127. According to Article 124(1) CCP every person is entitled to lodge a claim for the establishment of the existence or non-existence of a legal relationship or a right if he/she has an interest therein. One of the basic features of the ascertainment claim is that the request contained therein is that a civil law dispute be considered and determined through the force of res judicata. It is pointed out that it is a subsidiary one, because the legal disputes very quickly develop into disputes over violations of the law, and owing thereto the ascertainment claim is less common than the condemnation claim, and, besides that, the ascertainment claim is prevention

60. *See* J. Stalev, A. Mingova, V. Popova, O. Stamboliev, R. Ivanova, *Balgarsko ...* , *supra*, pp. 169, 862.

against the violation of the right in issue. It seems to me that in modern legal reality the ascertainment claims are not a rare phenomenon.[61] Depending on whether the ascertainment claim states or challenges the existence of a right or a legal relationship, the ascertainment claims are qualified as positive and negative ones.

The incidental ascertainment claim under Article 212 CCP is a specific claim in Bulgarian procedure law. It is lodged in the course of pending proceedings and its subject matter is a legal relationship which is prejudicial with respect to the subject matter of the case. This claim might be a positive or a negative one depending on whether the existence or the non-existence of a prejudicial legal relationship is claimed.

128. In principle the subject matter of the ascertainment claim can be any civil legal relationship or right regardless of the branch of civil law which regulates it: property law, contractual law, family law, inheritance law or commercial law. Future legal relations cannot form the subject matter of an ascertainment claim. Usually, the subject matter of the ascertainment claim is a legal relationship that is claimed to be existing at the time of lodging the claim, i.e., in the present. However, it is possible for the subject matter of the ascertainment claim to be a legal relationship that used to exist in the past, and does not exist any longer, but has given rise to civil law consequences relevant to the present (e.g., Article 52 FC and Article 327(1) CCP).

Those potestative rights which are exercised through court by law also cannot be the subject matter of an ascertainment claim. They can form the subject matter of a constitutive claim (*see* paragraph 138). However, the potestative rights which are exercised out-of-court through a unilateral expression of will, addressed to the other party, can form the subject matter of an ascertainment claim in those cases where they are challenged.

As for the rights to claim, claimed by the bearer thereof, in principle they cannot be the subject matter of an ascertainment claim if they are executable and, apart from their being challenged, non-performance is present. In this case the claimant often has no legal interest in lodging an ascertainment claim because he/she could not achieve the defence required in non-performance – condemnation of the debtor, this being a judgment which can form grounds for enforcement and on the basis thereof a writ of execution can be obtained under Article 404(1) and the judgment could be enforced, on the grounds of the respective document he/she can request issuance of a writ of execution and commence the enforcement against the debtor. In order to have grounds for execution the creditor might use the order for payment proceedings under Article 410 CCP or Article 418 CCP in connection with Article 417 CCP. According to Article 415(1) CCP the court instructs the applicant that he/she can bring an action for the claim when: the objection under Article 414 CCP has been filed within the time limit (item 1); the enforcement order has been served to the debtor under the conditions of Article 47(5) and the serving party has collected information that the debtor does not live at the address, after an inquiry from the manager of the condominium, the mayor of the respective populated area or in

61. *See* V. Popova, *Vidove iskove i novijat GPK (Types of Claim and the New CCP)*, Ciela. Norms. (http://www.ciela.net).

another way, and has certified this by indicating the source of this information in the message (item 2); the court refused to issue an enforcement order (item 3) (*see also* paragraph 394). According to the legislator's concept explicitly expressed in Article 415(3) CCP the claim under Article 415(1) items 1 and 2 CCP is ascertainment, while the one under Article 415(1) item 3 – condemnation.

Where the debtor lodges an objection against the receivable, the creditor can bring in a negative ascertainment claim for establishing the non-existence of that right. Such are the claims under Articles 424(1), 439, 240(2) CCP.

Absolute rights, the right of ownership belonging to this category, can also form the subject matter of an ascertainment claim if they are challenged but not violated[62] contrary to the right to property in ID No. 8-2013 on com. c. No. 8/2012-GMCC and the Com.C. of the SCC.

129. In principle a claim for ascertaining the existence or non-existence of facts is inadmissible (arg. under Article 124(4) CCP). There can be lodged a claim for ascertaining the authenticity or the forgery of a document (Article 124(4), sentence I CCP). A claim for ascertaining the existence or non-existence of other facts of legal importance is admissible only in those cases which are explicitly provided for in the law (Article 124(4), sentence II CCP): claims for ascertainment and challenging the origin (Articles 60(2), 62, 68 and 69 FC); claims for ascertaining the length of service (Decree on ascertaining the length of service through the court).

130. A claim for ascertaining a circumstance of the crime, this circumstance being important either for a particular civil legal relationship or for reversing a judgment that has taken effect, is admissible only where the criminal prosecution either may not be commenced or has been suspended for any of the reasons specified in Article 24(1), items 2–5 CPC or has been discontinued for any of the reasons specified in Article 25 CPC or Article 26 CPC, and also where the doer has remained undiscovered (Article 124(5) CCP). In the cases under Article 124(5) CPC, the criminal circumstance can be subject to an ascertainment claim, if said circumstance has bearing on a particular civil legal relationship or reversal of a decision that has taken effect.

The following persons are legitimized as defendants to the claim under Article 124(5) CCP: (a) the person alleged to have committed the crime, and if the latter has died – his/her heirs; (b) the person against whom the circumstance of the crime can be used as grounds for overruling a judgment that has been favourable for him/her (e.g., on the grounds of Article 303(1), item 2 CCP); (c) the person who bears financial liability for the damages caused by the circumstance of the crime (e.g., the assignor of the job who bears responsibility under Article 49 OCA; the State – in those cases where it bears responsibility under the Act on the responsibility of the State for damages caused to citizens). If the doer has not been found the claim can be brought only against the persons under items 'b' and 'c'.

131. The legal interest provided under Article 124(1) CCP for submitting an ascertainment claim is clearly evident from the submission of the claim, when the

62. *See also* the reservations of the judges in the cited ID.

claimant submits a claim for his/her right, which is disputed by the defendant, respectively disputes a right, which is claimed by the defendant. As a rule legal interest is absent in those cases where the right in issue can be claimed through a condemnation claim or a constitutive claim, because in these cases the legal dispute will also be determined through the force of res judicata, but simultaneously the defensive objectives inherent to these claims will also be achieved – the ascertainment of the right through the force of res judicata and conviction, and the respective enactment of the legal change ensuing from the content of the potestative right. For instance, where the ownership of a real estate is challenged, and the person claiming the right of ownership is not in possession of the real estate, he/she can defend himself/herself through a condemnation claim and not through an ascertainment claim since the right has been violated and it cannot be defended adequately only by determining the legal dispute between the parties by the force of res judicata[63] contrary to the right to property in ID No. 8-2013 on com. c. No. 8/2012-GMCC and the Com.C. of the SCC. The situation regarding joint ownership is rather specific. It is through a condemnation claim that the joint owner can demand cessation of the groundless actions of another joint owner if these actions prevent him from exercising his/her right. However, the ascertainment claim of the joint owner who is not in possession is admissible[64] because through this claim he/she can interrupt the acquisition limitation and will be able to seek compensation for the use of that part of the real estate which he/she owns (Article 31(2) PA). In this case he/she has legal interest in lodging an ascertainment claim because he/she can also claim distribution of the use of the jointly owned real estate (Article 32(2) PA). The right to partition provided for in Article 34 PA does not remove the legal interest in lodging an ascertainment claim regarding joint ownership. This ascertainment claim is inadmissible only where a joint owner has already lodged a claim for partition, because the judgment upon the admissibility of the partition has an ascertainment effect regarding the joint ownership (Article 344(1) CCP).

132. The legitimization of the parties to an ascertainment claim is determined by their legal interest in ascertaining the real legal situation. Primarily, these parties are the subjects of the legal relationship in issue. A third person may also be legitimized to lodge an ascertainment claim in those cases where the relationship in issue directly affects his/her legal sphere. Even where the claimant is not a subject of the legal relationship in issue, forming the subject matter of the claim, the case is not one of procedural substitution (Article 26(2), (3) and (4) CCP). The legitimization of the claimant belongs to the category of typical ones. It is his/her own legal sphere, and not someone else's, that is directly affected by the legal relationship, and so the claimant defends his/her own legal sphere.

The spouse is entitled to lodge a claim requesting that it be established that a donation contract concluded by the other spouse is a simulated one and conceals a requital transaction – a sale or a contract for maintenance and attendance. This interest ensues from the matrimonial tenancy by the entirety (Article 21(1) FC), which

63. *See also* the reservations of the judges in the cited ID.
64. *See* all judges reservations in the cited ID.

also includes the personal property (Article 21(1) FC) acquired during the marriage under the legal regime of commonness in the property relationships between the spouses.

The heir having a reserved part in the heritage (Article 29 Inheritance Act (IA)) is legitimized to lodge a claim for ascertaining that a contract for the sale of a legator's property right concluded between the legator and another person (the latter might be another heir to the legator) conceals a donation. The heir is legitimized to lodge such a claim because, on the grounds of Article 30 IA in relation to Article 28 IA, the heir having a reserved part is entitled to request a decrease of the donation to such an extent that his/her reserved part is preserved.

According to Article 464(1) CCP, where one of the claimants challenges the existence of another claimant's receivable, he/she has to lodge a claim both against the latter and against the debtor. The claimant lodging the claim is not a subject of the legal relationship between the other claimant and the debtor, but the challenged receivable directly affects the possibility for him/her to get satisfied in the enforcement proceedings, because the amount received from the enforcement on the debtor's property will be divided between the two creditors. The claim under Article 694 C. Code is similar to the one under Article 464(1) CCP

It should also be noted that in the cases above the persons constituted as defendants are those whose legal relationship is challenged.

133. According to Article 124(1) CCP anyone is entitled to bring in a claim for *restoration of any right of his/hers that has been violated.* This text refers to the *condemnation claim.* The characteristic features of this claim are determined by the form of the unlawful development of the civil legal relationship – a violation of a civil right, or non-performance of a civil obligation, respectively. In this form of unlawful development of the legal relationship *the very determination of the legal dispute through the force of* res judicata *cannot provide the necessary defence* because the right has already been violated, and the obligation has not been performed. With the condemnation claim, the claimant requests from the court: (a) to consider the dispute *and to establish through the force of* res judicata *the existence of the right alleged by the claimant*; and (b) *to sentence the defendant* to perform what is due, and to stop violating the right, respectively. The effective *judgment which upholds a condemnation claim constitutes grounds for enforcement* (Article 404(1) CCP). It is on the grounds of this judgment that the bearer of the right established through the judgment is entitled to demand that a writ of execution be issued, and enforcement be commenced. Moreover, the sentencing intermediate appellate decisions that have not taken effect are also foreseen in Article 404(1) CCP (*see* paragraphs 192-194).

134. In principle, *the subject matter of a condemnation claim* can be only an *executable civil right to claim* (regardless of the branch of civil law which regulates it: property law, contractual law, family law, inheritance law or commercial law).

In the literature it is pointed out that the subject matter of this claim can also be the responsibility taken by the defendant through a piece of property of his/hers for someone else's debt (Article 149(2) OCA) i.e., the creditor is entitled to file a condemnation claim against a person that has created a mortgage or a pledge on a piece of property of his/hers for securing someone else's debt. In my opinion the condemnation claim against this person is inadmissible. Unlike the surety, the third person that has created a mortgage or a pledge on a piece of property of his/hers for securing someone else's debt *is not personally obligated* under this obligation. The said person bears responsibility for the other person's debt *only through the object on which security was imposed*. Because of that the said person cannot be sentenced. Hence, the condemnation claim against him/her *is not admissible. On* the grounds under in connection with Article 417, item 6 and Article 418 *the creditor secured may on the secured by a mortgage may on the grounds of the act for registering the mortgage request that the court issues an order of immediate enforcement and simultaneously with it a writ of execution.* If the pledgor, or the mortgager, respectively, challenges the receivable by raising an objection under Article 422 CCP, the creditor secured by such a pledge, a mortgage, respectively, should lodge an ascertainment claim under Article 415 CCP within the preclusive term under Article 415 CCP.

135. As it has already been mentioned, the subject matter of a condemnation claim can be only a civil right to claim. In the literature it is assumed that the condemnation claim for a non-executable right to claim is a prematurely lodged one, however, it is groundless and not inadmissible. If in the course of proceedings prior to closure of oral pleadings, the right, subject to claim, has become executable, the claim has to be upheld. In court practice it was assumed that the condemnation claim for a receivable, which is not due and payable is inadmissible[65] as the claim is prematurely lodged, because the right has not been violated yet, and owing thereto, there is no legal interest in lodging the claim, so it has to be disallowed as inadmissible. In my opinion the two hypotheses regarding the receivable, subject of the claim, as due and payable, should be differentiated: (a) where it is stated in the claim that the receivable is due and payable, but in the course of proceedings it is established that the receivable is not due and payable yet; (b) where it is stated in the statement of claim that the receivable is not due and payable yet. In adversary proceedings the rights and obligations are to be stated. Only in the judgment, with which the court determines the legal dispute, does the court establish the existence of the legal relationship between the parties as well as its respective elements and legal features that individualize it. Therefore, (a) if the statement of claim contains an allegation that the receivable is due and payable, but in the course of proceedings it is established that the claim is not due and payable yet, the claim should be disallowed as groundless. (b) Where the statement of claim contains an allegation that the receivable exists, but has not become due and payable yet, in my opinion the claim is inadmissible. The court has to disallow the inadmissible claim by way of a ruling. Where the claimant alleges that the receivable has not become due and payable yet, he/she has no legal interest in lodging a condemnation claim. At this moment he/she cannot request voluntary execution, much less a condemnation decision.

65. *See* Decision No. 1232-55-IV C. Ch. of the SC, Collection 1955, No. 594.

136. According to Article 124(2) CCP a claim can be lodged for sentencing the defendant to perform repeated obligations although their executability occurs after the judgment is rendered. In order for a condemnation claim under Article 124(2) CCP to be admissible, the first payment should have become executable. The executability of the subsequent payments should not depend on the execution of the consideration on the part of the creditor-claimant – an advance or a concurrent one. It should only depend on the expiration of the term. Because of that the most common claims under Article 124(2) CCP are the ones for alimony and interest for delay. The claim for a periodically specified obligation of indemnity in cases of damages from tort is also an admissible one.

A condemnation claim for a non-executable right to claim, even where this right has not occurred yet, can be arrived at in cumulative joinder of claims. Often a constitutive claim for the denunciation of a contract for sale, or a contract for transfer of ownership, or a contract for establishing property rights over real estates (Article 87(3) OCA) is joined with a claim for returning the receipts under the contract; the claim under Article 19(3) OCA for concluding a final contract is joined with the claim for transferring the possession of the object of the contract. This hypothesis also contains the counterclaim under Article 219(3) CCP, the subject matter thereof being the regressive right to claim of a supported party against a third-person supporter. What is special about this case is that if the counterclaim is upheld, the sentence thereunder will be conditional, the condition being that the supported party performs the obligation for which it is sentenced. In joinder of claims, the counterclaim of the defendant (Article 211 CCP) for improvements (Articles 72 and 74 PA) in those cases where a revendication claim under Article 108 OCA has been lodged against him/her is a specific case of a claim for a right that has not yet become executable.

As far as legal interest is concerned, condemnation claim has its particularities. It is possible that the defendant violates the right of the claimant without challenging it, or, respectively, the defendant fails to perform his/her obligations without challenging the existence and executability thereof. The creditor may in those cases request the issuance of an execution order under 410 CCP when he/she has any of the documents mentioned in Article 417 CCP. He/she may have issued an order of immediate enforcement and a writ of execution simultaneously with it. However, he/she does not lose his legal interest in lodging a condemnation claim. The usage of the order of payment proceedings is just one of the possibilities. It is not mandatory (arg. of Articles 410 and 418 CCP). Hence, no matter whether the creditor has or does not have a document under Article 417 CCP and the debtor challenges or not the receivable extra-procedurally, if he/she fails to perform his/her obligations voluntarily, although he/she does not challenge it, the said creditor should not have to defend himself/herself directly through order for payment and enforcement proceedings. If in the adversary proceedings the defendant acknowledges the claim, the court will render a decision, if the creditor being a claimant requests that (Article 237 CCP). If the defendant does not challenge the claim and does not submit a reply, does not appear in the court session and does not declare that he/she wishes the case to be considered in his/her absence, a decision by default may be issued upon the request of claimant (Article 238 CCP). Hence in the Bulgarian civil procedure the creditor has legal interest in lodging a condemnation claim, in the cases when his/her receivable is challenged extra-procedurally, when it is not challenged but is not executed as well.

As it is obvious from the wording of Article 124(1) CCP the only person legitimized to lodge a condemnation claim is the one that states to be the bearer of a right which has been violated. And the legitimized defendant in the case is the person alleged either to have violated this right, or to be obligated under the right to claim stated by the claimant. According to Article 26(2) CCP nobody is entitled to claim in court, on his/her behalf, someone else's rights except as otherwise provided in law. In those cases where a person claims someone else's rights, the person whose rights are claimed is also summoned as a party to the case (Article 26(4) CCP). For instance, according to Article 134(1) OCA the creditor is entitled to execute the property rights of the debtor in those cases where the omission of the latter endangers the satisfaction of the creditor, with the exception of those rights whose exercise wholly depends on the personal judgment of the debtor. In these cases it is obligatory that the debtor be summoned as a party (Article 134(2) OCA). Procedural substitution is present in this case. Through this condemnation claim the claimant-procedural substitute is entitled to claim sentence for the benefit of the debtor.

137. According to Article 124(3) CCP a claim for modification or termination of civil legal relations may be brought solely in the cases provided for in a law. By this regulation the statement adopted in doctrine and in practice their existence was adopted explicitly. It was and is undoubtedly accepted that the subject matter of a constitutive claim can be only a potestative (converting) civil right for which the law provides that it be exercised through the court. Owing thereto, the constitutive claim as a separate form of defence is admissible only in the cases provided for in the law[66] (e.g., the claim for divorce; Article 87(3) OCA for wiping out a contract for transferring the property right and establishing property rights on an immoveable property, Article 19(3) OCA; for announcing the preliminary contract for concluded).

138. Through the constitutive claim the court is requested to review the dispute regarding the potestative right, subject of the claim, to ascertain it with a res judicata effect and to rule the change in the respective civil relationship between the disputing parties which follows from the contents of the potestative right. With the entry into effect of the decision, which upholds the constitutive claim, the potestative right is extinguished, as it is already exercised, satisfied. That is why in the constitutive claim the connection between the substantive law and the procedure is

66. In principle, the potestative right is exercised out-of-court, through a unilateral will of its bearer, addressed to the counterparty under legal relationship. For example, the right to wipe out a bilateral contract (Art. 87 (1) OCA), the right to compensate between two counterparty claims. Where there is a dispute over the existence and proper exercise of this category of rights of attorney, they may be the subject of an ascertainment claim. When the legislator has determined that the right to apply is of particular importance; the way in which it is exercised should not affect the legal security, he has provided in the substantive law that this right is exercised by the courts.

especially clear. The decision through which the constitutive claim is denied has only a res judicata effect, which establishes the non-existence of the potestative right, subject of the claim.

139. What is typical of constitutive claims is that the request to the court is the dispute for the potestative right, subject of the claim, be reviewed and decided, and that the right be ascertained with the force of res judicata, and the court renders the legal change in the civil relationship between the parties to the dispute. This change follows from the content of the potestative right. These proceedings are typical adversary ones. In its judgment on the constitutive claim the court is not entitled to judge the expedience. As the potestative right is realized through rendering of the legal change, this judgment actually has the effect of satisfaction of the right. Once the decision for upholding the constitutive claim takes effect, the potestative right is extinguished because it has already been exercised and satisfied. And owing thereto, in the cases of constitutive claims the relationship between substantive law and procedure is strongly expressed. However, the judgment which does not uphold the constitutive claim has only the effect of res judicata, establishing the non-existence of the potestative right which constitutes the subject matter of the claim.

140. The person legitimized to lodge a constitutive claim is the one alleging to be the bearer of the potestative right which constitutes the subject matter of the claim. The claim can be lodged against a person whose legal sphere shall be affected by the legal consequences ensuing from the potestative right.

§3. Defendant's Defence Against the Claim

141. The defence of the defendant against the claim is defence against the admissibility of the claim (procedural defence), and defence against the reasonableness of the claim (defence on the merits). The current CCP neither contains explicit regulations on the procedural means of this defence nor does it contain a legal definition of the terms 'defence against the admissibility of the claim', 'defence on the merits' or 'objection'. Article 131(2) CCP stating the mandatory content of the reply to the claim (*see* paragraphs 148 and 156) points that the reply should contain 'a stand on whether the claim is admissible and well-founded'.

The procedural defence of the defendant is the system of his/her procedural actions by which he/she objects to the admissibility of the proceedings by challenging the right to claim or the due exercise. In the literature, these objections are called procedural objections or demurrers. In the law, these procedural actions are called objections (*see* Article 191 (2), (3) and (4) CCP as it was in Article 119(2), (3), (4) CCP and paragraph 145) and its consideration is called 'consideration of preliminary matters' (Article 143 (1) CCP)

Under the current CCP viewing the preclusion under Article 133 CCP the division of the procedural prerequisites of absolute and relative is of significant importance for the defendant's procedural defence against the claim so that the proceedings are terminated, if the defendant does not submit a reply to the statement of claim within the term foreseen by the law (*see* paragraph 149).

142. The defendant's defence on the merits is a system of procedural actions by which the defendant sets his/her legal allegation against the claimant's legal allegation regarding the disputed substantive law relationship and requests the court to affirm the legal situation he/she alleges. The means of defendant's defence on the merits include: challenge, disavowal, objection and legal argument. Through these means the defendant exercises in the proceedings commenced against him/her by the claimant his/her right to claim regarding the issue in litigation, the right to have the legal dispute determined by res judicata and the right to legal defence against the claim brought against him/her.

143. Disavowal consists in disavowing the facts alleged by the claimant. The challenging of the claim relates either to disavowal of facts or to objections or to legal arguments, considered jointly or separately. The disavowal of a fact requires that the claimant proves the fact alleged by him (arg. Article 153 CCP in relation to Articles 154 and 145 CCP). According to the Bulgarian Procedural Law non-contesting the fact is not equal to its admitting and does not alleviate the claimant from the burden to prove the alleged fact.

144. The legal argument as a means of defence consists in challenging the legal consequences alleged by the claimant by providing the legal arguments and interpretation of the legal norms. While objection is lodged and proved in order to be taken into consideration (Article 143(3) CCP; Article 153 in relation to Article 154(1); Article 439(2) CCP and Article 131(2) item 5 in relation to Article 131(2) item 3 CCP and the preclusion foreseen in Article 133 CCP), the first-instance court is obligated to apply the law regardless to whether a legal argument is presented by the defendant or not. The differentiation is of significant importance for the application of the preclusion foreseen in Article 133 CCP (*see* paragraph 149).

145. The objections, as a means of the defendant's defence on the merits, are procedural actions of the defendant addressed to the court, which can comprise allegations of facts, but cannot be identified with the facts. The facts have their existence outside the proceedings and are independent. The allegations can reflect the actual situation or not.

The procedural action of objection by which a substantive subjective right of the defendant is claimed, constituting a substantive law objection, contains an allegation of the right. Objection forms an element of the chain of civil procedure legal relationships between the party and the court, and its facts of the case, content, and legal consequences are regulated by the norms of civil procedure. The substantive law objection as a civil subjective right forms part of the civil law relationship between civil law subjects and is regulated by substantive law. Consequently, it can be the issue in litigation of a civil law dispute between the parties.

Objections claiming counter rights of the defendant also contain allegations of facts. However, their position here resembles the one of the factual allegations of the claimant contained in the recitals of the statement of claim. In this case, the facts alleged by the defendant in his/her objection are not directly objectionable to the right forming the subject matter of the claim. They oppose this right because they form the basis of the substantive law right alleged by the defendant, the defendant's substantive law objection brought in by the procedural action of objection. The admissibility of bringing in counterclaims of the defendant by the procedural action of objection is determined by the relationship between the right that forms the subject matter of the claim and the right that forms the subject matter of the objection.

The objection by which the defendant's counter right is claimed is a means of defence against the claim that is brought and against the counterclaim of the defendant. These two elements are closely and inevitably connected. In connection with the ex officio and truth verification during the trial according to Article 131(2) CCP, the court should instruct the defendant that he/she must claim all his/her objections to the claim and must adduce evidence in their support, or respectively – to submit written evidence. The court has not any right to plead on non-submitted objections, no matter whether those are objections whose subject matter consist of facts favourable for the defendant or objections against a claim on the merits. Thus, viewing the necessity to submit objections our legislator treats uniformly the two types of objections.

146. Bulgarian procedure law treats the objection of set-off and the objection of improvement, related to the right to retention, in a specific way. According to Article 298(4) CCP (borrowed from Article 221(2) CCP repealed), the decision of the court is also effective regarding the claims and objections of retentions and adjudged set-offs.

The subject matter of the objections under Article 298(4) CCP are the counter rights of the defendant: (a) in objections to the right of retention, the acceptance of improvements and the right to retention and in objections of set-off of the bona fide *possessor* (Article 72 PA), the right of retention and set-off in connection with keeping, maintaining, repairing and improving a property which he/she does not own or for damages caused on such property (Article 91 OCA) the counter receivable of the defendant and his/her compensation right. Article 298(4) CCP introduces an exception connected with the objective limits of res judicata as specified in Article 298(4) CCP that states that the subject matter of res judicata is the right forming the subject matter of the claim. In Article 298(4) CCP the legislator indirectly allowed that the defendant's counterclaims, objectionable to the right forming the subject matter of the issue, are brought in by objection and become an issue in litigation. What is special about this issue is its connection with the issue in litigation brought by the claim. The defence sought by the objections to the counter rights of the defendant is connected with and subject to his/her defence against the claim. The defendant can have the claim disallowed if the objection of set-off is upheld. If the defendant's receivable is larger than that of the claimant, the defendant cannot get a court decision regarding the difference between the amounts of the two receivables. He/she can only get it only if he/she brings a counterclaim under Article 211 CCP.

The objection to the right of retention in the set-offs mentioned in Article 72 OA and Article 91 OCA is admissible because the defendant can claim that, in connection with his/her receivable regarding the improvements, he/she has the right of retention. If the counter receivable of the defendant is not connected with the right of retention, he/she can only defend his/her receivable for improvements by a counterclaim. If the objection of improvements is approved, the defendant receives a decision according to which he/she has to render back the possession of the property if the claimant pays the defendant the counter receivable. In the case of an objection under Article 90 (1) OCA concerning a non-performed contract, the debtor may refuse to perform his/her counter debt to the creditor arising from the legal relationship until the creditor himself performs. From a procedural point of view the defendant may wish to be sued to perform only under the condition of simultaneous performance by the claimant. Respectively, if the claim of the claimant and the objection of the defendant under Article 90(1) OCA are upheld, the defendant is ordered to perform simultaneously with the claimant (Article 91(1), sentence II OCA).

147. The novelty in the Bulgarian procedural law is the establishing of 'exchange of papers'[67] (as it is known in the doctrine and practice) in the general adversary proceeding. Its elements are the reply to a claim as a defendant's means of defence as well as the early time barring with respect to the 'concentration principle' when no reply has been filed or the reply is incomplete.

Though the reply is not given as a uniform procedural action, it is a combination of several procedural actions, i.e., it unites several different procedural actions which are an element of the defendant's right of defence in the adversary proceedings.

According to Article 131(1) CCP having accepted the claim, the court sends a duplicate copy together with the attachments to the defendant, instructing him/her to submit a written reply within one month, specifying the mandatory content of the reply and the consequences of non-submitted reply or of non-exercised rights, as well as the possibility to use legal aid, if necessary and if entitled thereto. *The obligation of the court to give that instruction is provided for explicitly* in Article 131(1) CCP since the failure to submit a reply and exercise the rights, foreseen by Article 131 (1) CCP, like the mandatory content of the reply, cause precluding of the possibility to exercise those rights later (*see* paragraph 149).

148. Article 131 (2) CCP stipulates that the written reply of the defendant should contain (131(2) CCP):

(1) Position on the admissibility of the claim; through the claim the defendant exercises his/her right to procedural defence (*see* paragraph 141). When the defendant exercises successfully his/her procedural defence by the reply the court terminates the case with a decision according to which he/she could claim reimbursement of the costs on the case.
(2) Position *on the circumstances upon which the claim is grounded.* The defendant exercises his/her defence on the merits, i.e., substantive law defence (*see* paragraph 142).
   In the reply the defendant should:

67. Papers are not exchanged between the parties. Both the claim of the claimant and the reply to it of the defendant are brought in to the court.

(a) Make a statement on the circumstances upon which the claim is founded (Article 131(2), item 4 CCP). He/she should state, if he/she admits or disputes the facts alleged by the claimant. According to Article 175 CCP the admission of a fact, made by a party or by a representative thereof, is evaluated by the court considering all circumstances of the case. The report that the court should make at its first hearing states which facts are admitted (*see* Article 146(1), item 3 CCP). Non-contesting a fact is not identical to admitting a fact.

(b) Present the objections to the claim and to the circumstances upon which the claim is founded.

(3) According to Article 131(3) CCP the defendant must adduce evidence and the specific circumstances which he/she will prove thereby, and present all written evidence in his/her possession.

(4) According to Article 132 CCP the reply to the claim should contain the following attachments: a power of attorney, where the answer is submitted by an attorney-in-fact; duplicate copies of the reply and of the attachments thereto corresponding to the number of claimants.

(5) It is not expressly specified in Article 131 CCP that the defendant may recognize the claim. Upon recognition of the claim a judgment can be rendered (Article 237 CCP). Thus, the defendant will not be responsible for the costs. Within the term for the reply, the defendant may bring a counterclaim (Article 211 CCP), an incidental ascertainment decree (Article 212 CCP), as well as he/she may request impleading of a third party in order to assist him/her (Article 219 CCP). The matter in the case concerns independent procedural actions accompanying the defendant's reply to the claim and exceeding his/her defence against the claim (*see* paragraphs 335, 369) that should meet the requirements set thereof.

149. The term for the reply is preclusive. Under Article 133 CCP when the defendant fails, within the established term to submit a written reply, to take a stand, to file an objection, to contest the truthfulness of a document presented, to cite evidence, to present written evidence or to exercise his/her rights under Article 211(1), Article 212, and Article 219 CCP he/she forfeits the possibility to do so later, unless the omission is due to special unforeseen circumstances. In the latter case the defendant may request a resumption of the term according to Article 64(2) CCP.

Non-submission of a reply is not identical to admission of the claim. The admission of the claim is an express statement of the defendant and may have as a consequence rendering of a judgment upon the admission of the claim, if the claimant requests it (Article 237 CCP). The passive behaviour of the defendant manifested by his/her non-submission of a reply cannot be treated as a concluding action being a specific kind of admission of the claim. Non-submission of a reply to the claim is one of the prerequisites for rendering a judgment by default.

150. The literal interpretation of Article 133 CCP might lead to the conclusion that the possibility to give a stand on the admissibility of the claim may be precluded. That is beyond doubt so as far as the relative procedural prerequisites are concerned. The law provides in relation to these not to be observed by the court ex officio but only upon the defendant's request and for which the court has set the term of the reply to the claim as a preclusive term. The term of the reply is preclusive for a demurrer for territorial cognizance as well as for arbitration agreement (*see* Article 19 CCP and Article 8(1) ICAA). The court must observe ex officio the absolute procedural prerequisites for which obligation there has not been set any time limit. Therefore, this obligation of the court does not repeal the defendant's right of seizing the respective absolute procedural prerequisite to the court. That is why his/her right to contest the admissibility of the claim is not precluded with the expiration of the time limit due to the existence of a negative absolute procedural prerequisite or to absence of a positive absolute procedural prerequisite, respectively. Non-submission of a reply or non-contesting the admissibility of the claim on the grounds mentioned is not an obstacle for the defendant to do so even after the deadline for the reply.

151. The literal interpretation of the text of Article 133 CCP might lead to the understanding that the defendant could not express any stand on the admissibility of the claim later, if he/she has not specified so in the reply.

The stand on the claim is an admission of the claim. In my opinion, there is no doubt that this could be done after the deadline for the reply. That is obvious from Article 237 CCP establishing that if the defendant admits the claim, the court, acting on a motion by the claimant, shall terminate the trial and shall render judgment conforming to the admission.

The question is whether in the case when the defendant has not objected to the claim in his/her reply, he/she could do so later in the course of the trial (*see* paragraphs 148, 149, 150). According to Bulgarian procedural law and to the current CCP the non-objection of the grounds of the claim is not equal to the admission of the claim. The admission of the claim is an explicit stand. In connection with preclusion the particular means of defendant's defence on merits should be analysed separately with regard to their specifics and only then the respective conclusion should be drawn.

The adequate arguments that the defendant uses to object the claim can be brought in at the court hearing and by the termination of the oral arguments both at first and, at appellate and cassation instances. They are also his/her stand on the grounds of the claim but the application of the substantive law is a duty of the court. The court must do that regardless of the fact whether the parties interpret the law, respectively – bring in their legal arguments on its application.

Much different is the case of the possibility for the defendant to bring in his/her stand on circumstances that the claimant alleges to establish his/her claims. For example, the current CCP differs from Article 166 of the old CLPA and §138, Abs. ZPO of Germany and has not a norm stipulating that the facts that have not been contested are regarded admitted by their counter proving. The regulation is contradictory and elusive. In Articles 154 and 155 CCP the non-contested fact among those that should be proved, i.e., such that could be excluded from those to be proved. Moreover, according to the current CCP the admission of a fact is not binding upon the court. According to Article 175 CCP an admission of a fact, made by a party or by its representative, is evaluated by the court considering all circumstances of the case. Besides, the text of Article 109(4) CCP (repealed) is missing. It established that *the court viewing the explanations of the parties by this determination might declare that the fact did not need proving*. Article 146(1) item 3 CCP establishes that the court's report should indicate which rights and which circumstances are admitted. The court puts questions to the parties for clarifying the facts and points at their importance for the case (Article 145(1) and (2) CCP). It is accepted in the literature that under Article 143(3) CCP the defendant may contest the facts even after the deadline for the reply, at a court sitting inclusive. In my opinion, having in mind the norms of Articles 145(1) and (2); 146(1), items 3 and 4 and 147 CCP, the objection is admissible under Article 147 CCP. Otherwise, that will be in conflict with Article 3 CCP for justful proceedings. The court cannot consider facts that have not been presented by defendant as well as right he/she has not claimed. Therefore, the preclusion according to Article 133 CCP based on the criterion mentioned covers practically all defendant's objections as a means of substantive defence: those alleging facts, generating legal consequences favourable for the defendant as well as those for bringing his/her claims on the merits (*see* paragraph 145). The text of Article 146(1), items 4 and 5 CCP and Article 146(3) and (2) CCP deals with instructions on the burden of proving and on the necessity of setting for and presenting evidence in support of the objections brought in already, the facts he/she alleges inclusive.

According to Article 371 CCP is whether defendant may actually bring in an objection for set-off after the deadline for the reply, if it is not connected with the collection of new evidences, if it is an objection for set-off with a cash receivable. Is it admissible for the first time before an intermediate appellate instance. According to Article 371 CCP an objection for set-off may be raised prior to the conclusion of the trial in the Court of First Instance, where taking of new evidence is not required to prove the set-off, or prior to the conclusion of the trial in the court of intermediate appellate instance, where the existence or non-contestation of the set-off are established by an effective judgment of the court or by an enforcement order. The text is in the special part concerning the especial claim jurisdiction for judging commercial disputes (*see* paragraph 369) and is not reproduced in the part about the general adversary proceedings. The text is under the strong influence of the SCC statement in its ID No. 1-2000 of the SCC about admitting the objection for set-off in the appellate jurisdiction at the time CCP repealed[68] in connection with the then unlimited appellate. It was adopted in ID No. 1-2013 of the CMCC and the Com.C. of the SCC that Article 371 CCP is applicable in the general adversary proceedings. The application by the analogy of a norm in the particular procedure in the general adversary proceedings is not a common law construction.

152. The provision in Article 133 CCP does not refer to the possibility for the defendant to bring in, and respectively present, pieces of evidence in support to his/her objections in the reply after the deadline for the reply to the claim. The court must indicate in the written report on the case (*see* paragraph 151) prepared upon receiving the reply to the claim how the burden of proof is allocated to the evidence to be proved (Article 146(1), item 5). The court must also indicate to the parties

---

68. *See* about it V. Popova. *On the permission in ID No. 1/2000 of SSC to bring in the objection for set-off in appellate proceedings*. Commercial Law Journal, 2001, Iss.1, pp. 37–48 (In Bulgarian).

which of the facts they claim do not bring evidence. According to Article 146(3) the court must give the parties the possibility to present their stand on the instructions given in the report on the case as well as to undertake the respective procedural actions. If the parties do not place requests for evidence when realizing the said possibilities, they lose the possibility to do that later except for the cases under Article 147 CCP (*see* paragraph 151).

153. A specific means of defence of the defendant against a condemnation claim is provided for in Bulgarian civil procedure: the claim for deferral or rescheduling of the performance of the decision for upholding the claim. According to Article 241 CCP, the court, upon rendering the decision, is entitled to defer or reschedule its execution in view of the property status of the party or any other reasons of a social nature. This deferral is of an exclusive nature and can be applied only once.

Chapter 3. Sanctions on Procedural Irregularities

§1. Formal Requirements

154. The procedural actions of the parties have to comply with the legal requirements, and have to be performed within the time, form and way provided for in the procedure law. So, in those cases where these actions either have not been performed, or have not been performed in accordance with the requirements, the party bears the respective unfavourable consequences, some of them having the nature of sanctions.

As a rule, the defective procedural actions of the parties are repairable. The court sees to the due performance of procedural steps and has the obligation to notify the party of its duty to repair the irregularities within the time provided for in the law (Article 101(1) CCP). If these irregularities are repaired, the action is cured retroactively (Article 101(2) CCP). In those cases where the irregularities are not repaired the procedural step are deemed non-performed (Article 101(3) CCP). That results in unfavourable consequences for the party: suspension of the case if the irregularity concerns only the filing of the claim, or considering the action as a non-performed one in those cases where the irregularity concerns an internal procedure action.

155. Where the statement of claim does not comply with the requirements set forth in Articles 127(1)[69] and 128 CCP, a message is sent to the claimant notifying him/her of the obligation to repair the irregularities within a seven-day term as well as of the possibility to use legal aid, if necessary and if entitled thereto (Article 129(2) CCP). Where the claimant fails to repair the irregularities within the set term, the statement of claim and the supplements thereto are sent back, or, should the address be unknown, they are kept in the chancellery of the court at the disposal of the claimant (Article 129(2), sentence I CCP). The same actions are taken when the irregularities in the statement of claim are noticed in the course of conducting the proceedings (Article 129(4) CCP). Then, if the statement of claim is not repaired, the proceedings are suspended.

156. The court instructs the defendant on the mandatory content of the reply to claim by sending him a copy of the application and its enclosures. The court also instructs him/her on the term he/she should submit the reply and on the circumstances of not submitting a reply or of not exercising his/her rights. Failure to respond to the claim and its incompleteness results in a preclusion of the possibility for the defendant to rely later on the relative procedural prerequisites for inadmissibility of the claim as well as his/her objections to the groundedness of the claim (Article 133 CCP, *see* paragraph 149) In the event of non-observance of the requirement to state in the reply all the evidence of the objections raised by the defendant and the submission of the written evidence, the preclusion occurs later under the

69. The legislator does not treat as an unconformity of the statement of claim the failure to meet the requirement provided for in Art. 127(2) CCP (*see* Art. 127(2) and (4)).

conditions of Article 147 CCP in connection with the Article 146(2) and (3) and Article 146(1), items 4 and 5 (*see* paragraph 151).

157. Where the statement of appeal does not comply with the requirements regarding its regularity, these requirements being set forth in Article 260, items 1, 2, 4 and 7 CCP and Article 261 CCP or the statement of appeal is not signed the party is given a notification to repair the irregularities within a seven-day term (Article 262(1) CCP). The statement of appeal is returned if the specified irregularities are not repaired within the seven-day term (Article 262(2), item 2 CCP).

Where the cassation appeal does not meet the requirements of Article 284 CCP or does not contain a motivated exposure of the grounds for cassation, the court is obligated to send a message to the appellant for repairing the irregularities within a seven-day term (Article 285(1) CCP). Where these irregularities are not repaired, the cassation appeal is returned (Article 286(1), item 2 CCP).

158. According to Article 40(1) CCP the party living abroad or travelling abroad for more than thirty days is obliged to supply an address for service (a person to be serviced with communications and subpoenas) if it does not have an attorney in the Republic of Bulgaria. The legal representative, the guardian and the attorney of the party have the same obligation in case of travelling abroad. *If the persons under* Article *40(1) CCP fail to supply an address for service, all communications are attached to the case and are regarded as being served.*[70] *The court has to warn these persons of the above-mentioned consequences upon servicing of the first subpoena, or notification or any other paper* (Article 40(2) CCP).

The party which is absent for more than one month from the address, which it has provided under the case or where a message has already been served once, is bound to notify the court of its new address. The party has such an obligation also when it has provided an electronic address for serving (Article 41(1) CCP). The person whose address is supplied as an address for servicing court papers, the legal representative and the guardian have the same obligation. This obligation is entered in the subpoena. In cases of non-performance of this obligation the subpoena is attached to the case and is regarded as being served, including when the party has provided an electronic address for serving, but has changed it, without notifying the court, or has provided an inaccurate or non-existent address.

70. However, it should be noted that when the case requires the service of notices, summons and papers in another EU Member State, Regulation (EC) No. 1393/2007 on the service in the Member States of judicial and extrajudicial documents in civil or commercial matters (service of documents), applies. In the Alder case, the CJEU ruled that Art. 1(1) Regulation (EC) No. 1393/2007 on the service of documents must be interpreted as excluding the law of a Member State which provides that judicial documents addressed to a party with residence or habitual residence in another Member State shall be placed in the file and deemed to have been served if that party has not appointed a representative authorized to accept the service and residing in the first Member State of the proceedings (CJEU 19 December 2012, ECLI: EU: C: 2012: 824, C 325/11). Therefore, in these cases Art. 40(1) CPC will not find application.

§2. Time Limits

159. The law provides for preclusive terms regarding the performance of certain procedural actions, these preclusive terms bringing about the preclusion of the legal possibility of performing the respective procedural action (Article 8(1) ICAA; Articles 119(1)–(3); 131(1), 193, 211, 212, 218, 219(3), 259 CCP, Article 286(1), item 1 CCP, in connection with Article 283 CCP). The preclusive terms *cannot be extended.* There is a possibility of *recovery of the term. The party which has failed to observe the term is entitled to request the recovery thereof if it proves that the failure is due to special unforeseen circumstances it could not overcome* (Article 64(2) and (3) CCP). The application for recovery of the term has to be filed within seven days following the notification of this failure (Article 64(3) CCP). *The application for recovery of the term must have attached thereto the papers showing what the recovery of term is sought for, and in those cases where the payment of costs is concerned, the court specifies a new term for the payment thereof* (Article 65(2) CCP).

160. The early preclusions concerning the allegation of facts and presenting of evidence established in the new CCP also have the nature of sanctions (Articles 133, 147, 260, items 5 and 6, 266(2) CCP, *see* paragraphs 151, 171) in connection with the requirement under Article 13 CCP to consider and determine the case within reasonable terms and the connected with it concentration principle (*see* paragraph 36).

161. According to Article 92a CCP the party causing reasonless adjournment of the case regardless of the outcome of the case, bears the costs of the new session under Article 91 CCP. The ruling is appealable according to the procedure under Article 92 CCP.

Part IV. Proceedings

Chapter 1. Preparatory Procedures (Pretrial Proceedings)

162. In Bulgarian civil adversary proceedings, there are no preparatory procedures (pretrial proceedings). In Bulgarian civil procedure there is no preliminary exchange of papers between the parties to the case, which must precede the filing of the claim with the court. The so-called exchange of papers between the parties introduced by the new CCP is not a preparatory procedure (*see* paragraphs 147, 205). This phrase is not legally established. It is used in the theory and court practice. There is not a direct exchange of papers between the parties. The claim is filed with the court. If the claim is conforming and admissible, the judge sends a copy of it and its attachments to the defendant with instructions of the opportunities and necessities to submit a reply to the claim as well instructions on the mandatory contents of the reply, on the consequences if it is not submitted (Article 131 CCP). The reply is submitted to the court with a duplicate to the claimant (Article 132 CCP, *see* paragraph 148), which the court sends to the claimant.

Chapter 2. First Instance Proceedings

§1. Adversary Proceedings

I. Ordinary Proceedings

A. *Introduction of the Claim*[71]

163. First-instance proceedings commence by the claim. According to Article 125 CCP the claim is brought in with registering the statement of claim with the court.[72] According to Bulgarian Civil Procedure bringing in the statement of claim orally is not admissible.

It is admissible to present it in electronic form (Articles 102a, 102b, 102e, 102f CCP, in force from 30 June 2021). In this case, it must be signed with a qualified electronic signature. Scanned and written evidence shall be attached to it. In this case, copies of the statement of claim and the annexes to it are not submitted (*see* paragraph 164).

According to Article 127(1) CCP the statement of claim should be written in Bulgarian and contain the following: the designation of the court it is brought with; the names (personal surname and family) and address of the claimant and defendant (when the defendant is a physical person), the name of company, respectively, its headquarters' address (when the defendant is a trader, a trading company or another type of legal entity) their legal representatives or attorneys, if applicable, electronic address for serving under the conditions of Article 38 and 38a CCP and an application whether he wishes to be served at the indicated e-mail address, as well as the telephone number of the claimant and his representatives or proxies, the personal number of the claimant (a physical person), identity code of the claimant (a legal entity); the amount of the claim if it is possible to determine; statement of the facts the claim is grounded on[73] what the claim consists of and the signature of the person bringing the claim. The right subject matter of the claim should be strictly individualized via the grounds and petitum of the statement of claim.

According to Article 127(2) CCP, the claimant specifies all the facts and submits all the written evidence the claim is grounded on in the statement of claim. The

---

71. Bringing the claim gives rise to procedural consequences and substantive law ones. The procedural consequences are the following: the case becomes a pending case. According to Art. 126(1) CCP, where, either in the same court or in different courts, there are two pending cases between the same parties on the same claim and on the same grounds, the proceedings instituted later are terminated ex officio by the court. Bringing the claim leads to scission of the limitation and acquittal (Art. 116, item b OCA, Art. 84 PA). During the pending trial, the limitation period and the limitation period cease to run (Art. 115 (1), item g OCA, Art. 84 PA).

72. Under the argument of Art. 62(2) CCP the deadline is not omitted when the statement of claim is sent by post. The date of its bringing according to Art. 125 CCP should be considered the date of the postmark and when it is submitted electronically – its entry into the EPEJ (Art. 62(4) CCP).

73. These are the juridical facts that give rise to the substantive law right claimed by the claimant, called 'grounds of the claim'. This term is also used both in doctrine and practice and by the legislator in certain texts (e.g., in Art. 214(1) CCP in connection with changing the claim by changing the grounds, in Art. 298(1) CCP in connection with the individualization of the right over which the objective limits of res judicata of the court's decision.

claimant is not obligated to give a legal qualification of the right constituting the subject matter of the claim. His/her legal qualification is not binding on the court.

According to Article 127(4) CCP, in the case of a claim for money receivable the claimant should provide a bank account or specify a mode of payment.[74]

164. According to Article 128 CCP the claimant has to submit the following together with the statement of claim: the letter of attorney if the statement of claim is brought in by an attorney; proof of paid State fees and costs where such are due. Copies of the statement of claim and the enclosures in accordance with the number of defendants.

When the statement of claim is submitted by a procedural representative in electronic form, an electronic image of the power of attorney is submitted (Article 102h(1) CCP conjunction with Article 360g CSA). Copies of it and the written evidence attached to it are not submitted. The court reproduces the statement of claim and the annexes to it in the required number of copies on paper and after certification by a court employee sends them to the participants in the proceedings who have not stated that they wish to receive electronic statements from the court (Article 102h(3)).

165. The regularity of the statement of claim and the admissibility of the claim are verified by the court in camera (Article 129(1) CCP). According to Article 130 CCP it should verify whether the claim is admissible with regard to the absolute procedural prerequisites. Where it is regular, the court rules that a case is instituted and sends a duplicate of the statement of claim with its enclosures to the defendant instructing him/her to submit a written reply within one month, as well as on the mandatory contents of the reply; on the consequences if the reply is not submitted, non-exercising his/her rights, respectively; on the possibilities to have legal aid if he/she needs such and has the right to it (Article 131(1) CCP; *see also* paragraph 147).

166. According to Article 129(2) CCP, if the statement of claim does not comply with the requirements under Article 127(1) and Article 128 CCP, a notice is sent to the claimant informing him/her that he/she has to eliminate the flaws within a seven-day term. Failing to meet the requirement of Article 127(2) CCP specifying claimant's obligation to bring evidence and the precise circumstances he will be alleging by it, to submit written evidence does not lead to non-conformity of the statement of claim. The verification of the procedural prerequisites for instituting the case does not foresee neither an obligation nor a right of the court to instruct the claimant that he/she must bring evidence in support of the facts he/she alleges and to submit all his/her written evidence. The court gives this instruction to the claimant only in its report on the case (*see* paragraph 32).

The ruling of the court under Article 129(2) CCP with which the court points what irregularities it finds in the statement of claim cannot be appealed by a private appeal. If the claimant eliminates the flaws within the seven-day term specified

74. The legislator does not treat the particular requirement as an irregularity of the claim (*see* para. 155).

above, the corrected statement of claim is regarded as regular from the day it was brought (Article 129(5) CCP). They are regarded as pending since the day the statement of claim was brought.

If the claimant fails to eliminate the flaws within the specified term, the statement of claim and the attachments are reverted, and if the address is unknown, the statement of claim and the attachments are left with the office of the court at the disposal of the claimant (Article 129(3), sentence I CCP). A private appeal can be filed against this reversion of the statement of claim, without submitting a copy (Article 129(3), sentence II CCP). According to Article 129(5) CCP, if the flaws in the statement of claim happen to be noticed in the course of proceedings, the same actions are taken. If the claimant fails to eliminate the flaws, the court suspends the proceedings already instituted. This ruling, grounded on Article 129(3), sentence II and Article 274(1), item 1 CCP, can be appeal by a private appeal.

According to Article 130 CCP when the court verifying the statement of claim finds the claim inadmissible, it returns the statement of claim. The return of the statement of claim can be appealed by a private appeal without submitting a copy.

B. *Progress of Proceedings*

1. Preparatory Measures (Including Production of Documents, Exchange of Pleadings, Etc.)

167. If the claim is lawful and admissible from the point of view of absolute procedural prerequisites, the court institutes the case and sends to the defendant[75] a copy of the claim together with the enclosures, instructing him/her to file a written reply within one month, the mandatory content of the reply and the consequences of non-submission the answer or the non-exercise of rights, as well as the possibility to use legal aid, if necessary (Article 131(1) CCP). Although it is not explicitly provided for by law, the doctrine and practice requires a rational understanding that the court should send to the claimant a copy of the reply to the claim and its enclosures.[76]

The response to statement of the claim may also be filed electronically, under the same conditions as the statement of claim (cf. Article 102a-102e CCP, as well as paragraphs 163–164).

168. The Bulgarian legislator has specified the preparation of the case regarding the actions of the court and specified an especial closed session. According to

75. There is no exchange of papers between the parties to the case in Bulgarian Civil Proceedings. The exchange is performed through the case.

76. The legislator has provided for the so-called double exchange of papers which also takes place through the court (Arts 372 and 373 CCP), only for commercial cases (*see* paras 147, 162, 369). The claimant should file the so-called additional statement of claim in which he/she should give an opinion on the disputed matters and objections in defendant's reply to the statement of claim. Having admitted the additional statement of claim the court sends its duplicate with the attachments to the defendant who can submit a reply within two weeks.

Article 140 CCP the preparation for the case takes place in camera without subpoenaing the parties. It aims at concentrating the collection of evidence and parties' pleadings in one session. During the preparation for the case in camera the court should verify the conformity and admissibility of the brought claims and other requests and objections of the parties; render a ruling on all preliminary matters and on the admissibility of the evidence.[77] According to Article 140(2) CCP the court may render a ruling on the counterclaims (if there are such in the reply) and on the admissibility of some evidence at the first court session at which the parties are subpoenaed (*see* paragraphs 174).

According to Article 140(3) CCP the court schedules a hearing of the case in an open session at which the parties are subpoenaed and handled a copy of the ruling under Article 140(1) CCP. It is foreseen that the court may notify the parties and send them its draft report on the case.[78] In practice, most of the judges draw up a draft report at this session, as provided in Article 146(2) and (3) CCP, send them to the parties so that they can prepare for the open court hearing and avoid the prolongation of the case for another hearing. Moreover, although a special session for the preparation of the case is regulated in Article 140 CCP, the legislator has related a part in the preparation of the case (Articles. 143(2) and (3), 145, 146 CCP) to the hearing of the case in an open court session with summoning the parties, called a session for the hearing of the case. This regulation often leads to the inability of the case to be heard in a single session and is a common cause for rescheduling of the hearing.

2. Purely Written Procedure (If Any)

169. In the general prosecution process, the Bulgarian legislator did not envisage a purely written procedure. Only in commercial disputes (*see* paragraph 369) it is provided that when the application, the reply to it, the supplementary application and the reply to it are presented to the parties, all the evidence is presented and if it is assumed that the hearing of the parties is not necessary, the court may consider the case in a closed session, giving the parties the opportunity to present written defence and replies (Article 376(1) CCP). According to Article 376(2) CCP in such cases, the court examines and adjudicates the case in a closed session, when the parties so request.

77. Concerning the admissibility of the claimant's claim on the absolute procedural prerequisites the court is obliged under Arts 129 and 130 CCP to perform that verification with instituting the proceedings (*see* paras 165–166). Therefore, we face a second verification. However, the relative procedural prerequisites are verified for the first time at this session as the court verifies them only if the defendant has made the respective recusal in his/her reply to the statement of claim (*see* para. 150). For the first time the court renders a ruling on the admissibility of the evidence presented by the defendant and those brought by the claimant in his/her statement of claim.

78. The court may also recommend the parties to go to mediation or to use another manner of amiably settling their dispute.

3. Determination of the Trial Date

170. The parties must receive the summons of the scheduled open court session for consideration of the case and the ones referred to in Article 140(3) CCP at the latest one week prior to hearing the case (Article 56(3) CCP). Under Article 142(1) CCP, the non-appearance of one of the parties, which is regularly summoned, is not an obstacle to the examination of the case, but the court proceeds to its examination after examining the cases which parties have appeared. Under Article 141(2) CCP the court decides to adjourn the case if the party and its proxy cannot appear because of an obstacle that the party cannot overcome.

In Article 135a (in force since 30.06.2021) CCP it was provided that each party may request to participate in a court hearing via videoconference, when it is not able to appear directly before the court. During the videoconference, the party is present in a specially equipped videoconference room in a regional court, a place of imprisonment or arrest. The court shall notify the parties of the conditions for carrying out a videoconference.

4. Trial (Including Representation of Parties, Examination by the Trial Judge, Adjournment, Etc.)

171. According to Article 143(1) CCP, the court, having settled the preliminary matters, proceeds with clarification of the factual aspect of the dispute in an open session for hearing the case. Under the current CCP the preparation for the case consisting of verification of the admissibility and conformity of the claims and the other requests and objections of the parties according to Article 140(1) CCP (*see* paragraph 165) should be performed in camera. This session is especially for preparation for the case. In the part of the open court session, the parties also express their opinions about the admissibility of the court session itself in view of whether they are duly subpoenaed or not, duly represented, respectively. Besides, as I pointed above (*see* paragraph 122), the obligation of the court to monitor the absolute procedural prerequisites does not eliminate the party's right to raise the question. Here the questions about those prerequisites can be raised as they are not covered by the preclusion under Article 133 CCP (*see* paragraph 150). The defendant could not refer to relative procedural prerequisites e.g., venue jurisdiction, arbitrary clause during the open session for which the preclusive term is the term for submitting a reply to the statement of claim, if he/she has not done so in his/her reply to the statement of claim.

The claimant at this stage of the court session should refer to defendant's objections to the admissibility of the claim, as well as to the relative and absolute procedural prerequisites.

The ruling for proceeding with the case ruling is not subject to appeal by a private appeal.

172. Once the ruling for proceeding with the case is rendered, the clarification of the factual issues of the dispute is achieved by the following procedural actions of the parties and the court in an open session:

(a) First, the parties are obliged to make and substantiate the claims brought in by the statement of claim and the counterclaims and challenges brought in by the reply, respectively. According to Article 143(2) CCP the claimant may explain and complement the statement of claim, as well as cite and present evidence in connection with the defendant's contestations, and the defendant may bring and present new evidence which he/she was unable to cite and present in the reply to the statement of claim. This completion is not an amendment of the claim in the sense of Article 214 CCP (*see* paragraph 266). It just concerns completing the statement of claim with juridical and evidentiary relevant facts within the frames of claimed grounds. According to Article 143(3) CCP in this session the claimant should under the threat of preclusion bring facts opposable to the facts alleged by the defendant, to the counter rights claimed with challenges in the reply to the statement of claim.

(b) The legislator has provided that at the first open session each party is obligated to make and justify all demands and oppositions and to pronounce on the circumstances alleged by the opposing party (Article 143(3) CCP).[79] This is one of the disputed texts in the current CCP. It reproduced Article 109(1) CCP, repealed. It corresponded with the preparation for the case that used to take place in an open session, unlike nowadays when the preparation for the case is with exchange of papers in camera. The legislator has tried to combine the virtues of the two ways of preparation for the case. The result is an intrinsic contradiction of the regulation. The claimant has brought in his/her demands in the statement of claim. The defendant has brought in his/her demands and allegations in the reply to the statement of claim. At this session for the first time the claimant has the legal possibility to make a stand on the defendant's demands and objections brought in his/her reply to the statement of claim. In connection with the explanations and complements of the statement of claim the claimant made on the grounds of Article 143(2) CCP, the defendant may make new contestations, new objections, respectively. They are not covered by the preclusion under Article 133 CCP.

Regarding the newly found and newly occurred facts Article 147 CCP applies (*see* section (c) bellow).

(c) According to Article 143(2) CCP the claimant may bring in and provide evidence related to the contestations brought by the defendant and the defendant – to identify and submit new evidence which he/she could not point at and submit in the reply to the claim. Under Article 144(1) CCP the defendant can ask for additional term to make a stand on the evidentiary demands made by the claimant during this hearing and to cite additional evidence in connection with the contestations made.

79. It is the reproduced Art. 109(1) CCP, repealed, which corresponded to the preparation of the case, performed at the first open court session, unlike nowadays, when the preparation is done through the exchange of papers and in a closed court session. The legislator attempted to bring together the positive aspects of two different ways of preparing the case, what lead to an internal contradiction in the regulation. The defendant has made his/her claims and allegations in the reply to the claim.

Regarding the preclusion of the possibility to bring evidentiary demands one should have in mind Articles. 146(1), item 5 CCP Article 146(2) and, Article 146(3) CCP (*see* paragraph 173).

According to Article 147 CCP prior to the conclusion of the trial, the parties may allege: new circumstances and cite, and present new evidence, solely if they were unable to learn, bring and present them in due time; intervening circumstances, which are relevant to the case, and cite and present evidence of the said circumstances.

(d) The court poses questions to each of the parties regarding the factual allegations of the other party (Article 145(1) CCP). It may pose questions to each of the parties regarding both the factual allegations of the other party and the party's own allegations when they are unclear, incomplete or circumlocutory.

The court instructs the parties to specify their allegations and to cure their inconstancies (Article 145(2) CCP), provided the allegations are incomplete or circumlocutory. It is the court's obligation stipulated in Article 7(1), sentence I CCP, to assist the parties in the clarification of the factual and legal aspects of the case.

173. According to Article 145(3) CCP the court invites the parties to reach an agreement and points at its consequences. If an agreement is not reached, the court makes a report registered in the minutes.[80] According to Article 146(1) CCP the report on the case must contain: the circumstances wherefrom the claimed rights and oppositions arise; the legal qualification of the rights claimed by the claimant, of the counter rights and the objections of the defendant; which rights and which circumstances are admitted; which circumstances do not need proving; and of course the facts irrelevant to the dispute; how the burden of proving the facts to be proved is apportioned. According to Article 146(2) CCP the court instructs the parties for which of the facts alleged they do not present evidence.

According to Article 146(3) CCP the court gives the parties an opportunity to make a stand[81] in connection with the instructions given and the report on the case, as well as to undertake the relevant procedural steps. If the parties, realizing the given opportunity, fail to place a request for evidence, they lose this opportunity to do that later, but in the cases under Article 147 CCP (*see* paragraph 176). Therefore, the preclusion regarding the evidence occurs when the parties do not bring, respectively – do not present evidence, after the term they were granted under Article 146(3) CCP.

174. According to Article 146(4) CCP the court renders its decision by a ruling for admitting the evidence and the way of collecting it, admitting evidence that is relevant, admissible and requisite.

80. When the draft of the report on the case is prepared in a closed court session for hearing the case and its copy has been sent to the parties, a note citing the fact is put in the minutes from the session.

81. In connection with the stands of the parties on the report and particularizations and supplements on their allegations and claims made in those sessions, the court may make additions and the report, amend it, respectively.

The claimant has brought in his/her statement of claim, presented, respectively, with it according to Article 127(2) CCP, as well as on the evidence the defendant has brought in his/her reply to the statement of claim, presented, respectively, with it according to Article 131(2) CCP. In this case, on the grounds of Article 253 CCP in connection with Article 146(4) CCP, the court can render a ruling for modification, completion of the ruling under Article 140(1) CCP, if it finds that it has made an error or omitted something. On the evidence, thus brought in, presented, respectively, by the parties the court will render a ruling according to Article 146(4) CCP when it has determined to render a ruling on the admissibility of some evidence in an open session in the ruling under Article 140(2) rendered in a closed session in preparation for the case. The court will render a ruling under Article 146(4) CCP in the cases when the parties following the court's instructions under Article 146(3) CCP have brought evidence in the first court session and have required its admissibility.

175. Under the current CCP all evidence can and should be collected in the first chronologically open session of the court, unless the claimant has fulfilled his/her obligations in connection with Article 127(2) CCP and the defendant has fulfilled his/her obligations under Article 131(3) CCP and the court has conducted flawlessly its closed session in preparation for the case foreseen in Article 140 CCP and admitted the evidence brought by the parties. In this court session the case can and should be considered in full, including the collection of evidence and the oral pleadings of the parties. It is hard to achieve concentration of the hearings on the case in a single court session. Due to the contradiction cited above, the number of the cases conducted in several court sessions is not small. The threat of preclusion, in connection with the so-called concentration principle, has improved a lot the proceedings discipline.

The possibility of gathering evidence by videoconference (cf. paragraphs 318, 326, 327) is regulated in Article 156a CCP. Witnesses, parties and experts whose statements will be heard via videoconference are summoned for the date and time of the hearing, with an indicated court in which they are to appear, or the place of imprisonment or arrest where they will the video conferencing will be used.

176. The oral pleadings start, if only all the evidence sought by the parties and admitted by the court is collected and the trial has been concluded. The legislator has clearly outlined in the new CCP the trial stage that comprises of submission, admission and collection of evidence (arg. Article 439(2) CCP and Article 147 CCP, the title of Article 149 'Conclusion of the Trial). Under Article 439(2) CCP the conclusion of the trial is the moment determined for the ascertaining and precluding force of res judicata.

When the evidence indicated by the parties have been collected and admitted by the court, and they do not point to other evidence in the connection with Article 147, items 1 and 2 CCP, the court terminates the trial with a ruling. After that moment, the parties cannot bring in new allegations, requests and present new evidence, inclusive, within the first-instance proceedings under the conditions of Article 147, items 1 and 2 CCP.

According to Article 149(1) CCP once the trial is over the court should invite again the parties to reach an agreement. If such an agreement is not reached, the court on the grounds of Article 149(1), sentence II CCP should proceed with the oral pleadings. The possibility of replacing the oral pleadings with pleadings between the parties in a written form is specified in Article 149(3) CCP. It stipulates that when the case is factually and legally complex, the court, upon the request of any party, may set a suitable term for presentation of a written defence. The written defence is presented with duplicate copies according to the number of parties.

5. Opinion by the 'Ministère Public' (If Any)

177. According to Article 26(3) CCP the prosecutor may participate in the proceedings with the rights of a party to the case in the cases provided for by the law (*see* paragraph 292).

C. *Judgment*

1. Deliberation.Formal Aspects of the Judgment

178. According to Article 149(2) CCP, where the court finds that the case is absolutely clear, it closes the oral pleadings and announces the day when it will render its decision (*see* paragraph 182). According to Article 235(1) CCP, the court decision is rendered by the panel *that participated in the session where the consideration of the case was terminated.*

179. Upon rendering its decision, the court considers all the evidence collected in the case as well as the arguments of the parties following their own convictions (Article 12 CCP). Non-observance of this rule is a serious violation of procedure. According to Article 235(3) CCP, the court also considers the facts that occurred after the claim was brought, as long as they have bearing on the disputed right. The court should and can do this only if the parties stated these facts and submitted evidence in its support prior to the closure of the trail (*see also* Article 147, item 1 CCP). The court bases its decision upon the law and the established facts of the case (Article 235(2) CCP). According to Article 15(3) ANA, if the subordinate legislation act contravenes the law the court has to apply the law. In connection with Bulgaria's EU membership, Article 15(2) ANA specifies that an EC Regulation is applied where the regulation is in contradiction with the latter. The SCC decision on the compliance with the Constitution of a law which applies in the case is obligatory for the court (Article 14(6) CCA; Article 229(1), item 1 CCP).

180. The court decision is rendered in a written form (Article 235(4) CCP), a prerequisite for its validity. Its contents should be according to Article 236(1) CCP. The decision should be signed by the judge who rendered it (arg. under Article 236(3)).

181. According to Article 236(2) CCP, the court has to enclose to the decision the motives the decision was rendered on. In Bulgarian procedure doctrine the motives are not a part of the decision, although they are materialized in the same document. It is underlined that the wording mentioned is express, because the decision *is a judicial act*, and, in its capacity of an expression of will, the judicial act is something totally different from the considerations (the motives) on which grounds the expression of will was made. It is assumed that such a decision is not invalid. It can be attacked, in accordance with the cassation procedure, as wrongful because of considerable violations of the court procedure rules. The concept that the motives have no res judicata effect (item 18 of ID No. 1-2000-GMCC of the SCC) resulted into the provisions of both Article 212 CCP concerning the incidental ascertainment claim and Article 298(4) CCP concerning the objections regarding set-off and retention.

2. Notice and Service

182. According to Article 235(5), sentence I, CCP the court announces its decision with the motives within a one-month term following the session in which the consideration of the case was terminated. According to Article 149(2) CCP when the case is clarified the court announces the closure of the oral pleadings and is obliged to specify the day when its decision will be announced. The reasonability of the day according to Article 149(2) CCP in connection with Article 13 CCP, the court should set with regard to the factual and juridical complexity of the certain case as well as with the number of cases it has to deal with. But by all means it should be within the one-month term established by Article 235(5) CCP.

The decision is published in the register of court decisions, which is open to public and freely accessible to everyone (Article 235(5), sentence II CCP). They are published immediately after their issuance on the website of the respective court (Article 64 CSA). The court issues the decision in electronic form (Article 102a CCP; Article 360a CSA) and immediately announces it in the unified register of court decisions (360n, Article 360o), kept in the EPEJ system, which is also public. These announcements are made in compliance with the requirements for personal data protection and the Classified Information Protection Act.

After announcing its decision on the case, the court is not entitled to reverse or change it (Article 246 CCP). The CCP provides only for two exceptions. According to Article 248(1) CCP within the term for appealing, if the decision is non-appealable within a one-month term upon its rendering, the court upon the request of a party is entitled to make changes in the part of the rendered decision concerning the legal expenses. This ruling can be appealed as established to appeal a court decision. According to Article 249 CCP, the court is entitled to invalidate a decision it rendered, if prior to the time the decision takes effect, the parties state that they reached an agreement and request that the proceedings are terminated.

The court serves the parties with a copy of the decision (Article 7(1) CCP).[82] Since that moment starts the term for its appealing (Article 259(2) CCP).

3. Different Kinds of Judgments

183. There are neither any partial or temporary decisions in Bulgarian civil proceedings nor are there procedural decisions. The court renders rulings on procedural matters (*see* Article 252 CCP).

Of important practical significance is whether the court decision has only an ascertainment effect (only res judicata) or, in addition, it also has an enforcement effect or a constitutive effect – ascertainment, sentencing and constitutive ones. Ascertainment decisions are those that uphold or disallow an ascertainment claim, as well as the decisions disallowing sentencing claims and constitutive claims. Sentencing decisions uphold a sentencing claim. Constitutive decisions uphold a constitutive claim.

184. As stated above, in principle, the decision is made after a court hearing and oral hearing. These are the classic, typical court decisions. New to Bulgarian law are the decision in recognition of the claim (Article 237 CCP) and the decision by default (Article 238 CCP) in which there is no court trial and oral competition between the parties. The non-appearance of the party, who is regularly summoned, is not enough for the issuance of a decision by default. The preconditions for issuance and protection against the decision by default are regulated in Articles 238–240 CCP.

When the defendant recognizes the claim the claimant is entitled to request rendering of a decision at recognition of the claim. The court should *terminate the trial* and render a decision by which to solve the legal dispute with regard to the recognition (Article 237(1) CCP).[83] It is enough to point out in the motives that the decision is grounded on the recognition of the claim (Article 237(2) CCP).[84]

---

82. This happens at the address indicated by the party to the case. According to Art. 38a (in force from 30 Jun. 2021) CCP, the serving may be performed to an electronic address for serving provided by the party through: 1. the EPEJ; qualified electronic registered delivery service according to Art. 3(37) of Regulation No. 910/2014; to the e-mail address specified by the party, when the party has given its consent.
83. The court cannot render a decision at recognition of the claim when: (a) the recognized right is not in discrepancy with the law and the morality; (b) is a recognized right that the party cannot dispose of (Art. 237(3) CCP). A decision at recognition of the claim cannot be rendered on matrimonial cases (Art. 324 CCP); claims on civil status (Art. 334 CCP) and claims on interdiction (Art. 339 CCP).
84. The decision at recognition of the claim is subject to appeal. The specifics of this decision also reveal the particularities in the defects. When the recognition of the claim has been made by a procedural representative without power of attorney, the decision is inadmissible and should be invalidated Art. 34(2) CCP). It should be also invalidated in the cases of Art. 237(3) CCP, wherein the legislator does not allow ruling of a decision at recognition of the claim. When there are new facts and written evidence, he/she can request reversal of the decision on the grounds of Art. 303(1), item 5 CCP.

4. Interpretation, Rectification and Completing of Judgments

185. The court, either on its own initiative, or upon the request of a party, is entitled to correct the obvious factual mistakes (Article 247 CCP). The court informs the parties of the requested correction and instructs about a reply in a one-week term and summons them in an open session, when it is necessary. The decision on the correction is served with the parties and is appealable according to the procedure of appealing the decision. No changes are admissible to the decision as an expression of will under the pretext of correcting an obvious factual mistake. The corrected decision is valid from the day the decision containing the obvious factual mistake is rendered, and not from the day the decision of correcting the mistake is rendered.

186. According to Article 250(1) CCP the party is entitled to demand that the decision is supplemented if the court has not rendered a decision on the whole claim of the party. The request is filed within a one-month term following the day when the party was serviced the court decision or since the day it takes into effect. According to Article 250(2) CCP informs the opposite party of the requested supplement with an instruction to submit a reply within one week. The matter of supplementing the decision is considered in camera, and only when the court finds it is necessary, in an open session with subpoenaing the parties (Article 250(2) CCP). The court renders its supplementary decision, subject to appeal in accordance with the general procedure (Article 250(3) CCP).

The application to render a supplementary decision can be filed both by the claimant and the defendant. [85] In this case, it is not a new statement of claim, but a demand for determining the dispute over the claim, since the court failed to determine it. Until the term of Article 250(1), sentence II CCP expires, the case is pending. If the party fails to exercise its right within the term of Article 250(1), sentence II CCP, its right to demand the rendering of a supplementary decision is precluded. Due to the absence of a decision regarding the request upon which the court did not render its decision, no force of res judicata is formed. Consequently, upon the expiration of the term a new claim can be filed.

187. According to Article 251(1) CCP, the disputes over a decision that has taken effect are considered by the court that rendered it. The interpretation of the court decision in accordance with the procedure of Article 251 CCP is needed if the will of the State authority expressed is unclear. These cases are extremely rare in Bulgarian court practice. The will of the court is interpreted on the basis of the expressed motives of judicial act. No interpretation can be requested after the decision is enforced (Article 251(2) CCP). The parties to the case are legitimized to request it.

---

85. If the court has not pronounced on the defendants objection of the claim, the latter cannot file an application for a supplement decision, because that will lead to a breach of ban under Art. 246(2) CCP for pre-settling the dispute. Therefore, the defendant should file a complaint against the decision.

The court informs the parties about the requested interpretation of the decision with an instruction to submit a reply within one week (Article 251(2) CCP). Under Article 251(4) CCP the interpretation of the decision is as a rule considered in camera without subpoenaing the parties. It is considered in an open session with subpoenaing the parties only if the court finds it necessary.

The prohibition of Article 246 CCP cannot be violated or avoided by an interpretation that changes the actual will of the court, when given under the pretext that the decision is expressed in an unclear way. In these proceedings, the court is not entitled to examine the correctness of the decision. The interpretative decision is subject to appeal in accordance with the procedure for appeal against an interpretative decision (Article 251(3) CCP).

5. Res Judicata

188. Res judicata[86] is qualified as a public law consequence of a decision that has taken effect.[87] In the established view the content of res judicata comprises right-establishing effect, regulating effect and non-redetermination of the dispute. The *right-establishing effect* is expressed in establishing existence or non-existence of the disputed substantive law right of the case and the decision. According to Article 299(1) CCP, a dispute which is determined by a decision which has entered into force cannot be redetermined except in the event that the law provides otherwise.[88] A case brought in again is terminated ex officio by the court (Article 229(2) CCP). There is an established opinion that res judicata has no redetermination effect.

189. According to Article 298(1) CCP the provision outlines the subject matter and the objective limits of the force of res judicata – the disputed right, or the legal relationship, respectively, on which the court has rendered its decision (and has established the existence or non-existence of the relationship), using the same features which it has used when outlining the disputed right (Article 126 CCP and Article 127 CCP) with all its individual elements in their entirety – facts giving rise to a legal right, content, subjects of law, legal nature. It is assumed that the force of res judicata is formed only with regard to the right, or the legal relationship, respectively, which constitutes the subject matter of the claim, and not regarding the defence of the defendant, but in the cases under 298(4) CCP, or the prejudicial legal relationships, or the legally relevant facts in themselves. A view has been established that the motives do not have the force of res judicata (item 18 of ID No. 1-2000-GMCC of the SCC).

---

86. In Bulgarian procedural doctrine and practice, the term 'force of res judicata' is established.
87. According to Art. 296 CCP the court decisions that come into force are the following: (a) those which are not subject to appeal; (b) those against which no intermediate appeal or cassation appeal is brought within the term specified in law, or the appeal is withdrawn (item 2); (c) those against which the filed cassation is not upheld.
88. This is the reversal of decisions that came into force under Chapter 24 CCP (*see* paras 252–256), in the case of decision by default the claim under Art. 240(2) CCP and in the case of decision by default the reversal under Art. 240(1) and the claim under Art. 240(2) CCP (*see* paras 203–204).

Where a partial claim has been upheld, the decision establishes the existence of the right which constitutes the subject matter of the dispute at the respective amount that has been upheld. The non-claimed part of the receivable is neither included in the subject matter of the claim, nor is it included in the subject matter of the decision, and therefore, no force of res judicata can be formed for the unclaimed amount. Besides, from the viewpoint of substantive law, it is possible for the receivable to exist in its part which has been upheld, the other part thereof being non-existent. The ground introduced by the partial claim (the facts giving rise to the claim) is the same both for the part of the claim filed with it and for the unclaimed part. Therefore, the decision under a valid partial claim for a monetary receivable has the force of res judicata regarding the legal facts of the disputed subjective substantive right in another claim for protection of a receivable for the difference up to the full amount of the pecuniary claim arising from the same right (ID No. 3-2019 on ID No. 3-2016-GMCC and the Com.C. of the SCC). Where the partial claim has been disallowed, the force of res judicata establishes the non-existence of the whole receivable, including the part thereof which has not been claimed, although the latter has not been included in the subject matter of the claim or the case, because from the viewpoint of substantive law if the receivable exists as a whole, it is impossible that a part thereof does not exist.

The force of res judicata establishes the existence or non-existence of the right, or the legal relationship, respectively, constituting the subject matter of the dispute, as at the time of the closure of court trial. The force of res judicata is formed afterwards, as until that time the parties have the legal opportunity to allege facts and submit evidence, and the court is obligated to take into account the facts that have occurred and the evidence that has been submitted until that time (arg. under Article 235(3) CCP, Article 439(2) CCP) (*see also* paragraph 179).

Where the decision is at acknowledging the claim (Article 237 CCP) the ascertainment is at moment of the recognition of the claim. The facts that have occurred after the said moment cannot be affected by the precluding effect of the force of res judicata. The ascertainment effect of the force of res judicata occurs by the moment of the expiry of the term for submitting the reply, because by that moment the defendant could allege facts and submit evidence being threatened by the preclusion under Article 133 CCP. The ascertainment claim under 240(2) CCP based on newly discovered facts is a specific feature of res judicata effect of the decision by default (*see* paragraph 184).

According to Article 298(4) CCP the decision also comes into force regarding the claims and defence of improvements and set-offs upheld thereunder. The first case concerns the receivable related to the improvements which has been claimed together with the right to retention (Article 73 PA). It also covers the hypotheses of Article 91 OCA according to which a person who has an executable claim in connection with the preservation, maintenance, repair or improvement of the movable chattel of another, or for damages caused by such a chattel, the cases of defence under Article 90 OCA for an unfulfilled contract by which the defendant refuses to fulfil his/her obligation originating from a bilateral contract until his/her counter receivable originating from the same contract is executed, in other words on his/her right to concurrent enforcement. The force of res judicata is formed on the counter receivable of the defendant in respect of the points that are relevant to set-off, together with the features relevant to the set-off in itself (chargeability, compensability), and also in respect of the compensation right regarding the points relevant to set-off.[89]

190. The parties to the case are bound by the force of res judicata (Article 298(1) CCP), their heirs,[90] universal and private successors (Article 298(2) CCP), where the succession occurred after the completion of the proceedings (transferee of the disputed right upon its transferred right during the trial (Article 226(3) CCP).

The decision rendered on a civil status claim including a matrimonial claim has effect with regard to all persons (Article 298(3) CCP).

The creditor is not bound by the decision establishing the existence of the debtor's liability to another creditor (arg. Article 298(2) CCP, Article 464 CCP, Article 694 C. Code). Where the subject matter of the decision and res judicata concern the debtor's proprietary right the possibility for the creditor to obtain satisfaction from a certain proprietary right of the debtor depends on whether the right is owned by the debtor (Article 133 OCA and Article 442 CCP). Where this decision ascertains that the debtor owns the right, this decision can be pleaded against the creditor. In analogy with Article 135 OCA, the creditor can defend himself/herself by seeking that the decision is proclaimed invalid with regard to him/her (compare Article 299(3) CCP).

The liability of the surety ensues from the existence of the principal debtor (Article 138(2) OCA, Article 139, sentence II OCA). Consequently, if a decision with a force of res judicata rendered on a case to which the surety is not a party, renounces the existence of the principal debt, the surety can set this force of res judicata against the creditor that brought a claim against him/her. The surety cannot have a decision set against him/her if the decision establishes the existence of the principal debt with res judicata. According to Article 142 OCA, the surety is entitled to set against the creditor all defences of the debtor and to withhold a receivable due to the debtor by the creditor. The surety does not lose these rights even if the debtor waived them or admitted his/her debt.

191. The provision of Article 297 CCP is that the decision that came into force is obligatory for the court which issued it, and for all other courts, institutions and municipalities in the Republic to proceed from the substantive law relationship established by a force of res judicata, in its official actions regarding the persons bound by res judicata. Its recognition always presupposes the identity of the addressees of res judicata of the decision that came into force and the parties to the second case. It should refer to a legal relationship conditioning the issue of the State act, i.e., res judicata should concern a legal relationship prejudicial with regard to the legal relationship forming the subject matter of the second case (*compare* Article 298(1) and Article 299(1) and (2) CCP).

---

89. The decision that came into force cannot be contested by the party for being a decision rendered in false proceedings (Art. 299 (3) CCP).
90. If the inheritance is disclosed in the course of proceedings Arts 229(1) and 230 CCP are applicable.

6. Enforceability

192. Enforceability is the possibility to realize the court decision according to the enforcement procedure. As a rule, only the sentencing decisions have enforceability. Under argument 404(1) CCP constitutive decisions which constitute action or effect is enforceable right to claim also have enforceability (e.g., a decision of assigning an indivisible housing accommodation under Article 349(2) CCP, and a decision on portioning the actual use of a jointly owned real estate (Article 32(2) PA), a decision on using the family home after the divorce).

193. The addressees of the enforceability of the court decision are the bearer of the approved executable right to claim and the corresponding bearer of the legal liability. They are specified in the sentencing decision upholding the sentencing claim. These addressees are the claimant and the defendant. The court is not entitled to sentence an accessory party, a co-party, or a controlling party of the defendant.

Under the argumentation based on Article 429(1) in relation to Article 298(1) CCP, the heirs and the private successors of the surety are entitled to receive a writ of execution on the grounds of the sentencing decision and the document showing the occurrence of succession, if the inheritance and the private succession were disclosed before the issue of the writ of execution but after the rendering of the decision. The same applies to the surety and the joint debtor who paid the debt and subrogated himself/herself in the rights of the satisfied creditor.

In case of conveyance of the disputed right in the course of proceedings according to Article 226(3) CCP the decision constitutes a res judicata in respect of the assignee with the exception of the entry in the registers where an immovable property is concerned (Article 114 PA), or the acquisition of ownership by bona fide possession (Article 78 PA) of movable property.

Under the argumentation ensuing from Article 429(2) CCP, in connection with Article 298(2) CCP, the enforcement of the sentencing decision against the legator is also effective with regard to his/her heir if the succession occurred after the enforceability. The heir should have accepted the inheritance. Time of occurrence of enforceability.

194. The decisions that came into force as well as the sentencing intermediate appellate decisions have the quality of grounds for enforcement.[91] According to Article 282(1) CCP, the cassation appeal against a sentencing decision does not suspend the execution.

The immediate enforceability of intermediate decision is a significant deviation from the rule of Article 296 CCP that deals with decision's enforcement. The preliminary enforcement of *the first-instance decisions* is admissible. According to Article 242(1) CCP the court *enacts preliminary enforcement* of the decision if alimony or job remuneration or compensation is adjudicated. In this case, the so-called ex officio principle in Bulgarian doctrine and practice is manifested, as the court is

91. Those sentencing decisions not subject to cassation appeal under the explicit provision of Art. 280(3) CCP are not subject to cassation appeal (*see* para. 409) and, according to the general rule, they are enforceable from the time the decision comes into force.

obligated to admit preliminary enforcement in the hypothesis under Article 242(1) CCP even though the claimant did not make such a request. According to Article 242(2) CCP, *upon the claimant's request, the court can also admit* preliminary enforcement of the decision in the following cases: (a) if the court adjudges a receivable on the grounds of an official document, (b) if the court adjudges a receivable acknowledged by the defendant, and if the delay in enforcement might bring about considerable and (c) irreparable damages to the claimant, or the enforcement itself might be impossible or difficult to carry out. In the cases under Article 242(2) CCP, the court might oblige the claimant to submit due security in advance (Article 242(3) CCP). According to Article 243(1) CCP, no preliminary enforcement is allowed even if security is presented, if the enforcement might result in an irreparable damage to the defendant or a damage not subject to precise financial evaluation. This does not apply to decisions adjudging alimony or job remuneration.

The admission of preliminary enforcement of the first-instance decisions is done by an explicit act of the court, a ruling (arg. under Article 244 CCP) which can be appealed by a private appeal.

According to Article 245(1) CCP, with the exception of the cases under Article 242(1) CCP, the debtor against whom preliminary enforcement are admitted is entitled to suspension of enforcement if he/she submits to the claimant a security under Articles. 180 and 181 OCA. According to Article 245(2), the enforcement is also suspended if the appealed decision is reversed. According to Article 245(3) CCP, if the claim is disallowed by a decision that came into force, the enforcement is suspended.

The postponement of enforcement is regulated under Article 241 CCP (*see* paragraph 153).

7. Constitutive Effect

195. Constitutive effect is a civil law consequence of the constitutive decisions by which constitutive claims are upheld (*see also* paragraphs 137–139). It enforces the potestative rights, which the law provides to be exercised by the courts. (a) *The content of the constitutive effect is determined by the content of the potestative right*, which forms the subject matter of the upheld constitutive claim. The constitutive effect can be expressed in: (a) claims under Article 19(3) OCA for the conclusion of a final contract, claims under Article 33 PA for the buyout of a share of a jointly owned real estate, claims under Article 349(1) and (2) CCP for the assignment of a non-divisible housing estate in partition proceedings); (b) *cancellation or suspension of civil law relationships* (e.g., the decisions by which the following claims are upheld: those under Article 32 OCA for the invalidation of a wrongful transaction, claims under Article 87(3) OCA for the denunciation of a contract for the transfer of a proprietary right over a real estate as well as those for establishing and transfer of limited proprietary rights over such an estate, claims under Article 227 OCA for cancellation of a donation, claims under Article 318 CCP for a divorce and for the invalidation of a marriage, claims under Article 95(1) C. Code for the dissolution of an unlimited partnership, claims under Article 95(2) C. Code for the expulsion of a partner of an unlimited partnership, claims under Article 155 C. Code for the dissolution of a limited liability company, claims under Article 252(1), item 4 C. Code for the dissolution of a joint-stock company); (c) *alteration of an existing civil law relationship* (e.g., a decision that upholds the claim under Article 195 OCA for price reduction), *restoration of an existing legal relationship* (the claim under Article 344(1), item 2 LC for reinstatement in employment, joint with the worker's claim challenging the lawfulness of the dismissal).

196. The constitutive effect occurs at the time the constitutive decision comes in force, i.e., concurrent with the occurrence of res judicata (about entry into force of the decision *see* paragraph 188). However, the effect may be (a) *a future effect* (e.g., decisions upholding the claims: under Article 19(3) OCA for the conclusion of a final contract, divorce claims under Article 218 CCP, under Article 349(1) and (2) CCP for the assignment of a non-divisible housing estate in partition proceedings, and Articles 95, 155, 252(1), item 4 C. Code for the dissolution of the commercial company); (b) *a retroactive effect* (for instance, the decisions by which the following claims are upheld: those under Article 32 OCA for the invalidation of a transaction, or claims under Article 87(3) OCA for the denunciation of a contract for the transfer of ownership or establishing or transfer of limited proprietary rights over a real estate). Whether the civil law consequences the potestative right consists of will occur in the future or retroactively depends on what type of effect the legislator acknowledged for this right in question. The provisions concerning the latter are to be exercised by the court and its content to be realized by the constitutive effect of the court decision.

197. Res judicata upon the potestative right sustains and substantiates its constitutive effect, and consequently, it is always a precondition of an effective decision establishing the existence of a potestative right.

198. The addressees of the constitutive effect are not only those persons that were parties to the case, persons to whom the potestative right is valid, or persons whose civil law relationships are changed. The co-party, the controlling party and the procedural substitute are not addressees. The constitutive decision gives rise to a legal change in those legal relationships which have as a subject the bearer of the subjective potestative right and the person which is obligated to bear the legal change.

8. Penalty in Case of Non-compliance

199. The Criminal Code provides for criminal liability for: a) an official who fails to enforce an enforceable decision for the recovery of a wrongly dismissed employee (Article 172(2) CCP); a parent or other relative who fails to fulfil or in any way frustrates the execution of a judgment concerning the exercise of custody or personal contact with a child (Article 182(2) CCP); a person who is convicted of having his or her spouse, ascendant, descendant, brother or sister knowingly fails to meet his/her obligation in the amount of two or more monthly contributions (Article 183(1); a person who has intentionally been unable to provide maintenance either by transferring his property, either by not exercising his rights or otherwise (Article 183(2) CCP); a person who, in order to prevent or hinder the execution of a judicial decision, destroys, damages, hides or alienates a property to which this decision relates (Article 296(2) CCP).

II. Provisional Proceedings

200. In Part IV CCP, the securing proceedings are regulated as separate proceedings, functionally related to the claim and the enforcement (*see* paragraph 8). They are applicable during the first-instance proceedings for the examination of the application, the appeal proceedings for the examination of the appeal against the first-instance judgment until the completion of the judicial complaint (Article 389(1) CCP), as well as for securing a future claim (Article 390(1) CCP). In all three cases, the procedure for examining the application for admitting the security of the claim and issuing the precautionary order as well as for appealing the court order for admitting the security of the claim is the same.

According to Article 207 CCP, when there is a risk that some evidence may be lost or its collection may be difficult, the party may request that it be collected in advance. The legislator has called this procedure 'securing the evidence' (*see* paragraphs 332–333). It is not security proceedings.

§2. Default Proceedings

201. According to Article 238(1) CCP, if the defendant has failed to present a reply to the statement of claim in due time and fails to appear during the first hearing of the case without having made a request for examination of the case in his/her absence, the claimant may request rendering a decision by default against the defendant or may withdraw the claim. The court should instruct him/her on the consequences of his/her failing to present a reply to the statement of claim and to appear in a court session (Article 239(1), item 1 CCP). The explicit claimant's request made in the first court session is required to have a decision by default rendered.[92]

The legislator requires for rendering a decision by default under Article 239(1), item 1 CCP besides the prerequisites mentioned above, to have a claim eventually grounded[93] viewing the facts brought in *the statement of claim and the presented evidence*. There comes the problem because according to Article 239(2) CCP the decision by default is not motivated[94] on the merits. It is enough to point out that decision is grounded on the prerequisites for rendering a decision by default. According to Article 238(3) CCP when the court considers that the prerequisites for rendering a decision by default are not present, it rejects the request by a ruling and

92. If there is not such a request the court should continue the proceedings in the classical manner carrying out a court trial for collecting the evidence brought, presented, respectively, by the claimant followed by rendering of an ordinary classical decision.

93. The situation is analogous to the one in the case of securing the claim (*see* para. 401).

94. There is an internal contradiction in the cumulative availability of a requirement to verify the probity of the claim and the fact that the decision by default is not motivated.

proceeds with the examination of the case. Therefore, in the SCC practice (Decision No. N 306/2015, I CC of the SCC), it was accepted that the existence of the prerequisites for a decision by default, the probable merits of the claim must be judged by the court with a ruling at the hearing in which the request under Article 238 CCP was placed. If the request is made by the plaintiff and the court has found it to be well founded, it shall render a decision by default and uphold the claim. Where the evidence submitted does not create the probability of the merits of the claim, the court should reject the request by a ruling – Article 239 (3) CCP and proceed to examine the case following the general order by producing a report on the case in accordance with Article 146 CCP and indicate to the parties how the burden of proof is shared between them and in what circumstances evidence is not brought in. The court cannot in the decision by default, reassess the probable groundness of the claim and find that it is not grounded because it would be in breach of the rights of the defence of the party which has requested the decision by default by rendering a non-appealable court act which gives rise to res judicata effect in the absence of the prerequisites of Articles 238 and 239 CCP. The non-appealability of a decision by default at the request of the claimant is based on the rule that in the first court session and not in the decision itself, the court assesses the probable merits of the claim as a guarantee that it will be upheld without the need for the applicant to conduct full proof as provided for in Article 155 CCP. When a positive decision by default is rendered in the hypothesis under Article 238 (1) CCP, the claimant has no interest in appealing it, and in respect of the defendant against whom the decision by default was rendered, the law provides for non-appealability as a procedural sanction for his/her lack of interest in the case. The ruling by which the court rules on the request under Article 238 CCP is subject to withdrawing and if, after its observance, the court considers that the claim is likely not to be grounded, it is obliged to revoke the ruling and to continue according to the general order of the proceedings because the CCP does not provide a possibility for rendering a rejecting decision by default against the defendant upon the request of the claimant.

202. According to Article 238(2) CCP, if the claimant fails to appear during the first hearing of the case, has not presented a stand to the reply to the statement of claim and has made a request for examination of the case in his/her absence and, the defendant may request termination of the proceedings[95] and award of costs or rendering a decision by default against the claimant. The application of the consequences of Article 238(1) CCP requires the court should instruct the claimant on the consequences of his/her failing to present a reply to the statement of claim and to appear in a court session (Article 239(1), item 1 CCP). In the case of the mentioned omission the court can neither terminate the proceedings nor render a decision by default ex officio. The explicit defendant's request made in the first court session (Article 238(1) CCP).

Article 239(2) CCP specifies that the decision by default is not motivated, the existence of the prerequisite viewing the eventual unfoundedness of the claim

95. The legislator has assigned consequences to terminating the case under the said grounds as in the case of withdrawing the case (Art. 239(1), sentence II CCP).

should be stated in the grounds part of the decision. When the claimant has not presented evidence in support to his/her claim the situation is similar to the one of rendering a decision by default upon the request of the claimant in the hypothesis of Article 238(1) CCP when evaluating the probable unfoundedness of the claim the evidence presented by the claimant should not be ignored when judging the eventual unfoundedness of the claim as might lead the literate interpretation of Article 239(1), item 2 CCP on the criteria about establishing the eventual unfoundedness of the claim.[96]

203. According to Article 240(1) CCP within one month upon being served with the decision by default the party against which the decision by default has been rendered is entitled to request its reversal by the intermediate court on the grounds for reversal enlisted bellow that have deprived the party of participation: an inappropriate serving of the statement of claim or the subpoena for the court session; an impossibility to learn duly about the served duplicate of the statement of claim or the subpoena for the court session; an impossibility to appear in person or through counsel owing to special unforeseen circumstances which the party was unable to overcome. The court should render a decision only on the foundedness of the request, i.e., whether there is a ground for reversal of decision by default, foreseen in Article 240(1) CCP. If the court finds the request founded, it reverses the decision by default and should return the case to the first-instance court for a new hearing.

204. According to Article 240(2) CCP the party against which a decision by default has been rendered may claim the same right or may contest the same right, where newly discovered circumstances or new written evidence of material relevance to the case are discovered, which could not have been known to the said party upon adjudication of the said case or which the said party could not procure in due time. [97] The grounds for bringing a claim under Article 240(2) CCP are the same as the grounds under Article 303(1), item 1 CCP for reversal of decisions that have taken effect. There is a significant exception from the general rules for reversal of decisions that have taken effect which according to Bulgarian law is of the competence of the SCC (*see* paragraph 241) as well as a significant exception from the precluding effect of res judicata effect (*see* paragraph 189).[98]

An ascertainment claim based on new occurred facts is admissible on the basis of the general rule of Article 124(1) CCP (*see* paragraphs 128, 398).

---

96. For that reason, although Art. 239(2) CCP specifies that decision by default is not motivated, the existence of the said prerequisite viewing the eventual foundedness of the claim should be stated in the grounds part of the decision. The case is analogous with the security of the claim. The inner contradiction between the cumulative existence of a requirement for verification of the foundedness of the claim and the fact that the decision by default is not motivated.
97. Such a claim may be brought within three months from the date on which the new circumstance became known to the party or from the day on which it was able to obtain the new written proof but no later than one year of repayment of the receivable.
98. Art. 240(2) CCP is analogous to Art. 424(1) CCP, therefore item 4 of ID No.4/2013-GMCC and the Com.C. of the SCC is applicable (*see* para. 421).

205. According to Article 238(2) CCP if the claimant has not indicated and has not submitted evidence in his application and the defendant has not replied in time, both parties do not appear at the first hearing of the case without having requested the case to be heard in their absence, the case is terminated. By argument of Article 239(1), item 1 CCP, the court must terminate the case on this basis only if it has instructed to the parties on the consequences of non-observance of the terms of the exchange of papers and their failure to appear at a court hearing. By argument of Article 238(2), sentence II CCP in line with Article 323 CCP the consequences of such termination must be treated as a consequence of the withdrawal of the claim.

§3. Ex Parte Proceedings

206. There is no exequatur procedure in Bulgarian procedural law, which is conducted without the participation of the parties. It is also guaranteed in commercial cases in the hypothesis of Article 376 CCP (*see* paragraph 35). Where the exchange of papers (the application of the claim, the reply to the application, a further application and a reply to it, a copy of which the court handed over to the opposing party), all the evidence is presented and, if it is assumed that the parties are not required to be heard the court can hear the case in camera, giving the parties the opportunity to submit written defence and written replies.

However, there are ex parte proceedings which are functionally related to the claim and enforcement process. Transcript of the claim for securing the claim (Article 395(1) and (2) CCP); *see* paragraph 403); for issuance of a writ of execution (Articles. 410(2), 411(2), *see* paragraph 381); to issue a writ of execution (Article 405(1) and (2) CCP, *see* paragraph 410) is not served on the defendant, respectively the debtor, and the first-instance court examines it in a court hearing without the parties' summoning. The defendant can defend himself/herself by appealing against the order of admission of the security, the debtor may be protected by an appeal against the order to issue a writ of execution. The debtor in the order payment proceedings may challenge the order for execution with the objection under Article 414 CCP without the need to justify it.

Chapter 3. Review Proceedings

§1. Appeal

207. In Bulgarian procedure law, the appeal against decisions of first-instance courts before the second-instance courts is called 'appeal before the intermediate appellate court'. It is a regular remedy against invalid decisions of the first-instance court (*see* Article 270(1) CCP) or inadmissible (Article 270(3) CCP) or wrongful (Article 272 CCP). *All* the first-instance decisions of regional and district courts are subject to appeal. The only exception is the decision by default (Article 239(4) CCP). There are no limitations in view of the type of claim or the amount. The decisions of the regional courts are appealed before the district courts, while the decisions of the district courts as first-instance courts are appealed before the respective appellate courts (Article 258(1) CCP).

208. The intermediate appellate court is qualified in the literature as 'the second-in-order first instance' because where the decision is improper, this instance always decides on the merits of the case and does not refer it back for reconsideration. It is assumed that the activity of the intermediate appellate court is identical to that of the first-instance court and is aimed at rendering a decision on the merits of the substantive law dispute. *In the appeal before the intermediate appellate court the examination of the first-instance decision is a side effect and not a direct result of the activity of this court, which decides on the merits of the case.*[99]

In my opinion, the subject matter of intermediate appellate proceedings consists of the disputed substantive law relationship, forming the subject matter of the case and the examination of the first-instance decision. [100] These two components of the subject matter of intermediate appellate proceedings are closely connected to each other and the objective is the achievement of a flawless decision, a valid, admissible and proper decision. That is also shown by Article 271(1), sentence I CCP, wherein the legislator has revealed the logics of intermediate appellate proceedings, namely the intermediate appellate court arrives at its own decision on the merits of the case, deciding whether to confirm the first-instance decision or to reverse in whole or in part the decision appealed. Article 271(1), sentence I CCP outlines the procedure according to which court can the reach a reversal of the decision. The intermediate appellate court deals not only with the merits of the case. First, it examines whether the decision is valid, and if it is invalid the court announces its invalidity (Article 270(1) CCP), regardless to whether the defect is specified in the appeal or not. If the decision is valid, the court examines its admissibility and invalidates it, if it is inadmissible (Article 270(3) CCP) (*see* paragraph 221). Where the intermediate appellate court establishes that the first-instance decision is both valid and admissible, it proceeds to determining the dispute on the merits and to the examination of the propriety of the decision appealed (Article 271(1), sentence I CCP).

---

99. *See* A. Mingova in J. Stalev, A. Mingova, V. Popova, O. Stamboliev, R. Ivanova, *Balgarsko …*, *supra*, pp. 518–519; ID No. 1/2000-GMCC of the SCC; ID No. 1/2013-GMCC of the SCC.
100. V.Popova, *Civil Procedure. Bulgaria.* first ed., para. 233, second ed. para. 206.

209. According to Article 259(1) CCP, the appeal is filed with the court that rendered the decision, within two weeks of the date of serving party with the decision. This term is preclusive. If the decision is not appealed within the said term, it takes effect (Article 296, item 2 CCP) and it is not subject not only to intermediate but to cassation appeal as well.

Each party to the case has the right to appeal, regardless of whether the party was a main party, a co-party, typical or procedure substituent. The hypothesis of indispensable parties (Article 216(2) CCP) sometimes state the decision involves persons that did not participate in the first-instance proceedings. According to Article 304 CCP, the reversal of a decision that has taken effect can be sought by an indispensable party although it did not take part in the case. If in the first instance the indispensable joinder, whose participation in the proceedings is obligatory, was not constituted, the intermediate appellate court should invalidate the first-instance decision and return the case for reconsideration with the participation of the indispensable joinder (ID No. 1-2013-GMCC and the Com.C. of the SCC).

In the literature and in court practice, the person that brings the appeal is called an 'appellant'. The defendant under the appeal is called an 'appellee'. The appellant and the appellee are the parties to the intermediate appellate proceedings.

210. According to Article 258(2) CCP, the appeal can be filed either against the whole decision or against specified parts. If only a part of the decision is appealed, it is inadmissible that the intermediate appellate court should reverse the part that was not appealed, even if the grounds for reversal also concern that part, i.e., even where the relationship between the appealed part and the non-appealed part – is such that two contradictory decisions exist. This legislative solution is not pertinent at all. Unfortunately, that is the explicit will of the legislator (Article 269 CCP, item 13 of the ID No. 1-2000-GMCC of the SCC).[101] According to that ID, if the decisions on the two claims are contradictory, and only one of the decisions is appealed, and the intermediate appellate court rendered an opposite decision, and the other decision was not changed because it was not appealed, the contradiction can be overcome by a reversal under Article 303, item 3 CCP corresponding to Article 231, items 'c' CCP, repealed. [102] Thus, the SCC has turned the reversal of a decision that has come into force into substitute of an intermediate appeal which is inadmissible.[103]

211. In ID No. 1-2000-GMCC of the SCC is assumed that it is inadmissible a party to appeal only the motives for the decision, although the decision satisfies it.

In my opinion, the point here is whether the decision as a result satisfies the party, especially where the party is dissatisfied with the motives, for instance where the court dismissed the claim, but in the motives granted that the arguments of the defendant regarding the invalidity of the contract were groundless, i.e., the contract

101. See critique of the legislator's decision and IDV. Popova, *Civil Procedure. Bulgaria*. First ed., para. 233.
102. It is assumed in practice that item 13 of ID No. 1–2000–GMCC of the SCC is valid under the new CCP.
103. *See* J. Stalev, A. Mingova, O. Stamboliev, V. Popova, R. Ivanova, *Balgarsko …* , *supra*, p. 366.

from which the receivable claimed by the claimant ensues, and also granted that the set-off claim was well-founded and dismissed the claim on these grounds. This does not satisfy the defendant. The grounds on which the claim is dismissed matters to him. Consequently, the decision as a result does not satisfy him. A similar situation occurs for a claimant whose claim is upheld, but in the motives the court granted that the sales contract that the claimant alleges his property right ensues from, is invalid and the court upholds the claim on the grounds of the expiration of the acquisition limitation, while the claimant wanted it to be upheld on the grounds of eventuality. The party has a legal interest in appealing the decision itself, the disposition of the decision and not the motives themselves, in the decision apart. The court is obligated to state in the decision the grounds for upholding the claim, and the grounds for dismissing it.

212. The intermediate appeal should contain the following: name and address of the party filing it, designation of the appealed decision, an indication of the nature of the defect of the decision, what the request consists of, the newly discovered and newly occurred facts the appellant wants considered in the course of determining the case in the intermediate appellate instance and an exact listing of the reasons which have prevented the appellant from citing the newly discovered facts; the new evidence which the appellant wants to be collected in the course of examining the case in the intermediate appellate instance and a list of the reasons which have prevented him/her from bringing or presenting it and a signature of the appellant (Article 260 CCP).

According to Article 261 CCP the attachments to the appeal are: duplicate copies of the appeal and of the attachments thereto according to the number of persons who participate in the case as an opposing party; a power of attorney, where the appeal is lodged by an attorney-in-fact; the new written evidence cited in the appeal; documentary proof of payment of stamp duty.

The appeal is lodged with the first-instance court that has rendered the decision (Article 259 CCP). It carries out the verification on the admissibility of the appeal (Article 262(1) CCP), if the appeal does not meet the requirements specified in Article 260, items 1, 2, 4 and 7 CCP[104] and Article 261 CCP, the party is notified that it has to eliminate the flaws within a seven-day term. The appeal is reverted: where it was filed after the expiration of the term for appeal and the flaws under Article 262(2) CCP are not eliminated. The ruling of reverting the appeal can be appealed by a private appeal (Article 262(3) CCP).

According to Article 260, item 5 CCP the appellant may bring only newly *occurred*[105] and newly discovered[106] facts. The first group is the one of the newly

104. The failure to meet the requirements under: Art. 260, item 3 CCP regarding the errors in the judgment, due to which it is appealed; Art. 260, item 5 CCP regarding the facts and those under Art. 260, item 6 CCP regarding the evidence does not make the appeal inadmissible. Those requirements are not mandatory as far as the regularity of the appeal is concerned. The failure to meet those requirements might cause disallowing of the appeal as groundless due to the preclusion of the possibility for alleging the facts specified in Art. 260, item 5 CCP and for presenting evidence under Art. 260, item 6 CCP.

105. Those are facts that have occurred following the closure of the court trial at the first instance (arg. under Art. 147, item 2 CCP in connection with Art. 235(3) CCP).

occurred ones. If they are not cited in the appeal, the possibility to do so later during the intermediate appellate proceedings is precluded (Article 266(2) CCP). By arg. of Article 266(3) CCP (*see* paragraph 217) facts which the appellant could not have indicated to the Court of First Instance because of a procedural violation committed by the court may be mentioned in the appeal. By argument of Article 303 (1) item 5 CCP where the applicant has not been able to appear in person or through a trustee due to special unforeseen circumstances which he/she could not overcome he/she can bring in the appeal. Due to the commitment of the appellate court to that contained in the appeal (Article 269, sentence II CCP), the complainant must indicate and substantiate in the appeal the procedural violation committed by the court, which led to its inability to indicate the facts alleged by it. The same applies to the one referred to in Article 303(1) item 5 CCP objective impossibility.

The evidence under Article 260, item 6 CCP may concern both newly discovered facts as well as facts under Article 303(1) item 2 CCP (*see* paragraph 243). Unlike the reversal of a decision that has taken effect, not only written, but oral evidence and experts' conclusion are admissible in intermediate appellate proceedings. The evidence under Article 260, item 6 CCP may concern both newly discovered facts as well as facts under Article 260 item 5 CCP.

According to Article 266(3) CCP evidence that was not admitted by the Court of First Instance because of a procedural violation committed by the court may be mentioned, provided, respectively, in the complaint. Furthermore, due to the binding nature of the appellate court as set out in the appeal (Article 269, sentence II CCP), in order to apply Article 266(3) CCP the appellee must state in the appeal the procedural offence committed by the court, as well as the evidence itself, to present the written evidence, respectively. In ID No.1-2013-GMCC and the Com.C. of the SCC it was accepted that when the procedural violation consists of an incomplete or inaccurate report of the first-instance court, it is sufficient to state that the report is inaccurate or incomplete. The appellate court is obliged to correct the inaccuracies in the report by allowing the party to indicate the new evidence by indicating the burden of proof. The appellate court is required to distribute the burden of proof (without making a report) and to give guidance on what circumstances the complainant must prove, what the defendant in the complaint and then the parties can bring in evidence.

213. When the court receives the appeal, it sends a copy of it together with the attachments to the other party entitled to submit a written reply within a fourteen-day term. The regulations of Article 259(2)–(4) CCP and Article 260, items 1, 2, 4 and 7 CCP and Article 261 CCP (Article 263(3) CCP), respectively, are applicable to the reply. The reply is not filed with the intermediate appellate court through the first-instance court. The appellee is entitled to object the admissibility of the appeal, e.g., its regularity or omitted deadline, legitimization, etc. As a rule the objections

106. The notion of 'newly discovered facts' under Art. 260, item 5 CCP is the same as that under Art. 303(1), item 1 CCP concerning the reversal of decisions that have taken effect, i.e., the party had not known and which could not have known. In the case of Art. 260, item 5 CCP those facts should have been discovered and could have been discovered following the closure of the court trial at the first instance till the lodging of the appeal.

of defendant against the filed claim are not precluded with the term for filing the reply under Article 131(1) CCP, hence they cannot be brought in for the first time before the intermediate appellate court. That also concerns the objections against the redeem limitation. They can be brought for the first time before the intermediate appellate instance only if the party could not bring them in before the first instance due to violation of the legislation rules (e.g., its depriving from participation in the first-instance proceedings. It was adopted by ID No. 1-2013-GMCC and the Com.C of the SCC that the objection against set-off could be brought in before the intermediate appellate court, if it is a substantive law compensation of two executable and liquid receivables, which are extinguished by the amount of the lesser receivable on the day when there were conditions for their compensation. If the cross receivable is disputable, the objection against set-off could be brought in before the intermediate appellate court for the first time. It was also adopted by ID No. 1-2013-GMCC and the Com.C of the SCC that the objection against set-off (the objection under Article 90 OCA) is precluded with the expiry of the term for the reply to the claim which subject is a non-liquid receivable. When the receivable is liquid, e.g., it has been ascertained by a court decision or an enforcement order, as well as when the objection is brought in as an accessory right against the counterclaim could be brought in before the intermediate appellate court for the first time.

214. Within the term for submitting the reply, the appellee to the initial statement of an intermediate appeal is entitled to file an intermediate cross-appeal. It should meet the requirements for an intermediate appeal (Article 263(2) CCP). The intermediate cross-appeal has as a subject matter the part of the decision which the defendant on the initial statement of an intermediate appeal has not appealed within the lawful deadline. The right to a cross-appeal arises after the preclusion term and only under the condition that the opposite party has appealed the other part of the decision. Having admitted it the court sends it together with its attachments to the opposite party which following the service is entitled to file a reply within a one-week term (Article 263(3) CCP). The statement of the intermediate cross-appeal has an accessory character. It is not examined, if the statement of an intermediate appeal is withdrawn or returned (Article 263(4) CCP).

215. After expiry of the deadlines specified in Article 263(1) and (3) CCP, the statements of intermediate appeal and cross-appeal and the replies are sent to the intermediate appellate court (Article 263(5) CCP) which is not bound to the statement of the first-instance court on the admissibility of the appeal. It has to examine again its admissibility by a three-judge panel (Article 267(1) CCP).

The intermediate appellate court sits in a closed session for preparation of the case (Article 267 CCP). In this session the intermediate appellate court verifies the admissibility of the appeals applying Article 262 CCP, pronounces on admission of the new evidence cited by the parties, and schedules an examination of the case in an open session (Article 267 CCP). According to Article 267(1), sentence II, CCP the issues on the admissibility of the appeals and the requests for evidence may alternatively be addressed during the first hearing of the case, if the court determines that the oral explanations of the parties must be heard as well. Utilizing the second possibility inevitably leads to postponing the case for the next court session.

216. Each of the joint parties in the case is entitled to join the appeal filed by his/her co-appellant or co-appellee no later than the first session of the second instance. The party joins by filing a written application with copies for the opposing party according to the number of persons in that party (Article 265(1) CCP). It is assumed that the indispensable joint parties of the appellant are constituted as parties to the intermediate appellate proceedings regardless to whether they have joined the appeal or not (Article 265(2) CCP). However, in order for the indispensable joint parties to be constituted as parties to the intermediate appellate proceedings, it is necessary that they have joined the appeal in accordance with the terms and procedure in Article 265(1) CCP.

217. Prior to the conclusion of the trial, the parties may: allege any new circumstances and bring in and present any new evidence, only if the parties were unable to learn about them and to bring in and present such evidence prior to filing the statement of appeal or within the term for a reply (Article 266(2) item 1 CCP, *see also* paragraph 212); allege any circumstances which have occurred after the statement of appeal had been filed or after expiry of the deadline for the reply, respectively, circumstances which are relevant to the case, and cite and present evidence of any such circumstances (Article 267(2) item 2 CCP). According to Article 266(3) CCP it is possible to request collection of evidence which was not admitted by the first-instance court due to procedural breaches. In line with Article 269(2), sentence II CCP it was accepted in ID No. 1-2013-GMCC of the SCC that for these violations, the appellate court does not monitor ex officio (*see* paragraph 221). That is why, in order to use the possibility provided by Article 266(3) CCP, the complainant must have made a substantiated complaint in the application for the existence of a procedural violation referred to in Article 266(3) CCP.

218. In principle, the evidence collected in the first instance is not collected again in the intermediate appellate instance. According to Article 267(2) CCP, the intermediate appellate court is entitled to question the witnesses and the experts again only if it finds it necessary to question them directly. The court should collect the evidence collected ex officio (expertise, inspection, certification) only if complaint about procedural breaches committed by the first-instance court what left the case undetermined concerning its factual aspect, or the factual conclusions ungrounded in the motives of the first-instance decision, or if the evidence is need for application of the imperative substantive law norm (ID No. 1-2013-GMCC and the Com.C. of the SCC).

219. According to Article 268(1) CCP the intermediate appellate court in a three-judge panel sitting in an open session with subpoenaing the parties at which the statements of appeal and the replies are reported. The evidence is collected according to the general rules. Having settled the matter under Article 267 CCP and collected the evidence the court opens the oral pleadings. Article 149(3) CCP is applicable in the case, i.e., the oral pleading can be replaced by written pleadings in the form of written defences.

220. According to Article 270(1) CCP, if the decision is *void*, the intermediate appellate court *proclaims the invalidity* and, if the case is not subject to termination, it is referred to the first-instance court for a new decision. It should examine whether the decision is valid, even when there is no complaint about the invalidity of the decision in the statement of appeal (Article 269, sentence I CCP). According to Article 270(3) CCP, if the decision is *inadmissible* the intermediate appellate court *annuls* the decision by terminating the case. Where the termination is grounded on the lack of jurisdiction of the dispute, the case is submitted to a competent court. If the court considers a non-claim, the decision is annulled, and the case is referred to the first-instance court for a decision on the claim that is brought. The decision of the district court cannot be annulled just because the claim was under the jurisdiction of the regional court (Article 270(4) CCP). On the grounds of Article 269, sentence I CCP when only a part the decision is appealed, the court cannot examine the admissibility of the non-appealed part.

221. According to Article 269, sentence II CCP when verifying the validity of the decision the court is bound by what is stated in the complaint. Verifying the validity of the first-instance decision the intermediate appellate court can apply the imperative substantive law norm, even when its breaching has not been pointed as grounds for appeal (ID No. 1-2013-GMCC and the Com.C. of the SCC).[107] The intermediate appellate is not limited by the stated in the complaint when it supports ex officio the interest of a party to the case (e.g., placement under guardianship or the interest of the minor children when pronouncing on the measures for exercising the parents' rights, the personal relationship, the allowance of the children and the usage of the family home). The intermediate appellate court does not verify ex officio the breaches committed at the first instance when the case was reported. In case the statement of appeal contains grounded complaint about procedural breaches concerning the report that have been committed by the first-instance court, the intermediate appellate court should instruct the parties about the possibilities to undertake the procedural steps for bringing in evidence related to the case, that they had omitted to do at the first instance due to a lack, incomplete or inappropriate instructions in the report. When the intermediate appellate court finds a wrong qualification of the first instance that lead instructing incorrectly the parties concerning the facts subject to proving, the former court without being seized by such a complaint, has to ensure ex officio the proper application of the imperative substantive law norm by instructions about the facts that should be proven and of the necessity to bring in the respective evidence (ID No. 1-2013-GMCC and the Com.C of the SCC).

On the basis of the evidence collected at the first and second instances (*see* paragraphs 218 and 219) the court comes to its own determination on the merits of the dispute. This decision is compared to the appealed one. If it is the same as the decision of the first-instance court, the intermediate appellate court confirms the

107. An ID No. 1-2020-GMCC and the Com.C. of the SCC was formed regarding the issue 'Is the court obliged to monitor ex officio whether the legal transactions that are of importance for resolving the legal dispute are void, or should it rule on the issue only if the interested party has made a corresponding objection for voidness?'

appealed decision (Article 271(1), sentence I CCP) and does not render a separate dispositive on substantive law dispute. In that case it should motivate its decision, and may refer to the motives of the first-instance court (Article 272 CCP). In the practice of the SCC it was correctly accepted that the possibility to refer to the motives of the first-instance court does not release the appellate court from the obligation to present its own motives by ruling on the arguments of the parties in the appeal and the response against it. If the opinion of intermediate appellate court differs from that of the first-instance court, the former reverses the appealed decision. Upon the reversal of the decision as wrongful the situation of the appellant cannot deteriorate when it is not appealed by the opposing party (Article 271(1) sentence I CCP).

222. According to Article 271(3) CCP, the court also reverses the decision with respect to the appellant's indispensable joint parties that did not appeal the decision. In the cases of indispensable joint parties the court cannot reverse the decision with respect to joint parties that have not filed an appeal even when the reverse concerns the joint facts (*see* paragraph 280).

223. According to Article 271(2) CCP, if the decision on the principal claim is reversed, those claims that are eventually joined with it and the first-instance court has not rendered a decision become pending. However, the law does not explicitly specify before which instance they are pending. In practice the intermediate court is entitled to render the first decision on the merits of an eventual claim on which the first instance did not render its decision. In this hypothesis, the first-instance court did not render a decision on the eventual claim because the condition, on which the rendering of a decision depends, did not occur. However, this eventual claim is already considered in the first instance, evidence is collected and oral pleadings are conducted.

§2. Appeal to the Intermediate Appellate Court Against Rulings

224. The appeal of the rulings is regulated in Article 274 CCP:[108]

(a) Article 274 CCP provides the opportunity of bringing private appeals against rulings that are: barring the further conduct of proceedings (rulings for suspending the case (Article 229 CCP); refusal for reopening of suspended proceedings (Article 230 CCP); rulings which appeal is explicitly provided for in law, e.g., the rulings regarding subservience of the case after the court accepted it for consideration – Article 15(2) CCP, the rulings in connection with the jurisdiction – Article 121 CCP; and the rulings disallowing the intervention or joinder of a third-party accessory – Article 220(1), sentence II, CCP.

108. *See* V. Popova, *Njakoi normi za obzhalvane na opredelenijata (Some norms of appealing the rules)*. Ciela. Norms. At http://www.ciela.net; ID No. 6/15.01.2019 under ID No. 6/2017 of the GMCC and the Comm.C. of the SCC.

It was adopted by ID No. 1-2013-GMCC and the Com.C. of the SCC in connection with Article 274(2), sentence I CCP that the refusal of the first-instance court to admit for joint considering the incidental ascertainment claim is not subject to appeal. The ruling on disallowing the increasing of the amount of the claim which was not brought in as a partial claim is subject to appeal. The ruling of the first-instance court by which the cross-claim was returned due to a failure to cure its irregularities is subject to appeal under Article 274(1), item 2 CCP and Article 129(3) CCP.

(b) According to Article 274(2), sentence I CCP rulings rendered by a court of intermediate appellate instance under Article 274(1) CCP are appealable by a private appeal before the SCC. When the rulings are rendered by the district court, they are appealable before the respective intermediate appellate court. Those are rulings of the intermediate appellate court by which it rules for the first time on the admissibility of the intermediate appellate proceedings, suspending the proceedings because of the inadmissibility of the statement of appeal and disallowing the cassation appeal because of its invalidity, inadmissibility or delay, and refusal to institute intermediate appellate proceedings; the intermediate appellate proceedings are suspended or the suspended proceedings are not resumed, bar the further conduct of proceedings (Article 273 CCP).

According to Article 274(2), sentence II CCP the rulings rendered by SCC under Article 274(1) CCP are appealable before another panel of the same court. Those are rulings ruled for the first time by a panel of the SCC suspends the cassation proceedings due to a delayed, lack of legitimization, the ruling is on a case which decision is not subject to a cassation appeal (Article 274(4) CCP); the cassation proceedings are suspended, the suspended proceedings are refused resuming, respectively (Article 229 CCP).

For appealing the rulings under Article 274(2) CCP *the SCC acts as a second instance.*

ID No. 2-2018-GMCC and the Com.C. of the SCC is pending. The interpretative decision has to give interpretation of the question whether the ruling of the intermediate appellate court which confirms barring of the proceedings progress by a ruling or an order of the district court acting as an intermediate appellate instance is subject to cassation appeal.

225. According to Article 274(3), item 1 CCP, when the prerequisites in Article 280(1) CCP exist, the intermediate appellate court rulings subject to cassation appeal are those which do not upheld private appeals against the rulings barring the further development of the proceedings.

According to Article 274(3), item 2 CCP, when the prerequisites in Article 280(1) CCP exist, the intermediate appellate court rulings subject to cassation appeal are the ones deciding on the merits other proceedings or bar their further progress. In ID No. 5-2015-GMCC and the Com.C. of the SCC the SCC accepted that rulings, which resolve other proceedings within the meaning of Article 274, paragraph 3, item 2 CCP on the merits, are those with which the court rules on an application for protection and assistance of personal or property right in independent proceedings with a separate subject, which develops outside or within the claim process and has no temporary character. The cited ID lists the rulings, which according to this criterion are subject to cassation appeal under Article 274(3), item 2, proposition 1 CCP and which are not subject to cassation appeal. There is a large list of rulings to be interpreted.

According to Article 274(4) CCP cassation appealability does not apply to any rulings in civil cases which decisions are not subject to cassation appeal.

226. Private appeals are filed within a one-week term following the announcement of the ruling. If the appealed ruling is rendered in a court session, this term starts running on the day of the session for the party that attended the meeting (Article 275(1), sentence I, CCP). The court is obligated to attach ex officio a copy of the appealed ruling. After receiving the appeal, the court sends a copy to the other party, and he/she can submit a written reply to the appeal within a seven-day term of receiving this copy (Article 276(1) CCP). After the expiration of this term the appeal, together with the reply and its attachments, if any, are submitted to the higher court. The court encloses a duplicate of the appealed ruling according to Article 276(2), sentence II, CCP.

According to Article 277 CCP, a private appeal neither suspends proceedings, nor does it discontinue the enforcement of the appealed ruling, unless the law provides otherwise. However, the intermediate appellate court is entitled to suspend the proceedings and the enforcement of the appealed ruling until the private appeal is determined.

227. Private appeals are considered in a closed session. If the court finds it necessary, the appeal can be considered in an open session (Article 278(1) CCP). According to Article 278(2) CCP, if the intermediate appellate court reverses the appealed ruling, the court has to render its decision. The court is also entitled to collect evidence, if necessary. The ruling rendered on a private appeal is obligatory for the lower court (Article 278(3) CCP).

§3. Cassation

228. The cassation appeal in Bulgarian procedure law is its proviso as a regular (ar. Article 296 CCP), but not always possible due to the admissibility under Article 280 (1) (am. SG No. 86/2017) (2) (newly added SG No. 86/2017) CCP third instance of control. The decisions subject to cassation appeal to the SCC[109] are the intermediate appellate decisions (Article 280 CCP) [110] of the district and appellate courts. According to Article 280(3) CCP (amended several times Latest amendment SG No. 86/2017) decisions that are not subject to cassation appeal are those: on cases with a claim price of up to BGN 5,000 – for civil cases and up to BGN 20,000

109. *See* V. Popova, *Kasacionnoto obzhalvane i novijat GPK (The Cassation Appeal and the New CCP)*. Ciela. Normi. At http://www.ciela.net and the literature and practice cited therein.

110. The decisions of the first-instance court that are not appealed in accordance with the intermediate appeal procedure are certainly not subject to cassation appeal.

for commercial ones,[111] with the exception of judgments on property claims and other real rights over real estate and related claims, which have a decisive effect on the property claim (item 1); on appellate actions on maintenance claims, matrimonial claims, claims under Article 322(2) CCP, except for the issues under Article 59(2) FC in the cases in which, on the date of the announcement of the appellate decision on the marriage, there is a juvenile child, proceedings under Article 126(2) Article 127a and Article 130(3) FC, claims under Article 11(2) Ownership and Use of Agricultural Land Act and such under Article 13(2) Law for Restoration of the Ownership of Forests and Lands from the Forest Fund, proceedings for distribution of the use of own property under Article 32(2) PA, claims under Article 40 Condominium Property Management Act, applications for change of name under Article 19(1) CRA and claims under Article 17(1) Law on Settlement of Collective Labour Disputes (item 2); decisions on appeals in labour disputes, with the exception of decisions on claims under Article 344(1) item 1, 2 and 3 LC and on claims for labour remuneration and benefits under an employment relationship with a claim price of over BGN 5,000.

In ID No. 1-2001-GMCC of the SCC, it is stated that the decisions subject to cassation appeal are (a) not only the intermediate appellate decisions on the merits but also the intermediate appellate decisions proclaiming null or invalidating the first-instance decisions, both where the case is terminated and where the case is referred for reconsideration; (b) decisions of the appellate courts disallowing the entry of circumstances to be entered in the court register are also subject to cassation. In this aspect the ID cited is also valid under CCP, current.

229. Article 280(1) CCP (am. SG No. 86/2017) specifies that the intermediate appellate decisions are subject to cassation appeal provided the court has pronounced on a substantive law matter which: (1) has been determined in conflict with the obligatory practice of SCC and SC in IDs and ordinances, as well as in conflict with the practice of SC; (2) has been determined in conflict with act of the CC of the Republic of Bulgaria or the Court of the Justice of the EU; (3) is relevant to the accurate application of the law, as well as to the progress of law. Article 280(1) CCP outlines the grounds for admitting a cassation appeal and creates a filter which sets limits to the cassation appeal. The wording of Article 280(1) CCP has been the subject of severe discussions. It was attacked before the CC. With a majority of only one vote it disallowed the request for pronouncing the text as contradicting entirely the Constitution and pronounced as a contradicting only the part on the word 'significant' (DCC No. 4/2009 – SG 49/2009). It was simply because of a dispute in CC on the meaning of the word 'significant', whether the matter should be significant for the case or significant for the society. Since the opinion that the word 'significant' means significant for the society, not for the particular case, prevailed, the part on the word significant was found as contradicting the Constitution. However,

111. An ID No. 3-2019-GMCC and the Com.C. of the SCC has been formed on the question: 'Is the case which regards legal relations arising under a contract for carrying out of construction works concluded between a natural person and a commercial trader in connection with his occupation civil or commercial and what is the threshold for access to cassation appeal of the appellate decision in such a case?'

the lawyers practising civil proceedings had no doubts that the problem concerned a matter significant for the particular case. By the cited DCC No. 4/2009 to overcome the contradictory court practice ID No. 1 of 19 February 2010 was passed at GMCC and the Com.C. of SSC for imposing a unified interpretation of the texts cited with some dissents of supreme judges. After the said ID was repealed, a project for repealing Article 280(1) CCP was adopted at a first reading by the National Assembly. Meanwhile Article 280(1) CCP was amended and Article 280(2) CCP was created (SG No. 86/2017):

a. In order to avoid using the word 'significant' the wordings 'substantive law or procedure law matter relevant to the outcome of the case' have been adopted in practice (ID-No. 1-2010-GMCC and the Com.C. of the SCC), i.e., the said matter should have determined the outcome of the case. The cassation court should pronounce on whether the legal matter brought by the cassator, has determined the legal conclusions regarding the subject of the dispute, but it should not pronounce on their rightness and lawfulness. *The verification of the rightness and lawfulness of the appealed act is performed only after it has been admitted to cassation appeal* (Article 290(1) CCP). It was adopted in ID-No. 1-2010-GMCC and the Com.C. of the SCC that the cassator must indicate the legal matter relevant to the outcome of the case as a manifestation of the dispositive principle in the civil procedure. Not indicating the legal matter relevant to the outcome of the particular case is itself sufficient grounds for inadmissibility of the cassation appeal without considering the indicated additional grounds.

(b) Besides the general grounds for admitting the cassation appeal discussed already in item 'A' Article 280(1) CCP comprises several additional grounds being interrelated under the conditions of eventuality:

  (a) The substantive law or procedure law matter relevant to the outcome of the case has been settled in conflict with the practice of the SCC (Article 280(1), item 1 CCP). The amendments in Article 280(1) CCP were in connection with ID No. 1-2010-GMCC and the Com.C. of the SCC. The ID cited was based on the mandatory practice of the SC and the SCC. It was accepted in the cited ID that, the interpretative decisions of the General Meeting of the Colleges of the Council, rendered under the action of Article 52(1) ASC (repealed), which decisions serve as guidelines of the courts. There is disagreement of the supreme judges that item 1 should also cover the Guiding Practice of the SC – Interpretative Decisions adopted under the Act on the Structure of the Courts (ASC-1952 and ASC-1976). These interpretative decisions were rendered on controversial or controversial issues solved in the application of the law and serve as guidelines of the courts – Article 17(2) ASC-1952 and Article 52(1) ASC-1976. The fact that the interpretative decisions rendered under ASC and Article 212 CPC (repealed) were and continue to be (those regulating current legal relations) guidelines for the courts, and namely based on them existing constant practice has also been established. The contrary understanding leads to a complete deletion of the significance of the interpretative decisions made by the GMCC of the SCC, which college had the same specialization as the current Civil College of the SCC. That means the spoilage of the decades of accumulated, generalized and unconfirmed experience and legal culture in civil matters, with unchanged legal regulation of the relevant civil law. That is why I believe that the new version of Article 280(1) CCP should include the ID of the SC, during the operation of the above-mentioned ASC, which provided that they are guidelines to the courts.[112]

It is provided in Article 290(3) CCP (new, SG No. 86/2017) that, the decisions under Article 290 CCP are not mandatory law practice. That is why the quoted ID of the GMCC and the Com.C. has lost its effect. In item 1, however, the contradiction with the practice of the SCC remained. The aim is to cover consistent practice of SCC, so there was no need of ID.[113] In practice, if the complainant relies on that part of item 1 and presents decisions of the SCC panels to which the contested decision is in conflict and the defendant to the appeal presents other decisions of SCC panels, or the appellate court cites a contradictory practice of the SCC under Article 290 CCP or such practice is known to the SCC ex-officio, on the grounds of 292 CCP, panel of the SCC should still have to suspend the proceedings and propose to the General Meeting to render an ID (ID No. 2 of 28 September 2011 GMCC and Com.C. of the SCC).[114]

(b) The substantive law or procedural matter of relevance to the outcome of the case has to be resolved in contradiction with acts of the SC of the Republic of Bulgaria or of the CEC (Article 280 (1) item 2 CCP). The contradiction with the acts of CEC was adopted to overcome the incorrect practice of the SCC panels in which it was assumed that the SCC did not, in the examination of the admissibility of the cassation appeal, make preliminary rulings to the CEC because that phase was not judicial, but for the selection of complaints and regarding the SCC facultative phase.[115]

(c) The substantive law or procedure law matter relevant to the outcome of the case should be relevant to: (a) the precise application of the law when its consideration contributes to a change in the court practice created due to imprecise interpretation of the mandatory court practice and the practice on the particular case, in order to overcome the adopted legal solutions for the application of the legal norm, or for its updating and interpretation with regard to the changes in the legislation and social environment; (b) to the progress of law when the laws are incomplete, unclear or in conflict in order to create court practice on the application of new laws or to update it with regard to the changes in the legislation and social environment (Article 280(1), item 3 CCP; ID No. 1-2010-GMCC and the Com.C. of the SCC). In the amended Article 280(1) CCP, item 2 of the previous wording in which the grounds for admission of the cassation appeal provided that the formulated substantive or procedural law questions relevant for the outcome of the case should be decided contradictory

112. What is in accordance with the common sense of the judges concerning the cited ID.
113. It is in accordance with the disagreement of the judges regarding the cited ID.
114. *See* V. Popova, Civil Procedure. Bulgaria, second ed., para. 238.
115. V. Popova, Actual matters of the European civil procedure and Part VII of CCP, S. 2011, p. 224.

by the courts, was abandoned.[116] However, there is an opinion that this ground will fall within the scope of item 3 for the correct application of the law and the development of jurisdiction. In the ID No. 1-2010-GMCC and the Com.C. of the SCC it was accepted that in order for this reason to exist, the legal matter must be resolved in contradiction with another enforced decision of a first-instance, appellate court or a decision of the SCC on the same legal issue, rendered in compliance with the repealed CCP.

230. It has been established in Article 280(2) CCP (new, SG No. 86/1917) that, regardless of the prerequisites under Article 280(1) CCP the appeal decision is admitted to a cassation appeal in case of probable nullity or inadmissibility, as well as in case of obvious irregularity:

- The probable nullity or inadmissibility was introduced as a basis for allowing the cassation appeal under the influence of ID No. 1-2010-GMCC and the Com.C. of the SCC. It was accepted that the SCC is obliged to allow the appeal of the appellate court decision to cassation control, where the inadmissibility and the nullity of the appeal decision were not misled by the applicant under the grounds for admission of a cassation appeal. ID No. 1-2010-GMCC and the Com.C. of the SCC was mechanically reproduced in ID No. 1-2001-GMCC of the SCC, in which, under the old CCP (repealed) it was accepted that the SCC had to carry out an official examination of the nullity and inadmissibility of the contested decision. It ignores the fact that under the CCP, repealed there was no prior selection of complaints, as is now regulated in Article 280(1) and (2) CCP, which is why the SCC examined in open court with the participation of the parties the presence as grounds for cassation, in terms of nullity and inadmissibility, inclusive.

The provision of Article 280(2) CCP and ID No. 1-2010-GMCC and the Com.C. of the SCC regarding the possible nullity or inadmissibility contradict the promulgated in Article 121(1) C constitutional principle for the equality of parties in the process. Nullity and inadmissibility are provided in Article 281(1) and (2) CCP, grounds for cassation appeal (*see* paragraph 232).[117] They are an element of the substantive appeal which is dealt with at a sumptuous hearing by summoning the parties. In the hypothesis of Article 280(2) CCP at an open hearing the defendant is placed in a disadvantaged position with that of the applicant in whose favour the definition under Article 288 CPC has already ruled that the decision is probably null and void, respectively unacceptable. The provision also contradicts Article 4 JSA on impartiality of the judge and as established in Article 112 JHA prohibition to give

116. *See* the grounds V. Popova, Civil Procedure. Bulgaria, second ed., para. 227, section B, item 2.

117. Moreover, even nowadays Art. 284(1), item 3 CCP requires the cassation complaint to contain precise and motivated presentation of the cassation grounds (*see* para. 234).

preliminary opinion on the case, as well as the provision in Article 22(1), item 6 CCP grounds for dismissal of the judge.[118]

The new Article 280(2) CCP provides that, regardless of the prerequisites under Article 280(2) CCP, the appeal decision is admitted to a cassation appeal in case of obvious irregularity. With Decision No. 15/2018 under constitutional case 10/2018 the CC rejected the request of a three-member panel of the SCC to establish the unconstitutionality of this provision. Several of the constitutional judges signed the decision with a dissenting opinion.[119]

231. According to Article 288 CCP the SCC in a panel of three judges pronounces on the admissibility of the cassation appeal under the grounds of Article 280 CCP in a closed session. In Article 280 and following CCP there is not an explicit text concerning the appeal of the ruling on the admissibility of the cassation appeal, the one that panel of three judges assumed the cassation appeal inadmissible. Under Article 274(2), sentence II of the CCP that ruling should be appealable before another panel of the SCC. But in SCC practice it was adopted to be non-appealable.

232. According to Article 281 CCP, entitled Grounds for Cassation Appeal a statement of cassation appeal is lodged, if the decision is: (a) void; (b) inadmissible; (c) improper due to a violation of substantive law, a material breach of court procedure rules or groundlessness. Thus, the law specifies the grounds for cassation appeal:

(1) The decision is invalid where it does not comply with the requirement regarding validity of the decision. The cassation grounds are present only where the intermediate appellate decision itself is invalid on its own grounds (for instance, if rendered by a panel of one judge and not by a panel of three judges or a member of the panel has no capacity of a judge) as well as when the first-instance decision is invalid, but the intermediate appellate court failed to perform its powers under Article 270(1) CCP and failed to declare the invalidity of the first-instance decision, leaving it in force, or reversed it as improper and decided on the merits of the case.
(2) The intermediate appellate decision can be inadmissible on its own grounds, without the inadmissibility of the first-instance decision. This is the case where the intermediate appellate court considered the statement of intermediate appeal and determined the dispute although the statement was not filed in due time, where the statement was improper and the intermediate appellate court failed to observe the requirements of Article 262 CCP in connection with Article 267(1) CCP regarding rectification, where the statement was filed by a non-legitimized person, where the appellant appealed a part of the decision

118. *See* V. Popova The grounds for admitting a cassation appeal foreseen in the new Art. 280(2) CCP (SG No.86/2017) – June, 2018. On-line edition Apis-Time, Commentary Column, volume 1, available at http://online.apis.bg.
119. *See* V. Popova, Grounds for admitting …, v. 2; Bulgaria, IEL Civil Procedure, III Ed., 2019, para. 227

only, and, in breach of the principle of disposition, the intermediate appellate court reversed it including the non-appealed part, where, in its capacity of an instance on the merits, the court reversed the first-instance decision and rendered a decision on a claim that was not lodged, and where the party withdrew its appeal, but the intermediate appellate court did not suspended the intermediate appellate proceedings and rendered its decision on the withdrawn appeal, and reversed the appealed decision. It is possible for both decisions, the intermediate appellate and the first-instance decisions, to be inadmissible, for instance, any of the following can be missing: the right to claim, the proper procedural legitimation, or subservience. Moreover, the subject-matter jurisdiction can be violated or, instead of invalidating the inadmissible first-instance decision, the court preserves its force or reverses it as improper and decides on the merits of the case.

(3) Improperness of the decision is cassation grounds due to a violation of substantive law, violation of the court procedure rules or to groundlessness:
   (a) The term 'substantive law' includes all legal norms regulating substantive law civil relationships between the parties regardless of which private law branch they belong to, once they regulate the relationships between the subjects by the method of equality.
   (b) *A significant material breach of court procedure rules* is a violation of procedural norms regulating the procedure of clarifying the case and a guarantee of proper establishment of the facts relevant to the dispute. The breach of these procedural rules itself should also be material, i.e., it should bring about impropriety of the decision or to the right of defence of the cassator. The procedural breach should have been committed by intermediate appellate court. A procedural breach on the part of the first-instance court does not in itself constitute grounds for its reversal by the intermediate appellate court, and, consequently, for the reversal of the intermediate appellate decision by a cassation appeal, unless an argument has been made before the appellate court for a procedural breach and it has not remedied it.
   (c) Groundlessness is present if the court's conclusions regarding facts are defective and this is not due to a breach of procedural rules, but to a breach of rules not regulated in law, such as the rules of logical thinking, experience rules, the causal relation between events, or the achievements of science and arts.

233. The persons legitimized to lodge a cassation appeal are the ones constituted as parties in adversary proceedings in the first and the intermediate appellate instance, regardless of whether they were a main party or a secondary one. The other condition stipulating legitimization is the legal interest in the appeal where the intermediate appellate decision is unfavourable for the claimant. In the cases of impropriety of the decision due to a material breach of the court procedure rules, the breach should affect the appellant and not the opposing party.

234. The cassation appeal is lodged via the intermediate appellate court which has rendered the decision within one month following the service of the decision to parties (Article 283(1) CCP). It must contain: the name and address of the lodging party; an indication of the judgment appealed; an accurate and reasoned narrative of the cassation grounds; formulation of the prayer; signature of the appellant which is countersigned by a lawyer or a legal adviser, except where the appellant or his/her representative possesses a licensed competence to practice law (Article 284(2) CCP). The enclosures to the statement of the cassation appeal are: *description of the grounds for cassation appealability under* Article *280(1), which is countersigned by an attorney*; duplicate copies of the appeal its enclosures according to the number of persons who participate in the case as an opposing party; a power of attorney, where the appeal is lodged by an attorney-in-fact; a document proving the paid fee (Article 284, item 4). The SCC rules upon the grounds stated in the appeal concerning the inappropriateness of the decision (ID No. 1-2001-GMCC of the SCC, Article 290(2) CCP). However, the cassation instance can adopt a legal qualification differing from the offence stated in the appeal, i.e., this instance can change the qualification of the cassation grounds without going beyond its limits. The SCC is obligated to examine ex officio the validity and admissibility of the appealed decision (ID No. 1-2001-GMCC of the SCC, Article 290(2) CCP).

235. According to Article 285(1) CCP the intermediate appellate court through which the appeal is filed verifies its conformity and if it does not meet the requirements under Article 284(3) CCP, the party is notified about the irregularities within a seven-day term. According to Article 286(3) CCP, the appeal is reverted: (a) if it is lodged after the term for appeal expired; (b) if the irregularities are not cured within due time; the decision of the intermediate appellate court is not appealable under Article 280(2) CCP. According to Article 285(2) CCP, if the appeal is regular the appellate court sends to the other party a copy together with the enclosures. The other party is entitled to give a written reply within a one-month preclusion term after receiving it. Afterwards, the case together with the appeal and the reply are sent to the SCC. Articles 259(2)–(4) and 284 CCP are applicable concerning the written reply. It is filed with the SCC through the appellate court that has rendered the decision appealed. The appellant must state his/her objections to the decision in the written reply.

According to Article 287(2) CCP a statement of cross-appeal may be filed within the term for submitting the reply. The statement of cross-appeal is the statement of appeal of the opposing party against the part of the decision which is unfavourable to it and the party has not appealed it within the one-month preclusive term following the service of the decision. It is assumed that the said party would not appeal and would agree with the decision if the opposing party had not appealed the other part of the said decision. According to Article 287(4) CCP the statement of cassation cross-appeal is not examined if the statement of cassation appeal is not examined.

If the initial statement of appeal is regular, the statement of cross-appeal, too, the appellate court sends the exchanged papers and the case to the SCC. The stand of the appellate court does not bind the SCC. Prior to instituting a case, the SCC repeats the verification whether the appeal is admissible regarding it being lodged in due time, its meeting the requirements for content and enclosures and whether the decision is subject to a cassation appeal viewing the limits set in Article 280(2) CCP.

236. According to Article 289, sentence I CCP, until the first day of the month the SCC announces in the SG the dates of sessions and the cases to be considered during the month. Article 289, sentence II CCP provides that if the circumstances require a change in what was announced, the parties are notified. The circumstances 'can generally be defined as *reasons that bring about a postponement of the consideration of the case* until the session *announced in the SG'* (ID No. 2-2004-GMCC).

237. According to Article 290 CCP, the cassation appeal against the intermediate appellate decision is considered on the merits regarding the grounds provided for in Article 281 CCP by a panel of three judges of the SCC, in an open session with subpoenaing the parties. It is inadmissible to consider again the matter of the admissibility of the cassation appeal regarding the grounds specified in Article 280(1) CCP. The matter is settled once and ultimately with the ruling under Article 288 CCP. In the cassation instance the parties conduct oral pleadings regarding the cassation appeal and the reply to it on the merits of the cassation proceedings, namely the existence of the grounds for cassation foreseen in Article 281 CCP. In practice, these pleadings are often replaced by or supplemented with the presentation of written defence under Article 149(3) of the CCP.

238. According to Article 293(4) when the appealed decision is invalid or inadmissible, the rules in Article 270 CCP apply (*see* paragraph 220). According to Article 290(2) CCP, the SCC verifies only the regularity of the appealed decision of intermediate appellate court with regard only to the grounds brought in the statement of appeal.

239. If the SCC establishes that the appealed intermediate decision is valid, admissible and proper, it preserves its force. The decision itself comes into force at the time of its rendering, since it is not subject to appeal (Article 296, item 1 CCP). However, this decision is also a precondition for the appealed intermediate appellate decision to enter into force (Article 296, item 3 CCP) and for res judicata to give rise to (regardless of the type of the intermediate appellate decision, an ascertainment or a sentencing or a constitutive decision (*see* paragraph 188)), and for the constitutive effect of the decision (of course, this applies if the decision is constitutive (*see* paragraph 195). As far as the enforceability of sentencing intermediate appellate decisions is concerned, the amendment to Article 404 CCP provides that it occurs at the time of their rendering and as for enforceability, the decision of the SCC has a stabilizing effect.[120]

120. According to Art. 282(1) CCP, the cassation appeal against sentencing decisions does not suspend the execution. According to Art. 282(2) CCP, the appellant is entitled to seek suspension of the execution of the decision. In this case, he/she is obligated to submit due security. The amount of security is determined for a) decisions on money receivables – the adjudged amount; b) regarding

240. The decision is reversed when it is erroneous, when the substantive law is breached or significant violations from the court procedure rules have been committed or when the decision is groundless (Article 293(2) CCP). The court returns the case for a new examination by another panel of the intermediate appellate court only if any procedural actions should be repeated or new such actions should be performed (Article 293(3) CCP). The court to which the case was referred considers it in accordance with the general procedure, the proceedings starting from *the unlawful action that formed the grounds for the cassation of the decision* (Article 294(1), sentence I CCP). Consequently, the scope of the new consideration of the case can be different depending on the significant violation from the court procedure rules. The instructions of the SCC regarding the interpretation and application of the law are obligatory for the court to which the case is referred (Article 294(1), sentence II CCP). According to Article 295(1), sentence I CCP, when *the prerequisites under* Article *280(1) CCP exist*, the second decision of the intermediate appellate instance can be appealed over violations committed upon the reconsideration of the case. The access to the cassation appellate procedure on the merits of the appeal when appealing the second decision of the intermediate appellate court is under the same conditions as those of the first cassation appeal, i.e., under the same strict evaluation for admissibility (Article 280(1) and (2) CCP). The appeal against a decision rendered a second time is considered by another panel of three judges of the SCC and this panel decides on the merits regardless of the grounds for reversal (Article 295(1), sentence II CCP).

§4. Extraordinary Appeals

241. The reversal under Articles 303–309 CCP is *the only* extraordinary remedy against *defective decisions that have taken effect.*[121] Reversal is defined as *independent proceedings* for out-of-instance control and reversal of court decisions that have taken effect, where the decisions are *improper* ones due to any of the reasons specified in Article 303(1) CCP. It should be underlined that reversal does not constitute a stage in adversary proceedings. *In the course of assessing the grounds for the reversal claim, the only thing the SCC examines is whether the grounds for reversal specified in the claim are present and whether they are provided for in the law.* The SCC does not assess whether the reviewed case under the order for reversals is in actuality correct or not (with the exception of Article 303, item 4 in connection with Article 234(4) CCP, *see* paragraph 247 and 255).

242. The following must be indicated regarding the entered into force judgments subject to reversal:

proprietary rights over chattels – the amount of the claim appealed, (*see* ID No. 8–2012–GMCC of the SCC). According to Art. 282(3) CCP, in all other cases the amount of security is determined by the court.

121. *See* V. Popova, *Civil Procedure. Bulgaria.* first ed., para. 273.

(a) Both in doctrine and practice there is a well-established view, according to which the reversal under Article 303 CCP is a way of out-of-instance control only in respect of *those decisions in which the legal dispute between the parties has been determined through the force of* res judicata. Unlike Article 280(3), item 1 CCP (*see* paragraph 115), the legislator has not specified any limitations depending on the amount of the claim or the subject matter of the case for reversal under Article 303 CCP. The law *does not differentiate* between first-instance decisions, intermediate appellate ones and cassation ones, unless some of the grounds under Article 303(1) CCP exist. *Those decisions of the first-instance court and those of* the intermediate appellate decisions which have taken effect and the decisions of the SCC that have been rendered in cassation proceedings are also subject to reversal (Article 307(2), sentence II CCP).
(b) In practice of the SCC it is assumed that the reversal of inadmissible decisions that have taken effect is inadmissible. In my opinion the admissibility of the defence against an inadmissible decision should not be made absolute.[122] The rejection used to have its stable support under the CCP, repealed, prior to 1997, when the effective inadmissible decisions were subject to invalidation by a review under the rules of supervision which does not exist under the CCP, current. The inadmissible decision that has taken effect has determined the substantive law dispute through the force of res judicata. An inadmissible decision cannot have the defects under: (a) Article 303(1), item 1 CCP; (b) the first hypothesis of Article 303(1), item 2 CCP; (c) Article 303(1), item 3 CCP. The decision can have the defects under: (a) the second hypothesis of Article 303(1), item 2 CCP (*see* paragraph 245); (b) Article 303(1), item 5 CCP (*see* paragraph 248); (c) Article 303(1), item 6 CCP (*see* paragraph 249); Article 303(1), item 7 CCP (*see* paragraph 250) in the same way as the wrongful decision. Besides, it should be borne in mind that Article 303(1) CCP uses the term 'a decision that has taken effect' and not the explicit term 'an improper decision'. The emphasis is put upon two issues: the grounds and the nature of the decision to have taken effect. The existence of the grounds foreseen in Article 303(1) CCP is relevant to the reversal of the decision. The necessary and sufficient condition for reversal of an effective decision is to establish the existence of such grounds. The case will be returned to the instance where the grounds have realized and where there is no obstacle for the defendant to realize his/her defence against the admissibility of the proceedings. There is no reason for refusing the reversal of an inadmissible decision that has taken effect, provided that all the grounds for reversal are present. It is irrelevant to the reversal of a decision whether it is improper or inadmissible. SCC will consider only the matter whether the grounds foreseen in Article 303(1) CCP exist.
(c) No reversal of a decision rendering divorce, marriage annulment or marriage is recognized as non-existent (Article 303(2) CCP is admissible. According to Article 303(3) CCP, no revocation of an enforceable decision can be demanded for a reason for which a cancellation could be sought or is required under Article

122. *See* V. Popova. *Problemat za otmjjanta na vlezli v sila nedopustimi sadebni reshenija (Problems concerning the reversal of inadmissible court decisions).* First electronic law issue Apis-Time, http: //online.apis.bg.

240(1) CCP, or could have been brought or a claim under Article 240(2) CCP (*see* paragraph 204). ID No. 7-2014 of 31 July 2017 of the SCC on Com.C. No. 7/2014 it was accepted that the decisions of the district court pronounced on an appeal against the actions of the bailiff (item 3), the enforced judgments in the controversial court administration (item 4), the judgments barring the further development of the case, with the exception of the termination of the case due to the waiver of the claim (item 6) are not subject to reversal in accordance with the provisions of Chapter 24 CCP.

The reversal of *security instruments* is *inadmissible*. These instruments are challenged through the adversary procedure (Articles. 537 and 604 CCP).

243. Article 303(1) CCP contains an *exhaustive* enumeration of grounds for cassation what is an *essential feature* of the extraordinary nature of the reversal of decisions that have taken effect. The court is not bound by the qualification the interested party has given to the grounds for reversal. It is bound only by the circumstances stated in the claim substantiating the said grounds (item 13 of Decree No. 2-1977 of the Plenum of the SC).

244. According to Article 231(1), item 1 CCP, the interested party is entitled to seek a reversal of a decision which has taken effect if either *new circumstances*[123] *or new written evidence that is essential to the case are discovered, and these circumstances and evidence could not have been known to the party:*

(a) *The newly discovered circumstances* must be *relevant in law or in evidence in respect of the case*. They must have occurred prior to the termination of the court trial (prior to the moment until which they could have been stated by the party having in mind the preclusions under Articles 133, 147, item 1, 260, item 5 and Article 266(2), item 1 CCP). In spite of not being known to the party, they are precluded by the force of res judicata, and owing thereto no new claim can be brought in on the basis thereof. The reversal under Article 303(1), item 1 CCP provides the possibility of a new consideration of the case, taking account of the newly discovered circumstances. The newly discovered circumstances are not precluded by the force of res judicata. A new claim can be brought in on the basis thereof (arg. Article 439(2) CCP) and a decision that has taken effect cannot be reversed. It is necessary that the alleged newly discovered circumstance *could not have become known to the party in the course of hearing the case in spite of the party's activeness in collecting the evidence*. It is not enough for the circumstances to be newly discovered. The party has to support its allegations with *written evidence*. In general, this evidence is also newly discovered after the termination of the court trial (Having in mind the preclusions under Article 133 CCP, Article 147, item 1 CCP Article 260, item 5 CCP and Article 266(2), item 1 CCP). The written evidence might be newly created, for example a written out-of-court admission of the opposing party.

123. The Bulgarian legislator often uses the term 'circumstances' as a synonym of 'facts'.

(b) The second hypothesis concerns newly discovered or newly created evidence concerning circumstances alleged by the party in the course of hearing the case, the party being unable to prove them at that time (item 3 of Decree No. 2/1977 of the Plenum of the SC, which is also valid under the CCP, current. Though, the preclusions established in Article 133 CCP, Article 147, item 1 CCP Article 260, item 5 CCP and Article 266(2), item 1 CCP). New written evidence of major importance for the case forms grounds for the reversal of the decision if the said evidence could not have been known to the party although the latter has acted with reasonable care for the proper conduct of the case; also the evidence which the party was aware of in the course of proceedings, however, in spite of its acting with reasonable care for the proper conduct of the case, it was unable to procure.

245. According to Article 303(1), item 2 CCP, reversal can be sought in those cases where, in accordance with the due court procedure, any of the following has been established: untruthfulness of the testimony of the witnesses, or the conclusions of the experts that the decision is based on, or a crime committed by a party, or a representative thereof, or a member of the panel of judges or a server, this crime being related to the determination of the case:

(a) The crime must have been established in accordance with the due court procedure, i.e., through a judgment that has taken effect and has been rendered in a criminal case; and where the criminal proceedings cannot be commenced or have been terminated on the grounds under Article 24(1), items 2–5 CPC, or where the criminal proceedings have been suspended for any of the reasons under Article 25, item 2, or Article 26 CPC through a decision that has taken effect and has been rendered on the claim under Article 124(5) CCP (*see* paragraph 130).
(b) The decision has to be grounded on the untruthful testimony of the witnesses, or the wrongful conclusion of the expert, respectively.

Where the crime has been committed by a judge (or by a member of the panel of judges, respectively), who is considering the case, or by a party to the case, the law requires that it be committed in relation to the case. It is indispensable and sufficient to establish that the crime *has been committed in relation to the case*. It is not necessary to prove that the commitment of the crime has affected the outcome of the case.

246. According to Article 303(1), item 3 CCP, the interested party is entitled to seek a reversal in those cases where the decision is grounded either on a document which, in accordance with the due court procedure, has been found forged *or* on a decree of the court or another State institution which has subsequently been reversed:

(1) It was adopted by ID No. 5-2012 that a claim for the authenticity of a document under Article 124(4) sentence I CCP is inadmissible, if the claimant has

a legal interest in establishing the falsity of the document and using the decision on the said claim as grounds for its reversal of the decision under Article 303(1), item 2 CCP where the document was presented but the party has missed the deadline for establishing its forgery set forth in Article 193 CCP. It was also adopted that the due procedure in the sense of Article 303(1), item 2 CCP should be only a sentence for documentation crime or it being established by a civil court, when the prosecution cannot be instituted or terminated on grounds provided for in the cited legal norm.

(2) The second hypothesis is present in those cases where the decision is grounded on a decree of the court or another State institution and has subsequently been reversed:

(a) What is meant under decree is any court act that has taken effect regardless of it being a decree on a civil, administrative or criminal case, which has subsequently been reversed according to the procedure of the special means of reversal. The reason for the grounds for the reversal of a decision in those cases is the binding effect of the force of res judicata of the court decision on a prejudicial matter or the binding effect (Article 297 CCP); an effective sentence rendered on a criminal case (Article 300 CCP in connection with Article 413 CPC); the binding effect of the force of res judicata of the administrative act (Article 302 CCP).

In the ID No. 7-2014 of 31 July 2017-GMCC and the Com.C. of the SCC on Com.

C. No. 7/2014, it was considered that a subsequent interpretative decision, which gave a mandatory interpretation of a law applicable to the case in a way different from that adopted in the judgment, does not justify the annulment of an enforceable judgment. This view can hardly be shared, especially in combination with the one adopted in ID No. 8-2013 of 7 May 2014-GMCC and the Com.C. of the SCC on com.c. No. 8/2013, according to which, when an interpretative case before the SCC is instituted, the proceedings in pending cases may be suspended only at the cassation instance on the basis of Article 292 CCP and not at the appellate and the first instance (*see* paragraph 269). On the grounds of Article 130(A) CSA, however, IDs are mandatory for the courts.

(b) Article 303(1), item 3 CCP foresees that grounds for the reversal of an effective decision is it being based upon a decree by a court or by another government institution which has subsequently been reversed. Article 303(1), item 3 CCP has the same content as Article 231(1), item 'c' CCP which was not amended after the adoption of the Constitution in 1991. Viewing the separation of powers and the new normative realities phrase the 'decree by another government institution' in the regulation quoted should be understood an individual administrative act in the sense of Article 21 APA, or a general administrative act in the sense of Article 65

APA issued by an administrative authority or another authority or organization empowered to do so by a law.[124] The grounds for the reversal of an effective decision due to the reversal of an effective administrative act is connected with the obligation of the court to observe compulsoriness of the administrative act that has taken effect (Article 17(2) CCP). The effective administrative act should be reversed according to Articles 99–106 APC.

(c) What is meant in the law here is that the decision of the court, the effective administrative act, respectively (Article 21 APC), or the general administrative act (Article 65 APC), is reversed retroactively. Where the law establishes a new legal situation, which is effective for the future, the reversal is inadmissible.[125]

The act issued by the respective administrative body should not be a normative one. Even where a normative act has been given retroactive effect, it establishes a new legal situation and a new claim can be grounded thereupon, however, no reversal under Article 303(1), item '3' CCP can be sought of an act which has been issued prior to it being rendered.[126]

In relation to the strong principle of disposition in adversary proceedings it has been assumed in ID No. 1-2000-GMCC of the SCC, item 13 that where the appellant has appealed to the intermediate appellate instance only against the principal claim and not against the conditioned one, the court is not entitled to reverse the first-instance decision's part which refers to the conditioned claim. Besides, due to the interrelation between the two decisions and the contradiction between them, the party may seek remedy in accordance with the procedure for reversal of an effective decision on the conditioned claim on the grounds of Article 303(1), item 3 CCP. However, it was adopted in item 5 of ID No. 5-2014 of 31 July 2017-GMCC and the Com.C. of the SCC on com.c. 7/2014 that in this hypothesis the grounds are in item 4 (*see* paragraph 247). Item 13 of ID No. 1-2000-GMCC of the SCC is not repealed, which leads to the prerequisites for different practices of certain SCC panels.

247. According to Article 303(1), item 4 CCP, a reversal of a decision can be sought in those cases where another decision has been rendered prior to the said one, *the first decision having taken effect* and the second one being *contrary* to the first one, both decisions being rendered between *the same parties*, on *the same claim* and on *the same grounds*.

---

124. The reversal of an administrative act in the sense of Art. 75 APA is not grounds under Art. 303(1), item 3 CCP for the reversal of an effective decision. According to Art. 195(1) APA the reversal of an administrative act is for the future since it is considered reversed as from the day of decision's taking effect.
125. *See* item 6 of Decree No. 2–77 of the Plenum of the SC, which is still valid under the CCP, current.
126. *See* item 5 of Decree No. 2–77 of the Plenum of the SC, which is still valid under the CCP, current; *see also* the practice under the CCP, current, (Decision No. 365 of 3 May 2009 on c. c. No. 1022/2009, III-C.Ch. of the SCC; Ruling No. 417 of 25 Jun. 2009 on com. c. No. 339/2009, II-Com. Ch. of the SCC).

(a) This hypothesis violates the prohibition under Article 299(1) CCP on determining anew the dispute in those cases where it has already been determined by the force of res judicata, or under Article 126 CCP, respectively, according to which if there are two pending cases between the same parties (either in the same court or in different courts) and on the same grounds and on the same claim, the latter of the cases is suspended by the court ex officio. Strictly viewed, the second decision in this hypothesis is inadmissible, because of the violation of the absolute procedural prerequisites. However, in view of procedural economy, the legislator has not provided for invalidation of the later decision, but has provided for the reversal of the wrongful decision instead (Article 307(4) CCP).
The other element of the set of facts under Article 303(1), item 4 CCP is that the decisions should be *contradictory*. If the decisions are not contradictory ones, there is no way of eliminating the presence of two decisions that have taken effect. There are two possible hypotheses: both decisions are proper ones; both decisions are improper ones. There are no such problems where the decisions are establishment ones, i.e., the same establishment claim has been upheld, or the decisions have been constitutive ones with retroactive effect. However, where the decisions have been sentencing ones, there are actually two executive grounds, and, therefore, two writs of execution might be issued on the same pretence. Where the decisions are constitutive ones with effect for the future, one and the same judicial change will be rendered, however, the time it will take effect will be different for the two cases, what will cause uncertainty in the civil law relationships. There will also be a problem where the two decisions are improper ones, but are the same. According to the legal norms that are operative in our country now, these two decisions could be challenged if they are based on any of the grounds for reversal provided for in Article 303(1) CCP.
(b) In spite of putting the stress on the identity of the cases, the term of objective identity has been extended by assuming that it is enough for the *subject matter of one of the cases to be implicitly included in the subject matter of the other one* (e.g., where two effective decisions have been rendered on two cases involving the same parties, one of these decisions repudiating the joint ownership, and the other decision acknowledging the right to a*pro indiviso*; one of the decisions admitting the partition of a matrimonial tenancy in equal shares, and the other decision acknowledging the greater share of one of the spouses; one of the decisions acknowledging one of the co-partitioners as being the exclusive owner of the real estate, and the other decision admitting the partition of the said real estate).

It was assumed in Decree No. 2-77 of the Plenum of the SC, CDID of the SC. 'The term "the same parties" denotes not only those persons on behalf of which and against which the proceedings are held specifies, i.e., the appellant and the appellee) but also all those for which the decision has the force of res judicata. This ensues from the principle that a dispute determined through an effective decision cannot be determined anew. The term "the same parties" denotes the appellant and the appellee, the joint parties in the proceedings, the intervening third parties and the third parties that have joined, the heirs and legal successors to the original parties, and the acquirers of the disputed right. Besides, in view of the same considerations, if there are two cases, the admission of a reversal does not depend on whether any parties that are joint ones have participated, together with the appellant and the appellee, in one of the cases.'

In view of the principle of disposition in item 16 of the ID No. 1-2000-GMCC of the SCC (*see* paragraph 209) it is assumed that where the appeal has not been brought in against all the formal joint parties and the intermediate appellate court reverses the first-instance decision in respect of the appellee and renders an opposite decision, the court is not entitled to do the same in respect of a formal joint party that the appeal has not been brought in against. Therefore, it has been assumed that in this case, if a contradiction arises between the intermediate appellate decision and the first-instance decision in connection with the facts that are common for all the joint parties, it is in accordance with the procedure for reversal of effective decisions that remedy can be sought.

It was accepted in item 5 of the ID No. 7-2014 of 31.07.2017 GMCC and the Com.C. of the SCC on com.c. 7/2014 that, the identity in the subject of the enforced court decisions, as grounds for annulment of an incorrect decision in the sense of Article 303(1) item 4 CCP exists not only in the case of full objective and subjective identity with respect to the subject matter and the parties to the cases but also where different legal issues are addressed in the subject matter of the case in which the res judicata is formed, when the underlying claim and solutions in the controversial dispute contradict.

248. According to Article 303(1), item 5 CCP the interested party is entitled to seek reversal of a decision that has taken effect if the said party, in consequence of a breach of the respective rules, has been deprived from the opportunity to participate in the case or has not been duly represented or was unable to appear in court either personally or through an attorney, this failure to appear being due to an obstacle which the party was unable to remove. The decision has to be unfavourable for the party making the claim for its reversal, and the defect should affect the said party and not the opposing one, the latter being the party that the decision is favourable for:

(1) The first hypothesis under Article 303(1), item 5 CCP is present when the party, in consequence of a *breach of procedural rules has been deprived of the opportunity to participate in the proceedings.* Unlike in the hypothesis under Article 304 CCP (*see* paragraph 255) in the hypothesis under Article 303(1), item 5 CCP the party has been constituted as a party to the case, however, because of procedural breaches committed by the court, it has been deprived of the opportunity to participate in the case (e.g., it has not been duly subpoenaed). In the SCC practice, it was accepted that this ground was applicable only when the violation was admitted in the appellate instance because if admitted at first instance, the party could refer to it and appeal the decision before the appellate court.

(2) The second hypothesis under Article 303(1), item 5 CCP is present in those cases where the party *has not been duly represented* (for instance, the representative did not dispose of the power of representation as he/she did not have the power of attorney in the case, or has gone beyond the limits of the power of representation granted to him/her; or does not belong to the persons specified in Article 32 CCP, which are entitled to be representatives under a power of attorney; or the legal entity was not represented by the respective legal representative; or a juvenile has not performed the actions personally with the consent of his/her parent and the parent has appeared in person as a legal representative; a minor has been represented by another person and not by his/her parent; a person under interdiction has not been represented by his/her custodian, etc.).

(3) The third hypothesis under Article 303(1), item 5 CCP is present in those cases where *the party was unable to appear due to an obstacle which the party was unable to overcome.*

249. According to Article 303(1), item '6' CCP in the case of breaching the respective rules the party was not represented by a person under Article 29 CCP. The norm cited includes three hypothesizes: (1) the defendant was subpoenaed by SG and had a special representative appointed, although it had a registered permanent or current address; (2) the defendant did not have a registered permanent or current address, but had not been subpoenaed by SG; (3) the defendant did not have a registered permanent or current address, was not subpoenaed by the SG and had not had a special representative appointed under Article 29 CCP; was summoned by the order of Article 47(1) CCP (*see* paragraph 27) the party did not appear in the court to receive the papers, but the court did not appoint a special representative (Article 47(6) CCP in connection with Article 47(3) CCP).

250. According to Article 303(1), item 7 a reversal can be sought where a decision of the ECHRP has found a violation of the European Convention on Human Rights and Basic Freedoms Protection or of its Protocols and the new considering of the case is necessary to cure the consequences of the violation. The effective decision of the ECHRP establishing a violation under the European Convention on Human Rights *on the specific case*. The decision of the ECHRP sentencing the Bulgarian State to pay an indemnity to the party because of its case not having been considered within a reasonable term may not constitute grounds for reversal, although Article 6 of the Convention has been violated.

251. Article 303(1) CCP provides that a claim for reversal can be submitted by the interested party. A person that has not been constituted as a party to a certain case does not have the legitimization to institute proceedings for reversal on the grounds specified in Article 303(1) CCP. This is a common case as the decision rendered in the said proceedings may not be opposed thereto (Article 298(1) CCP). Where a person having an assured right to claim regarding the disputed right has not been constituted as a party to the proceedings and, in spite thereof, is bound by the force of res judicata, he/she is entitled to demand reversal on the grounds of Article 304 CCP.

In order for the party to be legitimized to seek reversal, that party should have been affected by a defect provided for in Article 303(1) CCP and the decision should be unfavourable thereto. The party may not invoke a defect which concerns the opposing party to which the decision has been a favourable one. Even though the grounds under Article 303(1) CCP affecting the party might be present, the party has no legal interest in the reversal if the effective decision is favourable thereto.

It is assumed that reversal can be sought by any party regardless to whether the party is a principal party or an accessory one (a co-party or a controlling one). In the cases of indispensable joint parties it is not necessary for the claim to have been filed by all the joint parties – by analogy with Article 264 CCP the other joint parties may get involved later. If the decision is reversed with respect to one of the joint parties, it has to be reversed with respect to the others as well.

252. According to Article 305(1) CCP, the reversal claim can be brought in within a term of three months following the day on which (1) the claimant learnt of the intervening circumstances, or from the day whereon the petitioner could procure the new written evidence: in the cases referred to in Article 303(1), item 1 CCP; (2) of entry into effect of the decision or of learning of the sentence, but not later than one year after the entry into effect of the said sentence: in the cases referred to in Article 303(1), item 2 CCP; (3) of learning of the act of reversal, but not later than one year after the entry into effect of the said act: in the cases referred to Article 303(1), item 3 CCP; (4) of entry into effect of the last judgment: in the cases referred to in Article 303(1), item 4 CCP; (5) of learning of the judgment: in the cases referred to in Article 303(1), items 5 and 6 CCP and Article 304 CCP. According to Article 305(2) CCP, in the cases under Article 303(1), item 7 CCP the reversal petition is brought in within a term of six months following the day on which the decision of the ECHRP has become final. The terms provided for in Article 306(1) CCP are preclusive ones and the court sees ex officio to their being observed.

253. According to Article 306(1) CCP the reversal claim should comply with the requirements specified in Articles 260 and 261 CCP (*see* paragraph 212) and contain a precise and motivated description of the grounds for reversal. Where the reversal claim fails to comply with these requirements, a notification thereof is sent and the irregularities should be eliminated within a one-week term (*see also* ID No. 7-2014 of 31.07.2017-GMCC and the Com.C. of the SCC on com.c. 7/2014). According to Article 306(2) CCP (new – SG, No. 64/1999) if the irregularities of the reversal claim are not eliminated within the said term, it is the provisions of Article 286 CCP that shall become applicable (*see* paragraph 235). The SCC is bound by the grounds for reversal specified in the reversal claim. As the legal qualification is not binding on the court, in item 13 of Decree No. 2-77 of the Plenum of the SC it is assumed that if the circumstances stated by the claimant in support of his/her reversal claim do not come within the scope of the grounds he/she has formulated under Article 303(1) CCP the claim, instead of being disallowed, is upheld on the basis of the actual grounds which have to be stated by the claimant after their being established. It was adopted in item 10 of ID No. 7-2014 of 31.07.2017 GMCC and the Com.C. of the SCC on com.c. 7/2014 that an application lacking particular and reliable allegations for the existence of any grounds in the sense of Articles. 303(1) and 304(1) CCP is inadmissible. The SCC pronounces with a ruling leaving it with no consideration.

According to Article 306(3) CCP, the claim is filed with the first-instance court. The claim has a copy enclosed thereto which is delivered to the opposing party. It is entitled to reply within a seven-day term following the receipt of the copy.

254. The SCC pronounces on the admissibility of the claim for reversal sitting in camera (Article 307(1) CCP). It is considered by the SCC in an open session within which the parties are heard and the requisite evidence is taken. Where a reversal of a decision of the SCC is sought, the claim is examined by another three-judge panel of the SCC. According to Article 307(3) CCP, where the claim is found to be a well-grounded one, the SCC *reverses* the decision either in whole or in part and *renders the case back for being reconsidered by the due court in another panel of judges, also specifying where from the new consideration of the case should begin.* According to Article 308 CCP, it is the general rules that apply in the further consideration of the case the decision upon which has been reversed. According to Article 307(4) CCP, in the cases under Article 303(1), item 4 CCP, the SCC reverses the improper decisions (*see* paragraph 247).

255. According to Article 304 CCP, the reversal of the decision within the term set forth in Article 232 can also be sought by any *person if the decision is effective thereto, although the said person might not have been a party to the case* (Article 216(2) CCP). The three months term begins on the day the decision became known (Article 305(1), item 5 CCP):

(a) Reversal under Article 304 CCP can also be sought by a *person that has not been a party to the case, provided that the rendered decision is effective thereto and is unfavourable for him.* The said provision contains *a renvoi* to Article 216(2) CCP, which shows that the reversal under Article 304 CCP refers to the indispensable joint parties. Hence, no reversal can be sought of an effective decision by a third person that is not in the position of an indispensable joint party of a party to the case terminated by the decision. DPSC No. 2/1977 established the understanding that the reversal under Article 304 CCP can be sought only by a person having the right of participating in the case, this right being assured in law, and having been constituted as a party to the case, i.e., in the case of indispensable joinder. In ID No. 7-2014 of 31.07.2017-GMCC and the Com.C. of the SCC on com.c. 7/2014 without a change in the legislation and without convincing arguments, a deviation from these rules was allowed. It was assumed that, regarding a claim by a spouse on property or property acquired under a matrimonial property regime, the spouses are facultative indispensable joinders and not dispensable joinders, but the spouse who has not been constituted as a party to the proceedings has the right to seek annulment of the enforceable judgment of the court on the grounds of Article 304 CCP. The view that in this hypothesis there is a facultative indispensable joinder, combined with the possibility of reversal under Article 304 CCP can hardly be shared, but on the grounds of Article 130(2) CSA, it is mandatory for the courts.

In item 2 of the ID No. 1-2000-GMCC of the SCC it has been assumed that the intermediate appellate court is obligated ex officio to constitute as a party to the intermediate appellate proceedings those indispensable joint parties of the appellant which have been constituted in the first-instance proceedings. In items 2 and 16 of the said ID it has also been assumed that where the appellee has its indispensable joint parties, in view of the requirements regarding the regularity of the appeal, the appellant has to bring it in with a number of copies, this number being equal to the number of the indispensable joint parties. Therefore, the persons that have been indispensable joint parties in the first-instance proceedings, have to be necessarily constituted as parties to the intermediate appellate proceedings. Owing thereto, if the intermediate appellate court has failed to observe this requirement, the indispensable joint party which has not been constituted in the intermediate appellate instance is entitled to seek reversal of the effective decision on the grounds of Article 304 CCP, which corresponds to Article 233(2) CCP, repealed, provided that he/she is interested therein, i.e., if the decision affects him/her.

(b) The grounds for reversal under Article 304 CCP consist only in the failure to constitute a third person as a party to the case, the said person being legitimized to participate in the case as a party, and having an assured right to participate in the case as a party, this right ensuing either from the law or from the legal relationship. In order for the said grounds for reversal to be proved, it is neither necessary, nor admissible to establish whether the decision has been a proper one or not. It was accepted in ID No. 7-2014 of 31.07.2017-GMCC and the Com.C. of the SCC on com.c. 7/2014 that, where, regarding a claim for property brought by the spouse or for property acquired under the matrimonial property regime, one spouse is not constituted in the case, that is sufficient for seeking the annulment of the SCC decision. According to Article 304 CCP, if the claim of the other spouse is rejected, respectively the claim against him is upheld, although the spouses are facultative indispensable joinder and that spouse has no guaranteed right to participate in the process as a party (*see* section 'A' above).

(c) Where the reversal claim under Article 304 CCP is upheld, the case has to be referred back to the first-instance court, because the third person has the right to participate in the hearings of the case in all instances, and here the proceedings start from the very beginning. Only in the hypothesis in which the indispensable joint party has been constituted in the first-instance proceedings, however, in breach of items 2 and 16 of the ID No. 1-2000-GMCC of the SCC, the intermediate appellate court has not constituted the said party in the intermediate appellate proceedings the case is returned thereto.

256. The filing of a reversal claim does not suspend the execution of the decision. However, upon the request of the party, the court may suspend the execution under the terms specified in Article 282(2–6) CCP (*see* paragraph 396) (Article 309(1) CCP). If the decision is reversed, the execution thereof is suspended. Where the new decision is different from the previous one, it is the provision of Article 245(3) CCP (Article 309(2) CCP) that applies.

Part V. Incidents

Chapter 1. Special Cases in the Development and Completion of General Adversary Proceedings

§1. Withdrawal of the Claim

257. The claimant is allowed to withdraw his/her claim. The proceedings have to be terminated. According to Article 232, sentence I CCP, *prior to the closure of the first court session in the case the claimant is allowed to withdraw his/her claim without the consent of the defendant.* If the claim is withdrawn *after that time, the defendant's consent is required* in order for the proceedings to be terminated. On the grounds of Article 232, sentence II CCP, if the proceedings are terminated due to the withdrawal of the claim, *the claimant preserves his/her legal possibility of bringing the same claim against the defendant.* Hence, he/she has the rightful legal interest in seeking the consideration and determination of the dispute *res* judicata, Article 34(3) CCP provides that the procedural representative, should have *an explicit power of attorney* in order to withdraw the claim. According to Article 232 CCP, if the claimant brings in the same claim again, he/she is entitled to use the collected evidence in the new case, *though only under the condition that an obstacle hard to overcome bars collecting the evidence once more. When the defendant is represented by a procedural representative, the latter should have an explicit power of attorney for defendant's consent on withdrawing the claim (*Article *34(3) CCP).*

§2. Waiver of the Claim

258. What is typical of the waiver of a claim in Bulgarian law (Article 233 CCP), is that the court does not render a decision disallowing the claim as groundless, and instead renders a ruling with which it terminates the proceedings, because it is de-seized by the claimant by his/her waiver of the claim. The reasons and motives for the waiver of the claim are irrelevant to the termination of the case. According to Article 233, sentence II CCP, where the claimant has made a waiver of the claim, he/she is not entitled to bring in the same claim again. Hence, no consent is required on the part of the defendant for the termination of proceedings. Where the waiver is made by the claimant's procedural representative, he/she should have an explicit power of attorney (Article 34(3) CCP).

259. The waiver of a claim can be made at any time in the course of proceedings while they are pending, including the time they are pending before the intermediate appellate instance or the cassation instance. According to Article 233, sentence III CCP, it is made before the intermediate appellate instance or the cassation instance the appealed decision is invalidated. Where the claim is waived in the course of cassation proceedings, the SCC has to invalidate both the intermediate appellate decision forming the subject matter of the cassation appeal and the first-instance decision.

260. Whether or not *res judicata*-effect is formed in the cases of waiver of a claim is a matter of dispute in literature. There is an opinion according to which the law gives *res judicata* to the waiver of a claim, concerning the denial of the right alleged by the claimant or the assertion of the right which the claimant denied by the claim that is brought.[127] According to the opposite opinion,[128] no *res judicata* effect is formed in the cases of waiver of a claim. The only consequence is that it is impossible for the claimant to seize the court with the same claim. According to this view, the waiver of a claim does not form a ground for the extinguishment of the disputed right (where it really exists), and the defendant is the bearer of the obligation. The defendant can fulfil his/her obligation to the claimant voluntarily. However, the claimant cannot seek the enforcement, because it has turned into a natural obligation.

The second understanding equates in terms of consequences the waiver of a claim with the prescription limitation. But those are completely different. The extinguishing limitation gives rise to defendant's substantive legal objection to refuse to fulfil. The exercising of this subjective right of his/hers does not lead to extinguishing the right to claim but to extinguishing the right to enforcement. Unlike the waiver of a claim the extinguishing limitation suggests the existence of an executable receivable. Therefore, when the objection to extinguishing limitation is upheld, the condemnation claim is disallowed on the merits (*see* paragraph 123). This decision ascertains the existence of the receivable and the extinguishing of the right for enforced remedy of the said receivable.

The waiver of a claim is a waiver of the procedural right to request the legal dispute to be considered and settled by res judicata. The consequence is explicitly pointed in Article 233 CCP – impossibility to bring in the same claim. It contains one of the elements of res judicata effect – the non-redeterminability of the same legal dispute, brought in by the same claim. The article establishes the inadmissibility of bringing the same claim – *between the same parties, on the same substantive legal right, on the same grounds with the same request and for the same period of the existence of the said right.* For that reason, the waiver of a claim may lead indirectly to consequences characteristic of waving a substantive legal right, only if it has really existed. However, the matter is about the impossibility of bringing the same claim on the same right for the same period of time. That is why I assume that

127. *See* J. Stalev, A. Mingova, V. Popova, O. Stamboliev, R. Ivanova, *Balgarsko ...* , *supra*, pp. 451–457 (the matters regarding withdrawal and waiver of a claim are worked out under the co-authorship of J. Stalev and A. Mingova).

128. *See* A. Mingova, *Otkazat ...* , pp. 223–263.

Article 233, sentence II, CCP is not an obstacle the claimant to the case that was terminated upon waiver of the claim, in another case on defendant's (to the first case) claim against him/her to bring an objection to set-off with his/her receivable, because of which he/she has waived the claim, alleging that the said receivable existed before the waiver of the claim and a set-off was performed before the waiver of the claim. That is due to the specifics of the objective limits of res judicata effect of the decision rendered on an objection for set-off which is determined by the particulars of the very set-off (*see* paragraph 369) as well as because the there is no need to examine the reasons of the waiver.

§3. Withdrawal and Waiver of an Intermediate Appeal and a Cassation Appeal

261. According to Article 264(1) CCP, the party is entitled to waive the appeal, either in full or in part, at any time during the proceedings. According to Article 264(2) CCP, a preliminary waiver of the right to appeal is invalid.

Argument of Article 296 item 2 CCP, they apply to cassation appeal as well. Decisions against which the appellate or cassation appeal filed within the term specified by law is withdrawn enter into force on the day of entry into force of the ruling terminating the case. Where the waiver is made by the appellant's procedural representative, he/she should have an explicit power of attorney (Article 34(3) CCP).

§4. Court Agreement

262. According to Article 145(3) CCP, the court has to invite the parties to reach an agreement as early as the first session in the case, once each of them presented all its claims and challenges, and gave its opinion of the matters of fact stated by the other party, it has asked them questions for clarifying the facts and curing the discrepancies in them According to Article 149(1) CCP, i.e., after terminating the trial, the court again invites the parties to reach an agreement. If it is not reached the court opens the oral pleadings.

263. According to Article 234(1) CCP, the court agreement should be concluded between the parties *in a court session.* The statements of the parties are entered into the minutes of the court session and the parties sign the agreement. The court is obligated to check whether the agreement contravenes the law or good morals, and where no such contravention is present, the court approves the agreement. The approval of the court agreement is given by a ruling of the court.

According to Article 234(4) CCP, once the court approved the achieved agreement, the court terminates the proceedings, and if the agreement concerns only a part of the case the court only terminates those proceedings with regard to this part.

264. According to Article 234(3) CCP, the court agreement[129] has the effect of a decision that has taken effect and is not subject to appeal to a higher court. That means that the court agreement has a *res judicata*-effect regarding the legal dispute settled by it and, where potestative rights are concerned, it also has an enforcement effect (Article 404(1) CCP) and a constitutive effect, if it refers to potestative rights. The Decree No. 7-73 of the Plenum of the SC (1973 Collection, No. 1)[130] the same under the CCP current[131] provides that, the court agreement is not subject to challenge by the extraordinary means of the judicial review or those of the reversal of effective decisions. A court agreement can be challenged by a claim, the contract can be challenged as void or voidable, and its denunciation can be sought. The court's ruling for approving the court agreement can be challenged by the claim under Article 431 CCP, repealed, which corresponds to Article 537(2) CCP, current.

§5. Alteration of the Claim

265. The alteration of the claim[132] is a procedural action of the claimant addressed to the court. The alteration of a claim can be manifested in three forms: an alteration of the grounds for the claim, the petition of the claim, or the parties. In the alternation of the claim in all its forms the elements of the initial claim are preserved and there is an impossibility to have a completely new claim differing in the grounds and in petition. Moreover, the actions performed so far retain effect.

266. Article 214(1), sentence I CCP, provides that the claimant is entitled to change the grounds for the claim in the first court session, provided that the court finds it appropriate in view of the defence of the defendant. What is meant by 'grounds' in Article 214 CCP in relation to Articles 127(1) and 298(1) CCP, is the facts upon which the claim is based, i.e., the factual content giving rise to the right forming the subject matter of the claim. The change of the legal qualification does not constitute a change of the grounds for the claim. Article 143(2) CCP provides the possibility in the first court hearing before the court report for the defendant *to make a supplement to his/her statement of claim* which is not an alternation of the claim and is admissible following the procedure of wand which are not grounds of another different from the initial grounds of the claim (*see* paragraph 172). The alteration might consist in the replacement of the grounds for the initial claim or in the adding of new grounds. In the second case, there is an objective joinder of claims, possible in most cases. If the alteration of the grounds consists in the

129. There are different views on the juridical nature of the court agreement and its elements as well as on the way they should be attacked (*see* details in Popova, V. Civil Procedure. Bulgaria. First Edition, paras 293–294).
130. *See* on an ID of the SCC prior to said Decree in Popova, V. Civil Procedure. Bulgaria, first ed., paras 293–294
131. *See* J. Stalev, A. Mingova, A. Stamboliev, V. Popova, R. Ivanova, *Balgarsko ..., supra*, pp. 491–492 (the matters regarding withdrawal and waiver of a claim are worked out under the co-authorship of J. Stalev and A. Mingova).
132. *See* about this institution and the opinion in doctrine V. Popova, *Izmenenie a iska i noviyat GPK (Alternation of the claim under the new CCP).* Ciela.Norms, http://www.ciela.net.

replacement of the grounds for the initial claim by new claims, the court examines whether the claimant waives or withdraws the claim based on the initial grounds. The provision of Article 214(1) CCP cannot be interpreted separately from Articles 232 and 233 CCP. Since *the procedural actions connected with the initial claim preserve their effect* the court assesses whether the alteration of the grounds will considerably encumber the defendant's defence. Therefore, I share the court practice where, if the grounds are altered, the court notifies the defendant and seeks his/her opinion regarding the alteration of the grounds for the claim.

Under the argumentation of Article 214(1), sentence II CCP, the claimant is not entitled to a simultaneous alteration of the grounds for the claim and the petition of the claim.

267. According to Article 214(1), sentence II CCP, the claimant is entitled, without changing the grounds, to alter his/her claim. The petition could be altered in the following forms: alternation of the very nature of the claim by alternation of the alleged right; alternation of the claim by diminishing or extending the claim; alternation of the requested defence by a transformation from an establishment claim to a condemnation one and vice versa. Prior to the closure of court trial at a first instance, the claimant is entitled to alter only the amount of the claim as well as to proceed from an establishment claim to a condemnation one and vice versa (Article 214(1), sentence III CCP):

(a) If the claimant diminished the amount of the claim, even if his/her claim happens to be upheld, it is upheld up to the diminished amount, and the possibility of lodging a claim for the part exceeding the upheld amount of the claim is precluded by res judicata (*see* paragraph 189), only if the diminishing of the claim does transfer it into a partial claim.
(b) The extension of a claim is an alteration of the petition, consisting of extending the amount of the alleged right and extending the resulting claim. According to Article 214(3) CCP overdue interest or of yields of the thing collected after the claim is brought are not treated as an extension of the claim.
Article 214(1), sentence III CCP specifies the term within which the alteration of the claim could be made – alternation of its amount in its two manifestations, i.e., diminishing the claim, extending the claim, and alteration of the type of the defence sought – a change from an establishment claim into a condemnation claim and vice versa. It is the closure of the court trial at first instance. Specifying the same moment for all the alternations of the claim, provisions of Article 214(1), sentence III CCP – diminishing of the claim, extending of the claim or change of the establishment claim into a condemnation claim and vice versa, the legislator has accepted the statement of the interpretative decision ID No. 1-2000-GMCC, item 9 of the SCC that there is not a change in the right a subject of the claim. These hypotheses should be treated the same way viewing the moment at which the respective alternation of the claim could be made. But the legislator has not accepted the stand in the ID on the admissibility of the said alternations at an intermediate instance. That is hardly reasonable having in mind that according to Article 266(2), item 2 CCP that the newly presented facts that have caused the extension of the claim (e.g., deterioration of the claimant's

health after the closure of the first-instance court trial on compensations on damages resulting from an employment accident, a disallowed damage, etc.) should be considered at an intermediate instance also in connection of the res judicata effect (*see* paragraph 217).

(c) According to Article 214(1), sentence III CCP, the claimant is entitled to change the establishment claim into a condemnation claim and vice versa until the closure of the court trial at first instance. The change consists of the alteration of the type of the defence sought. There is no alteration of the disputed substantive law right.
Concerning the ownership claims it was adopted by item 2B of ID No. 4 of 14 March 2016 on comm. c. No. 4/2014 of CMCC of the SCC that, it is inadmissible for a positive ascertainment claim or a revendictive claim to be transformed into a negative ascertainment claim and vice versa, since the subject matter of the former two claims is the ownership right of the claimant, while the subject matter of the negative ascertainment claim is the ownership right of the defendant. Thus, an alternation of the claim would lead to a simultaneous alteration of the grounds and the petition, what is inadmissible according to Article 214(1), sentence II CCP.

(d) The alteration of the petition can also consist of an alteration of the content. For instance, a claim for awarding a chattel can be altered into a claim for awarding the equivalent because of it being lost or destroyed. The alteration of the content of the petition can consist in adding a new petition (usually grounded on eventuality) and as a result of the alteration of the claim we are faced with an objective joinder of the claims or in the replacement of the initial petition by a new one. Article 214(1), sentence II CCP does not specify the term within which the alteration of the claim as a content (changing the content of the right alleged) could be made. The closure of the court trial at first instance is the deadline set only for the alterations of the claim amount, as well as for a change of the establishment claim into a condemnation claim and vice versa (Article 214(1), sentence III CCP). The first court session is the final possible deadline for alteration of the claim content (ID No. 1-2002-GMCC of the SCC), because in both cases when the grounds and when petition are changed, the right which is subject of the claim changes as well. It is due to the fact that the grounds provide the factual content giving rise to that right, while the petition provides the content of the right.

268. According to Article 228(1) CCP, the alteration of a claim by replacing a party by another person is admissible at any time during the first-instance proceedings, provided that the two parties and the person intervening as a party to the case give their consent. A characteristic feature of the alteration of the parties is that it results in the voluntary procedural succession in the proceedings, i.e., the procedural actions carried out until that time also preserve their effect regarding the new party. The reason it is that Article 228(1) CCP provides that the alteration of the claim consisting of the replacement of a party by another person is admissible at any time during the first-instance proceedings, *provided that the two parties and the person intervening as a party to the case give their consent.* Article 228(2) CCP provides that the consent of the first defendant is not required if the claimant waives his/her claim against the defendant. According to Article 228(3) CCP where the condition of Article 228(2) CCP is present, the claimant is entitled to address his/her claim against a defendant who is unwilling to join the proceedings but the claim against the new defendant is regarded as brought on the day the statement of claim against him/her was received by the court. The procedural actions carried out until that time cannot have effect regarding the new defendant, and because of that, the proceedings shall have to start from the very beginning. In these hypotheses a real alteration of the claim is not present.

In all the events of altering the parties, the claim against the new defendant or by the new claimant ensues from the same grounds and contains the same petition as the one against the first defendant (item 5 of ID No. 1 of 23 Dec. 2015 on comm. c. No. 1/2014 of CMCC of the SCC). The alteration of the parties is extremely important: the new party should be legitimized to be a party to a case whose subject matter is the same disputed right or obligation as the one forming the subject matter of the initial claim.

Article 228 CCP does not mention anything about the form of the alteration of a party. When considering this matter, it should be kept in mind that the alteration of a party is double-addressed. It concerns both the initial party and the new party. The latter did not participate in the proceedings and was not subpoenaed to a court session. Consequently, the request for constituting a new party to the case should be made in writing and a copy should be sent to the new party, together with a copy of the statement of claim. A copy of the petition should also be delivered to the defendant no matter if he/she attended the court session where the alteration was made.

§6. Suspension, Resumption, and Termination of Proceedings

269. According to Article 229(1) CCP, the court suspends the proceedings: by mutual consent of the parties; in the case of the death of a party; if it is necessary that guardianship or custody is established over a party; if a case is considered, either by the same court or by another court, and the judgment has bearing on the proper determination of the claim;[133] if circumstances of a crime are found in the course of civil proceedings, and the ascertainment has bearing on the determination

133. It was assumed in ID No. 1–2001–GMCC, item 8 of the SCC that the proceedings cannot be suspended in the cassation instance because no evidence can be submitted. Although it is obligatory for the courts, this opinion is difficult to share. It is not the submission of evidence that the cases relate to, but the need to have the proceedings suspended and the obligatory effect of the respective court act observed (Arts 297, 300 and 302 CCP). If the suspension of the proceedings before the cassation court is inadmissible that will lead to the necessity after its taking effect to request again the reversal of the decision by the SCC on the grounds of Art. 303(1), item '2' CCP.

It was adopted by ID No. 8 of 7 May 2014 on comm. c. No. 8/2013 of CMCC and the Com.C. of the SCC that, when an interpretative case on a determining legal matter is initiated before the SCC, the proceedings on the pending case can be suspended only at the cassation instance (Art. 292 CCP) and not at first or appellative instance. It is hard to share the statement although it being obligatory for the courts (Art. 130(2) CSA). The need to suspend the proceedings is also obvious if the aim of the ID is to unify the practice by imposing the right interpretation of the law. By the system of preliminary selection (Art. 280(1) and (2) CCP) the access to cassation is strictly limited (*see* paras 229–230). Cassation is absolutely inadmissible (Art. 280(3) CCP – *see* para. 228).

of the civil dispute; if the CC admitted the consideration on the merits of a claim for challenging the compliance with the Constitution of a law applicable to the case; in the cases explicitly provided for in the law (e.g., Article 637 CCP).

270. According to Article 230(1) CCP, the proceedings are resumed ex officio or upon the request of a party after the obstacles for conducting the proceedings are eliminated. In the case of the claimant's death[134] and in the cases under Article 229(1), items 3–6 of CCP the court takes the necessary measures itself. The resumption of proceedings starts from the action when they were suspended (Article 230(3) CCP).

271. According to Article 229(3) CCP, a suspension of the case by common consent of the parties is admissible only once in the course of proceedings in a certain instance.

If the proceedings are suspended by the parties' common consent and neither party requests their resumption within a six-month term following the suspension, the proceedings are terminated. If a court decision is rendered, it is invalidated (Article 231(1) CCP). In such cases of suspension Article 232, sentence II CCP, applies (Article 231(2) CCP, *see* paragraph 253).

272. The ruling with which the resumption of the proceedings is suspended, terminated or denied bars the further progress of the proceedings, due to which according to Article 274(1), item 1, CCP it is subject to appeal by a private appeal (*see* paragraph 122).

§7. Transfer of the Disputed Right in the Course of Pending Proceedings

273. Article 226(1) CCP provides that if in the course of proceedings the disputed right is transferred to another person, the case continues its course as a case between the initial parties. The disposal of the right forming the subject matter of the claim has no direct procedure law effect. The party transferring the disputed right preserves its capacity of a party, but the nature of its procedural legitimation changes. It changes into a procedural substitute (Article 226(1) CCP). In the case the procedural substitution is of the type of procedural subrogation (*see* paragraph 282), because the transferee of the disputed right is not constituted.

274. According to Article 226(2), sentence I CCP, the transferee is entitled to intervene in the case or join it as a third-person accessory. The transferor of the disputed right becomes a procedural substitute while the transferee as a bearer of the

134. According to Art. 230(2) CCP, in the case of the defendant's death, within a six-month term following the notification, the claimant is obligated to specify the defendant's legal successors and their addresses, to take measures for the appointment of a trustee of the heritage, or for having the legal successors subpoenaed in accordance with the procedure of Art. 48 CCP. If the claimant fails to perform this obligation, the proceedings are terminated.

disputed right, actually becomes a co-party and not a principal party. According to Article 226(2), sentence II CCP the transferee of the disputed right is entitled to replace his/her transferor only where the conditions under Article 222(1) CCP are met (*see* paragraph 288). The party of an untypical procedural legitimation is replaced by a party of a typical procedural legitimation.

275. According to Article 226(3) CCP, in any event the rendered decision also has a *res judicata*-effect regarding the transferee, with the exception of the actions of registration where a real estate is concerned (Article 114 PA) or where the acquisition of ownership by bona fide possession of movable property is concerned (Article 78 PA). Article 226(3) CCP envisages where the judgment is a sentencing judgment it spreads not only its *res judicata* but its enforcement effect upon the transferee of the disputed right as well.

Chapter 2. Special Cases Connected with the Parties to General Adversary Proceedings

§1. Subjective Joinder of Claims (Joinder of Parties)

276. Subjective joinder of claims in adversary proceedings is present if the claims of several claimants or the claims against several defendants are united in order to be jointly considered. According to the terminology used in the law, the co-claimants, and the co-defendants, i.e., the persons who are on the same side in the adversary proceedings are called *joint parties*. Each joint party has its own legal relationship with the court. Depending on the type of joinder of parties, and the nature and the level of connection between the cases of the separate joint parties, the procedural actions carried out by a joint party can have bearing on the other joint parties as well (*see* paragraphs 278, 279).

277. Article 215 CCP provides that a claim can be brought by several claimants or against several defendants if the subject matter of the dispute consists of their common rights and obligations, or rights or obligations ensuing from the same grounds.

The rights and the obligations are *common* if the claims brought either by or against the joint parties *have the same object,* no matter whether the common right or the common obligation ensues from the same juridical fact, i.e., whether its grounds are the same or not.

According to Article 215, item 2 CCP, the same grounds are present if the rights or the obligations *ensue from the same factual content*. If it consists of several elements, *the identity of only several juridical facts is sufficient.*

It is also necessary the claims to fall within the jurisdiction of the court, and should be subject to consideration in accordance with the same procedure, and should be within the generic jurisdiction of the same court.

278. Article 216(1) CCP regulates formal joinder of parties. The provision states that each of the joint parties acts on its own and its procedural actions and omissions neither favour nor harm the others. According to Article 217 CCP, if the joint parties' factual allegations regarding the common facts are inconsistent, the court assesses them in connection with all the circumstances related to the case. According to Article 265 CCP, prior to the first session in the second instance, each of the joint parties to the case is entitled to join an appeal brought by a party's co-claimant or co-defendant. Under the argument of Article 216(2) CCP (*see* paragraph 279) in the case of formal joinder the withdrawal, waver, amendment of the claim, the court agreement could occur only for one of the joint parties. That should be valid where there is a request for rendering a decision upon admission of the case (Article 237 CCP) and a decision by default (Article 238 CCP). Under the argument of Article 217 CCP the inaction of one of the formal joint parties cannot be grounds for rendering a decision by default.

279. According to Article 216(2) CCP, when, in view of the nature of the disputed relationship or by order of the law, the court's decision must be the same regarding all joint parties, there is an indispensable joinder of parties, and the actions taken by some of them are also valid for those who have not acted. There may be a contradiction between the allegations and actions of the individual parties. According to Article 17 CCP, if the factual statements of the parties on the general facts contradict each other, the court judges them in relation to all the facts of the case. In the case of indispensable joinder of claims, due to the nature of the disputed relationship, all facts are general. Therefore, according to Article 217(2), sentence II CCP for concluding an agreement (*see* paragraphs 262–264) and for withdrawal (*see* paragraph 257) and for waiver of the claim (*see* paragraph 258), all parties must give their consent. The same applies to the request for a decision on the recognition of the claim (Article 237 CCP, *see* paragraph 184) and an default decision (Article 238 CCP, *see* paragraph 201). The inaction of one of the parties in the indispensable joinder cannot be grounds for rendering a decision by default regarding it.

Article 216(2), sentence II CPC is applicable by analogy to the amendment of the request, the suspension of the case by mutual consent (Article 229(1) CCP), refusal of appeal or withdrawal of the appeal.

280. There are two types of indispensable joinder of parties, the obligatory and the optional (*see* paragraph 276). It seems as if the obligatory joinder of parties is more frequently encountered. It is present where, due to the inseparability of the cases, due to the nature of the dispute or due to an explicit legal provision, the law requires an obligatory joint procedural legitimation as a procedural prerequisite for lodging the claim (*see* the motives of ID No. 3-2017 on com.c. No. 3 of 2016-GMCC and the Com.C. of the SCC, but it is provided that this is an exception). The optional indispensable joinder of parties is less frequently encountered in Bulgarian law (opposite from the cited ID). For instance, it is present where a claim is brought by several legitimized persons for placing a person under interdiction (Article 336 CCP), and a claim is brought by several co-heirs under Article 3 IA for declaring one of the co-heirs unworthy of the inheritance. In ID No. 3-2017 on com.c. No. 3 of 2016-GMCC and the Com.C. of the SCC it was maintained that spouses are optional indispensable parties under an ownership claim lodged by or against them over possessions or properties, which are obtained under marital property community.

If one of parties in the indispensable joinder appeals against the decision, the parties that did not are compulsorily constituted to the case and without the need to join the complaint (Article 265 (2) CCP, ID No. 1-2000-GMCC of SCC). If the indispensable joinder is on the opposite side of the complainant, the complaint must be presented in as much copies as the number of parties in the indispensable joinder is, because of their legal right to participate in the process (Article 261, item 1 CCP, ID No. 1-2000-GMCC of SCC). If a party in an obligatory indispensable joinder has not been constituted at first instance, the appellate court must cancel the decision and return the case for a new hearing at the first instance (ID No. 1-2013-GMCC and the Com.C. of SCC).

§2. Procedural Substitution

281. According to Article 26(2) CCP explicitly regulates that no one is entitled to claim on his/her own behalf someone else's rights before the court. The person to whom the law acknowledges the right to a claim for the defence of another person's right is called 'procedural substitute'.

Article 26(4) CCP explicitly states that if a person claimed another person's right, the person whose right was claimed is also subpoenaed as a party to the case. That is the general rule in procedural substitution.[135] It guarantees that the bearer of the right is not deprived of the right to claim or the right to participate in the proceedings conducted by the procedural substitute in defence of the bearer's right. This type of procedural substitution is called 'procedural intercession' and a specific type of obligatory joinder of parties is present.

Typical examples of procedural substitution under the conditions of procedural intercession are the following: the claim under Article 134 OCA and Article 510 CCP.

282. Article 226 CCP regulates a typical case *of procedural substitution under the conditions of procedural subrogation.* As already pointed out (*see* paragraph 273), where the disputed right is transferred in the course of proceedings, it continues between the same parties (Article 226(1) CCP). A procedural substituent under the terms of procedural subrogation is the assignee as a claimant of the revocable claims under Articles 646, 645, 647 C. Code and Article 135 OCA, which are in the interest of the creditors of the debtor, for whom insolvency proceedings have been opened. However, in the absence of such action, such claims may be brought by any bankruptcy creditor (Article 649 C. Code).

§3. Co-party (Third-Person Accessory)

283. The co-party,[136] also called 'third-person accessory' in Bulgarian law, is a subsidiary party to the proceedings. Where the Constitution as a party to the proceedings takes place on the initiative of the third-person accessory (Article 218 CCP), an intervention is present, and where this Constitution takes place on the initiative of a principal party (Article 219(1) CCP), joinder is present of the third-person accessory as a subsidiary co-party to the adversary proceedings. The intervention, subsidiary co-party, respectively, could be at the side of the claimant or at the side of defendant.

---

135. The exceptions from the rule in Art. 26(4) CCP are a few. These are the cases where procedural subrogation is present (*see* para. 282).

136. *See* V. Popova, Tretoto lice pomagach prez pogleda na novija GPK i evropejskoto pravo (The Third Party – Accessory regarding the new CCP and the European Law). Ciela. Norms, http://www.ciela.net.

284. In order for the intervention or joinder to be admissible, adversary proceedings should be pending between other persons, which are the principal parties to the proceedings.

According to Article 218 CCP, *the intervention is admissible until the closure of court trial in the first instance*. This term is preclusive. According to Article 219(1) CCP, the joinder can be sought by the claimant in the first session in the case at the latest, while by the defendant with the reply to the statement of claim. The preclusive term set in Article 219(1) CCP guarantees the rights of the third person providing him/her with the possibility to participate in the proceedings in the first instance, so that he/she could not be bounded to the motives of the decision without being able to affect the proceedings' outcome.

It is established in Article 219(2) CCP that intervention is inadmissible, if the third person does not have a permanent address in the Republic of Bulgaria or lives abroad.[137] The regulation is applicable both when the person has a permanent address or lives in a non-EU Member State and when he or she has a permanent address or lives in an EU member state. According to Article 65(2) Regulation 1215/2012, the competence specified in Article 8(2) and Article 13 in cases related to actions for granting a guarantee or security or in connection with any other actions of a third party, may be applied in the Member States, included in the list, which the Commission prepares according to Article 76(1), item b) and Article 76(2) only to the extent permitted by their national law. For Bulgaria referred to in Article 219(2) CCP, inadmissibility is reflected in List 2 for Rules on the notification of third parties, specified in Article 65 of the Regulation.

A legal interest is required (*see* paragraph 285) for accession of the third-person accessory. The third person being a subsidiary co-party has the right to perform all procedural actions except the actions which are dispositional with the subject matter of the dispute (*see* paragraph 288). The rendered decision to the case has a *res judicata*-effect in the relationships between the third-person accessory and the opposing party (Article 223(1) CCP). In the relationships between him/her and the supported party the rendered decision finds manifestation in the binding effect of the motives (Article 223(2) CCP).

By the ruling for admission of joinder (*see* paragraphs 257, 287), the third person becomes a party to the proceedings regardless to his/her will and to whether he/she actually participated in the proceedings or not and is bound by the judgment (Article 223(1) and (2) CCP) (*see* paragraph 289).

285. The following should be mentioned in relation to the legal interest for joinder.

---

137. This text is also applicable to the third party where it is a legal person and has its registered office in a non-Member State. The restriction is not to hamper the defence of the third party since being constituted he/she becomes a party (though auxiliary one) to the case regardless of its will and will bound by the res judicata effect in the relationship with the opposing party (Art. 223(1) CCP), while with the assisted party – by the binding effect of the motives (Art. 223(2) CCP). Moreover, the intervention of a third person is often connected with bringing a cross-claim to which this person is a defendant.

(a) Article 218 CCP explicitly provides that the third person is entitled to intervene in the proceedings in support of one of the parties provided that *he/she is interested in having the judgment rendered in favour of that party*, i.e., the concern here is a *legal interest*. A person has a legal interest in intervention if: (a) as an exception, the judgment has res judicata – effect or enforcement effect regarding that person, although he/she did not participate in the proceedings (for the transfer of a disputed right, *see* Article 226(3) CCP, Article 523 CCP, Article 429 CCP); (b) the judgment unfavourable to the supported party would provide grounds for that party to bring in a recourse claim. Consequently, the following persons are entitled to intervene: the principal debtor under the case against the surety (arg. under Article 143 OCA), the delinquent under the case against the assignor of responsibility under Article 49 OCA (arg. under Article 54 OCA), the joint co-debtor under a case against the other joint co-debtor (arg. under Article 127 OCA) and the seller (because of his/her responsibility for eviction) under a revindication claim brought by or against the buyer, if he/she happens to be removed by the court (arg. under Articles 188, 189 OCA), etc. The legal interest in the intervention is present if the disputed legal relationship between the principal parties has a direct legal connection with the legal relationship between one of the principal parties and the third person willing to intervene in the proceedings. By intervening in the other persons' proceedings, the third-person- accessory defends not only another person's right, but also his/her own legal sphere. There might even be an inconsistence between the interests of the third-person accessory and the supported party (*see* Article 221(2) CCP, paragraph 288). For instance, in the case of a claim against the assignor of the job under Article 49 OCA, he/she is entitled to prove that the delict was not committed in the course of performing the assigned job or in connection with its performance.

(b) Article 219(1) CCP states that *any party is entitled to have a third person join the proceedings* provided that *that person is entitled to intervene in the proceedings* in order to support the party. However, it is pointed out that, while in the case of intervention the third person should be interested in the intervention, in the case of joinder, it is the party willing to have *the third person join the proceedings that should be interested in the joinder*. In practice, the legal relationships that give rise to the legal interest in intervention and joinder are the same (*see* above).

286. The joinder should be sought by a written request, and a copy is to be delivered to the third person whose joinder is requested as well as one for the opposing party (arg. Article 131(2) CCP, Article 100, sentence II, CCP and Article 102 CCP; Article 8(1) CCP in connection with Article 100, sentence II, CCP and Article 102 CCP). The matter is of constituting a third-person accessory as a party to the case.

The request for intervention should be made in writing with duplicates for the opposing and supported party (arg. Article 100, sentence II, CCP).

287. According to Article 220, sentence I CCP, the court renders a ruling on whether the third person is admitted or not. According to Article 220(1), sentence II CCP, the ruling that does not admit the third person is subject to appeal by a private appeal (for the appeal against rulings, *see* paragraphs 224–227). It was assumed in ID No. 1-2013 of the GMCC and the Com.C. of the SCC that the ruling of the intermediate appellate court with which the first-instance ruling which disallows constituting of a third-person accessory is not a subject to cassation appeal. The ruling admitting the third person is not subject to appeal.

288. According to Article 221(1) CCP, the third person is entitled to carry out any procedural actions except those that constitute disposal of the subject matter of the dispute.[138]

According to Article 221(2) CCP, in case of inconsistency of the party's actions and explanations with those of the third person, the court assesses the actions and explanations in relation to all the circumstances in the case. With the consent of both parties, the third party who has intervened or who has been impleaded may substitute himself or herself for the party assisted thereby and may excuse the said party (Article 222 CCP).

According to Article 219(3) CCP the party who has a cross-claim against the third party may bring the said claim for joint examination simultaneously with the motion for impleader (*see also* paragraph 298).

289. According to Article 223(1) CCP, the judgment rendered by the court has an ascertainment effect *(res judicata* effect) regarding the relationships between the third person and the opposing party. If the judgment is a sentencing one, it is not enforceable against the third-person accessory.

The binding effect of the motives applies to the internal relationships between the supported party and the third-person accessory. According to Article 223(2) CCP, what the court established in the motives for its decision is obligatory for the third person in his/her relationships with the party he/she supports as well as for the party that made him/her join the proceedings, and the third-person accessory is not entitled to challenge it under the pretext that the party conducted the proceedings badly, with the exception of those cases where, either wilfully or because of gross negligence, he/she failed to submit evidence or facts which are unknown to the third person.

§4. Primary Intervention: Dispute Between Creditors

290. According to Article 225(1) CCP, the third person, who has his/her own rights upon the subject matter of the dispute, is entitled to intervene in the proceedings by bringing in a claim against the two parties. This type of intervention of the third party in the proceedings is termed as 'primary intervention':

---

138. The third-person accessory is not entitled to waive or withdraw the claim. Generally, he/she cannot conclude an agreement. In my opinion, the third-person accessory can also participate in the agreement provided that he/she is a subject of the disputed legal relationship, e.g., if the creditor's claim is brought against one of the joint co-debtors, while the other intervened or joined as a third-person accessory on the first joint co-debtor's side. However, if the court agreement is only valid between the principal parties and the third-person accessory does not participate, it is unenforceable against the third-person accessory.

(a) For the primary intervention to be admissible it is required that the primary intervener alleges his/her independent rights upon the object forming the subject matter of the disputed right, which exclude the rights of the parties to the case. This precondition is present when he/she claims to be the holder of the disputed right or part of it (e.g., he/she is a co-owner of the property). It is also present when he/she claims another right, which excludes the rights of the parties to the case. For example, if a revindication claim is brought in the case, the holder of the real right of use has a legal interest in the primary intervention. If in case of a claim under Article 19(3) OCA for announcing a preliminary contract for establishment of a real right over real estate, a third party claims to be the owner of the property, his request under Article 225(1) CCP is procedurally admissible.
The filing of the claim by a third party (the primary intervention) is admissible until the end of the court search in the first instance. The request for primary intervention must be made in writing, which must meet all the requirements for a statement of claim, including for its supplements. A copy of it and the supplements must be served to the claimant and the defendant on the initial claim, giving them the term for a written response to this request provided in Article 131(2) CCP.
(b) The court renders its decision on the admissibility of primary intervention by a ruling subject to appeal. It was adopted in ID No. 1-2013 of GMCC of the SCC that the ruling of the appellate court, which upheld a first-instance ruling refusing the Constitution of primary intervener, is subject to cassation appeal.
(c) In the case of primary intervention, three claims are being joined: the original claim and the claims which the primary intervener had brought against the claimant and against the defendant in the original claim. There is a subjective joinder of claims (*see* paragraph 276) and objective joinder claims (*see* paragraphs 293–294).

291. Article 224 CCP states that the defendant is released from participation in the proceedings provided that he/she deposits the sought amount or a chattel in accordance with the instructions of the court and has the person claiming independent rights joined the proceedings. The proceedings continue between the two creditors only. If the joining person does not intervene in the proceedings, they are terminated, and the deposited amount or chattel is delivered to the claimant. When the claimant makes a request for joining with the reply to statement of claim he/she is not responsible for the costs (Article 224(3) CCP).

§5. The Public Prosecutor in Civil Adversary Proceedings

292. According to Article 26 (3) CCP the public prosecutor is entitled to participate in the proceedings with *the rights of a party only when the law provides for them*:

(a) According to Article 336(1) CCP, the public prosecutor is legitimized to bring a claim for placing a person under interdiction. This claim can be brought in defence of a public interest or in defence of the person whose placement under interdiction is sought. *In both cases, the person whose placement under interdiction is sought is a defendant under the proceedings.*

According to Article 336(2) CCP, the public *prosecutor's participation is obligatory* in proceedings regarding placement under interdiction where the *claim* for placing a person under interdiction is *brought* by a person legitimized under Article 336(1) CCP (spouse, close relatives) Article 336(2) CCP provides *the obligatory participation of the public prosecutor in these proceedings* and he/she is obligated to participate in the entire proceedings, including the collection of evidence, so his/her participation is not limited to only giving his/her conclusion on the proceedings (arg. under Article 26(3) in connection with Article 336 CCP).

(b) According to Article 537(3) CCP, the public prosecutor is entitled to bring a claim for the reversal of a security act if is rendered in violation of the law. The claim is addressed against those persons for whom favourable legal consequences ensue from the challenged security act.

(c) Article 552(1) CCP provides for the public prosecutor's right to claim the reversal or modification of the judgment declaring the absence or death of a person, if it is established that that person is alive or the date of his/her death is different from the one announced by the court.

(d) By virtue of Article 604 CCP, *the public prosecutor is legitimized to bring a claim establishing the inadmissibility or invalidity of the entry, or the non-existence of a circumstance entered in the respective public register.*

(e) According to Article 47(1), items 3 and 4 FC, the public prosecutor is entitled to bring a claim for the termination of a marriage in the cases under Article 7(1), items 1, 2 and 3 FC as well as in the cases under Article 7(2) FC.

(f) The public prosecutor may bring claims for dissolution of the company for invalidity due to the reasons referred to in Article 70(1) C. Code (Article 70(2) C. Code); to terminate the company when its activity is offending the law (Article 155(2) C. Code).

Chapter 3. Particularities in General Adversary Proceedings Related to the Objective Joinder of Claims

§1. Objective Joinder of Claims: General Characteristics – Types

293. An objective joinder of claims[139] is present if several claims *with different subjects between the same parties are joined in order to be jointly considered in common proceedings.*[140] The general conditions for admissibility of joinder of claims are not introduced by a general norm. They are deduced form the interpretation of Article 210 CCP (*see* paragraph 295), proceeding from those aims – procedural economy and non-conflicting determination of the cases under joint claims – and also from the provisions of Articles 211, 212, 213, 219(2) CCP.

(a) *The claims should fall within the jurisdiction of the same court.* Subservience and subject-matter jurisdiction should be observed, but according to the rules of venue jurisdiction, the court does not necessarily have to be the same.
(b) The claims should be subject to consideration in accordance with the procedure concerning the same proceedings. According to Article 210(2), sentence I CCP, where the claims are not subject to consideration in accordance with the procedure concerning the same proceedings, the court rules that they should be separated. This ruling is not subject to appeal (arg. Article 247(1), items 1 and 2 CCP).
(c) The admissibility of objective joinder of claims is the presence of connection among the single disputed subjects. Article 210(2), sentence II CCP provides that where the court finds that the joint consideration would create considerable difficulties, it rules that the claims should be separated.

294. The Bulgarian legislator set the types of objective joinder of claims according to how the joinder is made by: bringing several claims by one claimant against the defendant (Article 210 CCP – *see* paragraph 295); bringing in a defendant's counterclaim against the claimant (Article 211 CCP – *see* paragraph 296), by bringing an incidental ascertainment claim by the defendant or the claimant (Article 212 CCP – *see* paragraph 297); bringing a principal party's cross-claim against the third-person accessory (Article 219(3) CCP – *see* paragraph 298), and by a joinder of cases between the same parties where there is a connection between the cases, taking place on the initiative of the court where the cases are pending before (Article 213 CCP – *see* paragraph 299).

---

139. *See* V. Popova. *Civil Procedure. Bulgaria,* first ed., para. 395 and the literature and court practice cited therein.

140. In the cases of a cross-claim under Art. 219(2) CCP, neither the claimant nor the defendant are the same as those under the initial claim. This cross-claim is brought by the principal party under the initial claim against a co-party, so he/she should be constituted as such in the proceedings (*see* para. 298).

An important division of the objective joinders of claims is the one reflecting the relationship between the various types of claims: cumulative, eventual and alternative joinder. The type of objective joinder is really determined by the connection between the rights and legal relations determining the legal interest in the type of joinder and its admissibility:

(a) Cumulative joinder of claims – the claimant requests the court to consider and render a decision on each one of the claims. It is admissible, if the connection between the rights and legal relationships, alleged in the joint claims makes it possible for them to coexist, and the sought remedies of the two rights or legal relationships are compatible.
(b) Eventual joinder of claims – one of the claims is principal and the decision on the eventual claim depends on the outcome of the proceedings regarding the initial claim. In these cases, the proceedings regarding both claims are pending. Therefore, in the hypothesis under Article 210 CCP (*see* paragraph 295), the claimant actually makes an objective eventual joinder of claims for the case in which his/her principal claim is not upheld. In the hypothesis under Article 211 CCP (*see* paragraph 296), the defendant brings the counterclaim as an eventual claim for the case where the court finds that the claim brought against him/her is well-grounded. In the hypothesis under Article 219(2) CCP, the principal party brings a cross-claim against the third person-accessory as an eventual claim for the case where the court upholds the claim against the principal party, i.e., where the court finds that the principal party's allegation is groundless (*see* paragraph 298).
(c) Alternative joinder of claims is present if the claimant leaves it to the court to decide which of the joint claims should be upheld. It is admissible only where the relationship between the rights (and the legal relationships) alleged in the two claims provides the court with the possibility of choosing the claim to be ruled upon. The alternative joinder of claims is admissible only under Article 131(3) OCA, in the cases of alternatively defined obligations with a right to choose, granted to a third person and he/she fails to make a choice within the specified term, the court makes the choice. In this case, the alternative joinder of claims is not only admissible, but also necessary. In my opinion when bringing in claims in the presence of competing grounds or competing pretences, the eventual joinder is admissible and no the alternative one. In practice there are no alternative joinders of claims, except for in the cases under Article 131(3) OCA.

§2. Separate Hypotheses of Objective Joinder of Claims

295. According to Article 210(1) CCP, the claimant is entitled to bring several claims by one statement of claim against the same defendant provided that these claims fall under the jurisdiction of the same court in accordance with the generative jurisdiction and are subject to consideration in accordance with the procedure concerning the same proceedings.[141] According to Article 210(2), sentence II CCP, if the claims are not subject to consideration in accordance with the procedure concerning the same proceedings, the court rules that they should be separated.

The subjects of the claims should be different. There should be a legal or factual connection between the alleged legal relationships, giving rise to the legal interest in the joinder of claims, as the objective of joining the claims for joint consideration in common proceedings consists in procedural economy and non-conflicting determination of the disputes.

296. According to Article 211(1) CCP, within the term for submitting the reply the defendant is entitled to bring a counterclaim provided that it is within the subservience of the same court according to the rules of generic jurisdiction and is connected with the initial claim or set-off can be performed under it.

The reply to the statement of claim and the counterclaim are separate procedural actions of the defendant but are interrelated. The counterclaim can be brought simultaneously with the reply or after it, but before the deadline for replying has expired. The term under Article 211(1) CCP is *preclusive*. According to Article 133 CCP when the defendant does not exercise his/her rights under Article 211(1) CCP within the set term, then he/she loses the possibility to do so later (*see* paragraph 151), unless the omission is due to especial unforeseen circumstances. The omission of the preclusive term for bringing in the counterclaim means preclusion of the possibility to bring in only the counterclaim, but not the legal possibility for bringing a separate claim with a substantive right, subject of the belated counterclaim.

According to Article 211(2), sentence I CCP, the counterclaim is brought according to the rules of bringing a claim.[142] The court should send the duplicate of the statement of claim to the defendant and to set a term for his/her submission of a reply to the statement of claim under Article 131 CCP. According to Article 211(2), sentence II CCP, when the court finds that the joint consideration of the counterclaim will be hampered, it renders its separation. The ruling by which the court does not admit the joint consideration of the counterclaim of the defendant is not subject to appeal because it does not belong to the category of court acts which bar the further progress of the proceedings and the law has provided explicitly their appeal.

The subject of the counterclaim should be a disputed right related to the right forming the subject of the initial claim or a right by which set-off can be performed under the right forming the subject matter of the initial claim (Article 211(1) CCP). There is a relationship between the two disputed rights where they ensue *from the same legal fact* (e.g., a contract or tort in a crash between two vehicles), but also where they concern *the same object* (e.g., the defendant under an initial claim brings a claim according to which he/she is the owner of a movable or immovable property, while the initial claim is one for the ownership of a chattel, a revindication claim, or a claim for establishing the right of use of the property). The presence of

141. *See* the exceptions in Art. 322 CCP on the matrimonial proceedings; Art. 332 CCP about the claim for establishing the origin and the claim for alimony.

142. It was adopted by ID No. 1-2013-CMCC and the Com.C. of the SCC that the ruling of the first-instance court disallowing the statement of counterclaim due to the failure to fulfil the instructions for curing its irregularities is subject to appeal under Art. 274(1), item 1 CCP in connection with Art. 129(3) CCP.

an *everyday relationship* between the two claims is sufficient. The possessor or holder of the property brings a counterclaim for the improvements against a revindication claim for ownership. The holder of the property and the unconscionable possessor are entitled to seek the receivable for the improvements by a counterclaim, and not by an objection, because they do not have the right of retention.

In the second hypothesis, the subject of the counterclaim should be a receivable by which set-off can be carried out if the receivable forms the subject of the initial claim. The subject of the counterclaim also includes the right of set-off. It provides the connection between the initial claim and the counterclaim required under Article 211(1) CCP and substantiates the legal interest in bringing the counterclaim. Where the defendant's receivable is greater than the claimant's, the defendant is entitled to demand that the claimant is sentenced for the excess between the two receivables on the grounds of Article 211(1) CCP.

The counterclaim can be brought under the conditions of cumulativeness, provided that the defendant did not challenge the initial claim. However, the counterclaim can also be brought under the conditions of eventuality if the defendant challenges the initial claim and brings a counterclaim requesting the court to uphold his/her counterclaim if the claim brought against him/her is deemed well-grounded.

297. According to Article 212 CCP, in the first court session the claimant and the defendant are entitled to request the court to pronounce in the decision its ruling upon the existence or non-existence of a disputed legal relationship, upon which the outcome of the case depends in whole or in part.

The subject of an incidental ascertainment claim can consist of *a right or a legal relationship which is prejudicial for the subject of proceedings*. The institute of the incidental ascertainment claim is well-established in Bulgarian legislation due to the conception, adopted by the legislator, that res judicata of the decision rendered on the case is formed only on the subject of the claim, and not on the prejudicial legal relationships. An incidental ascertainment claim for ascertaining a fact relevant to the case is inadmissible (arg. Article 124(4) CCP). The incidental ascertainment claim can be a positive or a negative ascertainment claim.

The term to bring in an incidental ascertainment claim under Article 212 CCP is *preclusive*. It is inadmissible for an incidental ascertainment claim to be brought in the intermediate appellate instance or the cassation instance. According to Article 133 CCP, when the defendant fails to exercise his/her rights under Article 212 CCP within the established term, he/she forfeits the possibility to do so later (*see* paragraph 149). If the term for submitting a reply is resumed, that means the term for bringing in an incidental ascertainment claim is resumed as well.

Unlike the case of a counterclaim, in the case of an incidental ascertainment claim, it is *not laid down explicitly that it should be brought in accordance with the rules on bringing a claim*. However, it is a matter of claim. Consequently, when there are no special rules for its bringing, the general rules concerning the form and ways of bringing a claim should be observed, i.e., it should be brought in a written form with the enclosures to the statement of claim specified in Articles 127, 128 CCP (*see* paragraphs 163, 164). It was adopted by ID-No. 1-2013 of the GMCC and the Com.C. of the SCC that the ruling of the first-instance court disallowing the joint consideration of the incidental ascertainment claim is not subject to appeal.

298. According to Article 219(3) CCP, a principal party that has a cross-claim against the third-person accessory is entitled to bring it to be considered together with the pending case simultaneously with the request for impleading. The specifics of the cross-claim consists of the deviation from the general requirement that an objective joinder of claims should be between the same parties. The prerequisite for admissibility of the cross-claim is the Constitution of a third-person accessory in the proceedings. The subject of the cross-claim is the recourse pretension of the principal party against the co-party, connected with the right forming the subject of the initial claim and, consequently, it is brought in for joint consideration.

According to Article 219(3) CCP, the cross-claim can be brought no later than simultaneously with the request for joining. It is also admissible to bring in a cross-claim against the intervener if that is done within the term for joining. Otherwise, the third person intervening would void the bringing of a cross-claim against him/her.

The cross-claim should be brought in observance of the requirements regarding bringing of a claim. It is *usually* brought as *an eventual claim.*

299. According to Article 213 CCP, if there are several cases pending before the court, and the same persons participate on the part of the claimant and the defendant, or there is an interrelation among the cases, the court can join these cases in joint proceedings and render a common decision on them. The provision should get a corrective interpretation. It is worth sharing the opinion maintained both in doctrine and practice, that in the hypothesis under Article 213 CCP the parties to the cases should be the same, and there should be a relationship between the cases. *The cases should be pending before the same court.* The court does not have the right to join the cases if they are subject to consideration in accordance with a different procedure, in spite of the fact that they are cases between the same parties and a relationship is present between them.

Part VI. Legal Aid and Legal Costs

§1. Legal Aid

300. The LAA regulates the legal assistance provided in civil cases in all court instances. The legal aid is rendered by attorneys and is financed by the State (Article 2 LAA). *It is provided to individuals on the grounds specified either in the LAA or in other laws* (Article 5 LAA). *The funds for legal aid come from the national budget* (Article 4 LAA). According to Article 6(2) LAA, legal assistance is organized by the National Bureau for Legal Aid (NBLA) and the Councils of Attorneys. The NBLA is an independent State body – a legal entity funded by the budget under the Minister of Justice (Article 6(3) LAA).

According to Article 18 LAA the Lawyers' Councils organize the provision of legal aid in the relevant judicial region. Legal aid is provided for consultation on how to reach an agreement before the commencement of the proceedings or the filing of a case, including consultation under Chapter Five 'a'; preparation of filing documents; procedural representation (Article 21 LAA).

According to Article 22(1), items 1-10 and (2) LAA, legal aid under Articles. 21, item 1 and 23 LAA is provided to those persons who meet the requirements for receiving monthly social benefits in accordance with the procedure set forth Article 9 and 10 Rules on the Application of the Social Support Law (RASSA); persons and families eligible for targeted assistance to afford heating for the previous or current heating season; to those persons who have been placed in specialized institutions for social services, as well as to those or who are using a social service – a resident type or a social service 'Mother and baby' under Article 36 RASSA; children placed in foster families or families of kinsmen or relatives where a child has been placed under the provisions of the ChPA; a child at risk within the meaning of the ChPA; persons under Article 143 and 144 SG and persons under 21 years of age, in accordance with Reg. No. 4 of 2009 on jurisdiction, applicable law, recognition and enforcement of judgments and cooperation in matters relating to maintenance obligations and the Convention on the International Recovery of Child Support and Other Forms of Family Maintenance (OJ L 192/51 of 22 July 2011); victims of domestic or sexual violence or people trafficking who do not have the means and wish to enjoy legal protection; persons seeking international protection under the Law on Asylum and Refugees, for whom granting of legal aid is not due to another legal basis; foreigners who have been subjected to a compulsory administrative measure and foreigners accommodated in a special home for the temporary accommodation of foreigners under the Law on Foreigners in the Republic of Bulgaria (LFRB) who do not have the means and wish to enjoy legal defence; persons who have been refused or withdrawn status of stateless person in the Republic of Bulgaria, or the procedure for granting status of a stateless person under the LFRB has been terminated, who have no funds and wish to enjoy legal defence.

According to Article 23(1) and (2) LAA, the system of legal aid under Article 21(3) LAA refers to those cases in which the attorney's defence or representation is necessary in law, as well as to those cases in which a party to civil proceedings does not have the funds needed for paying an attorney, and is willing to have an attorney, the interests of justice requiring that the party should have an attorney. On the grounds of the evidence submitted by the respective competent bodies, the court judges whether the party has the funds needed for paying the attorney's remuneration or not, taking the following into account (Article 23(3) LAA): the incomes of the person and his/her family; the person's financial state certified by way of a declaration; his/her family status; his/her health condition; his/her employment; his/her age; other circumstances.

Article 24 LAA regulates those cases in which the provision of legal aid is refused under Article 21, items 1, 2 and 3 LAA: where the provision of legal aid is unjustified from the viewpoint of the benefit resulting from it to the person applying for legal aid; where the pretence is obviously groundless, unfounded or inadmissible; in the cases of commercial proceedings and proceedings on taxes under the TSPC, except in the cases when the party applying for legal aid is a natural person and meets the requirement for provision of legal aid.

In the cases under Article 21, items 1 and 2 LAA, the decision for providing legal aid is taken by the body which administers the procedural actions, either upon the request of the interested person or by virtue of law. The person is explained in writing by a declaration in a form approved by the NLAB that, in the case of a conviction the person shall be obliged to reimburse the expenses. The refusal to provide legal aid is motivated and subject to appeal in the appropriate manner. In the cases under Article 21, items 1 and 2 LAA (Article 25(2) LAA) the decision regarding the provision of legal aid is made by the President of the NBLA. The refusal of legal aid may be appealed against in accordance with the procedure set forth in the APA. The act for the provision of legal aid is sent immediately to the respective Council of Attorneys for the nomination of an attorney from the National Register for legal aid (Article 25(4) LAA). If possible, the Council of Attorneys nominates the attorney specified by the person to whom the legal aid is provided. According to Article 26(1) LAA, the Council of Attorneys notifies the body under Article 25(1) or (2) of the nominated attorney and he/she is appointed a special representative for all court instances, unless there exists an objection against that. The appointed attorney is entitled to reauthorize another attorney from the National Register for legal aid. The appointed special representative may be replaced if so requested by the body under Article 25(1) or (2) LAA, in accordance with the procedure through which he/she was appointed (Article 26(5) LAA).

According to Article 31 LAA, the NBLA maintains the National Register for legal aid listing the attorneys nominated for the provision of legal aid in the court regions of the respective district courts. The register is public and drawn up either in a hard copy or in an electronic one and is published on the Internet (Article 32(1) LAA).

LAA has a special procedure for the provision of legal aid before all instances in international disputes regarding civil or commercial matters. According to Article 41(2) LAA, within the meaning of Article 41(1), 'an international dispute' is one in which the party requesting legal aid is either a citizen of an EU Member State, or a person legally residing in an EU Member State, and the dispute is determined in another EU Member State. According to Article 42(1) LAA, EU citizens and the legal residents in any EU Member State are provided with legal aid in those cases where their property status is not above the social level specified in Article 22(1) LAA. According to Article 42(2) LAA, if the property status of the persons under Article 42(1) is above the social level specified in Article 22(1) LAA, however, the said persons claim that they cannot pay the court costs, the NBLA judges whether the said persons are able to pay the court costs or not. The Ministry of Justice in the Republic of Bulgaria is the body with which the competent bodies of EU Member States file their applications for legal aid in international disputes. That is the Bulgarian body which sends the applications for the provision of legal aid in international disputes, these applications being sent to the competent bodies of EU Member States. (Articles 43 and 44 LAA).

301. Article 83(1) CCP provides that *no fees or costs* for proceedings are paid by the claimants who are: workers, employees and members of cooperatives – under claims from labour contracts; claimants under claims for alimony; the claimants under claims brought by a prosecutor; claimants under claims for damages sustained as a result of a tort or delict, for which a sentence has entered into effect; especial representatives of a party whose address is unknown.

302. According to 83(2) CCP, no fees or costs for proceedings are due by natural persons who *have been acknowledged by the court* as not having sufficient funds for paying the fees and costs on the grounds of an application for waving the fees and cost.

303. Article 83(3) CCP provides that in the cases under Article 83(1) and (2) CCP *the costs for the proceedings are paid out from the amounts, allocated in the court's budget.* According to Article 78(1) CCP the fees paid by the claimant, costs of proceedings and remuneration for one lawyer, if any, are paid by the defendant in proportion to the upheld part of the claim. Where the case is solved in favour of a person exempted from a State fee or costs, the sentenced person is obliged to pay all due fees and expenses. The corresponding amounts are awarded to the court. (Article 78 (6) CCP). It is foreseen in Article 78(7), sentence I CCP that, if the claim is upheld, the lawyer's remuneration paid is awarded to the NLAB in proportion to the upheld part of the claim. Article 78(7) sentence II CCP provides that, in the case of a conviction, the person who has received legal aid owes expenses in proportion to the rejected part of the claim. In the SCC practice the following understanding was imposed: 'Article 78(7) sentence I CCP regulates the substantive right of the NLAB to award the lawyer's remuneration paid by him for legal aid provided in respect of the claim of the person who received it but against the counterparty under the general rule of Article 78 CPC on the responsibility for costs depending on the outcome of the case.' Since the liability for the costs in the proceedings concerns the parties, the provision in that regulation is an exception and the second hypothesis – sentence II concerns the liability of the legal aid recipient for the costs incurred by the opposite party in a judgment rendered in proportion to the rejected part want. In the hypothesis of Article 78(7) sentence II CCP, the person who received legal aid does not owe expenses to the NLAB, which provided free legal aid financed by the State meeting the requirements for providing legal aid – Article 94 CCP and Articles. 2 and 22 LLA.

304. According to Article 84 CCP, payment of fees but not of court costs is waived for: State and government institutions (except claims on private State receivables and rights on chalets – private State property), municipalities except claims on private municipal receivables and rights on chalets – private municipal property) and the Bulgarian Red Cross.

305. According to Bulgarian procedure law the party's representation by an attorney is not obligatory. In all types of cases the party is entitled to represent and defend itself in person in any instance. However, the representation of the party by an attorney guarantees better defence in the case. According to Article 38(1) AB, the attorney or the one from the EU may render his/her assistance free of charge to: persons entitled to alimony; financially embarrassed persons; his/her relatives and kinsfolk, or another lawyer. In these cases, if the opposing party has been sentenced to pay the costs, the attorney or the one from the EU has the right to attorney's remuneration (Article 38(2) AB). The court determines the remuneration, which cannot be lower than the one specified in the Ordinance under Article 36(2) AB, and sentences the other party to pay it.

306. Article 29 (1), (3) CCP provides for cases in which the court is obligated to appoint *a special representative of the party:* for the missing persons whose whereabouts are unknown; persons whose permanent and current residence is unknown; where the interests of the represented person contradict those of his/her legal representative. Where a special representative is appointed the remuneration thereof is determined by the court in accordance with the factual and legal complication of the case. The remuneration could be less than the minimal amount for the particular work under Article 36(2) AB, but not less than half of it. It is paid to the budget account of the court which considered the case. If the opposing party loses the case, it will be sentenced to pay the said remuneration in favour of the court to the respective account of the budget thereof.

§2. Legal Costs

307. Article 71(1) CCP lays down that where proceedings are conducted, *State fee on the claim amount and costs* for them should be collected. Thus, the Bulgarian legislator distinguishes the State fee from the other costs on the proceedings and uses the term 'costs' in its narrow sense. However, when providing on the responsibility on the costs (Article 78 CCP) he uses the term 'costs' in its broad sense. In its broad sense, 'costs' comprises all the expenses for the case: the State fee and the other costs for the case. 'Costs' in its *narrow sense* (Article 71(1) CCP) means those expenses *which are not included in the State fee, and comprise the costs for collecting the evidence and those for attorneys' remuneration.*

308. State fee is collected when filing for defence or assistance (Articles 71 and 73(3) CCP; Article 1(1) ASF).[143] The State fee must be paid upon filing the statement of claim (Article 128, item 2 CCP). The non-payment thereof makes the statement of claim an invalid one. According to Article 71(1) CCP, the State fee is collected upon the amount of the claim and when the claim cannot be appraised, the State fee is determined by the court. Where the subject matter of the case is a right of ownership or other rights in rem to an immovable, the amount of the State fee is determined on one-fourth of the cost of claim (Article 71(2) CCP). Where the amount of the claim is reduced the fee which has already been paid is not repaid (Article 74 CCP). Where the amount of the claim is increased the fee upon the difference is additionally paid.

According to Article 72(1) CCP for the claims filed in a single application for protection of one interest, one State fee on the protected interest is collected *irrespective of the number of defendants*. This rule applies to the eventual and alternative objective and subjective joinder of claims as well as to the cumulative joinder of claims against several defendants in cases of joint and several liabilities. In case of cumulative objectively united claims against the same person, a State fee is charged for each claim. According to Article 72(2) CCP, the minimum fee is levied on all interests filed in a single application for the protection of various interests.

309. As it has already been pointed out (*see* paragraph 307), the legislator differentiates between the narrow sense of costs on the proceedings from the State fee. The costs in the narrows sense are divided into two groups: costs for the evidence (*see* Articles 75, 76, 160 CCP) and attorney's remuneration (*see* Article 78(1) CCP). According to Article 76 CCP, each party makes an advance deposit to the court for the costs for the actions which the said party has requested. The amounts for costs for steps on a motion by both parties or on the initiative of the court are deposited by both parties or by one party depending on the circumstances. According to Article 160 CCP, where costs have to be incurred on the taking of evidence, the court sets an amount and a term for depositing of the said costs. The said term begins to run as from the day of the court hearing during which the said term was set, and this applies as well to the party that did not appear. The evidence is taken after presentation of documentary proof of making the deposit set for costs. The term for depositing of costs is interrupted by the submission of a petition for waiver of the depositing of such costs and does not run while the said petition is examined.

310. According to Article 36(1) AB the attorney is entitled to receive remuneration for his/her work. According to Article 36(2), sentence I AB, the amount of remuneration is determined in the contract between the attorney and the client. The said amount should be a fair and well-grounded one and cannot be lower than the amount provided for in the Ordinance of the Attorneys' Supreme Council regarding

143. Which is determined according to the tariff of State fees collected by the courts under the CCP.

the respective type of work (Article 36(2), sentence II AB). According to Article 36(4) AB, the remuneration can be agreed as an absolute amount and/or a percentage of the specified interest in view of the outcome of the case, with the exception of the remuneration in civil cases with non-pecuniary interest.

311. According to Article 78(1) CCP, the fees and costs for the proceedings as well as the attorney's remuneration (if there is such) are paid by the defendant in proportion to the upheld part of the claim. In favour of legal entities and sole traders is also awarded remuneration to the amount determined by the court, if they were defended by a legal counsellor. The amount of the awarded remuneration may not exceed the maximum amount for the respective type of case determined by the order of Article 37 LAA (Article 78(8) CCP). According to Article 78(3) CCP, the defendant has the right to seek the refunding of the expenses he/she has made in proportion to the disallowed part of the claim. He/she also has the right to have his/her costs refunded upon the termination of the case (Article 78(4) CCP). According to Article 78(2) CCP, where the defendant's conduct has not provided cause to the institution of proceedings, and the defendant has recognized the claim, the costs are adjudged to the claimant. According to Article 78(9) CCP, if the case is concluded by an agreement, half of the State fee deposited is refunded to the claimant. The costs in the proceedings and on the agreement are borne by the parties as they have made them, unless the agreement provides otherwise. According to Article 78(10) CCP, the third-person accessory is neither due nor adjudged to any costs.

According to Article 78(4) CCP, where the amount paid by a party to the attorney exceeds the amount corresponding to the actual legal and factual complexity of the case, the court might adjudicate a lower amount of costs upon the request of the opposing party, however, the latter cannot be lower than the minimum amount specified in Article 36 AB.

According to Article 92a CCP, where a party has caused a deferral of proceedings pays a fine under Article 91 CCP. A petition for cancellation of a fine as imposed may be submitted within one week to the court which has imposed the said fine. The term begins to run as from the day of the court hearing, and in the cases where the person does not attend the hearing, as from the day of the communication. The court examines the petition in camera and, if it finds the reasons set forth valid, the court reduces or vacates the fine, as well the compelled attendance. The said ruling is subject to appeal by a private appeal (Article 92 CCP).

Where the case has been adjudicated in favour of a person for whom payment of State fee or of costs of the proceeding is waived, the sentenced is obligated to pay all fees and applicable costs due. The respective amounts are awarded in favour of the court (Article 78(6) CCP).

In cases when the party has been granted legal aid Article 78 (7) CCP is applied (*see* paragraph 303).

The receivable on the costs can be claimed only in the pending proceedings but not by a separate claim. The court does not pronounce ex officio on the receivable on the costs. It pronounces only on the petition of the interested party. The party that requests adjudicating of the costs should present to the court a list of the costs not later than the closure of the last session at the respective instance. The non-performance of this obligation does not render the request on the costs irregular or ungrounded. The court will adjudicate the due costs, but the party that fails to present the list of the costs, cannot request modification of the rendered decision on the part of the costs (Article 80 CCP).

The party can appeal decision on the part of the costs only if the decision on the nature of the case is appealed meanwhile. Otherwise, the party can defend itself against the incorrect adjudicating of the costs only following the procedure under Article 248(1) and (2) CCP, if the party has presented the list specified in Article 80 CCP. According to Article 248(1) CCP, within the term for appeal and, if the decision is unappealable, within one month after rendition of the said decision, the court, acting on a request by the parties, may amplify or modify the decision as rendered in the part thereof concerning the costs, only if the party has presented the list specified in Article 80 CCP. The court pronounces on the modification in a closed session with a ruling with which the parties are served. The said ruling is appealable according to the procedure applicable to the decision (Article 248(3) CCP).

Part VII. Evidence

Chapter 1. Burden of Proof

312. Article 154(1) CCP provides that either party is obligated to state the circumstances upon which it bases its claims or objections. The party's role (a claimant or a defendant) in the procedure is of no importance to the distribution of the burden of proof.[144] What is determinant here is whether the facts the party alleges give rise to legal consequences which are favourable to it, regarding the disputed legal relationship. The burden of proof also concerns the facts from which conclusions can be drawn regarding the existence or non-existence of the legally relevant facts. In this case the distribution of the burden of proof is determined on the grounds of whether conclusions favourable to the party can be drawn from the evidentiary fact. This is true where, through the said fact, the party seeks to prove a legally relevant fact, and the legal conclusions drawn from the latter are favourable thereto.

313. Even after Article 154(1) CCP (Article 127(1) CCP, repealed) was redrafted, no veritable obligation can be spoken about, but about a burden. The party also has the right to prove the facts it alleges. If the party fails to prove them, it will bear the unfavourable legal consequences – the court is obligated to assume that the fact alleged by the party is unproved, and, because of that, it is unrealized, and therefore, the court has to assume that the legal consequences alleged by the party have not occurred. These unfavourable consequences are not a real sanction. They are too close to the unfavourable consequences in those cases where a right is not exercised, and therefore, it is more precise to speak about burden of proof.

314. The court must apply the consequences of burden of proof when it finds that the fact is not proven, only when it has given the instructions foreseen in Articles 146(1), item 5 and 146(2) CCP on the burden of proof and on its distribution and the party has been given a term under Article 146(3) CCP to make its evidential requests according to the instructions on the burden of proof, but has failed to do so. The party can avoid the consequences from the burden of proof only by evidential requests under Article 147 CCP. According to Article 147, item 1 CCP the parties may allege any new circumstances and cite and present any new evidence solely, if they were unable to learn of such circumstances and to cite and present such evidence in due time. The preclusion in Article 133 CCP is valid for

144. The terms 'proof' and 'evidence' are used as synonyms in the CCP.

the defendant's possibility allege facts and bring in objections. The preclusion of the possibility of citing and presenting evidence, i.e., the evidential requests of the parties, it occurs under the conditions Articles 146(3) and 147 CCP.

According to Article 153 CCP, the contested facts relevant to adjudication of the case and the links there between are subject to proving. Therefore, the party bears the burden of proof of the contested facts. In my opinion, Article 146(1), items 3 and 4 CCP in connection with Article 153 CCP specifies the court's obligation of rendering an explicit ruling on differentiating the disputed and non-disputed facts and for declaring the facts alleged by the party and acknowledged by the opposing party. The court should state as a mandatory element of the report which rights and facts are admitted, and which facts need proving. Moreover, Article 175 CCP foresees that an admission of a fact, made by a party or by a representative thereof, is evaluated by the court considering all circumstances of the case, i.e., the admission of the fact does not bind the court.

According to Article 155 CCP only those facts which are either generally known or ex officio known by the court (the court is obligated to communicate them to the parties) are not subject to being proved.[145] For those facts in particular the party does not bear burden of proof.

On the grounds of the said above, I think that the party bears burden of proof for all the facts it alleges, wherefrom it derives favourable legal or evidential conclusions, excerpt for the facts admitted explicitly by the opposing party, as well as for the facts declared as needing no proof under Article 155 CCP. The court does not have the right to refer to facts which the parties do not allege, to collect evidence for which the parties have not made the respective evidential request. The only exception concerns the conclusion of the expert witness (Article 195 CCP).

315. Article 154(2) CCP provides that it is not necessary to prove those facts for which there exists a presumption established in law. It is sufficient for the party to prove the presumptive prerequisite in order for the presumed fact to be deemed proved. Such rebuttable presumptions are set forth in the regulations of substantive laws (Article 69 PA, Article 45(2) OCA, etc.). Their nature is a procedural one, as they regulate the distribution of the burden of proof. According to Article 154(2), sentence II CCP, the rebuttal of such presumptions is admissible in any event, except where the law forbids it. The rebuttal of a presumption is called contraposition and should be made with complete proof, i.e., the court should be firmly convinced that the presumed fact has not been realized.

145. In my opinion, ex officio known facts and facts needing no proof in the sense of Art. 155 CCP should be considered under the new normative reality those facts which should be verified by the court ex officio (e.g., Art. 24 CRA).

Chapter 2. Admissibility and Administration of Evidence

§1. Admissibility and Deposition by Witnesses

316. According to Article 164(1) CCP, *the testimony of witnesses is admissible in any event, except where the following is concerned*: (1) the ascertainment of a legal transaction for the validity of which a written instrument is required in law; (2) the rebuttal of the content of an official document; (3) the ascertainment of circumstances for the evidencing of which a written instrument is required in law, and the ascertainment of contracts the value of which exceeds BGN 5,000, except where the said contracts have been concluded between spouses or lineal relatives, or collateral relatives within the fourth degree, or relatives by affinity within the second degree inclusive; (4) the extinguishment of money receivables ascertained through a written instrument; (5) the ascertainment of written agreements in which the party requesting the witnesses has participated, or an amendment to or a reversal of such agreements; (6) the rebuttal of the content of a private document with a destination abroad. According to Article 164(2) CCP, where cases under items 3, 4, 5 and 6 are concerned, testimony of witnesses is admissible only with the explicit consent of the parties. According to Article 165(1) CCP, in those cases where a written document is required in law, testimony of witnesses is admissible provided that it is proved that the document has been lost or destroyed through no fault of the party. According to Article 165(2) CCP, testimony of witnesses is also admissible if the party seeks to prove that the consent given in the document is only a seeming one, and provided that there is written evidence in the case, this evidence either originating from the opposing party or certifying its statements before a State body, and the evidence makes the party's statement regarding the seeming consent a credible one. This restriction neither concerns third persons, nor does it concern the successors in those cases where the transaction is intended against them.

317. The witness has the procedural obligation to testify once he/she has been admitted as a witness, and has been subpoenaed as such, respectively. His/her failure to perform this obligation gives rise to the respective sanctions. According to Article 85(1) CCP in connection with Article 91(1) CCP, if a witness fails to appear in court without a reasonable excuse, the court imposes a fine on him/her and orders that the person be compulsorily brought to the next session. According to Article 85(2) CCP in connection with Article 91(2) CCP, where a witness refuses to testify without reasonable excuse, the court imposes a fine on him/her. Article 166(1) CCP provides that nobody is entitled to refuse to testify with the exception of: (a) the attorneys-in-fact of the parties to the same case and the persons who were mediators in the same dispute (item 1); the parties' lineal relatives, brothers and sisters and the relatives by affinity within the first degree the spouse and the former spouse, as well as the de facto cohabitee with a party (item 2); those persons who, through their answers, would cause direct harm, or disgrace, or criminal prosecution either to themselves or to their relatives specified in 166(1), item 2 CCP (item 3). Where the persons under Article 166(1) items 2 and 3 CCP agree to testify, their testimony is assessed in accordance with the criteria set forth in Article 172 CCP Where classified information must be presented, the court should question the witness behind closed doors (Article 136(1) item '1' CCP). According to Article 166(2) CCP, the witnesses in the case cannot be attorneys-in-fact of the parties to the said case.

318. In order to admit the witnesses, which the party has requested the court has to decide whether, in view of Article 164 and Article 165 CCP, the testimony sought is legally admissible and whether it is relevant to the said fact. The testimony of the witnesses is collected through questioning them in a court session. On the grounds of Article 140(2) CCP, according to Bulgarian procedure law the case with collecting the evidence is heard in a court session with subpoenaing the parties. The witnesses are questioned in a court session (arg. Article 163(1) CCP). The only exception is provided for in Article 163(2) CCP when due to an important reason, the questioning of the witness may be conducted even before the day assigned for the hearing, as well as outside the premises of the court. The parties should be summoned to attend this questioning.

According to Article 170 CCP prior to questioning the witness, the court ascertains his/her personal identity and reminds him/her of the responsibility provided in law in the event of perjurious testimony. According to Article 170(2) CCP, the witness promises to tell the truth. Bulgarian procedure law does not provide for sworn testimony. This has been the traditional legislative solution for decades and it is an expression of the tolerance of Bulgarians towards the various beliefs and views of people. In return thereof, however, the PC provides for penal responsibility for perjurious testimony (Article 290(1) PC). According to Article 171(1) CCP, each witness is questioned separately in the presence of the parties which have appeared in court. Those witnesses who have not yet given their testimony are not entitled to be present at the questioning of the other witnesses. According to Article 171(2) CCP, a witness can be questioned anew in the same session or in another session either at his/her own request, or at the request of the party, or upon the initiative of the court. Upon the request of a party or on its own initiative the court may enter into the minutes specific features of witness's behaviour during the questioning (Article 171(3) CCP). According to Article 174 CCP, in the cases of discrepancy in the witnesses' testimony, the court might order that a confrontment be made. A confrontment might also be ordered between a witness and the parties.

In Bulgarian procedure law it is inadmissible to collect witnesses' testimony through the deposition of written testimony of witnesses, even where this testimony is notarized. It is inadmissible for the court to invoke witnesses' testimony collected in another case. The only exception is set forth in Article 232, sentence II CCP (where the first case has been terminated due to the withdrawal of the claim), and accordingly, if the claimant brings in the same claim again, he/she may use the collected evidence in the new case only if its repeated collection is barred by an obstacle which is hard to overcome (*see* paragraph 257).

Pursuant to Article 156a(1) and (2) CCP, at the request of a party, a witness may be interrogated by videoconference, when the witness is unable to appear in person before the court in the case and is outside the district of the regional court, whose seat coincides with the seat of the court.[146] The court shall determine the date and

146. In view of the witness's obligation to testify in the case, I consider that de lege fenenda this should also be admissible at the witness's request.

time of the hearing in which videoconferencing will be used, after examining the possibility of holding it with the nearest district court to the place of residence of the witness; indicates the place where the witness must appear (Article 156a(4) and (5) CCP). In this case, the identity of the witness shall be verified by the employee under Article 150(3) CCP, who is present at the videoconference. The party can participate in the videoconference from the courtroom, so he/she is summoned to the court hearing.

§2. Admissibility, Deposition and Forced Production of Documents

319. The written evidence is a document – a chattel upon which a statement is materialized through written signs. Written evidence can be either dispositive or testimonial depending on whether it materializes an expression of will or a statement of knowledge.

The new reality was taken into account in the CCP, current, and rules for collecting written evidence have been created depending on whether the document is a paper-based or an electronic one (*see* paragraph 324). According to Article 3(1) EDETSA, an electronic document is an electronic document within the meaning of Article 3, item 35 of Regulation (EU) 910/2014 on electronic identification and trust services for electronic transactions in the internal market and repealing Directive 1999/93/EC. According to Article 3(2) EDETSA the written form is observed if an electronic document, containing an electronic statement, is created. According to Article 2(1) EDETSA, an electronic statement is a verbal statement presented in digital form through a generally accepted standard for conversion, reading and presentation of information. The electronic statement can contain non-verbal information (Article 2(2) EDETSA).

320. According to Article 178(1) CCP, the force of the written evidence is determined in compliance with the law which was effective at the time and place of drawing up the written evidence (*see* paragraph 322).

According to Article 178(2) CCP, *the court assesses the evidential effect of a document* containing any crossing-outs, erasures, additions between the lines or other visible defects, in view of all the circumstances in the case. The rule is not applied to the signed electronic document (Article 178(2), sentence II CCP). The special rules of the EDETSA are applied in the case.

321. The written evidence consists of *official documents and private ones.* According to Article 179(1) CCP, an official document issued by an official[147] within the scope of his/her official duties, and in accordance with the established forms and procedure *constitutes evidence of the statements made before his/her and the actions carried out before him/her.* According to Article 188 CCP, a document

147. It is not necessary for the certifying body to be a body of State authority. It should be a body which has acknowledged the right (either in law or in a subordinate legislation instrument) to issue the respective official document.

which has been issued by an incompetent body or has not been issued in the prescribed form has the effect of a private document if signed by the parties. That aim is for the document signed by the parties (e.g., a contract of sale) to preserve its nature of a private document if the official one has any of the said defects (for instance, a notary deed has been drawn up by the notary's assistant, and not by the notary himself/herself, the assistant not being vested with this power under the ANNA. In this case, on the grounds of Article 188 CCP, this document might be used for proving bona fide possession).

According to Article 180 CCP, the private documents signed by the persons who have issued them constitute evidence that the statements contained therein have been made by the said persons, i.e., these documents have only the so-called formal evidential effect regarding the authorship, i.e., the authenticity thereof.

The special rules of EDETSA are valid for the electronic signature. The law makes a difference between an electronic signature (Article 13(1) EDETSA), an advanced electronic signature (Article 13(2) EDETSA) and a qualified electronic signature (Article 13(2) EDETSA) under an electronic document.

According to Article 189(1) CCP, a private document issued by an illiterate person should contain a fingerprint of his/her right thumb instead of a signature, and should also be countersigned by two witnesses. If it is impossible for the fingerprint of the person's right thumb to be affixed to the document, the latter should specify the reason for it and should also specify the finger from which the fingerprint affixed to the document has been taken. According to Article 189(2) CCP, a private document issued by a blind literate person should be countersigned by two witnesses.

An unsigned private document is also a document and constitutes worthy written evidence (arg. under Article 193(3), sentence II). On the grounds of Article 193(3), sentence II CCP, however, the burden of proving the authorship of the document rests on the party which has submitted it (*see* paragraph 325).

According to Article 181(1) CCP, the authoritative date of a private document regarding third persons is the date of it being certified, or the date of death, or the date on which it became physically impossible for the signer to sign the document, or the date on which the content of the document was reproduced in an official document, or the date of occurrence of any other fact which undeniably proves that the document has been drawn up prior thereto. The authoritative date signifies that on that date the document already existed and could not have been drawn up or changed after this date.

According to Article 182 CCP the entries in accounting records are judged by the court according to their regularity and in the light of the other circumstances on the case. They can also serve as proof of the person or organization who kept the books.

322. According to Article 31 PILC Bulgarian courts assess the validity of foreign official documents in accordance with the laws of the State in which the said documents have been executed or issued. Under Article 178(1) CCP the same is valid for the private documents provided the foreign law does not contradict the Bulgarian legal norms. The foreign law will be also applicable where it has a norm of authenticity of a deal or action. According to Article 185 CCP, the documents submitted in a foreign language have to be accompanied by an accurate certified translation in Bulgarian. If it is impossible for the court to check the fidelity of the translation, it appoints an expert to check it. If the foreign document has been drawn up in an EU Member State, according to Article 4, items 2 and 3 and Article 5 of Council Regulation (EC) No. 1206/2001 of 28 May 2001 on cooperation between the courts of the Member States in the taking of evidence in civil or commercial matters it is enough for the document to be accompanied by a translation made by a licensed sworn translator in any Member State. The same is valid where the foreign document has been drawn up in a State which has ratified the Hague Convention on collecting evidence abroad on civil and commercial cases dated 18 March 1970, it is not necessary for the document or its translation to be legalized (Article 3(2) Hague Convention). If the foreign document has been drawn up in a country which has not ratified the Hague Convention, but there exists a bilateral treaty for legal assistance signed between the said country and the Republic of Bulgaria, it is the provisions of the respective treaty that apply to the translations. If the foreign document has been drawn up in a State which has not ratified the Hague Convention and has not signed a treaty with Bulgaria for legal assistance, it is the rules on legalization, certifications and translations of documents and other papers that apply.

However, the genuineness of a document is challenged in accordance with the procedure set forth in Article 193 CCP (*see* paragraph 325). In relation to Article 185, sentence II CCP, the fidelity of the translation might also be challenged (*see* paragraph 321).

323. The written evidence is collected through it being submitted in court. The claimant is obligated to submit the written evidence in support of the facts alleged by him/her (Article 127(2) CCP and paragraphs 163, 166). The defendant is obligated to do so in the reply to the statement of claim (Article 131(3) CCP, paragraphs 145, 147–148). These terms are not preclusive ones. In the report on the case (Articles. 140(1) and (3) and 146(3) CCP) the court must specify how the burden of proof is apportioned (Article 146(1), item 5 CCP) and instruct the parties as to the facts alleged thereby in respect of which they do not cite evidence (Article 146(2) CCP). According to Article 146(3) CCP the court provides an opportunity for the parties *to undertake the relevant procedural steps*. If they fail to do so, the possibility is precluded, but in the cases under Article 147 CCP (*see* paragraphs 152, 156, 172–173).

The court renders its ruling upon the admissibility of written evidence submitted together with the statement of claim and the reply to it in a court session for preparation of the case. A copy of the ruling is sent to the parties (Article 140(1) and (3) CCP). If they are presented later, the court admits the evidence at court session to which the parties have been summoned (Article 157 CCP).

According to Article 186 CCP, the official documents and certificates are submitted by the parties, however, the court is entitled either to seek them by a request of a party from the respective institution or to provide the party with a court certificate on the grounds of which the latter can receive them. The institution should either issue the requested documents or explain the reason for not having issued them. According to Article 190 CCP, after explaining the importance of the document for the dispute, each party is entitled to request the other one to present a document in the other party's possession. The failure to present a document is assessed according to Article 161 CCP (Article 190(2) CCP). According to Article 191 CCP presentation of a document may be refused where: the content of the document concerns circumstances of the personal or family life of the party and this would lead to defamation or to criminal prosecution of the party or of any relatives thereto within the meaning given by Article 166 CCP. According to Article 192(1) CCP each party can request through a written request a person non-participating in the case to present a document, within its possession. According to Article 192(2) CCP, a copy of the request is sent to the third person and a term for submitting the said document is specified therein. According to Article 193(3) CCP, a third person who unjustifiably fails to present the requested document, bears responsibility under Article 87 CCP and is also answerable to the party for the damages caused. The grounds to refuse presentation of the requested document established in Article 191 CCP are also valid in favour of the third person who does not participate in the proceedings.

324. According to Article 183(1) CCP, where documents are presented as paper-based, they can be submitted also as a copy certified by the party, however, in this case, upon request, the party is obligated to submit the original of the document or an officially certified copy thereof. If the party fails to do so, the submitted copy is excluded from the evidence in the case. Article 183(2) CCP (in force from 30.06.2021) prescribes that the copy, certified by the party under Article 183(1) CCP can be presented also as an electronic version, certified by the party through a qualified electronic signature. According to Article 179(2) CCP, officially certified copies or extracts from official documents have the same evidential effect as the originals. According to Article 32 AB, within his/her official duties, an attorney is entitled to certify copies of documents presented to him/her in connection with or on the occasion of the defence of the rights and legal interests of his/her client. These certified copies have the effect of officially certified documents before the court.

Article 184 CCP provides that an electronic document may be presented reproduced on a paper-based data medium in the form of a duplicate copy authenticated by the party. In practice until the amendments of XI 'a' 'Procedural actions and acts in electronic form' (in force from 30 June 2021) of the CCP, the document is presented in the very court session as a printed copy signed by its issuer. According to Article 184 CCP, upon request, the party is obligated to present the document on an electronic data medium. If the court does not have at its disposal technical means and experts making it possible to reproduce the electronic document and to duly verify the electronic signature in the courtroom in the presence of the persons who appeared, electronic copies of the document are furthermore presented to each of the parties to the case. In such case, the genuineness of the electronic document may be challenged during the next succeeding court session (*see also* paragraph 325).

325. According to Article 193(1) CCP, the interested party is entitled *to challenge the genuineness* of a document in the reply to the litigation action by which the latter is submitted. When the document is presented in a court session is the genuineness can be challenged not later than the end of the session in which the latter is submitted. As said in paragraph 324, in such case, the genuineness of the electronic document may be challenged during the next session succeeding the one wherein the electronic document is presented. The terms set forth in Article 193 CCP and Article 184 CCP are preclusive ones.[148]

According to Article 193(2) CCP, the court has to order that an examination of the genuineness of a document be made in those cases where the opposing party states its desire to make use of it. According to Article 193(3) CCP, the burden of proving that a document is not genuine rests on the party which challenges it. Where the genuineness of a private document is challenged, and the said document is not signed by the party challenging it, the burden of proving that a document is authentic rests on the party which has submitted it. According to Article 194 CCP, the court makes an examination either by comparing the document with other documents which are indisputable ones, or by questioning witnesses, or through experts. Court expertise is the most common means used.

According to Article 18, item 1 EDETSA a person other than the holder, respectively the creator, has no right to access the data for creating the electronic signature. Therefore, Article 18a EDETSA contains special rules for contesting the electronic signature. An expertise is appointed, which must comply with these special norms.

According to Article 194(2) CCP, having carried out the examination, the court renders a ruling which acknowledges that either the challenge of the document has not been proved or the document is not a genuine one. In this latter case the court excludes the document from the evidence and sends it to the public prosecutor together with the ruling it has rendered. According to Article 194(3) CCP, the court is also entitled to render its decision on the challenging of the document through the decision on the case.

§3. Expert Evidence

326. In Bulgarian law the terms 'court expertise' and 'conclusion of an expert' are used as synonyms. According to Article 195(1), sentence I CCP *an expert* is appointed where the clarification of certain questions arising in the case requires *special knowledge*[149] in the field of science, arts, crafts, etc. The appointment of an

148. It was adopted in ID No. 5-2012-GMCC and the Comm. C. of the SCC that in connection with Art. 193 CCP the party may bring in a claim under Art. 124(4), sentence I CCP only if it has another legal interest in establishing the non-genuineness of a document, because this claim is not grounds for suspending the proceedings. The decision on this claim is also not grounds for a reversal under Art. 303(1), item 2 CCP. It was adopted that the claim under Art. 124(4), sentence I CCP for establishing the geniuses of a document is inadmissible where the claimant's legal interest is based on the possibility to use the decision on the ascertainment claim as grounds for reversal under Art. 303(1), item 2 CCP of an effective decision on the case wherein the said document has been presented but the claimant omitted the deadline for challenging it Art. 193(1) CCP.

149. Therefore, the expert should possess the respective qualification (Art. 198 CCP).

expert in legal matters is inadmissible.[150] An expert should also be appointed in those cases where the judge has knowledge in specialized matters other than the legal ones (for instance, apart from his/her education in law, the judge either has education in the respective specialized matters or deals with them as a hobby). The expert is necessary not only for the court, but also for the parties in clarifying the factual aspects of the dispute.

The expert might be appointed either *upon the request of a party, or upon the initiative of the court.* The court is obligated to appoint an expert even in those cases where the party has not requested it, however, the clarification of certain facts in the case requires specific knowledge and the court does not have it. Otherwise, a serious procedural breach would be committed.

According to Article 197 CCP, the ruling for the appointment of the expert should contain: the subject and task of the expertise; the materials the expert will be provided with; the name, education, specialty, place of work and position held by the expert. The court gives the expert a suitable term for preparation of the conclusion. The expert witness notifies the court when he/she is unable to prepare the conclusion within the term set, and states the time he/she needs (Article 197(2) CCP).

It is inadmissible to use a conclusion of an expert given in another case, even where the latter is between the same parties and is heard by the same court. Besides, the so-called private expertise is inadmissible, this being expertise given by specialists who have not been appointed as experts in the case, and the expertise thereof has been made out of proceedings, upon the request of a party.

The provisions of Article 22(1) CCP (relating to the grounds for recusal of the judge) shall apply accordingly to the expert. Each of the parties may request his removal if any of the provided grounds are present.

The expert has the right to examine the case and participate in the collection of evidence, as well as to ask questions to witnesses through the court. Moreover, pursuant to Article 206(2) CCP, he may replace the court during the inspection and certification.

The expert must present his written conclusion at least one week before the court hearing (Article 199 CCP) and must be summoned and questioned in open court (arg. Article 200 CCP). He/she must be heard directly by the court and the parties, and they may be asked questions. Hearing of an expert by videoconference is admissible when due to official engagement or other objective circumstances the expert cannot appear before the court in the case and is outside the district of the district court, whose seat coincides with the seat of the court in the case (Article 156a(3) CCP). The court determines the date and time of the videoconference, after checking the possibility of holding it with the nearest district court at the place of residence of the expert and calls on the expert to appear at that place and time. The parties to the case participate in the videoconference from the courtroom, where the court hearing is held, for which they are also summoned (Article 156a(4) and (5) CCP).

According to Article 202 CCP, the court is not obliged to accept the conclusion of the experts, but discusses it together with the other evidence in the case.

---

150. Except in the cases for establishing the contents and interpretation of a foreign law, which should be applied for solving the case (Art. 43(1) PILC).

According to Article 195(2) CCP, where the subject of the study is a complex one, the court might appoint more than *three experts when required by the circumstances in the case*. According to Article 203, sentence I CCP, where the opinions of the experts are inconsistent with each other, each group states its own opinion. If the court is unable to form its own opinion, it either requests the same experts to perform additional studies or appoints other experts (Article 203, sentence II CCP).

§4. DEPOSITION BY THE PARTIES THEMSELVES

I. Explanations of the Parties

327. In Bulgarian procedure doctrine it is disputable whether the parties' explanations constitute a means of evidence in adversary civil proceedings. According to one of the views, the parties' explanations, as being a source of information provided for in law, constitute means of evidence regardless of whether facts which are favourable to the party are alleged therein, or facts which are unfavourable thereto are admitted. According to the other view, the party's allegations of facts which are favourable thereto are not a means of evidence, but give rise to the need of being proved. In my opinion, the view according to which the parties' allegations of facts which are favourable thereto constitute a means of evidence cannot be shared. In Bulgarian procedure law the institute of the so-called assertory oath neither exists, nor has any penal responsibility been laid down for untruthful allegations of the parties. The provision of 154 (1) CCP is clear and categorical – the party has to prove those alleged facts from which it draws legal or evidential conclusions which are favourable thereto (*see* paragraph 312). The fact that, when rendering its decision, the court has to consider the parties' allegations does not turn them into means of evidence. The court considers them in order to assess whether the alleged facts have been proved or not by the evidence on the case collected.

The explanations of the party are given in a court hearing, for which the opposing party is also summoned. Giving explanations by a party (e.g. in the cases under Article 176 CCP) by videoconference are admissible when it is not able to appear directly before the court and is located outside the judicial district of the regional court, whose seat coincides with the seat of the court in the case (Article 156a(2) CCP. The videoconference itself is conducted in the same way as that for the questioning of a witness (*see* paragraph 318) and hearing of an expert (*see* paragraph 326), in which case the opposing party may participate in it from the courtroom, for which court hearing it is also summoned.

328. It is in *special provisions* that the Bulgarian legislator has specified the *evidential effect* of the explanations of the parties:

(a) According to Article 146(1), item 3 CCP in its report on the case the court should state which rights and which circumstances are admitted; which circumstances do not need to be proved. Moreover, in the first court session the court questions the parties for clarification of the facts. *The replies* to these questions are dictated in brief by the chairperson in order for them to be entered in the minutes. Thus, the court discerns the disputable from the indisputable.

(b) The party's admission of facts which are unfavourable thereto is not binding on the court (Article 195 CCP), the admission made by the party or by the party's representative is assessed by the court in view of all the facts in the case. Where the defendant admits the claim, the court, acting on a claimant's request for rendering a decision upon admission of the claim, the court renders a decision conforming to the admission, the court trial is not carried out and if such has been already carried out, it is terminated (Article 237(1) CCP); paragraph 184). However, if the claimant has not requested rendering of such a decision, the admission of the claim is not binding on the court and it has to be adjudged according to Article 195 CCP.

(c) At any time in the course of proceedings upon the request of the party the court is entitled to *obligate the other party to appear in person in order to reply to particular questions that* are of great importance to the outcome of the case (Article 176 CCP). The court may also exercise its powers under Article 176 CCP upon its own initiative in case of a suspected simulative process or/and of unclear and evasive allegations of the party that has appeared in court. The party which is obligated to appear in person is informed by the court about the questions it will have to answer, with the court warning the party about the consequences of the non-performance of the said obligation (Article 176(2) CCP). According to Article 176(3) CCP, the court is entitled *to deem proved those circumstances for the clarification of which the party has failed to appear or regarding which it has refused to answer.* In order to protect the rights of the party that has not appeared, Article 176(4) CCP provides that where the party is unable to appear before the court owing to a hardly surmountable impediment, the explanations of the said party may be provided to a delegated court.
According to Article 177 CCP the following persons give explanations: natural persons personally,[151] the legal representatives of a legal entity; the partners in a general partnership, the personally liable partner in a limited partnership, respectively; the debtor against whom bankruptcy proceedings have been instituted; the trustee in cases relating to the bankruptcy estate.

(d) According to Article 161 CCP, in view of the circumstances in the case, the court is entitled to deem proved those facts regarding which the party has created obstacles to the collection of evidence admitted by the court. According to Article 190(1) CCP, each of the parties might request the other party to submit a document in its possession, having explained its importance to the dispute (*see* paragraph 323). If the court allows this request, and the opposing party possessing the document refuses to submit it, the court might apply the consequences of Article 161 CCP (Article 190 CCP).

151. Where a party is a minor or under a full legal guardianship, the court may hear its legal representative. When he/she is a minor or placed under limited guardianship, the court may interrogate him/her in the presence of his/her parent or guardian.

II. Deposition by the Parties Themselves

329. The parties must bring the evidence and the specific circumstances they will be proving with them and provide written evidence available to the claimant in the application (Article 127(2) CCP, *see also* paragraph 163 about the application), the defendant in reply to it (Article 131(2) CCP; *see also* paragraph 148 about the reply) about the burden of proof) to instruct the parties which of their alleged facts have a burden of proof; which do not provide evidence and should give them time to make requests of evidence. If the parties fail to do so, they lose the opportunity to do so later, except in the cases under Articles. 147 and Article 146(3) CCP. The court does not have the right to collect evidence not specified by the parties, except for the appointment of an expert (Article 195 CCP; *see* paragraph 314).

§5. Affidavit

330. The affidavit does not exist in Bulgarian law and is inadmissible.

§6. Inspection by Judge

331. Here, it should be noted that:

1. The rules for visual inspection and certification are laid down in Articles 204 to 206 CCP.

According to Article 204(1) CCP, *upon a request of the parties, or in its own discretion* (*see* paragraph 32 and ID No. 1-2000-GMCC of the SCC), the court is entitled to appoint an inspection of movable and immovable property, or examination of persons with or without the participation of experts. The subject of the inspection might be movables or immovable properties, while the subject of the examination might be only persons (e.g., in the cases of a tort). Expertise is usually appointed for the examination, the expert examines the person and gives the respective conclusion (Article 206(2), sentence II CCP). In the cases of examining a person the court should act in a way which does not hurt the dignity of the person under examination.

In Article 204(2) CCP, the legislator determines the inspection and certification (*see* paragraph 323) as means of gathering and verifying evidence. It is ruled that they are carried out by the entire panel of the court, by a delegated member of the court or by another delegated court. However, in practice, instead of inspection and certification, forensic expertise is often appointed.

2. The rules for document verification

The verification of a document disputed by the opposing party (Article 193 CCP), shall be carried out by the order of Article 194 CCP (*see* paragraph 325).

3. Inspection by judge

The evidence admitted by the court is collected in a court session involving the court and the parties (Article 148 CCP). Therefore, the ‘inspection by a judge’ procedure existing in other legal systems does not exist in the Bulgarian procedure law. It is inadmissible for evidence to be gathered by the parties outside the proceedings, without the participation of the court, as well as to be inspected by the court. On the grounds of Articles. 235 and Article 12 CCP, when rendering a decision the court is obliged to discuss all the evidence in the case collected. Failure to comply with this rule is a material procedural violation that may lead to an inaccurate decision which might be repealed by the appellate court (Article 269 CCP). If this violation is committed by the appellate court, there is a ground for cassation under Article 281, item 3 CCP.

Chapter 3. Securing the Evidence

332. In Bulgarian law '*securing the evidence*' *means the collection thereof in advance.* Article 207 CCP provides that where there is a risk that any evidence might be lost or the collection thereof might become difficult, *the party is entitled to seek the collection of the said evidence in advance.* According to Article 208(1) CCP, the request for securing the evidence is filed with the court which hears the case, and where the case has not yet been instituted, it is filed with the regional court either by the permanent address of the person who will be questioned or by the location of the real estate which will be inspected. It is through a ruling that the court renders its decision on the request for securing the evidence. The ruling of the court which disallows the request is subject to being appealed against by way of a private appeal (Article 208(3) CCP).

333. A copy of the request for evidence securing is delivered to the other party (Article 208(2) CCP), if the person filing the request is unable to specify the name and address of the other party, the court appoints a representative thereof (Article 208(5) CCP). The same should be done where the permanent address of the party is unknown. According to Article 208(6) CCP, it is the general rules that apply both to the procedure for collecting the evidence and to the effect thereof. It should be carried out in an open court session that the parties have been subpoenaed to. Because of the promptness sought, in this case it is appropriate to use the ways of subpoenaing by telephone and fax provided for in Article 42(3) of the CCP. According to Article 208(4) CCP, if the evidence stated by the other party is closely related to the evidence stated by the person filing the request, the court is entitled to collect it in the same proceedings.

Part VIII. Particular Proceedings

Chapter 1. Particular Adversary (Claim) Proceedings

§1. Summary Proceedings

334. According to Article 310(1) CCP, the claims considered in accordance with the procedure for summary proceedings are:

(a) for labour remuneration, to pronounce a dismissal wrongful and to revoke such dismissal, for compensation for the period of unemployment due to the dismissal, and for correction of the grounds for the dismissal as entered in the work book or in other documents;
(b) for eviction from premises leased or loaned for use;
(c) for establishment and cessation of an infringement of rights under the Copyright and Related Rights Act (CRRA), the Patents and Utility Models Registration Act, the Marks and Geographical Indications Act, the Industrial Designs Act, the Topographies of Integrated Circuits Act and the Protection of New Plant Varieties and Animal Breeds Act;
(d) for ascertainment and cessation of violation of rights under the CPA;[152]
(e) other claims regulated in a law (e.g., claims for maintenance under Article 146(2) FC).

Summary proceedings are not admissible considering a joinder of a claim belonging to the list in Article 310(1) CCP with a claim subject to consideration according to the general adversary procedure (Article 310(3) CCP). The joinder of a claim subject to consideration according to the summary procedure with a claim for an ancillary receivable (e.g., interests, penalties) is admissible.

---

152. In Art. 113 CCP (suppl., SG 100/2019) it was ruled that the cases initiated under claims of and against consumers shall be considered as civil following the order of the general claims process. For example: in case of claims against a consumer under Art. 422 CCP, for the price due by him; in case of consumer claims / resp. consumers for compensation or for reducing of the price due to defects of the item.

Art. 310, item 4 CCP will be applicable when the claim is filed by a consumer (resp. in case of subjectively joined claims of consumers) for establishment and termination of violation of rights under the CPA. When the claim is of this type but is filed as a collective claim for protection of collective interests of consumers, it will be considered under the order of consideration of collective claims (*see* paras 370–377).

335. On the day of receipt of the statement of claim, the court verifies the conformity thereof and the admissibility of the action Article 311(1) CCP; gives instructions to the claimant to complete and particularize the allegations thereof and to eliminate the contradictions therein, where the said allegations are obscure, deficient or imprecise (Article 311(2) CCP). *There is nothing particular concerning the term for submitting a reply to the statement of claim.*

The preparation of the case is carried out in closed chambers without subpoenaing the parties. It should be on the day of receipt of the defendant's reply or of the expiry of the term for submitting the said reply. The court:

(a) schedules a hearing of the case for a date within three weeks;
(b) prepares a written report on the case;
(c) invites the parties to reach an agreement and explain thereto the advantages of the various procedures for voluntary resolution of the dispute;
(d) pronounces on the requests for evidence, admitting the evidence which is relevant, admissible and requisite;
(e) determines an amount and a time limit for depositing of the costs of evidence collecting.

The court serves the parties with a duplicate copy of the order, and, in addition to the said duplicate copy, serves the defendant with a duplicate copy of the written reply and the evidence attached thereto, and instructs the parties to provide a position, within one week, in connection with the instructions given and the report on the case and to undertake the relevant procedural steps, as well as advises the parties of the consequences of non-compliance with the instructions (Article 312(2) CCP). The court rules on the timely requests made in connection with the instructions and the case report on the day of their receipt. The order under the requests shall be communicated to the parties (Article 312(3) CCP). Where the parties fail to comply with the instructions of the court within the term set, the said parties forfeit the possibility to do so later, unless the omission is due to special unforeseen circumstances (Article 313 CCP).

The claimant may, by his/her position on the report of the court, and the defendant may, by the written reply, bring in an incidental ascertainment claim (*see* paragraph 127). Counterclaims may not be brought, third parties may not be impleaded, and actions may not be brought against any such third parties according to the procedure of this proceeding (Article 314(2) CCP). Article 314(3) CCP provides that in cases of claims for eviction from premises leased or loaned for use, objections as to ownership and to improvements made in the immovable are inadmissible.

The cases considered according to summary procedure are heard in an open session with subpoenaing the parties. During the said session the court reinvites the parties to reach an agreement, and if no such agreement is reached, the court collects the brought in and presented evidence and hears the oral pleadings (Article 315(1) CCP). According to Article 315(2) CCP the court sets a day whereon the said court is to announce its decision and which shall be the day as from which the term for appeal of the said decision shall begin to run. *The court is obligated to announce its decision, together with the motives for it, within a two-week term following the session in which the consideration of the case was concluded.*

In ID No. 12-11.03.2013-SCC under interpretative case No. 12/2012, the GMCC accepted that the term for appeal of a decision announced under the conditions of Article 315(2) CCP, runs from the date on which the court has indicated that it will issue its decision. The serving under Article 7(2) CCP of transcripts of the decision changes the beginning of the term for filing an appeal only if a copy of the decision with other instructions is sent to the parties or the decision is announced after the date specified in advance under Article 315(2) CCP.

§2. Matrimonial Proceedings

336. The claims considered according to the procedure of particular adversary proceedings are: claims for divorce, claims for the invalidation of marriage and ascertainment of the existence or non-existence of marriage between the parties (Article 318 CCP). The claims regarding personal or proprietary consequences of marriage or the termination thereof are not matrimonial ones, even where they are joined in order to be considered jointly with matrimonial claims (Article 322(2) CCP). The disputes forming the subject matter of matrimonial claims cannot be determined incidentally on the occasion of objections against other claims (arg. under Article 46(2) FC).

337. The legitimation regarding the bringing in of matrimonial claims is strictly limited, this being due to the specific personal nature thereof. The claim for divorce can be brought in only by a spouse against the other spouse. According to Article 47(1) FC, a claim for the invalidation of the marriage can be filed in the following cases: (a) violation of Article 6 FC – only by the juvenile spouse; (b) the cases under Article 46(1), item 2 – only by the threatened spouse; (c) the cases under Article 13(1), item 1 – by either spouse, or the public prosecutor, or the spouse in the first marriage; (d) in the cases under Article 7(1), items 2 and 3, and Article 13(2) – by either spouse or the public prosecutor. The public prosecutor's claim for the invalidation of a marriage under Article 47(1), item 4 FC in the cases under Article 7(1), items 2 and 3 FC, and Article 7(2) FC are brought in against the two spouses, and in the cases under Article 7(1), item 1 FC – against the two spouses and the spouse in the first marriage. Matrimonial proceedings are inadmissible if they do not involve both spouses.

338. Article 319 CCP provides that juvenile spouses as well as the ones under limited interdiction are entitled to bring in matrimonial claims on their own and to be defendants thereto. Article 6(4) FC provides that the juvenile person becomes legally capable upon contracting a marriage. *Owing thereto, it is reasonably assumed that the juvenile person who has contracted a marriage has full legal capability, including where he/she is a party to cases regarding matrimonial claims, and the special procedural capability laid down in* Article *319 CCP concerns only those persons who are placed under limited interdiction.*

339. According to Article 320 CCP, matrimonial proceedings are suspended upon the wife's request in those cases where the latter is pregnant, and until the child becomes twelve months old.

Neither a decision by default nor a decision upon recognition of the claim is rendered (Article 324 CCP). The legislator has allowed to transform adversary matrimonial proceedings into matrimonial proceedings on mutual consent when the parties do not dispute and conclude an agreement under Article 51 FC (*see* paragraph 346).

340. In the first session of matrimonial proceedings the parties should attend in person to be heard (Article 321(1) CCP). Where the claimant has failed to attend the said session without having a reasonable excuse the proceedings are terminated.

The court should guide the parties to mediation or to another procedure for voluntary resolution of the dispute. If they reach an agreement on commencement of mediation or another procedure for voluntary resolution of the dispute, the case is suspended (Article 321(3) CCP). Each of them may request a resumption of the proceeding on the case within six months. Unless such a request is made, the case is terminated (Article 321(4) CCP). If the parties fail to reach agreement on a mediation procedure or another procedure for voluntary resolution of the dispute, the examination of the case continues (Article 321(6) CCP). It is provided in Article 321(5) CCP that where an agreement is reached, depending on the content of the said agreement, the case is terminated or proceedings for a divorce by mutual consent are proceeded with. The case will be terminated, if the claim has been duly withdrawn or waived. The proceedings for a divorce by mutual consent will be proceeded with, if the parties request that and present the agreement required under Article 51 FC.

According to Article 49(4) FC at any stage of the suit the spouses may submit to the court an agreement regarding all or any of the consequences of the divorce. The court approves the agreement, having been assured that the children's rights are protected. It may request a statement from the Social Support Directorate (Article 49(5) FC).

341. According to Article 322(1) CCP, in the cases of divorce the claimant has to state all the grounds for the profound and irretrievable breakdown of the marriage. The grounds which have occurred prior to the closure of the court trial *and have been known to the spouse*, but the latter has failed to state them, cannot constitute grounds for bringing in a new claim for divorce. In procedural doctrine this consequence is called 'procedural consumption' and it expresses the principle of singleness and exhaustiveness of matrimonial proceedings. The facts which were not known to the claimant are not precluded by the decision when the claim is disallowed in divorce adversary proceedings. A new claim can be brought in on the grounds of the said facts.

According to Article 322(3) CCP, the provisions of Article 322(1) and (2) CCP also apply to the defendant's claims which he/she could have brought in. The defendant is also entitled to seek the termination of the marriage on the grounds of its profound and irretrievable breakdown, as well as on the grounds of other facts from the life of the spouses. Besides, he/she is also entitled to bring in claims for the invalidation of the marriage. In literature and practice the claims brought in by the defendant in the adversary proceedings instituted by him/her are treated as his/her counterclaims. However, the requirements under Article 211 CCP (*see* paragraph 296) regarding the bringing in of a counterclaim do not apply thereto.

The text of Article 322(1) CCP, in connection with Article 322(3) CCP opened the crucial question about the applicability of the preclusions foreseen in Article 133 CCP (*see* paragraphs 149–152); Article 147 CCP (*see* paragraph 152) and Article 266 CCP (*see* paragraphs 212, 217, 244). Article 322(1) CCP concerns both the facts constituting grounds for bringing in a claim for divorce because of the profound and irretrievable breakdown of the marriage and the objections of the defendant.

According to Article 322(2), sentence I CCP, all matrimonial claims can be joined. According to Article 322(4) CCP, once the divorce claim has been disallowed, no claim can be brought in for invalidating a marriage because of a violation of the age conditions under Article 6 FC, or because of intimidation under Article 46(1), item 2 FC. Therefore, bringing in the claims specified in Article 322(4) CCP is also necessary, if the party is not willing to have the possibility of bringing in such a claim precluded.

In the case of a divorce, the spouses solve on mutual agreement the matters of upbringing the underage children born during the marriage in their interest and the court approves the agreement under Article 49(5) FC (Article 59(1) FC). If such an agreement is not reached, the court ex officio rules who the children will live with, who will exercise the parental rights, and determines the measures regarding the exercise of these rights and the regime of personal relationships between the children and parents, and the maintenance of the children. The court rules on those matters having evaluated all circumstances in accordance with the children's interests, namely the abilities of the parents to bring up the children, the care provided at the moment. The court hears the parents and the child under Article 15 ChPA. The opinion of the Social Support Directorate is also taken into consideration and if appropriate other persons are also heard. When there are data of parental alienation syndrome, the court hears and expert psychologists. On the grounds of Article 322(2), sentence II CCP, Articles 56(2) and 59(2) and (3) FC in matrimonial proceedings when there are minors and underage children born in the marriage, the court should consider the matters of the exercise the parental rights, the personal relationships between the children and parents the child support and the usage of the family home when the parties have not lodged the respective claims.

The claims for spousal support and the family name, as well as that for usage of the matrimonial home when there are no minor and underage children born to the marriage, can be brought in the matrimonial proceedings, although those are not matrimonial claims. Article 322(1) CCP is valid for the matrimonial claims but not for the non-matrimonial claims. Therefore, the general rules of Articles 133, 147, 260 item 1, 266 CCP should be valid for those claims. The same should be valid for the claim on the fault. On the grounds of Article 56 FC and Article 326 CCP the spouse who has changed his/her family name upon conclusion of the marriage is entitled to require the court to rule on restoration of his/her pre-marriage family name.

342. According to Article 323(2) CCP, upon the request of the parties the court with which the claim for divorce or invalidation of a marriage has been filed rules on the temporary measures regarding the alimony, the matrimonial home, and the use of the property acquired during the marriage, and the care for and maintenance of the children. The court is obliged to rule on in the court session in which the request has been filed whereas no additional evidence should be collected. Otherwise, a new session is scheduled within a two-week term (Article 323(2) CCP). The said ruling is not subject to appeal and ruling is enforceable (Article 323(3) CCP). It can be amended or revoked by the court, which has issued it (Article 323(3) CCP).

343. According to Article 49(3) FC, through its decision admitting a divorce *the court rules on the fault* regarding the breakdown of marriage, if any of the spouses has requested that. The decision on the divorce takes effect even when its part on the fault is appealed (Article 325 CCP).

344. If the claimant dies in the course of the proceedings the heirs or the parents are entitled to continue the proceedings in order to establish the reasonableness of the claim which has been filed, if the latter is grounded on the faulty conduct of the surviving spouse (Article 52(2) FC). According to Article 327 CCP, the court sets a term of two weeks to the heirs or the parents to state whether they are willing to continue the proceedings; the same is also valid for a claim for invalidation of a marriage if the surviving spouse has been unconscionable. The proceedings are terminated if within the set term none of the heirs states that he/she is willing to continue the case.

According to Article 328 CCP, in the cases of death of the defendant it is possible for the proceedings to be continued by persons under Article 327 CCP only where the claim is connected with Article 13 FC and the claimant was the unconscionable party when the marriage took place.

Under Article 52 FC, Articles. 327 and 328 CCP the proceedings continue on the ascertainment claim seeking to establish that, prior to the termination of the marriage due to the death of their testator, the latter was entitled to a divorce, or to an invalidation of the marriage, respectively, due to the grounds specified in the said texts.

345. According to Article 303(2) CCP, no reversal of a decision is allowed in those cases where the decision prescribes a divorce, invalidation of the marriage, or the decision declares the marriage a non-existent one. The decision rendered on a matrimonial claim is binding upon all persons (Article 298(3) CCP).

346. According to Article 50(1) FC, in the cases of the spouses' *serious and firm consent to the divorce*, the court allows the divorce without examining their motives for the termination of the marriage. The divorce on mutual agreement is also rendered by the court. These proceedings are not adversary but non-contentious ones, as no dispute between the spouses exists regarding the termination of the marriage.

According to Article 51(1) FC, in the cases of a divorce by mutual consent the spouses have to submit their agreement regarding the residence of the children, exercise of parental rights, personal relationships and the maintenance of children, as well as the proprietary relationships, the use of the matrimonial home, the alimony of the spouses and the family name. The parties may agree on other consequences of the divorce. According to Article 51(2) FC the agreement is approved by the court, the latter having examined whether the interests of the children are protected. The court may request the statement of the Social Support Directorate. Where the agreement is incomplete or the interests of the children are not protected properly the court sets a term within which the defects of the agreement should be eliminated. Where the defects are not eliminated within the specified term the court disallows the request for divorce (Article 51(1) FC).

According to Article 330(1) CCP, where a divorce by mutual consent is sought the spouses have to attend the court session in person. In those cases where a spouse fails to appear in either the reconciliation session or the court session without having a reasonable excuse for it, the proceedings are terminated (Article 330(2) CCP).

Once the court has got convinced that the consent of the spouses to have a divorce is a serious and firm one, and deems that the agreement under Article 51 FC does not contradict the law and is in the best interests of the children, it allows the divorce and approves the agreement by way of a decision (Article 330(3) CCP). Two non-contentious acts, united in a single decision, are concerned here. The decision terminating the marriage by mutual consent constitutes a non-contentious act with constitutive effect, the latter being manifested in the termination of the marriage. The agreement between the parties on the matters under Article 51 FC which has been approved by the court is enforceable.

According to, the decision allowing a divorce by mutual consent is not subject to appeal (Article 330(5) CCP). The same applies to the decision approving the agreement reached by the parties. The decision which disallows the request of the spouses for a divorce by mutual consent is subject to appeal. The appeal has to be filed by the two spouses.

§3. Proceedings Regarding Civil Status Cases

347. According to Article 331(1) CCP, the claims for establishing or challenging the origin, and the claims for the termination of adoption are considered in accordance with the particular adversary proceedings regarding civil status.

The legitimization and the terms for the claims for establishing challenging the origin are regulated in Articles. 60(3), 62(1), (2) and (3), 67, 68 and 69 FC. The origin from the woman, who has given birth to the child in case of assisted reproduction, may not be challenged on these grounds (Article 60(5) FC). No challenging the fatherhood is allowed where the child was born under the conditions of assisted reproduction, if the husband of the mother has given consent in writing about its performing Article 62(5) FC. According to Article 335 CCP, the proceedings regarding the challenging of fatherhood are terminated upon the death of the child.

In 2020 (SG, issue 103 of 2020) several amendments were made to Chapter Six 'Origin' of the FC (*see* Article 62(1), Article 62(4), Article 62(5), Article 63(2) and Article 66(1), (5) and (6) FC) and the possibility for filing part of the claims was expanded. According to Article 62(4) FC (amended, SG No. 103/2020) the child may challenge paternity from the age of 14 up to one year from the age of majority. This provision is also in accordance with the special procedural capacity established by law in civil status cases (Article 331 CCP).

Neither any claim for seeking the origin can be brought in, nor can owning be carried out until the existing origin is rebutted in accordance with the adversary procedure, the existing origin being established through a birth certificate, or through the presumption under Article 61 FC, or through owning (Article 71 FC). It is possible for the two claims to be joined.

The claim for establishing the fatherhood or motherhood might have a claim for the child's maintenance joined thereto, however, no temporary maintenance can be adjudged in these cases (Article 332 CCP). Where the court upholds the claims under Articles 68 and 69 FC, it enacts ex officio with whom of the parents the child should live, the measures regarding the exercise of parental rights and determines a regime of the personal relations between the child and the parents, and his/her maintenance, applying Article 59 FC, respectively (Article 70 FC).

The grounds of the claims for termination of adoption are listed in detail in the FC (Articles 64(1) and 106(1) FC). The legitimization of bringing in such clams is restricted (Article 106 (2), (3), (4) and (5) FC). There are set preclusive terms for nullifying adoption. Where public interests are concerned, the termination of the adoption can also be sought by the public prosecutor (Article 106(6) FC). Social Aid Directorate is entitled to seek termination of the adoption under Article 106(1) FC where it is against the child's interest (Article 106(7) FC). According to Article 106(9) FC, the participation of a public prosecutor in the cases of termination of adoption is obligatory but in the case under Article 106(8) FC. According to Article 106(8) FC the adoption may be terminated by the regional court upon mutual consent of the adoptive parent and the adopted child, when both of them are in judicial ability.

348. The heirs are not entitled to bring in the claims specified in Chapter IV FC (claims for establishing or challenging the origin, claims for challenging or invalidation of owning a child), however, they are entitled to continue the proceedings regarding the claim brought in by their testator (Article 72(1) FC). Where the adoptive parent or the adopted person dies during the proceedings regarding the termination of adoption under Article 106(1) FC, the proceedings can be continued by the heirs of the claimant (Article 108 FC). Where the court upholds the claim, the defaulting surviving adoptive parent or adopted person does not inherit the deceased one.

349. According to Article 331(2) CCP and Article 319(2) CCP in this category of proceedings the juveniles and the persons placed under limited interdiction have special procedural capability. According to Article 34(2) CCP, an explicit power of attorney is necessary for bringing in a civil status claim. The minors and the persons placed under complete interdiction should be represented by their legal representatives. Owing to the specificity of these proceedings, the interests of the representative are often in conflict with those of the represented person. Therefore, the court often appoints a special representative according to Article 29(4) CCP.

350. The claims regarding the establishment or challenge of the origin, as well as those regarding the termination of adoption fall within the jurisdiction of the district court as a first-instance court (Article 104(1) CCP).

The Bulgarian courts have jurisdiction over proceedings for (a) establishment and challenging of origin except pursuant to Article 4 PILC and where the child or the parent, who is a party, is a Bulgarian national or is habitually resident in the Republic of Bulgaria (Article 9(1) PILC); (b) annulment or termination of adoption, except in the cases covered under Article 4 PILC and where the adopter, the adoptee or one of the parents of the adoptee is a Bulgarian national or is habitually resident in the Republic of Bulgaria. According to Article 1(2), item 'a' of Regulation 1215/2012 on jurisdiction and the recognition and enforcement of judgments in civil and commercial matters this regulation is not applicable with respect to civil status cases. According to Article 1(3), items 'a' and 'b' of Regulation 2201/2003 concerning jurisdiction and the recognition and enforcement of judgments in matrimonial matters and the matters of parental responsibility, the regulation is not applicable with respect to: determining or disproving parental connection and the decisions for adoption, measures preparing adoption or termination of the adoption.

351. The parties to the case are obligated to cooperate upon the preparation of the conclusion by the expert witness, unless the research involves a substantial or sustained risk to the life or health of the said parties (Article 333 CCP). *The court pronounces on a refusal to cooperate by a ruling which is subject to a separate appeal.* Where the refusal is rightful, the court determines another method of research into filiation which does not involve any such risk. In event of necessity, the court determines application of proper compulsory measures for obtaining samples through methods by which the body inviolability is kept (Article 333 (3) CCP).

There are no special norms in Chapter 27 CCP, providing explicitly the application of the rules for the reply to the statement of claim, the preclusion under Articles 133, 147 and 266 CCP. That is an unintentional omission of the legislator, if he has excluded the applicability of a decision at recognition of the claim and decision by default in Article 334 CCP. The lack of a reply to the statement of claim) does not enable the rendering a decision by default on cases from this category, then the lack of a reply should not be grounds for applying the preclusions under Articles 133, 147, 260(5) and 266 CCP.

352. According to Article 298(3) CCP, the decision rendered on a civil status claim (including the claims regarding the establishment or challenge of the origin, as well as those regarding the termination of adoption and the matrimonial claims) is binding on all persons (*see* paragraph 190). A decision by default and a decision upon recognition of the claim are not rendered on the civil status cases (Article 334 CCP).

§4. Proceedings Regarding the Placement under Interdiction and the Abolishment of Interdiction

353. The proceedings regarding the placement under interdiction[153] aim is to have the person placed under of interdiction protected; to protect the interests of the said person's relatives protected against his/her actions, through which he/she might harm them; to protect the public interests. The said interests might consist in the need to place a person under the respective type of interdiction. They also aim at having the said person protected from the unconscionable actions of those persons who are legitimized to bring in a claim for his/her being placed under interdiction in pursue of their own selfish aims, or for the purpose of harming or manipulating him/her.

354. The claims for placement under interdiction and those for the abolishment thereof fall within the jurisdiction of the district court as a first instance (Article 104, item 1 CCP). This legislative solution takes into account the social significance of these cases.

The claim for the placement of a person under complete or limited interdiction might be filed by the spouse, or the close relatives, or the public prosecutor, as well as by anybody who has a legal interest therein (Article 336(1) CCP). The participation of the public prosecutor in these proceedings is obligatory when the claim has been filed by any of the persons legitimized under Article 336(1) and (2) CCP).

355. The defendant in the proceedings regarding the placement under interdiction is the person whose placement under interdiction is sought.[154] He/she participates in the proceedings in person. He/she is not legally incapable until he/she is placed under interdiction by way of a decision which has taken effect. According to Article 337(1) CCP, he/she has to be questioned in person and, if necessary, he/she is brought to the court forcibly. According to Article 337(2) CCP, if after the questioning the court finds it necessary, it appoints a temporary custodian of the person, and the latter has to take care of his/her personal and proprietary interests. The aim consists in having his/her personal and proprietary interests protected. The appointment of a temporary custodian does not affect his/her procedural legal capacity in the proceedings regarding his/her placement under interdiction, he/she participating therein in person. He/she might hire an attorney and have competent legal assistance in the proceedings instituted against him/her.

According to Article 338(1) CCP, the court rules on the claim after questioning the person whose placement under interdiction is sought, and after questioning his/

153. There are two types of placement under interdiction in Bulgarian law – complete and limited (Art. 5 FA).

154. If the defendant dies while the proceedings are still pending, they have to be terminated, and where a decision has been rendered but has not taken effect yet, the said decision has to be invalidated because of it being pointless. There is no opportunity of having the proceedings continued for the purpose of establishing whether the person has been in any of the States envisaged in Art. 5 PFA, and owing thereto, he/she should have been placed under interdiction (Decree No. 5–79 – Plenum of the SC).

her relatives as well.[155] Where this turns out to be insufficient, the court proceeds to collecting other evidence and hearing out the experts.

According to Article 339 CCP (*see* paragraph 352) the rules for a reply to the statement of claim and for the preclusion under Articles. 133, 147 and 266 CCP do not apply.

356. The effective decision for placing a person under interdiction has a constitutive effect and deprives the person of legal capability. According to Article 338(3) CCP, the court notifies the custodian body thereof, so that the guardianship or custody is established.

It is the person's mental state that determines whether the court will place the person under complete or limited interdiction (*see* paragraph 353).

On the grounds of Article 298(3) CCP, the decision rendered on claims for the placement under interdiction has the force of res judicata regarding everybody (*see* paragraph 190).

According to Article 339 CCP neither a decision by default nor a decision upon recognition of the claim can be rendered on claims for placing a person under interdiction.

357. According to Article 340(1) CCP the regulations of Chapter 28 are also applicable to proceedings on abolishment of the interdiction (*see* paragraph 353). The claim for the abolishment of the interdiction may be also brought in by the custodian body or by the custodian or by the person placed under limited interdiction in person (Article 340(2) CCP, Amend. SG No. 86/2017).[156]

In these cases the claim has to be brought in against the persons on whose request the decision for placement under interdiction has been rendered. The claim may also be brought in by the persons under Article 336(1) CCP, including the public prosecutor. Articles 337(2) and 338(3) CCP do not apply to these proceedings because of their being pointless. Article 336(2) and Article 337(1) CCP providing examination in person of the one to be interdicted must apply in these proceedings.

The abolishment of the placement under interdiction may be sought in those cases where new facts are alleged, that brought about the recuperation of the person placed under interdiction, hence there is no more need of his/her being under interdiction.

§5. Juridical Partition

358. Juridical partition is characterized as *particular adversary proceedings*, in the course of which the right to partition is both established and enforced. Partition

155. In view of the new social realities and the increased number of factual cohabitation, the cohabitant with whom the person lives as a spouse should also be questioned.
156. With the amendment of Art. 340(2) CP (SG, No. 86/2017) the special legal capacity of the person subject to the interdiction of his/her claim for abolishment of his/her placement under limited interdiction was recognized. However, he/she may have a lawyer. In view of his condition, he/she should be provided with due legal assistance under the Legal Aid Law.

cases fall within the subject-matter jurisdiction of regional courts, regardless of the amount of the claim (Article 341(1) CCP).

Each of the co-owners has his/her own right to partition (Article 34 PA), and partition proceedings are aimed at putting an end to the co-ownership. Therefore, all co-owners should take part in partition proceedings. Otherwise, the partition is void (arg. Article 75(2) IA). In partition proceedings indispensable parties are present, and each of the co-partitioners has the quality of a claimant regarding his/her right to partition, and the quality of a defendant regarding the other partitioners' rights to partition.

In ID No. 3 of 19.12.2013 of the SCC under interpretative decision No. 3/2013 GMCC it was accepted that in case of disposition of the disputed right by a co-owner (co-partitioner) in favour of another person in the course of the partition proceedings in the phase of admitting the division, the provisions of Article 226 CCP.

359. Partition proceedings have two stages. The first stage is of admitting the partition. The purpose of this stage consists in establishing the right to partition. In the first court session each one of the co-partitioners is entitled to bring an objection either against another co-partitioner's right to participate in the partition, or against the amount of his/her share, or against the inclusion of certain property in the partition estate (Article 342 CCP). Article 343 CCP provides that in the course of partition proceedings the following is considered as well: challenging the origin, or adoption, or testimony, or the genuineness of written evidence, and demands for diminishing testamentary dispositions and donations. The legal relationships concerned here are prejudicial both to the co-ownership and to the right to partition. The challenges under Article 342 and Article 343 CCP may not be brought in those cases where they have been determined through the force of res judicata or have been brought in accordance with the adversary procedure. If there is a pending case regarding a prejudicial legal relationship, the partition proceedings have to be suspended (Article 229(1), item 4 CCP).

The rule of Article 133 CCP is not applied in the partition proceedings, as it is excluded by the special provision of Article 342 CCP. Procedural preclusion occurs with the expiration of the term referred to in Article 342 CCP.

360. According to Article 344(1), sentence I CCP, in its decision admitting the claim the court rules on the following matters: which persons and estates will the partition concern, and what each co-heir's part is. This is a decision of independent nature. It puts an end to the first stage of partition proceedings. It is subject to being appealed against in accordance with the general procedure for appeal against decisions. Only after this decision takes effect can the second stage of partition proceedings begin, this being the stage of carrying out the partition. In this stage the court is obligated to acknowledge the force of res judicata of the decision regarding both the admitting of the partition, this decision having taken effect, and the matters it has determined in relation to the right to partition of the co-owned property, the co-owners and their parts in the co-owned property, these being matters that cannot be redetermined in the second stage.

361. The second stage of the juridical partition is of carrying out the partition. Disputes over payments can be also considered and determined in this stage. According to Article 346 CCP, it is in the first session following the admitting of the partition that the co-partitioners are entitled to bring in claims for payments among themselves, producing the evidence thereof. This is a preclusive term for bringing in the said claims in partition proceedings. However, they may also be brought in separate proceedings, and will be considered in accordance with the general adversary procedure. The claims concerned here are the ones regarding those contractual pretensions among the co-partitioners *which have arisen in connection with the co-ownership of property.*

362. It is specific of Bulgarian law is that the legislator has put the accent on the need for having each of the co-partitioners receive a real share, if possible. According to Article 347 CCP, where there are estates for all co-partitioners, the court draws up the partition record on the grounds of the expert's conclusion. When drawing up the partition record the court is obligated to acknowledge the decision regarding the admitting of the partition, this decision having taken effect, and determining the estates, the co-partitioners and the shares thereof. The difference between the quota and the value of the share is equalized in money. After drawing up the draft record of the partition, the court summons the parties in order to present it to them and to hear out their objections against it. Afterwards the court draws up and announces the final record of the partition (Article 352 CCP).

Once the decision regarding the partition record takes effect, the court summons the parties for drawing lots where the co-partitioners' quotas are equal and the property is of a type which allows that real shares of equal value be formed.[157] According to Article 353 CCP, the court is entitled to carry out the partition by way of distributing the co-owned estates among the co-partitioners without drawing lots, if the formation of shares and the drawing of lots turns out to be either impossible or rather inconvenient. The partition is carried out in this way in those cases where the quotas of the co-partitioners are different, and owing thereto, it is necessary that the record be drawn up in such a way that the amount of the real share of each co-partitioner corresponds to the amount of the quota.

363. According to Article 347 CCP, in those cases where an estate is indivisible and it is impossible for it to form part of any of the shares, the court rules that it be put up for public sale. In the hypothesis set forth in Article 347 CCP, upon the termination of adversary proceedings the partition has not been carried out and the co-ownership is not over. The public sale was added to partition proceedings. It is held after the decision for putting up the property for public sale takes effect (*see* paragraphs 358, 361) but no enforcement proceedings are present.

According to Article 354 CCP, where the property is put up for public sale as indivisible, each of the co-partitioners is entitled to buy it out in observance of the

157. The Court of First Instance to draw a lot is subject to appeal before the intermediate appellative court; the ruling of the intermediate appellative court allowing it is subject to a cassation appeal under Art. 274 (3), item 2 CPC (ID No. 5-2015 of 12 Jul. 2018, on inter. dec. No. 5/2015).

conditions laid down in Article 505(2) CCP. If a co-partitioner takes part in the bidding, he/she is proclaimed buyer provided that in the course of having the record under Article 492(1) CCP drawn up, he/she states that he/she is willing to buy the estate at the highest offered price. According to Article 354(2) CCP, in those cases where several co-partitioners are willing to buy out the estate under the conditions of Article 505(2) CCP, a new sale is held among them only, the initial price being the highest one offered in the course of the first sale. The second sale continues for seven days and is held in accordance with the general rules. According to Article 354(3) CCP, if in the course of this sale none of the co-partitioners buys out the estate, the latter is awarded to the bidder – a third person in the sale who has offered the highest price in the course of the first sale.

364. According to Article 349(1) CCP, where the indivisible estate is a housing accommodation which used to be under matrimonial ownership in common terminated upon the death of one of the spouses or upon a divorce, and the surviving spouse, or the former spouse who has been granted the exercise of parental rights regarding the children born in the marriage has no housing accommodation of his/her own, upon the request of the latter the court is entitled to place it in a share, equalizing the shares of the other co-partitioners through other estates or money. Under the argument of Article 349(2) CCP, it is assumed that, in those cases where the co-ownership of a housing accommodation results from a transaction, the partition is carried out by way of putting it up for public sale. Items 4 and 5 of the ID No. 1-2004-GMCC of the SCC are still valid. Article 349(1) CCP regulates two hypotheses of awarding in share of an indivisible housing accommodation, acquired under the regime of matrimonial ownership in common – where the co-ownership occurs either because of the death of one of the spouses, or because of a divorce of the parties. The requirements of the law are specified in detail and the cumulative presence thereof is needed.

365. According to Article 349(2) CCP, in those cases where the indivisible estate is a housing accommodation, each of the co-partitioners who was living in it at the time the inheritance was disclosed and does not own another housing accommodation is entitled to demand that it be placed in his/her share, and that the shares of the other co-partitioners be equalized with other estates or money. In those cases where several co-partitioners meeting the requirements specified in the preceding sentence bring in pretences for having the estate placed in their shares, preference is given to the one who offers the highest price. Item 7 of the ID No. 1-2004-GMCC of the SCC is still actual.

The legislator *has not laid down a specific procedure for determining the priority offer*. By *analogy with the bidding in enforcement proceedings* (Article 498(1) and (2) CCP), without co-partitioners' depositing earnest money, in order to guarantee the equality of the parties, in the course of proceedings the court is obligated to *hold a secret bidding among the pretending co-partitioners*.

The surviving spouse who takes part in the partition of an indivisible housing estate which is under matrimonial ownership in common has a dual quality – he/she is an heir and a co-owner. *The presence of the prerequisites set forth in* Article *349(1) CCP for awarding the estate exclude the consideration of any possible pretences under* Article *349(2) CCP.*

366. Once the decision for admitting the partition takes effect, the request for the awarding can be made, prior to the first session of the court (Article 349(4) CCP).

367. According to Article 349(5) CCP in those cases where a pecuniary equalization is made it has to be paid together with the statutory interest thereupon, within a term of six months following the day on which the decision regarding the award takes effect. The co-partitioner in whose share the estate has been placed in accordance with the procedure laid down in Article 349(1) and (2) *becomes the owner thereof provided that he/she has paid within the term under* Article *349(6) CCP the pecuniary equalization and the statutory interest thereupon. If he/she fails to pay the equalization within the said term, the awarding decision is invalidated ex jure and the estate is put up for public sale.* The estate may not be put up for public sale, and be awarded to another co-partitioner who meets the requirements set forth in Article 349(2) CCP and has placed a request for awarding under Article 349(4) CCP, provided that he/she pays the price immediately, the said price being reduced by the value of the co-partitioner's share in the estate. The amount thus calculated is distributed among the other co-partitioners in accordance with their quotas.

The law gives rise both to the substantive law (constitutive) effect of the decision and to the transformation of the co-owned property into individually owned property *upon the payment of a pecuniary equalization within the period set forth in law. It is only through the payment of a specific pecuniary equalization and the interest that the awarded co-partitioner becomes the owner of the estate, this period being six months following the date on which the awarding decision took effect.* In item 10 of the quoted ID it was assumed that where, following the expiry of the term under Article 288(6) CCP, repealed (Article 349(5) CCP, current) *no payment was made, in view of the ex jure invalidation of the awarding decision and the retroactive elimination of the grounds for the occurrence of the pecuniary liability.* In the ID No. 1-2004-GMCC of the SCC, it was assumed that, *in order for the pendency of the partition proceedings to be resumed, the co-partitioner who is also the creditor, and in whose favour the arrear of pecuniary equalization of a share has occurred, should seize the court by way of a written request.*

It was also assumed that the court decision should necessarily contain an explicit disposition ascertaining the invalidation of the award of the indivisible housing accommodation. Once the decision proclaiming the ex jure invalidation of an awarding decision under Article 349(1) and (2) CCP has been rendered, the principal way of carrying out the partition is putting up the estate for public (Article 349(6) CCP, current). In sentence III the legislator has provided for an exception in those cases in which another co-partitioner meeting the requirements of Article 349(6) CCP immediately pays the price of the estate as determined in the evaluation thereof.

§6. Commercial Disputes

368. Article 365 CCP contains a thorough list of the claims considered following the special adversary procedure for considering commercial disputes which are under the generic competence of the district court as a first instance. Where claims do not exceed BGN 25,000, the disputes are considered under the general adversary procedure. They do not meet the generic jurisdiction criterion. Thus, cases that have the same subject matter are considered by a different procedure depending on the amount of the claim.

Claims regarding subject matter rights or legal relations, which are not commercial, are also considered under the order of proceedings on commercial disputes. According to Article 365(1), item 2 CCP, by way of this special claim procedure, disputes regarding a right or legal relationship arising from or relating to a privatization contract, a public procurement contract and a concession contract are also considered. The privatization contract is not a commercial transaction, but a special civil transaction with administrative elements, but the disputes related to it are subject to consideration under the procedure for commercial disputes (ID No. 1-15.06.2010 of the SCC under interpretative decision No. 1/2009, GMCom.C.).

According to Article 113 CCP (supplemented, SG No. 100/2019), however, the claims of and against consumers are considered as civil cases under the general claim procedure, although these rights and legal relations may arise from a transaction with a trader which under Bulgarian commercial law is treated as a unilateral commercial transaction. An interpretative decision No. 3/2019 of the SCC on the issue of civil or commercial case with a subject of legal relations arising under a contract for construction works concluded between a natural person and a trader in connection with his occupation, and what is the threshold for access to cassation appeal of the appellate decision in the case is formed, on which there is still no ruling.

369. But the general requirements that a statement of claim should meet, Article 366 CCP specifies a requirement for the claim for a money receivable – an attachment containing the calculations required for determination of the amount of the receivable. If the statement of claim conforms and the claim is admissible, the court sends its duplicate with the attachments to the defendant giving him/her instructions on submitting a written reply within a two-week term, on mandatory content of the reply and on consequents of his/her failing to submit a reply or non-executing his/her rights.

According to Article 369(1) CCP the objection that the dispute is not subject to examination according to the especial adversary procedure for commercial disputes may be lodged solely by the defendant with the reply to the statement of claim at the latest or may be raised ex officio by the court within the same term. A ruling that the dispute is subject to examination according to the standard procedure can be appealed by a private appeal Article 369(2) CCP.

The mandatory content of the reply to the statement of claim and its attachments foreseen in Article 367(1) CCP is the same as the one of the defendant's reply in the general adversary procedure (Article 131(2) CCP, *see* paragraph 148). The nature of the preclusion under Article 370 CCP is the same as that under Article 133 CCP in the general adversary procedure. According to Article 371 CCP the objection to set-off may be lodged prior to the conclusion of the trial in the first-instance court, where taking of new evidence is not required to prove the said set-off, or prior to the conclusion of the trial at the intermediate appellate instance, where the existence or non-contestation of the said set-off are established by an effective decision of the court or an enforcement order (*see* the objection against set-off in the general adversary procedure paragraphs 146, 213 and item 4 of inter. dec. No. 1-09.12.2013 on inter. dec. No. 1/2013, GMCC and the Com.C. of the SCC). Within the term for bringing in a reply the defendant may bring in a cross-claim and impeded third persons and bringing in claims against the said third persons (compare Articles 367(4) and 211; 219(1) and 133 CCP).

The court having received the reply to the statement of claim and verified its conformity, sends its duplicate to the claimant who can file an additional statement of claim within two weeks (Article 372(1) CCP). In the additional statement of claim the claimant can clarify and complement the initial claim. Within the term for the additional statement of claim he/she can alter the claim, involve third persons, file claims against such persons, request the court to pronounce by the decision itself *inter alia* regarding the existence or non-existence of a legal relation disputed in the reply to the statement of claim upon which the outcome of the case depends in whole or in part, as well as cite and present new evidence which he/she was unable to cite and present by the statement of claim (Article 372(2) CCP).

Having admitted the additional statement of claim, the court sends its duplicate with the attachments to the defendant who can submit a reply the within two weeks (Article 373(1) CCP). The defendant should reply to the additional statement in the additional reply. Within the term for an additional reply, the defendant can request the court to pronounce on the existence or non-existence of a legal relation disputed in the additional statement of claim upon which the outcome of the case depends, as well as cite and present new evidence which he/she was unable to cite and present by reply to the statement of claim.

The preparation of the case is in camera without subpoenaing the parties and conducting the double exchange of papers. The court schedules a hearing of the case in an open session, sending the additional reply to the claimant. The court communicates its ruling under Article 373(1) CCP to the parties. The court may furthermore communicate to the parties the court's draft of a report on the case, as well as direct the parties to mediation or another procedure for voluntary settlement of the dispute (Article 374(2) CCP).

The case is considered in an open session with subpoenaing the parties as it is done in the general adversary procedure (compare paragraphs 171 and 172, Article 375 CCP). An exception is specified in Article 376(1) CCP: when all the evidence is presented by the exchange of papers, the court may find that no hearing of the parties is necessary and consider the case in a closed session, provides the opportunity to present written defences and replies.

According to Article 377 CCP, as there are no special rules for the proceedings on commercial cases, the general proceedings rules for considering a case at the first instance are applied. According to Article 378 CCP, the special rules for considering commercial disputes at the first instance are applied in the intermediate appellative proceedings, respectively.

§7. Collective Claims Proceedings

370. The collective claim can be brought on behalf of persons who are harmed by the same infringement where, according to the nature of the infringement, the circle of the said persons cannot be defined precisely but is identifiable (Article 379(1) CCP). It aims at protecting the collective interests of a wide circle of persons.[158] They are definable regarding the feature of infringement that affects them, e.g., the territory affected by the environmental pollution; discrimination policy of the respective State or municipality institution towards employing staff of a certain gender; certain poor quality of goods sold to the customers. The defendant to collective claim is the person who committed the infringement under Article 379(1) CCP (Article 379(2) CCP). That claim can be: for cessation of the infringement (Article 379(2) CCP), for rectification of the consequences of the infringement of the harmed collective interest, or for compensation for the damages inflicted on the said interest (Article 379(3) CCP).

371. The affected persons are not obliged to accept the defence via a collective claim. They are entitled to bring in a claim for protection of their individual rights in separate proceedings. For this purpose they should declare their unwillingness to be defended in the said proceedings (Article 383(1), item 2 CCP, *see* paragraph 373). That is aimed both by the publication of the statement of claim, foreseen in Article 382(2), item 2 CCP and by the ruling on excluding the persons unwillingness to be defended in the said proceedings (Article 383(1), item 2 CCP, *see* paragraph 373). The goal is to avoid an unfavourable decision if the legitimated persons do not conduct the proceedings adequately (Article 386(1) CCP, *see* paragraph 375).

The legitimated are either persons pretending to be harmed by the infringement specified in Article 379(2) CCP or organizations for the defence of the harmed persons or organizations of defence against such infringements. It is provided explicitly that the claim against the offender is brought in on behalf of all persons who are harmed by the same infringement. *The legislator has not adopted the figure of the substituent in the proceedings* (Article 26(2) CCP, paragraphs 307–309) who in the Bulgarian Procedure Law is a suitable defence of collective interest and is a more appropriate legislative solution. The said substituent has admitted right to a claim for defending the substantive law rights of other persons. The procedural representation in the collective claims originates from the law and there is no need of particular authorization by the harmed persons. The associations for consumer protection, included in the list under 164(1), item 7 CPA are entitled to bring in a claim for termination or banning actions or trade practices that harm the collective

158. The existence of an identifiable collective interest which is common to the whole group of persons on whose behalf the claim is brought is decisive for the classification of the claim as collective (Decision No. 198 of 2 Oct. 2013, on c.c. No. 1420/2012, of the SCC). Only collective, but not individual, interest can be defended via a collective claim. The existence of several individual pretences which are claimed together only because of the identity of the damage suffered by individuals do not justify a collective interest within the meaning of Art. 379 CCP. There is a subjective joinder of claims then. The claim for damages caused to the collective interest is not a claim for damages to each of the individuals (Decision No. 198 of 2 Oct. 2013 on c.c. No. 1420/2012, of the SCC).

interests of the consumers. Where with a collective claim under Article 74 C. Code is contesting a resolution passed by the general assembly of an investment company of the open-end type the claim is considered according to the procedure of the particular collective claim proceedings. Exclusion from participation is inadmissible in the case.

372. The collective claims are under the jurisdiction of the district court as a first instance, regardless of the amount of the claim (Article 380(1) of CCP). There is no especial norm in the CCP setting a particular local jurisdiction for the collective claims. A particular local jurisdiction for the collective claims for consumer protection is foreseen in Article 190 CPA. It is the location where the infringement has occurred or the permanent address of the defendant or the seat of the defendant. The particular local jurisdiction foreseen in Article 113 CCP that is applicable to the individual claims of the consumers (*see* paragraph 368). It is not applicable to the collective consumer claims. The particular local jurisdiction under Article 115 CCP could be applied to the collective claims for compensation of the damages caused by the infringement – according to the location where the infringement has occurred or to the seat of the defendant – since in the said case the matter is also about damages by unlawful infringement.

373. The statement of claim should include apart from the circumstances on which the claim is grounded, the circumstances identifying the circle of harmed persons and the form in which publication of the bringing in claim is proposed (Article 380(2) CCP). Evidence of the capacity of the claimant to protect the harmed interest seriously and in good faith, as well as to incur the charges related to the conduct of the case, including the costs, should be enclosed to the statement of claim (Article 380(3) CCP). Having verified the admissibility of the brought in claim and the regularity of the statement of claim the court verifies ex officio the capacity of the person or persons who have brought the action to protect the harmed interest seriously and in good faith and to incur the charges related to the conduct of the case, including the costs (Article 381(1) CCP). The court may hear the person or persons who have brought the action in an open session (Article 381(3) CCP). The court does not admit consideration of the case if someone of the persons who brought in the claim does not meet the requirements under Article 381(1) CCP, or if all of them do not meet the said requirements (Article 381(3) CCP). The ruling of the court disallowing its consideration is subject to a private appeal (Article 381(4) CCP).

The preparation for considering the case (Article 382 CCP) is in an open session with the parties being summoned. The court hears the stands of the parties regarding the circumstances which identify the circle of injured persons and the form of publication of bringing in the claim. The courts rules on: (a) an adequate form of publication of bringing in the claim: number of announcements, through which media and how long the said announcements must be made; (b) an adequate term after the publication within which the injured persons may declare that they will participate in the procedure or will pursue a remedy independently. The ruling is appealable by a private appeal (Article 382(3) CCP).

The said publication aims at ensuring the defence of the persons on whose behalf the collective claim is brought in and viewing the possibility foreseen in Article 383

CCP for accepting new participants in the procedure or the exclusion from participation in the procedure. The court, sitting in camera: accepts for participation in the procedure other injured persons, organizations responsible for the protection of the injured persons, of the harmed collective interest or for protection against such infringements, who or which have declared, within the time limit set, a motion for participation in the procedure; excludes the harmed persons who have declared, within the time limit set, that they will pursue a remedy independently in a separate procedure. The ruling on disallowing inclusion of new participants or exclusion of participants is appealable by a private appeal (383(2) CCP). This specific feature does not find expression in admitting the evidence.

374. Upon a request of the claimant, the court may rule on adequate interim measures for protection of the harmed interest. It is not bound by the claimant's request. The ruling may be modified or vacated by the same court consequent to a change in circumstances, an error or an omission (Article 385(3) CCP). It is subject to intermediate and cassation appeal regardless of the prerequisites for admitting a cassation appeal under Article 280 CCP. The ruling does not suspend its execution, only if the court renders something else (Article 385(4) CCP).

375. If no agreement is reached, the court considers the case and settles the dispute by a decision. The court may order the defendant to perform a specific act, to refrain from performing a specific act, or to pay a specific amount (Article 385(1) CCP). Special measures are foreseen in Article 187 CPA. The court is not bound by the measures for protection cited by the claimant. Considering the specifics of the case and after taking into account the stand of the defendant, the court may render other measures which ensure adequate protection of the harmed interest (Article 385(4) CCP). The decision of the court has an effect in respect of the infringer, the person or persons who have brought in the claim, as well as in respect of those persons who claim that they are harmed by the established infringement and who have not declared that they wish to pursue a remedy independently in a separate procedure (Article 386(1) and (2) CCP). Therefore, a list of the excluded persons is attached to the decision of the court with which the claim is upheld. The decision is subject to an intermediate and cassation appeal regardless of the prerequisites for cassation appealability covered under Article 280(1) CCP (*see* paragraph 229). It cannot be reversed under Article 304 CCP (*see* paragraph 255).

376. When adjudging a compensation on the damages caused by the infringement[159] the court may render that the compensation be credited to an account of one of the persons who have brought in the claim, to a special account jointly disposable by the persons who have brought in the claim, or to a special account jointly disposable by the injured persons (Article 387(1) CCP). Having rendered the decision, the court may obligate the persons who have brought in the claim to transfer

159. This is not a compensation for the damages suffered individually by the members of the collective, but is compensation for the damaged collective interest (Arts 387–388 CCP; Ruling of the SCC No. 456 of 15 Jul. 2013 on c.c. No. 4140/2013).

the compensation to a special account jointly disposable by the harmed persons, taking adequate measures to secure the execution of this obligation (Article 387(2) CCP).

377. The first-instance court may convene a general meeting of the injured persons by publishing the notice in the form in which bringing in the claim has been published. It is presided over by the judge and may act if at least six injured persons present themselves. (Article 388(1) CCP). The general meeting of the injured persons elects a committee to dispose of the assets on the special account and may resolve on the acts which the said committee is assigned to perform (Article 388(2) CCP).

Chapter 2. Order for Payment Proceedings[160]

§1. General Characteristics

378. Order for payment proceedings (OFPP)[161] are especial proceedings for creating grounds for execution (Article 404, item 1 CCP) when the receivable is not fulfilled although not contested.[162] They aim at establishing that the receivable is not contested and the court does not verify its existence which should be due and individualized.

The legislator termed the parties in those facultative proceedings 'applicant' and 'debtor'. This type of proceedings are facultative.[163] When filing a contest under Article 414 CCP, the case does not transform ex officio into adversary proceedings. According to Article 415 CCP he/she has a one-month preclusive term to file an ascertainment claim. The enforcement order does not replace the writ of execution which is judicial grounds for its issuing.

The order for payment proceedings are classified provisionally into two different order proceedings (Article 410 and Article 418 CCP in connection with Article 417 CCP).[164] Some of their prerequisites are different (compare Article 410 and Article 417 CCP). In the hypothesis of Article 410 CCP the writ of execution is issued when the enforcement order takes effect, and in the hypothesis of Article 418 CCP in relation with Article 417 CCP – simultaneously with the issuance of the enforcement order. Most rules are the same.

It was adopted in ID No. 4/2013 of the GMCC and the Com.C. of the SCC that, the rulings of the intermediate appellative court on complaints against court acts rendered in order of payment proceedings are not subject to appeal before the SCC.

§2. Order for Payment Proceedings under Article 410 CCP

379. Several categories of receivables are foreseen in Article 401 CCP: for money receivables and for delivery of fungible movable chattels the legal grounds and qualification are irrelevant. One can request issuing an enforcement order for the delivery of a movable chattel the debtor has received with an obligation to return

160. In 2017 (SG No.86/2018) and 2019 (SG No.100/2019) significant supplements and amendments to this type of proceedings were conducted.
161. *See* details In: V. Popova, V. Order for Payment Proceedings in Bulgarian Civil Procedure Law, Civil Procedure Review, v.2, n.3: 17-97, September-December, 2011, ISSN 2191-1339, www.civilprocedurereview.com. Upon the amendments of 2017 (SG No.86/2018) those specifics augmented. See V. Popova In: Stalev, A. Mingova, V. Popova, O. Staboliev, R. Ivanova, *Balgarsko … , supra*, pp. 907–997.
162. However, there are significant differences between the order of payment proceedings and those under Art. 418 CCP in connection with Art. 417 CCP (*see* para. 386).
163. Depending on the defendant's behaviour the debtor can achieve a court settlement (Art. 234 CCP), a decision upon admitting the claim (Art. 237 CCP) or a decision by default (Art. 238 CCP) depending on the defendant's behaviour in the case.
164. On the grounds of Art. 425(1) CCP the Ministry of Justice adopted Ordinance No. H-2 which is currently in effect and which specifies the standard forms of enforcement order, application for issuing of enforcement order and the other papers connected with those proceeding.

it or which is encumbered by a pledge or has been transferred to the debtor with an obligation to surrender possession, when the claim is under the regional court jurisdiction. The common feature of all hypotheses under Article 410 CCP is that the receivable should be claimed before the regional court. The lodged claims up to BGN 25,000 (arg. Article 104, item 4 CCP) are under the jurisdiction of the regional court. Though, the legislator has foreseen many exceptions in the CCP's TCPs.

380. The application[165] is lodged with the regional court where the permanent address or the seat of the debtor is; when he/she has the status of a consumer – with the court where his/her current address is, and if he/she does not have a current address – where his permanent address is (Article 411(1) CCP). Since the application is considered in a closed session without subpoenaing the parties, the court should observe both the generic and venue jurisdiction. Upon issuance of the order the matter of venue jurisdiction cannot be reconsidered (ID No. 4-2013-GMCC and the Com.C. of the SCC).

The application contains the request for issuing a writ of execution and should meet the requirements of Article 127(1) and (3) and Article 128(1) and (3) CCP (*see* paragraph 163–164). The receivable must be individualized by the grounds, content and size with the same criteria as in the application. It must be chargeable. In the order of payment proceedings under Article 410 CCP it is not required to provide evidence and to indicate such evidence for the alleged receivable, unless the receivable arises from a contract concluded with a consumer. Then the contract, if it is in writing, together with all its annexes and amendments, as well as the applicable general conditions, if any, is attached to the application (Article 410(3) CCP). The application should also indicate a bank account or other payment method (Article 410(2) CCP). The application should be lodged in the standard form in Application 1 to Ordinance No. H-2/2020 what is a condition for validity of the request for issuing a writ of execution. When the applicant did not use it or used a wrong one, the court attaches the standard form to the written instruction for curing the non-conformity (Article 425(2) CCP).

The court should give instructions to the claimant for curing the non-conformity of the application within a three-day term upon receiving the notice (Article 411(2), item 1 CCP).

381. The court considers the application in a closed session without subpoenaing the parties. It should pronounce on the application for issuing an enforcement order within three days following its service (Article 411(2) CCP). The court issues an enforcement order, except when: the request does not comply with the requirements under Article 410 CCP and the claimant does not cure the non-conformities within the three-day term upon receiving the notice; the request confronts the law or with good morals; the debtor has not a permanent address or a registered office on Bulgarian territory; the debtor has not a habitual residence or a place of business on Bulgarian territory (Article 411(2) CCP).

When the application for issuing an enforcement order is disallowed, the court pronounces with a motivated writ (Article 413(2) CCP). The writ is subject to

165. The defendant is not served with its copy.

appeal before the SCC according to the procedure for appealing rulings (Article 279 CCP) but the debtor is not served with a copy of the appeal.

After the entry into force of the motivated writ by which the court has refused to issue an enforcement order, it gives instructions for filing a claim (Article 415(1), item 3; (2), (3)). These rules also apply to the proceedings under Article 418 in conjunction with Article 417.

382. When the application is upheld, the court issues an enforcement order and the debtor is served with its copy[166] (Article 411(3) CCP). It is not motivated and is issued in the standard form established in Ordinance No. H-2/2020. Its content is foreseen in Article 412 CCP indicating the obligation that the debtor must comply, and the costs to be paid; an invitation to the debtor to comply within one month after service of the order; an instruction that the debtor can lodge an objection within the term under item 7; an instruction that if he/she fails to lodge objection to the issuer of the order or to comply, the enforcement order will take effect and coercive enforcement will be proceeded.

The debtor is serviced with a duplicate of the enforcement order. The enforcement order cannot be appealed except its part concerning the costs (Article 413(1) CCP).

§3. The Objection under Article 414 CCP and the Claim under Article 422 CCP in Connection with Article 415 CCP

383. The debtor can object in writing the enforcement order within a one-month preclusive term after service of the order (Article 414(2) CCP). Justification of the objection is not required (Article 414(2) CCP). Item 3 of Standard Form No. 7 gives the debtor instructions that he/she can optionally give reasons for his/her contesting the receivable.

The objection is lodged in the standard form which is not specified as a condition for the validity of the objection (Article 425 CCP). Its aim is to facilitate realization of the debtor's right to objection. This defence objection has a great intensity. For that reason, the enforcement order under Article 410 CCP does not take effect and the applicant should bring in an ascertainment claim under Article 422 in connection with Article 415 (1), item 1 CCP. The debtor's failure to lodge an objection under Article 414 CCP in the due term makes him/her unable to lodge a negative ascertainment claim based on facts which have occurred by the expiry of the said term, only if he/she did not know or could not have known about them.

When the objection is lodged in the due term, the court instructs the applicant that he/she can lodge an ascertainment claim for his/her receivable within a one-month term, paying the due State fee (Article 415(1), item 4 CCP). Article 415(5) CCP provides that when the applicant fails to present evidence that he/she has brought the

166. When the enforcement order is issued on the grounds of Art. 410 CCP, the debtor is served with its duplicate. The bailiff serves a duplicate of the immediate enforcement order under Art. 418 CCP (Art. 418(5) CCP).

action within the due term, the court invalidates the enforcement order in part or in whole, as well as the writ of execution issued under Article 418 CCP.

384. When an objection has not been lodged in due time or has been withdrawn, or the court decision for ascertainment of the receivable has taken effect, the enforcement order under Article 410 CCP enters into effect (Article 416 CCP). When a claim is lodged under Article 422 CCP in connection with Article 415(1), item 1 CCP, the order takes effect upon a decision on an upheld ascertainment claim under Article 415 CCP has taken effect. As seen from Article 415(3) and 416, sentence II, CCP, due to the explicit will of the legislator the enforcement order remains. The decision that has come into force has *res judicata*, but no enforcement effect. The writ of execution should be issued by the court that has issued the enforcement order. The adversary proceedings under Article 422 CCP in connection with Article 415(1), item 1 CCP follow the rules of the adversary procedure.

385. There is a new hypothesis on the necessity to lodge a claim under Article 422 CCP in connection with Article 415 provided for by the amendments to the order payment proceedings of late 2017 and 2019. When the debtor is served with the order for execution under the terms of Article 47(5) CCP and the server has collected data that the debtor does not live at the address, after a reference from the manager of the condominium, from the mayor of the respective area or in another way and has certified this by indicating the source of these data in the message, the court instructs the applicant that he/she can bring a claim for his/her receivable, which is ascertainment claim (Article 415(1), item 2, Article 415(3) CCP). This rule applies to both enforcement proceedings. The aim is to avoid damaging the interests of the debtor and to secure the right of defence in the process. The legislator came from the presumption that when the order is served under Article 47(5) CCP and data that he/she does not live at his/her registered permanent or current address has been duly collected, the debtor could not actually receive it and therefore has not filed an objection under Article 414 CCP.

§4. Order for Payment Proceedings under Article 418 CCP in Connection with Article 417 CCP

386. The hypothesis of Articles 417 and 418 CCP (called 'order for immediate enforcement') a writ of execution is issued simultaneously with this order without hesitating for it to take effect. The amount of the receivable is irrelevant (Article 417 CCP). It should be executable meeting the same requirements as in the case of lodging an application under Article 410 CCP. The order for immediate enforcement could be issued only on the grounds of a document admitted as grounds for its issuance (Article 417 CCP) which should be enclosed to the application.

387. The documents, grounds for issuing an order for immediate enforcement are enlisted in Article 417 CCP:

(1) An act of an administrative authority according to which the admission of the enforcement is assigned to the civil courts.

(2) A document or a statement from account books ascertaining the receivables of the State establishments and municipalities or an extract from the bank's books of accounts to which the document from which the bank's receivable is derived is presented, together with all its annexes, including the applicable general conditions.[167] In connection with Article 417(2) CCP amendments were made in Article 53(2) of LNBB, Article 111(2) Health Insurance Act, Article 60 CIA, Article 67(4), sentence II of the Law on Patents and Utility Model Registration, Article 11b Privatization and Post-privatization Control Act (PPCA), etc.

In practice the order for payment procedure under Article 417, item 2 CCP is used mostly by the banks. However, it is not enough to present only the loan contract. Besides, the executability of the receivable should be also written in the statement of account books. ID No. 4-2013-GMCC and the Com.C. of the SCC provides that a receivable originating from a bank loan, when contracted the entire loan to be executable, if a certain number of instalments are unpaid or any other terms, the creditor has the right of collecting his receivables without notifying the debtor. The receivable becomes executable under the above conditions set in the contact; even when the bank used its right of making the loan preliminary executable notifying the debtor about it.

Article 417 item 2 CCP is applicable only to the entities mentioned. According to ID No. 4-2013-GMCC and the Com.C. of the SCC when grounding the execution on Article 417 item 2 CCP viewing the special nature of the creditor, the private rights holder should possess the same quality for issuing an order of immediate execution in his/her favour.

(3) A notary act, an agreement or another contract bearing notarized signatures with regard to the obligations contained therein to pay sums of money or other fungible things, as well as obligations to deliver particular chattels. The said documents cannot serve as grounds for issuing an order for immediate enforcement for other pretence rights, although certifying those rights. According to ID No. 4-2013-GMCC and the Com.C. of the SCC there are also grounds for issuing an order for immediate enforcement under Article 417 CCP concerning accessory receivables for remedy of unexecuted main receivable, as set by the grounds and determined or to be determined in the deed under Article 417 CCP. During the verification under Article 418(1) CCP the court cannot verify the genuineness of the deeds and testimonies that the documents under Article 417 item 3 CCP contain. The verification is only on the formal regularity of the document, i.e., whether the type of document meets the standards and norms for its issuance. The executability of the receivable occurs depending on the occurrence of another circumstance, then Article 418(3) CCP applies. That should be attested by an official document or a document originating from the debtor.

167. The request of the Ombudsman of the Republic of Bulgaria for ascertainment of the anti-constitutional Art. 417(2) CCP was disallowed with Decision No. 12/12 Oct. 2012 of the CC.

(4) A statement of the registered pledges registry on a recorded security interest and on commencement of foreclosure: in respect of the delivery of pledged chattels as grounds for issuing an order for immediate enforcement order under Article 417, item 4 CCP. The text does not correspond to Article 35(1) RPA in its latest wording on a statement of the registered pledges registry and on commencement of the execution as a direct execution grounds for delivery of the pledged property according to Article 521 CCP. In its present wording Article 35(1) RPA is a law newer than Article 417, item 4 CCP, so Article 35(1) RPA should be applied and the said entry should be used as direct grounds for execution.

(5) A statement abstract of the registered pledges registry on an entry of a contract for sale with retention of title until payment of the purchase price or a lease contract: in respect of the return of corporeal things sold or leased (*see* ID No. 4-2013-GMCC and the Com.C. of the SCC).

(6) A contract of pledge or a mortgage deed under Articles 160 and 173(3) OCA. Article 417, item 6 CCP is grounds for issuance of an order for immediate enforcement against: (a) the debtor who has pledged or mortgaged his/her chattel for securing his/her own obligation; (b) a third person who has a pledge or mortgage for securing an obligation of somebody else. This is the text saving the creditor when principal debtor is insolvent, because under the argument of Article 638 CC neither order for immediate enforcement nor can a writ of execution be issued against him/her. The disposition of the writ of execution against the third person should contain an ascertainment that he/she is responsible for the debt of the principal debtor by pledging or mortgaging his/her particular property (Ruling No. 378 of 10 February 2010 on comm. c. No. 1481/2009 Comm.Ch. of the Varna District Court; Ruling No. 557 of 7 Jul. 2010 on comm. c. No. 557/2010 I – Comm.Ch. of the SCC).

(7) An effective act for ascertainment of a State or municipal receivable, where its enforcement is performed according to the procedure established by the CCP (Article 14b(2) Law for Social Support).

(8) Mandatory prescriptions that have taken effect of bodies of the Executive Agency of the General Labour Inspectorate given to an employer for payment of monetary obligations under a labour relationship delayed more than two months.

(9) Act of deficiency (Article 418 item 8 CCP and Article 27(4) PFIA). According to Article 27(4) PFIA the inspected organization sends the act of deficiency to the respective court issuance of an order for immediate enforcement under Article 418 CCP. The provision of Article 22(5) PFIA is that factual findings in the act of deficiency are regarded true until proven false. Though, the debtor can by his/her objection under Article 414 CCP object the enforcement order without having to ground his/her objection. The lodged objection causes the necessity the creditor to act of deficiency (the damaged legal entity) to lodge a positive ascertainment claim under Article 415 CCP for ascertainment of the receivable subject of the deficiency act. The adversary proceedings under Article 422 in connection with Article 415 CCP should apply the rule of Article 22(2) PFIA. The objection under Article 414 CCP does not lead to suspending the enforcement. It can be suspended only under the conditions of

Article 420 CCP (*see* paragraph 392). The court should also suspend the enforcement in the cases when the creditor is served with the order according to the procedure provided for in Article 47 (5) CCP.

(10) A promissory note, a bill or exchange or another negotiable security payable to order which is equivalent thereto, as well as a bond or coupons attached thereto. When the security secures a claim arising from a contract concluded with a consumer, the contract is attached to the application, if it is in writing, together with all its annexes, including the applicable general conditions.

388. To have an enforcement order issued under Article 417 CCP, one should file a written standard application according to Annex No. 4 to Ordinance No. H-2/ 2020, presenting a document under Article 417 CCP. Filing the application in the standard form is a condition for its validity. When the applicant has not used a standard form or has used a wrong one, the court gives him/her instructions for curing the irregularity enclosing the relevant standard form to the written instruction (Article 425(2) CCP). If the irregularities are not cured within the set term, the application is disallowed. The writ disallowing the application is appealable by a private appeal (Article 279 CCP in connection with 274(1) item 1 CCP). The writ disallowing entirely or partially the application for issuance of an enforcement order is appealable by a private appeal without serving the opposing party with a copy of it (Article 413(2) CCP). The writ disallowing entirely or partially the application for issuance of a writ of execution is appealable by a private appeal within a one-week term. A copy of the appeal is not presented for serving the opposing party with (Article 418(4) CCP).

389. The proceedings under Article 418 CCP are characteristic of issuing the writ of execution *simultaneously* with the enforcement order (Article 404, item 1 is its enforcement ground), although it has not taken effect yet. That is why the enforcement order under Article 418 in CCP in connection with Article 417 CCP is called 'order for immediate enforcement'. When issuing a writ of execution, the court puts down a due note on the enforcement order and on the document presented under Article 417 CCP (Article 418, sentence I CCP). The writ of execution is issued after the court verifies whether the document is prima facie conforming and ascertains the enforcement receivable against the debtor (Article 418(2) CCP). In the order for payment proceedings the court is not entitled to verify whether the receivable exists and is executable. For the proceedings under Article 418 CCP the document under Article 417 CCP has evidential effect regarding the executable right it certifies. The document should comprise the data about the receivable's executability. When according to the document the executability depends on the performance of a counter obligation or upon the occurrence of another fact, the performance of the obligation or the occurrence of the fact, it has to be ascertained by an official document or the debtor's outgoing document (Article 418(3) CCP).

390. The enforcement order under Article 418 CCP in connection with Article 417 CCP includes the provisions of Article 412 CCP. Additionally, it includes: (a) it being subject to immediate enforcement; (b) possibility for the creditor to lodge a claim for the receivable against the debtor if his/her objection has been filed within a one-month term. If such a claim is not lodged the enforcement order will not take effect; (c) the debtor is instructed that the enforcement is suspended if he/she furnishes a due security before the court following the procedure of Articles 180 and 181 OCA and that the court can suspend the enforcement, if within the term for lodging an objection, the debtor presents convincing written evidence thus he/she has no obligation to perform; (d) the verification performed by the court of the document grounds for the enforcement order. A copy of the document is enclosed to the enforcement order. According to Article 418(5) CCP the order for immediate enforcement issued under Article 418 CCP and a copy of the document on which grounds the order has been issued are served by the bailiff. He/she sends immediately to the court a copy of the announcement with the documents served. Each of the latter has a notice of it being served.

391. The writ with which the application for immediate enforcement is upheld is appealable in a one-month term following the serving of the enforcement order Article 419(1) CCP. The statement of appeal against the writ for immediate enforcement is lodged together with the objection against the enforcement order and may be grounded only on facts taken from the acts under Article 417 (Article 419(2)) CCP. The complaint statement can be grounded only on allegations of wrongfulness of the writ regarding the prima facie conformity of the document under Article 418 CCP and its ascertainment of the due executable receivable. The debtor can also refer to violations under Article 411 CCP. He/she can object only the receivable and its executability and should file an appeal under Article 414 CCP with the court that issued the order. Its consequence is connected with the necessity of creditor's filing a positive ascertainment claim within the preclusive term under Article 415(4) CCP. The creditor's failure to keep the deadline under Article 415 CCP is grounds for invalidation of the enforcement order and the writ of execution issued on its grounds. Under Article 419(2) CCP the debtor cannot appeal the writ for immediate enforcement without lodging an objection against the enforcement order meanwhile.

The writ of the enforcement court with which the appeal for immediate enforcement is upheld is subject to appeal before the intermediate appellative court according to the procedure foreseen in Article 419 CCP.

392. The objection under Article 414 CCP does not suspend the enforcement except in the cases of Article 417, item 9 CCP (arg. Article 420 CCP). The proceedings can be suspended only following the procedure under Article 420 CCP:

(1) When the debtor has furnished duly the security for the debtor following the procedure of Articles 180 and 181 OCA. He/she will use the defence under (1) in connection with Articles 180 and 181 OCA when he/she does not possess convincing written evidence. That is an indication that the objection is a serious one when the security covers the entire receivable plus the interests, and furnishes the claimant with a doubtless right of preferable satisfaction. When the debtor is a consumer, the security is limited to an amount of one-third of the receivable. When the receivable is furnished by one of several debtors, the enforcement is suspended only against him/her (Article 421(1)

CCP). While the security does not cover fully the receivable, the suspending is limited to the amount of the security (Article 421(2) CCP). Having a security under Articles 180 and 181 OCA furnished duly in favour of the claimant and an imperatively set condition for suspending the court should suspend the enforcement proceedings.

(2) When a request for suspending the enforcement supported by convincing written evidence is filed within the term for objection, the court that has rendered an order for immediate enforcement can suspend it (Article 420 CCP). The request for suspending the enforcement should be grounded on objections supported by convincing written evidence that the enforcement right does not exist or is not executable.

(3) In the hypothesis of Article 417, item 9 CCP an objection filed under Article 414 CCP is enough.

According to Article 420(3) CCP the ruling on the request suspending of the enforcement is appealable by a private appeal but is subject to immediate enforcement, regardless of its appeal (Article 420(4) CCP).

393. The amendments from 2017 and 2019 to the order of payment procedure provided that, if no objection under Article 414 CCP has been filed, but the debtor is served with the order under the conditions of Article 47(5) CCP and the server has collected data that the debtor does not live at the address, after a reference from the manager of the condominium, from the mayor of the respective area or in another way and has certified this by indicating the source of these data in the message, the court is obliged to order suspension of the execution when a writ of execution has been issued under Article 418 CCP. The court should instruct the applicant to file a claim under Article 422 within the term under Article 415(4) CCP (Article 415(2) CCP). The claim is an ascertainment one (Article 415(3) CCP).

§5. Proceedings under Article 422 CCP: Sentencing Claim under Article 415(3) in Connection with Article 415(1), Item 3

394. As established in practice the applicant should lodge before the court a claim as well as present evidence of having done so within the one-month term under Article 415 CCP.

According to ID No. 4-2013-GMCC and the Com.C. of the SCC the procedural prerequisites for existence and duly exercise of the right to claim lodging following the procedure under Article 422 CCP, Article 415(1) CCP, respectively, do not exist when no objection under Article 414 CCP was filed within the term under Article 414(2) CCP or it does not contest the receivable. The court considering a claim under Article 422 CCP, Article 415(1) CCP, respectively, performs its own verification whether those procedural prerequisites exist and is not bound to the findings of the court in the order of payment proceedings.

If in the proceedings under Article 422 CCP in connection with Article 415 CCP the debtor fails to submit within the due term a reply to the statement of claim and does not object the facts presented in it, he/she suffers the consequences under

Article 133 CCP. It is admissible in the proceedings on the claim lodged under Article 422 CCP, Article 415(1) CCP, respectively, to consider the debtor's contestations against the receivable of the creditor grounded in his/her objection under Article 414(1) CCP, although no reply to the claimant's statement of claim was submitted; or he/she has not filed a detailed objection within the due term (ID No. 4-2013-GMCC and the Com.C. of the SCC).

The claim under Article 422(1) CCP in connection with Article 415(1), items 1 and 2 CCP is a positive ascertainment claim. The explicit legislator's concept is in Articles 415(2) and 416 CCP. The sentencing claim is inadmissible in those cases since as the claimant will have simultaneously two writs of execution for one and the same receivable. The enforcement order is the source of enforcement effect (Article 416 CCP). The decision on the claim under Article 422 CCP in connection with Article 415(1), items 1 and 2 CCP has a res judicata effect.

The claim for the receivable ascertainment is considered lodged since the moment of filing the application for issuance of enforcement order within the term under Article 415(4) CCP (Article 422(1) CCP). The limitation is also considered suspended since the moment of filing the application for issuance of enforcement order (arg. Article 116, item 'b' OCA in connection with Article 422(1) CCP), as well as the suspension of the limitation with pending proceedings (arg. Article 116, item 'g' OCA in connection with Article 422(1) CCP).

If the claim is disallowed by a decision that has taken effect, the execution is terminated (Article 422(3) CCP) and Article 245(3), sentence II CCP is applied. A contra writ of execution is issued on the sum collected as a result of the enforcement as well as on the fee related.[168] Under the argument of Articles 415(2) and 416 CCP the enforcement order should be invalidated. If the claim is disallowed via a decision that had taken effect the execution is terminated.

When the court has refused to issue an enforcement order (Article 415(1), item 3 CCP in connection with Article 411 CCC), it instructs the applicant that he/she can bring a claim for his/her receivable. In this case, the claim is sentencing (Article 415(3) CCP) but it must also be filed within the term under Article 415(4) CCP. This claim will be considered as lodged since the moment when the application for an enforcement order was filed, as for the interruption and suspension of the prescription. The same applies to the claim under Article 422 CCP.

§6. Objection Within the Period for Voluntary Execution / Article 414a CCP

395. The regulation of this objection is one of the most significant changes in the Bulgarian order of payment procedure that took place in 2017. It is related to the fact that the order for execution also contains a call for voluntary execution (Article 412, item 8 CCP). With the objection under Article 414a CCP the debtor

168. It was provided in Art. 422(4) CCP that contra writ of execution is not issued when the claim is disallowed due to non-executability of the receivable.

does not contest the claim subject to the order. On the contrary, he/she acknowledges it and claims to have fulfilled it within the given period of voluntary execution. This is the substantial difference with the objection under Article 414 and should therefore be motivated. There is a specific objection to the enforceability of the enforcement order.

It has been promulgated in Article 414a CCP that, a debtor who has fulfilled his/her obligation under the order for execution within the term under Article 412, item 8 CCP is entitled to object in writing against the enforcement order, claiming to have fulfilled all or part of his/her obligation. The evidence of the fulfilment of the obligation with a copy for the applicant is attached to the objection.

The objection, together with the enclosures, is sent to the applicant indicating that he/she may submit an opinion within three days, indicating the consequences of failure to provide an opinion (Article 414a(2) CCP). If the applicant does not submit an opinion within the specified term, the court invalidates the order for execution, in whole or partially, including in the part regarding the expenses (Article 414a(1) sentence I CCP). If a writ of execution pursuant to Article 418 CCP has been issued, the court nullifies it in the part where the enforcement order is invalidated (Article 414a(6) CCP).

It is stipulated in Article 414a(4), sentence II CCP that, if the opinion is submitted in due time, the court shall pronounce on the objection and on the opinion received. It is not foreseen by what act the court should pronounce. In practice, the correct understanding was established that, this should be a ruling via which issuance of a writ of execution is refused.

§7. Objection under Article 423 CCP

396. Article 423 CCP provides on defence before the intermediate appellative court by a written objection. Those are exceptional proceedings very close both to Article 20 of Regulation (EC) No. 1896/2006 and to the reversal under Article 303(1), item 5 CCP. The reversal used to be called 'reversal before the intermediate appellative court' prior to the 2008 amendment of Article 423 CCP. According to Article 423(1) CCP the debtor who was deprived of contesting the receivable is entitled an objection to the intermediate appellative court, when:

(1) He/she has not been duly served with the enforcement order.
(2) The enforcement order has not been served upon the debtor in person and on the day of the service he/she had not a habitual residence within the territory of the Republic of Bulgaria. In the case of a reversal under Article 423 CCP the enforcement order and the writ of execution are invalidated since the case was not under the international jurisdiction of the Bulgarian courts on a general basis (*see* Article 4, item 1 PILC and Article 6 of Council Regulation (EC) No. 1896/2006 in connection with Article 3 of Council Regulation (EC) No. 44/2001). The rule of Article 423(1) item 2 CCP in connection with Article 411(1) item 4 CCP excludes the international competence of a Bulgarian court in order for payment proceedings.

(3) The debtor was unable to learn of the service in due time owing to special unforeseen circumstances. Those are the cases when the debtor was not served with the enforcement order in person (Article 46 CCP) and there is no procedural breach committed by the court.
(4) The debtor was unable to lodge the objection because of special unforeseen circumstances which he/she was unable to overcome, although he/she has been served duly with the enforcement order and has learnt about it.

The preclusive term for lodging objection under Article 423(1) CCP is one month and starts on the date of learning about the enforcement order. It is also valid for the private appeal under Article 419(1) CCP lodged with the objection on the grounds of Article 423(1) item 2 CCP as well as for the request for suspending the enforcement.

According to legislator's concept, the objection under Article 423(1) CCP has also the role of an objection under Article 414 CCP. The admitted objection under Article *423 CCP* in the hypothesis of Article 410(1) CCP acts as an objection under Article 414 CCP. Therefore, the situation is restored, when the prerequisites under Article 423(1) CCP exist and the court admits the objection,[169] and the debtor has lodged the objection under Article 414 CCP on time. Lodging the objection before the intermediate appellative court under Article 423(1) CCP does not suspend the enforcement. Upon the debtor's request the court may suspend the enforcement under Article 282(2) CCP (Article 423(2) CCP).

397. It is stipulated in Article 423(3) CCP that the court admits the objection finding that the prerequisites under Article 423(1) CCP exist. Then the court also considers the private appeals filed under Articles 413(1) and 419(1) CCP with the objection. When the objection is admitted because no prerequisites under Article 411(2) items 3 and 4 CCP exist, the court invalidates ex officio the enforcement order and the writ of execution issued on its grounds. In the remaining cases admitting the objection has the following consequences:

(1) The execution of the enforcement order under Article 410 CCP is suspended (Article 423(1), sentence I, CCP) because the issuance of a writ of execution on the grounds of the enforcement order under Article 410 CCP presupposes that the order has taken effect (Article 416 CCP). Its taking effect is determined by the fact that no objection under Article 414 CCP has been lodged. In the hypothesis of Article 417, item 10 CCP the fact that an objection under Article 414 CCP has been lodged is an imperatively determined grounds for suspending the enforcement. Therefore, when the intermediate appellative court accepts the objection under Article 423 CCP it should suspend the enforcement even when the debtor has not placed an explicit request for suspension. Suspension of the enforcement order under Article 418 CCP in connection with Article 417, items 1–9 CCP is not a consequence of admitting the objection under Article 423 CCP. The writ of execution is issued immediately

169. The term is legal. It means the court has admitted the objection under Art. 423 CCP as grounded and has allowed it.

provided there is an enforcement order issued on the grounds of a document under Article 417, items 1–8 CCP. The debtor is entitled with the objection under Article 423 CCP to request simultaneously suspending of the enforcement on the grounds of Article 413(2) CCP (which is a special norm regarding Article 420(1) CCP) in connection with Article 282(2) CCP.

(2) Admitting the objection under Article 423(1) CCP does not lead to invalidating the enforcement order neither under Article 410 CCP, nor under Article 418 CCP in connection with Article 417 CCP. The case is sent back to the regional court. The proceedings are continued with giving instructions to the applicant that he/she should file a claim under Article 415 CCP (Article 423(4), sentence I CCP).

There is not a foreseen possibility for appealing the ruling of the intermediate appellative court under Article 423(1) CCP.

§8. The Claim under Article 424 CCP

398. The debtor is entitled to contest the receivable by an adversary procedure, when there is newly discovered evidence or new written evidence of material relevance to the case, which he/she could not have known by the time the term for filing the objection expired, or could not procure within the said term (Article 424(1) CCP). The prerequisites for filing the claim under Article 424(1) CCP are identical to the grounds for the reversal under Article 303(1), item 1 CCP (*see* paragraph 244) of a decision that has taken effect. It is applicable both in the hypothesis of Article 417 CCP and of Article 410 CCP. Article 424(1) CCP is a special regulation regarding Article 439(2) CCP and excludes its application.

The claim under Article 424(1) CCP can be lodged within a three-month term following the day on which the debtor learnt about a new circumstance or the day when a new piece of written evidence was procured, but not later than a year of extinguishing the receivable (Article 424(2) CCP). The term is preclusive.

Thus, the negative ascertainment claim on the grounds of newly occurred facts is admissible on the grounds of Article 124(1) CCP.

Lodging the claim under Article 424(1) CCP, Article 124(1) CCP, respectively, does not suspend the enforcement. The debtor being a claimant to this claim having presented convincing written evidence or/and due security according to the procedure of security proceedings (Articles 389–397 CCP), can request admittance of a security of his/her claim via suspension of the enforcement (Article 397(1), item 3 CCP).

Part IX. Seizure for Security and Enforcement of Judgments

Chapter 1. Seizure for Security[170]

§1. PROCEEDINGS

399. Security proceedings are employed where there exists a danger of impeding the forthcoming remedy which will be provided through the adversary or enforcement proceedings (*see* paragraph 8).[171] They proceed in two phases (admitting the security and imposing security measures). Where the claim is disallowed through an effective decision, the security measure is reversed and has just a temporary effect within the frames of pending proceedings. If the claim is admitted, it ensures the successful conduct of future enforcement proceedings.

If a distraint is imposed upon an item of immovable property with regard to a sentencing claim for a money receivable, we achieve an effective decision. No new distraint is imposed in the enforcement proceedings. The distraint imposed in the security proceedings will do as if it were imposed in the adversary proceedings. The relative invalidity of Articles 452(2) and 453 CCP protects us against the debtor's disposition actions performed after the distraint has been imposed and prior to the institution of enforcement proceedings and prior to our right to institute such. The suspension of execution (Article 397(3) CCP) is valid only till the adversary proceedings are pending. If the claim under Articles 124(1), 240(2), 424, 439 and 440 CCP is upheld by an effective decision, the enforcement proceedings should be terminated (Article 433(1), item 7 CCP).

400. Security is admissible in all types of claims (Article 389(2) CCP). It is most frequently used in condemnation and in negative ascertainment claims under Article 439, 240, 424 CCP and Article 124(1) CCP (*see* paragraphs 133–134, 398, 437–438)

170. For seizure of security *see* V. Popova in: J. Stalev, A. Mingova, V. Popova, O. Stamboliev, R. Ivanova, *Balgarsko ...* , *supra*, pp. 1325–1394.

171. The temporary measures in matrimonial proceedings (child support, temporary settling the problem of the housing, temporary measures regarding the children) are not security proceedings. Those are an act of the so-called in Bulgarian procedure doctrine and practice 'disputable judicial administration' (*see* para. 11). The main judgment is on the appropriateness regarding the children's interests in pending matrimonial proceedings between their parents. Those are temporary and are valid only in the course of the pending. After that they are replaced by consequences of the decision. Only the compulsory realization of the rights on the temporary measures takes place in the enforcement proceedings because the said ruling is valid enforcement grounds (Art. 404(1) CCP).

challenging the existence of the receivable which forms the subject matter of compulsory execution. According to Article 389(1) CCP, at any time in the course of proceedings, prior to the closure of the court trial in the intermediate appellate proceedings the claimant is entitled to demand that the court admits security for the claim, this court being the one the case is pending before. The security for the claim is also admissible where the case has been suspended Article 391(4) CCP.

According to Article 390 CCP, security can also be sought even prior to the time the claim is lodged. In this case the request for security should be filed either with the generically competent court by the permanent address of the claimant, or with the one by the location of the real estate which will serve as security for securing a future claim by suspending the execution is filed with the generically competent court by the place of enforcement (Article 390(4) CCP). When a future claim is secured, the court sets a term for bringing in the claim which cannot be longer than one month. Where no evidence that the claim has been brought in within this time limit the court withdraws ex officio the security (Article 390(3) CCP).[172] The grounds for withdrawal of the security are specified imperatively in Article 390(3) CCP. Securing a future claim by suspending the compulsory execution of the receivable challenged by the said claim is admissible only against a presented guarantee (Article 390(4), sentence I CCP). The requirement does not apply to claims under Article 440 CCP.

401. Security for a claim is admissible where, were it not for the said security, it would be either impossible or difficult for the claimant to enjoy the rights granted through the decision: (a) the claim should be supported by written evidence, or (b) a bond should be provided at the amount specified by the court in accordance with Articles 180 and 181 OCA (Article 391(1) CCP). In the cases under Article 391(1), item 1 CCP the court may also demand that the claimant submit a pecuniary or property bond at the amount the court has specified (Article 391(2) CCP). Those prerequisites are guidance regarding the probable grounds of the claim.

According to Article 391(4) CCP, State institutions and municipalities, as well as medical treatment establishments under Article 5(1) Medical Treatment Facilities Act (MTEA) are released from the obligation to provide a bond. When claims for maintenance are concerned, security is admissible even where the requirements of Article 391 CCP have not been observed (Article 392 CCP). In the case, the court may take measures ex officio for securing the claim.

According to Article 393 CCP, the security for a claim regarding money receivables (*see* paragraph 415) is inadmissible against State institutions or municipalities, or medical treatment establishments under Article 5(1) MTEA, as well as regarding money receivables medical treatment establishments within the National Health Insurance Fund. According to Article 393(2) CCP, in a case of a claim for a

172. For the moment from which the term for filing the future claim starts to run and for proving this filing, *see* item 1 and item 2 of ID No. 6-14.03.2014 under inter. dec. No. 6/2013-GMCC and the Com.C. of the SCC.

money receivable is inadmissible furnishing security by imposing a distraint upon the receivables against which compulsory execution is inadmissible.[173]

402. The request for security should specify the security measure and the amount of the claim. The opposing party is not given a copy of the request (Article 395(1) CCP). The request is considered and determined in a closed session held on the day of it being filed (Article 395(2) CCP). The court renders a ruling on the request for securing the claim. In it the court assesses the prerequisites provided for in Article 391(1) and (2) CCP justifying the probable merits of the claim whose securing is sought; the existence of a need of security; the admissibility of the security measure and its compliance with the need of security.[174] By the ruling through which the security is admitted, the court also indicates the security measure. On the grounds of this ruling, on the basis of it, but simultaneously with it, without waiting for it to enter into force, the court issues a security order. It is precisely on the basis of the security order and not on the basis of the ruling that the security measure is imposed.

403. Imposing[175] a security measure is a non-court phase of the security proceedings. Article 400(1) CCP provides that, upon the request of the claimant and in accordance with the court order, the distraint is *immediately* imposed by the bailiff, this being in accordance with Article 449(1) CCP; Articles 450(1) and (2), 507 and 515 CCP (*see* paragraph 412); and the defendant is delivered a message instead of an invitation to voluntary execution. In the cases of distraint imposed on a chattel the public or private bailiff makes a description and an evaluation of the chattel and deposits the chattel for it being kept under Articles. 465–472 CCP. According to Article 400(2) CCP, an attachment is imposed by way of entering the court order by the respective entry judge, in accordance with the procedure for making entries. The

173. The attachment on non-sequestrability of immovable property leads to limiting the disposal powers of a debtor only with the consequence for the relative non-existence with regard to the claimant and the joint creditors. The attachment is not an obstacle to the debtor's utilization of the immovable property. If the debtor despite the attachment disposes with the non-sequestrable immovable property, the non-sequestrability is eliminated (*see* para. 417) because the disposal with the said immovable property reveals that the debtor does not need it. The same is valid for unusable non-sequestrable chattels. Therefore, the distraint on the said chattels is admissible. Under the argumentation of Art. 393(2) CCP the distraint on non-sequestrable items of movable property ensuring the elementary living needs and whose usage is connected with their consumption (usable chattels) is inadmissible.

174. The types of security measures are provided for in Art. 397(1) CCP. It is set out that the security is provided by way of: (a) imposing an attachment on a real estate; (b) distraint on the debtor's chattels or receivables; (c) other appropriate measures the court has ordered, including suspension from operation of a motor vehicle and the suspension of execution. The court is entitled to admit several types of security, the total amount thereof being equal to the amount of the claim (Art. 397(2) CCP). The security measure has to correspond to the security need, as the measure is an expression of the protection-sanction provided through security proceedings. The security measure should ensure the future enforcement of a right which has been groundlessly rescinded, or the impeding of the current enjoyment of a right which has been groundlessly sought.

175. 'Imposing' is a legal term. Imposing a security measure is practically enforcement of a security order.

Office of Entries notifies the defendant of the entry that has been made. The distraint or attachment imposed for securing the claim gives rise to the effect provided for in Articles 451–453 CCP; Article 459(1) CCP; Article 508 CCP; Article 509 CCP and Articles 512–514 CCP (Article 401 CCP).

§2. Judicial Review

404. According to Article 396(1) CCP, the ruling of the court on the admission of security is appealable by a private appeal within a one-week term commencing on it being communicated (for the appellant), or on the day when the appellee[176] is served with the message from the bailiff, or the entry judge, or the court in the cases under Article 397(1), item 3 CCP. The opposing party is served with a copy of the private appeal to submit a reply within a one-week term. When a ruling on disallowing a request for securing the claim is appealed, the defendant is not serviced with a copy of the plaintiff's the private complaint (Article 396(2), sentence I CCP). According to Article 396(2), sentence III CCP when the intermediate appellate court admits the security, its ruling is appealable by a private appeal before the SCC, provided that the prerequisites under Article 280(1) and (2) CCP exist[177] (*see* ID No. 5-2015 of 12 July 2018 on com.c. No. 5-2015-GMCC and the Com.C. of the SSC). The restriction under Article 280(3) CCP regarding the price of the claim is not valid. The cassation appeal under Article 396(2), sentence II CCP is admitted quite rarely. Under the argumentation of Article 396(2), sentence II CCP, the ruling of the intermediate appellate court with which it disallows the defendant's appeal against the ruling of the court for admitting the security, is not subject to appeal before the SCC. The ruling of the intermediate appellate court with which it disallows the request for securing the claim is not subject to appeal as well. In this aspect ID No. 1-2010-GMCC of the SCC is valid (*see also* ID No. 5 of 12 July 2018 on com.c. No. 5-2015-GMCC and the Com.C. of the SSC).

The ruling of the intermediate appellate court with which it pronounced for the first time on the request for admitting the security that has been made for the first time before the said court under Article 389(1) CCP since the very adversary proceedings are pending before the intermediate appellate instance. The rules valid in the case are foreseen Article 274(2) CCP. When rendered by an intermediate appellate court it is subject to appeal before the SCC, and when the ruling is rendered by the district court, the appeal should be brought before the respective intermediate appellate court. The appeal of a ruling rendered by a higher instance is according to Article 396(2) CCP.

176. In item 6 of ID No. 6-14.03.2014 under inter. dec. No. 6/2013 of the GMCC and the Com.C. of the SCC legitimized persons who can appeal the ruling of the court regarding the seizure for security claim are the claimant in the event of refusal to impose security or in the event of its imposition under other terms, the defendant and any person, whose legal sphere is affected by the allowed security measure.

177. At first glance it seems the shortened appeal in a case of securing the claim adopted in the present wording to correspond to the requirement for equality of the parties in the procedure. Each party has one chance to appeal. However, the equality is illusory. Admission of cassation appeals in Art. 396(2), sentence II in relation with Art. 280(1) CCP is very limited.

According to Article 396(3) CCP, the ruling through which security for the claim is admitted cannot be suspended due to it being appealed by a private appeal.

405. Upon the request of one of the parties and after notifying the other party and taking into consideration its objections made within a term of three days following the communication thereof, the court is entitled to admit the replacement of one type of security with another (Article 398(1) CCP). According to Article 398(2) CCP, in the cases of security for a claim subject to being assessed in money, at any time and without the consent of the other party, the defendant is allowed to replace the security admitted by the court with a pledge in money or securities in accordance with Articles 180 and 181 OCA. This does not apply to security for ownership claims.

§3. Modification and Revocation of the Security Measure

406. The modification of the security measure could be requested not only by the defendant but the claimant as well. Article 398 CCP does not provide which court is competent on the modification of the security measure. In the literature and practice under the CCP, repealed, it used to be assumed that the competent court is the one that has rendered the security measure, when sought modification of the security measure is imposed under a future claim and the court considering the claim when the sought modification of the security measure is under a pending claim. In my opinion, in a case of securing a future claim, it should be foreseen that if the claim is brought, the proceedings should be transferred to the court hearing the case and is competent on the modification of the security measure rendered.

407. Withdrawal of security is ordered upon the request of the interested party, and a copy of the said request is handed over to the person whose claim is secured. The latter is entitled to file an objection within a three days' term following the receipt of the copy (Article 402 CCP). The withdrawal of the security measure under Article 402 CCP sets up the successive invalidation of the prerequisites for its admitting. The court considers the request and the objection in a closed session (Article 402 CCP). It withdraws the security after making sure that the reason for admitting the security does not exist anymore, or that the conditions set forth in Article 398(2) CCP (*see* paragraph 401) are present. The ruling of the court is appealed by a private appeal (Article 402(2) CCP). It was adopted in ID No. 1-2010- GMCC and the Com.C. of the SCC that the ruling of the intermediate appellate court on the said complaint is not subject to cassation control.

According to, the lifting of the distraint, the striking-off of the attachment and the discharge of other security measures is carried out on the grounds of an effective ruling of the court (Article 402(3) CCP).

408. If the claim for which the security was admitted is disallowed, or the claimant fails to lodge it within the specified term, or the proceedings are suspended, the defendant is entitled to demand that the claimant pay to him/her the damages caused as a result of the security (Article 403(1) CCP). In these cases, in order for the guarantee to be discharged, the interested person has to file a request with a copy to the defendant party. It is within a term of seven days following the receipt of the request that the defendant is entitled to file an objection against the discharge of the guarantee. Within a term of one month he/she is entitled to bring in a claim for damages sustained. Where the defendant fails to file an objection or lodge such a claim within the said terms the guarantee is discharged (Article 403(2) CCP).

The claimant might be willing to be released from the guarantee which he/she has provided in the cases under Article 391(1), item 2 and 391(2) CCP in those cases where his/her claim has been upheld by a decision that has taken effect.

Chapter 2. Enforcement of Judgments[178]

§1. Enforcement of Domestic Judgments[179]

409. The grounds for enforcement of the national law (Article 404(1) CCP) are:

A. The effective sentencing decisions of the courts (Article 404, item 1 CCP in connection with Article 296 CCP). Both in doctrine and practice it is assumed that grounds for execution are also those constitutive decisions, the constitutive effect of which consists in their giving rise to a right to claim which is being sought (e.g., for transferring the ownership according to division report under Article 348 CCP; the decision on assignment of the indivisible home under Article 349(1) and (2) CCP regarding entry into possession). The grounds for execution in the sense of Article 404, item 1 CCP are also the effective court decisions, rendered in proceedings on debatable court administration (Article 32 PA, Article 56 FC, Article 59 FC).
B. The sentencing appellate decisions are also grounds for execution (Article 404, item 1 CCP), before they become unappealable and before the arising of their res judicata effect. In practice writs of execution are also issued on the grounds of the constitutive decisions, which have not entered into force, rendered on the debatable court administration concerning the exercising of parental rights following the divorce (Article 59 FC) and granting the family home (Article 56 FC).
C. The decisions of the first-instance courts admitting preliminary execution pursuant to Article 242(1) and (2) CCP.

I. Proceedings[180]

A. *Proceedings for Issuance of a Writ of Execution*

410. The absolute procedural prerequisite for the admissibility of the enforcement procedure is the existence of a writ of execution (Article 426(1) CCP in

178. *See* V. Popova, in J. Stalev, A. Mingova, V. Popova, O. Stamboliev, R. Ivanova, Balgarsko … , *supra*, pp. 897–1325.
179. For the enforcement of the decisions rendered by the Bulgarian courts *see* paras 192–194. Grounds for execution grounds under Bulgarian law are also the entered into force convicting rulings of the courts, the court agreements, the entered into force orders for execution under Art. 410 CCP, the orders for immediate execution under Art. 418 in conjunction with Art. 417 CCP, as well as the decisions of the Bulgarian arbitration courts and the agreements concluded before them (Art. 410, item 1 of CCP).
180. The individual proceedings for enforcement of certain types of property rights, the satisfaction of which is aimed at the enforcement process, depend on the type of right, in the enforcement of monetary claims – on the property right of the debtor, which is aimed at enforcement (cf. §1, vol. I, items C and D, para. 415). In doctrine and practice, these procedures are called executive methods. By its nature, each method is a special enforcement process, which is governed by the special rules applicable to it, as well as by the general rules regarding all enforcement methods.

connection with Article 404 CCP).[181] It is the writ of execution that empowers and obliges the body of compulsory execution (the bailiff[182]) to carry out the actions of compulsory execution provided for in the respective method of execution.

The writ of execution is issued based on Article 405 CCP upon the written request of the petitioner on the grounds of any act listed in Article 404 CCP (Article 405(1) CCP). No copy of the request is delivered to the debtor. It is considered in camera. The court examines whether the act on the grounds of which the issue of a writ of execution is sought formally complies with the law and whether it certifies an executable receivable against the person against whom the issue of the writ of execution is sought, respectively the legitimization of the parties. In these proceedings the court is not entitled to check whether the receivable exists.[183]

The writ with which the request for the issue of a writ of execution is upheld or disallowed may be appealed with a private appeal within a two-week term (Article 407(1) CCP). The term for the applicant commences on the day on which the writ is delivered, and as for the debtor it commences on the day on which the invitation to voluntary execution is delivered. The appeal against the ruling through which the request is upheld does not suspend the execution (Article 407(2) CCP). The appeal against the ruling for issuance of a writ of execution is considered in accordance with the procedure for appeal against rulings (Article 407(1) CCP in connection with Article 279 CCP). In ID No. 5/12 July 2018 under interpretative decision No. 5/2015-GMCC and the Com.C. of the SCC it was upheld that the ruling of the appellate court under a private appeal against the ruling of the first-instance court under a request for issuance of a writ of execution is not subject to cassation appeal.

411. The parties in the enforcement proceedings are called claimant and debtor. The writ of execution may be used by the claimant specified therein for compulsory execution against the debtor specified therein. According to Article 429(1) CCP, the

181. That concerns all enforcement grounds, the court decision that has taken effect as well as the enforcement order that has taken effect, inclusive. The possibility to commence compulsory execution on enforcement grounds is foreseen Art. 426(1) CCP, only in the cases when it has been foreseen in a law (*see* para. 412).

182. In Bulgarian enforcement proceedings there are public bailiffs and private bailiffs (*see* paras 65–66).

183. The writ of execution is issued in one copy, signed by the judge (Art. 408 CCP). For its issuance he makes a note on the act (Art. 406(3) CCP). According to Art. 409(1) CCP, if the original writ of execution is lost or destroyed, the court that issued it, at the written request of the applicant, shall issue a duplicate of it on the basis of the act under which the original was issued. The application is considered in open court after a copy of it is served on the debtor (Art. 409(2) CCP). The debtor may oppose in addition to the lack of conditions under Art. 409(1) CCP, as well as objections for repayment of the debt, which occurred after the establishment of its existence (Art. 409(3) CCP). Objections not submitted are precluded. The court shall rule on the application for issuance of a duplicate with a decision, which shall be subject to appeal according to the general procedure before the appellate court, resp. the appellate decision of cassation appeal (ID No. 5/12.07.2018 under inter. dec. No. 5/2015.

heirs to the claimant, and his/her private legal successors, as well as the surety and the joint co-debtor who have paid off their debt, are entitled to seek execution on the grounds of the writ of execution issued in favour of the claimant. The succession, and the payment made by the surety or the joint co-debtor, respectively, is certified by way of written evidence. According to Article 429(2) CCP, the issued writ of execution against the legator may also be exercised upon the property of his/her heirs, save if they ascertain that they have renounced the inheritance or have accepted it in accordance with an inventory.

According to Article 429(3) CCP, the writ of execution against the debtor also has effect against the third person that has granted his/her property as a pledge or mortgage for securing the debt in those cases where the claimant directs his/her execution against the said property. The third person that has granted his/her property as a pledge or mortgage for securing the debt of somebody else is not a debtor to a substantive law relationship, but he/she is responsible with his/her property that has been pledged or mortgaged. Therefore, the said third person becomes a debtor in the compulsory execution when it is against the subject of the pledge, the mortgage, respectively (ID No. 4 from 11 March 2019 under interpretretative decision No. 4/2017).

B. *Commencement, Suspension, Termination, and End of Enforcement Proceedings*

412. The bailiff proceeds to the execution on the grounds of either the submitted writ of execution or another act which is subject to execution (Article 426(1) CCP). No copy thereof is delivered to the opposing party. It is delivered to the bailiff, whose territorial competence is determined in Article 427 CCP.

According to Article 428(1) CCP the bailiff is obligated to invite the debtor to voluntary execution within a two-week term. This also applies in the cases where an entered into force judgment is being executed.[184] When undertaking enforcement on the grounds of an enforcement order the bailiff invites the debtor to voluntary execution. All distraints and attachments are pointed in the invitation enclosing a copy of the enforcement act. There is ban on enforcement actions during the term for voluntary execution. According to Articles 449(2) and 450(2) CCP they may be imposed simultaneously with the servicing of the invitation to voluntary execution. This also applies to taking inventory of the item.

413. According to 432 CCP provides that the enforcement proceedings are suspended: by the court, in the cases referred to in Article 245(1) and (2), Articles 309(1), 397(1), item 3 CCP and Article 438 and 524 CCP; upon the request of the claimant; in the cases under Article 229(1), items 2 and 3 CCP with the exception of the sale of immovable property in those cases where an announcement thereof has already been made; in the cases under Article 282(2) CCP when the appealed intermediate appellative decision is reversed by the SCC; in the cases under Article

184. In case of enforcement on the basis of an enforcement order, the bailiff invites the debtor with its service, and when it has been served to him, a new term for its voluntary enforcement is not given.

624(4) CCP; in the cases under Article 627b(2) CCP; in other cases provided for in law (Article 420 CCP, Article 454(1) CCP, Article 502(1) CCP, Article 462(2) CCP, Article 464 CCP, Article 462(2) CCP, Article 638(1) CC).

414. According to Article 433(1) CCP provides that the enforcement proceedings are suspended in the following cases: when the debtor submits a receipt either from the claimant, the said receipt being duly certified and showing that the amount under the writ of execution has been paid off, or from the post office, or from the bank showing that the amount under the writ of execution has been paid off in favour of the claimant prior to the instituting of the enforcement proceedings; when the claimant has requested in writing that the enforcement proceedings be suspended; when the writ of execution is invalidated; when the act on the grounds of which the writ of execution is issued is either revoked or acknowledged as being forged; when the property cited by the execution creditor cannot be sold and other seizable property cannot be discovered; when the fees and costs related to the enforcement, due in advance, have not been paid; when an effective decision is presented, the said decision upholding the claim under Articles 439 and 240 CCP; Article 424 CCP; Article 124(1) CCP or Article 440 CCP; when, within a period of two years, the claimant does not demand that executive actions be carried out, with the exception of proceedings regarding financial support.

The bailiff issues a writ for ending of the enforcement proceedings when they have achieved enforcement of the obligations and collection of the fees for execution (Article 433(2) CCP).

The bailiff lifts the imposed distraints and attachments when the decree for the termination of enforcement proceedings comes into force. The termination of proceedings neither affects the rights acquired by third persons prior to that time on the grounds of executive actions, nor does it affect the regularity of the payment made by the third party-debtor to the bailiff (Article 433(4) CCP).

C. *Proceedings for Execution of Pecuniary Pretentions*[185]

1. Grounds for Execution

415. The CCP provides different means for execution of pecuniary receivables depending on whether the object of execution is movable, immovable property, receivables of the debtor, and namely: a) execution upon movable property (Articles 465–482 CCP); b) execution upon immovable property (Articles 483–500 CCP); c) execution upon a debtor's receivable (Articles 507–514); d) execution upon securities of the debtor (Articles 515–516 CCP); e) execution upon a share of the debtor in a commercial company (Article 517 CCP); f) execution upon a separate part of an enterprise (Article 518a CCP); g) execution upon objects of industrial property

185. The enforcement of monetary claims against the State and State institutions is not admissible (Art. 519(1) CCP; Art. 39(5) State budget structure act). Monetary receivables against State institutions are paid from the funds provided for this purpose in their budget. For this purpose, the writ of execution shall be presented to the financial authority of the institution concerned.

(Article 518a CCP). The law provides deviations from the general order for execution upon movable or immovable property regarding execution upon matrimonial tenancy (Articles 502–506 CCP). In Chapter 43, Articles 501a–501g CCP a new manner for execution was created – electronic public auctions. The ordinances for its implementations have not been issued yet.

416. Article 442a CCP provides that the security measures imposed by the bailiff and the enforcement methods undertaken must be proportionate to the amount of the obligation, taking into consideration all data and circumstances in the case, the procedural behaviour of the debtor and the possibility of the receivable remaining unsettled. In Article 441(2) CCP the imposed injunctions which are manifestly disproportionate to the amount of the obligation under the enforcement case are deemed as unlawful execution.

2. Sequestrability and Non-sequestrability

417. According to Article 442 CCP the claimant can direct the execution over every proprietary right of the debtor, unless due to the nature of the right, for instance the proprietary right to use (Article 56 PA, State ownership and municipal ownership) or due to an explicit legal provision it is non-sequestrable.

Articles 444–446 CCP regulate the non-sequestrability of belongings and receivables of the debtor – physical person. The non-sequestrability of the housing accommodation of the debtor – physical person is specific to Bulgarian law (Article 444, item 7 CCP), in those cases where neither he/she, nor any of the members of his/her family with whom he/she lives has another housing accommodation.[186] This non-sequestrability does not apply with respect to financial support obligations; claims for damages and financial statements. The labour remuneration or any other remuneration for work done, or upon pension, the amount of the said remuneration or pension not exceeding the minimum monthly labour remuneration are non-sequestrable. This non-sequestrability does not apply with respect to obligations for financial support.

Execution upon the bank accounts of the municipalities and other budget-subsidized establishments, received as a subsidy, transfer or temporary interest-free loan from the State budget, including through the municipal budgets or through other budgets, shall not be allowed; EU funds and other international programmes and contracts of municipalities and related national co-financing, as well as on the funds from advance financing, when provided at the expense of the State budget, including through accounts for EU funds (Article 520(2) and (3) CCP), is not permitted.

186. Up to the amounts determined in the Ordinance by the Council of ministers on housing needs and the members of his family.

3. Joinder of Claimants and Distribution of Collected Amounts

418. The joinder of claimants is specific to the enforcement proceedings. The attachment and distraint do not render the claimant (creditor) privileged.

At any time in the course of execution, until carrying out the distribution, other creditors of the same debtor are entitled to join the proceedings (Article 456(1) CCP). The claimant attaches his/her writ of execution or certificate issued by the bailiff to a written application, this certificate evidencing that the writ of execution has been used in other enforcement proceedings (Article 456(2) CCP).

Article 458 CCP and Article 191(3) TSPC provides that the State is always regarded as a joint claimant of the public and other receivables due to it by the debtor, the amount of the said receivables having been communicated to the bailiff prior to the distribution. He/she sends a notification to the National Revenue Agency (NRA) regarding each execution he/she has started, as well as regarding each distribution. In a term of no later than fourteen days following the said notification the NRA issues a certificate containing information on the amount of debtor's public receivables, the eventual measures imposed on his/her property for securing the said receivables, as well as on the property against which compulsory executions have commenced.[187] Thirty days after the notification under Article 191(2) TSPC, the bailiff can continue the enforcement proceedings (Article 191(4) TSPC).

According to Article 459(1) and (2) CCP, the creditor in whose favour a security has been admitted by way of imposing a distraint or attachment is regarded as a joint claimant in those cases where the execution is directed upon the object of security.

419. The claimant who has joined the enforcement proceedings becomes a party thereto. He/she has the same rights in the enforcement proceedings as the initial claimant (Article 457(1) CCP) and also benefits from those executive actions which have been carried out prior to the joinder (Article 457(2) CCP).

However, the communications and the subpoenas are sent only to the initial claimant (Article 457(3) CCP). According to Article 457 CCP, if a third person brings in a claim against the enforcement actions, then the initial claimant is subpoenaed as a party to the proceedings. The joint claimants are entitled to intervene in the proceedings as formal joint parties. The court decision is effective to them as well, although they have not intervened in the proceedings.

420. According to Article 460 CCP, in those cases where the amount collected under the enforcement proceedings is insufficient for satisfying all claimants, the bailiff carries out a redistribution pursuant to the order of Article 136 OCA.

According to Article 462(1) CCP, the bailiff should inform the debtor and the claimants about the distribution, summoning them on a day he/she has specified. If

187. Property on which measures for securing public receivables have been imposed before the initiation of enforcement proceedings under the Civil Procedure Code or against which enforcement has been initiated for collection of public receivables shall be realized by the public executor under the terms and conditions of the TSPC.

no complaint is lodged within a term of three days following it, the said distribution is regarded as a final one, and the bailiff delivers the amounts under it to those entitled thereto (Article 462(2) CCP).

In those cases where the distribution is appealed against, the case and the complaint are sent to the district court which regards it following the order of Article 278 (Article 463(1) CCP). The decision of the district court on the distribution is subject to being appealed against. The complaint is considered in accordance with the procedure set forth in Article 274 CCP. The decision of the appellate court is not subject to appeal (Article 463(2) CCP).

421. Article 464(1) CCP provides that where a claimant challenges the existence of another claimant's receivable, he/she has to bring in a claim against the latter and against the debtor. The bringing in of the claim suspends the delivery of the amount attributable to the creditor by virtue of the challenged receivable.

According to Article 464(2) CCP, it is also possible for the claim to be grounded on facts which precede the court trial in the proceedings wherein the act has been issued. When the enforcement grounds are a decision upon recognition of the claim (Article 237 CCP), the rival claimant is entitled to bring in a claim under Article 464(2) CCP grounded on facts which preceded the recognition of the claim. When the enforcement grounds are a decision by default, he/she may bring in a claim under Article 464 CCP being not bound by the restrictions under Article 240(2) CCP. If the enforcement grounds are an enforcement order, he/she, being not bound to the restrictions under Article 240(2) CCP may bring in a claim under Article 464 CCP grounded on facts which by the expiry of the term under Article 414 CCP were known or could have been known to the debtor.

D. Procedures for Execution upon Non-pecuniary Claims

1. Execution of a Pretension for the Delivery of Movable Property

422. If the debtor fails to deliver voluntarily the adjudicated movable property after the bailiff has demanded him/her to do so, he/she is forcibly deprived of the said movable property and the latter is delivered to the claimant (Article 521(1) CCP). The debtor should have been subpoenaed for this executive action. His/her presence is not obligatory. The bailiff is entitled to exercise the rights accorded to him in Article 431(1) CCP. The claimant should be present in order to receive the item of movable property which has been seized from the debtor.

423. According to Article 521(2) CCP, if the item of movable property is not in the possession of the debtor, or has been destroyed, the money equivalent thereof is collected from him/her. The same applies to those cases where only a part of the item of movable property is found. If the money equivalent of the item of movable property is not specified in the writ of execution, it is determined by the bailiff, after the parties have been heard out, and, if necessary, after witnesses and experts have been questioned. The decree for determining the money equivalent is subject to appeal before the district court (Article 521(3) CCP). The complaint does not suspend the collection of the money equivalent, but the court may render suspension. The court considers the complaint in an open session with subpoenaing the claimant and the debtor. The decision is subject to appeal before the appellate court, whose decision is final.

2. Execution of a Right to Claim the Delivery of an Item of Immovable Property (Repossession)

424. The repossession is a method of execution for compulsory satisfaction of all rights to claim the delivery of possession of an item of immovable property (Article 522 CCP). The bailiff schedules a day and time for repossession and notifies the parties. In those cases where the debtor fails to leave the item of immovable property voluntarily, he/she is removed from it forcefully (*see* Article 431 CCP).

425. In principle, in order for the repossession to be carried out, at that time the item of immovable property should be possessed by the debtor. However, Article 523 CCP provides that in those cases where the bailiff finds the adjudicated item of immovable property in the possession of a third person and the said bailiff gets convinced that the said person has assumed possession of the item of immovable property after the institution of the proceedings in which the executed decision was rendered, he/she puts the claimant in possession of the item of immovable property.[188] If the said third person who possesses the property after the institution of the case, the decision executed by the repossession, claims rights upon the adjudicated item of immovable property which exclude the rights of the claimant, the bailiff postpones the livery of seisin and fixes a term of three days within which the third person has to seek suspension of execution from the regional court (Article 523(2) CCP). The application should have enclosed written evidence of his/her claimed right upon the item of immovable property (Article 524 CCP). It is considered in an open court session to which the claimant, the debtor and the third person have been subpoenaed. In those cases where the court finds that the application is a well-grounded one, it suspends the execution and fixes a term of one week, within which the third person is obligated to bring in a claim with the respective court. If the third person fails to bring in a claim within the specified term, the suspension is reversed upon the demand of the claimant.

3. Execution of Liabilities for a Certain Action or Omission

426. Where the debtor fails to perform an action which he/she has been sentenced to perform and which can be performed by another person, the claimant is entitled to request from the bailiff to authorize him/her to carry out the action *at the*

---

188. No repossession may be made against a third party who has acquired possession of the property during the filing of the case on which the enforceable decision has been rendered. If such is done, the person can protect his/her rights by appealing it under Art. 435(5) CCP.

expense of the debtor (Article 526 CCP). He/she is entitled to demand that the court sentences the debtor to pay in advance the amount required for carrying out the action (Article 526(2) CCP).

427. Where it is impossible for the action to be carried out by another person, and the action wholly depends on the will of the debtor, upon the request of the claimant, the bailiff compels the debtor to carry out the action by way of imposing a fine on him determined in Article 527(3) CCP. If, even after that, the debtor fails to carry out the action, the bailiff imposes new consecutive fines on him/her in the same amount.

4. Execution of Liabilities for Delivering a Child

428. Liabilities for delivering a child may arise from different decisions (e.g., in connection with Article 59 FC and Article 322(2) CCP) on exercising the parental rights and personal relationships between parents and children after the divorce.

The claimant is the parent who has been granted to exercise the parental rights, the one whose rights determined by a decision on the measures and personal relationships between parents and children are violated (ID No. 3 from 10 July 2017 on interpretative decision No. 3/2015-GMCC and the Com.C.). The debtor is the person who violates the court decision regarding the granted exercise of the parental rights, the parent who violates the measures personal relationships between parents and children. *The child is neither a debtor in the compulsory execution, nor an object of that execution. The rights of the child should be respected and the CPA should not be violated.*

When undertaking the execution of liabilities for delivering a child, as well as execution of the liabilities for child's successive return the bailiff invites the debtor to comply voluntarily at the assigned place and time (Article 528(1) CCP). Within three days following the service with the invitation the debtor should inform the bailiff whether he/she is ready to deliver the child at the assigned place and time. If he/she thinks that there are obstacles to do so, he/she should point at those obstacles to the due execution of the liability, as well as to point the time and place he/she will be ready to deliver the child (Article 528(2) CCP). In case of non-performance of these obligations, the bailiff imposes fines and if required – requests his/hers mandatory bringing.[189]

If the debtor fails to comply voluntarily, the bailiff, acting with the assistance of the police authorities and the mayor of the municipality, borough or mayoralty, seizes the child compulsorily and delivers the said child to the claimant (Article 528(5) CCP). The enforcement executed by the bailiff may be directed against the executive debtor but not against the child.

189. He/she can request assistance from the 'Social assistance' directorate for removal of the obstacles and undertaking appropriate steps under the ChPA, and if necessary – to request that the police organs undertake the necessary steps under Art. 56 Ministry of Interior Act.

II. Judicial Review

A. *Judicial Review Through Appeal of the Actions and Omissions of the Bailiff*

429. Appealing is a measure of judicial review in the event of procedural illegality of the actions of the bailiff. In the new CCP this form of defence was highly limited. The appealable actions of the bailiff and the legitimized persons are in the limitative list in Article 435 CCP. Article 435 CCP is completed by other norms of the CCP on the distribution (Articles 462(2) and 463 CCP); the appeal of the execution upon an item of property which is matrimonial tenancy by the spouse who is not a debtor (Article 503(2) CCP in connection with Article 502 CCP) the bailiff's decree on determining the money equivalent of an adjudged item of movable property which was not found with the debtor or was damaged (Article 521(2) CCP), the award decree for the immovable property, subject to the public sale.

430. The claimant is entitled to appeal (Article 435(1) CCP): (a) the bailiff's refusal to perform enforcement, the bailiff's refusal to institute enforcement proceedings, inclusive; (b) a decree for suspending the enforcement proceedings; (c) a decree for terminating the compulsory execution.

431. The debtor may appeal (Article 435(2) CCP): (a) the decree for a fine (Articles 527(4) and 528(2) CCP); (b) the schedule[190] of an execution upon property he/she considers non-sequestrable; (c) the confiscation of a movable property or the removal from an immovable property due to the fact that the debtor has not been duly notified of the execution; (d) the refusal of the bailiff to perform a new assessment under Article 468(4) and Article 485 CCP; (e) the appointment of a third person as a guardian, if the requirements of Article 470, as well as in the cases under Article 486(2) CCP; f) any act of the bailiff, which determines the amount of the debtor's obligation for the costs of enforcement (ID No. 3-10.07.2017 under interpretative decision No. 3/2015-GMCC and the Com.C. of the SCC).

432. The award decree in the cases of public sale of an item of movable property is not subject to appeal (Article 474(5) CCP). The intermediate acts – attachment, evaluation, announcement, proclaiming of the buyer are not subject to separate appeal. The legitimized persons to appeal the award decree are: the bidder who has deposited earnest money by the last day of the sale (Article 435(3) CCP), the debtor, the claimant who has participated in the auction as a bidder without owing earnest money.[191]

The grounds for appeal are: if the bidding at the public sale was not done duly (*see* item 8 of ID No. 2 dated 26 June 2015 under interpretative decision No. 2/2013); if the property is assigned to a person who has not submitted the highest bid or to a person who has not paid the price offered by him. If the assignment is

190. *See* ID No. 2-26.06.2015 under inter. dec. No. 2/2013-GMCC and the Com.C. of the SCC.

191. The legislator has not given him/her the possibility of appealing when he/she has not participated in the auction as a bidder, although having an interest in the sale of the item of immovable property, as well as in its selling at as highest possible price.

not appealed, the public sale can be challenged only by way of a claim, and in case of two deficiencies: a) when the property has been assigned to a person who is not entitled to participate in the bidding; and when b) the property has been assigned, although the buyer has not paid the price (Article 496(3) CCP).[192]

433. According to Article 435(4) CCP, the third person is entitled to complain against the actions of the bailiff only where the latter has directed the execution upon items of movable property which are in the possession of the said persons. According to Article 435(4) CCP, the complaint is disallowed if it is found out that the item of movable property was owned by the debtor at the time the distraint or attachment was imposed. Where the term for appealing is omitted the third person can defend himself/ herself via a claim under Article 440 CCP (ID No. 3-10.07.2017 under interpretative decision No. 3/2015-GMCC and the Com.C. of the SCC).

It is possible for the repossession of an item of immovable property to be complained against only by the third person who was in possession thereof prior to the lodging of the claim, this being the claim the decision on which is executed. If the said third person misses the term for lodging the complaint, he/she is entitled to file a possessory claim, but cannot file a claim under Articles 523 and 524 CCP (ID No. 3-10.07.2017 under interpretative decision No. 3/2015-GMCC and the Com.C. of the SCC).[193]

434. The complaint against the bailiff's actions or omissions, respectively, are filed through him/her to *the district court* by the place of execution within a term of seven days following the day on which the action was performed in which the party either was present when the action was performed, or was subpoenaed thereto, in all other cases since the communication of the action (Article 436(1) CCP). As far as the third parties are concerned, the term commences at the time they learned about the action. The term for filing the complaint is a preclusive one. Lodging the complaint does not suspend the actions of execution, however, the court is entitled to order such suspension (Article 438 CCP).

A copy of the complaint is handed to the other party, and where the complaint has been lodged by a third person, copies thereof are handed to the debtor and to the claimant on whose request the enforcement proceedings have been instituted (Article 436(2) CCP). Having received a copy of the complaint, the party is entitled to file written objections within a term of three days following the receipt (Article 436(3) CCP). Once the said term has expired, the bailiff sends the complaint, together with the objections, if available, to the district court, and gives written explanations regarding the respective actions.[194]

---

192. In item 3 of ID No. 4-11.03.2019 under inter. dec. 4/2017-GMCC and the Com.C. of the SCC it was accepted that the invalidity of the public sale under Art. 496(3) CCP can be invoked through an individual assessment claim, as well as through invocation by the claimant and objection by the defendant in other proceedings.
193. Only the person who holds the property after the submission of the claim can protect himself following the order of Arts 523 and 524 CCP if he/she claims his/her rights, which negate the rights of the claimant (*see* para. 425).
194. All documents can be sent to the court in electronic form (Art. 436(3) CCP).

The complaints lodged by the parties are considered in a closed session, with the exception of those cases in which witnesses or experts should be heard out (Article 437(1) CCP). The complaints filed by third persons are considered in an open court session, to which there have been subpoenaed the complainant, the debtor and the claimant upon whose request the enforcement proceedings have been instituted (Article 437(2) CCP).

The court considers the request on the grounds of the data of the enforcement proceedings and the evidence submitted by the parties (Article 437(3) CCP). Its decision is not subject to appeal (Article 437(4) CCP) or revocation (ID No. 7-31 July 2017 under interpretative decision No. 7/2014-GMCC and the Com.C. of the SCC).

B. Judicial Review Through the Claim under Article 441 CCP

435. As a means of indirect judicial control for procedural legality of the enforcement procedure in Article 441 CCP, the legislator regulates the claim for liability for damages caused by the executive magistrate, which are a direct consequence of this illegality. Indirect judicial control is exercised through this claim proceedings. The private bailiff is liable, under the terms established by Article 45 OCA, for any damages inflicted on the debtor as a result of legally non-conforming compulsory execution. The liability for any such damages inflicted by the bailiff is under Article 49 OCA. The matter concerns the liability for any property damages that are directly connected to the procedural unlawful action or inaction of the bailiff and result particularly from the procedural unlawfulness of the said action (inaction). Illegal enforcement is present when the bailiff has imposed security which is clearly disproportionate to the amount of the obligation under the enforcement case (Article 441(2) CCP)

The proceedings under Article 441 CCP follow the general adversary procedure. The claim can be brought in against the private bailiff. The realization of regress responsibility of the State bailiff, it is advisable to implead him/her as a party helping the ministry and the regress claim to be brought in as a negative one (Article 219(1) and (3) CCP).

The bailiff is not liable in a case of substantive law illegality of the enforcement procedure which is a non-executable right. The bailiff obeys the writ of execution. The ascertainment of the existence of an executable right is beyond his/her powers.

The bailiff is liable for the damages caused by substantive law legality, if it results from the culpable bad execution of his/her powers under Article 426(4) CCP in connection with research on the debtor's property status, the execution was carried out upon a chattel or right, which did not belong to the debtor.

436. The liability for property damages is regarded as a substituent of the defence through appeal due to procedural unlawfulness, which is very limited in the new CCP (Article 435; *see* paragraph 433). Therefore, the lawfulness of the actions, inactions, respectively, of the bailiff which are not subject to appeal can be verified only in the adversary proceedings under Article 441 CCP. In the practice of the SCC a notion was established that that this inspection can be performed also when the action or inaction is subject to appeal, or when it has not been appealed and when it has been appealed. In ID No. 7-31 July 2017 under interpretative decision No. 7/2014-GMCC and the Com.C. of the SCC it was accepted that the decision of the district court under Article 435 CCP has no force of res judicata for the legality of the procedural activity of the bailiff, which should be taken into account in disputes in which the same procedural issue is dealt with.[195] Therefore, it is assumed that: Article 297 CCP for respecting the entered into force decisions issued by the order of Article 435 et seq. CCP is not applied in the process under Article 441 CCP; the proof of procedural illegality follows the general rules of burden of proof; if the general meeting has revoked a lawful act or omission of the JI and he has complied with the obligatory act of the general meeting, then he is not guilty and is not responsible.

C. Judicial Review in the Challenge of the Receivable under a Writ of Execution[196]

437. As a rule, the debtor can defend himself/herself against the compulsory execution, when he/she challenges the receivable, i.e., the substantive unlawfulness of the compulsory execution is via a negative ascertainment claim (Article 439(1) CCP).

Article 439(2) CCP provides that the claim can be only on the grounds of facts that occurred after the closure of the court trial in the proceedings under which the grounds for execution have been issued. This rule is valid for the cases when the grounds for execution are an effective court decision, i.e., an ordinary court decision.

When the grounds for execution are a decision by default (Article 238 CCP), no court trial is carried out (*see* paragraphs 201–203 regarding default decision). Article 240(2) CCP which provides that the debtor can challenge the receivable via a claim, where newly discovered circumstances or newly written evidence of material relevance to the case are discovered, which he/she could not have been known or could not procure in due time. The term is three months (Article 240(3) CCP).

On the grounds of Article 439(1) CPP and Article 124(1) CCP the debtor has the legal interest in bringing in a negative ascertainment claim on grounds of newly occurred facts without restrictions of the said term. When a decision with recognition of the claim is the grounds for execution (Article 237(1) CCP) a negative ascertainment claim can be brought in on grounds of newly occurred facts following the recognition of the claim.

195. This understanding could hardly be shared, because it makes the appealed meaningless and allows for the existence of contradictory decisions on the legality of the same action or inaction of the bailiff. But based on Art. 130(1) CSA the cited ID is mandatory for the courts.

196. Through the outlined procedure, indirect control is exercised over the substantive legality of the enforcement process.

438. The filing of a negative ascertainment claim under Article 439; 240(2); Article 124(1) CCP does not automatically lead to the suspension of the enforcement case. The debtor can in the order of the seizure for security process (*see* paragraph 400), to request from the court before which the claim has been filed, to order suspension of the execution (Article 397(1), item 3 CCP). This will ensure the substantive legality of the enforcement process.

D. *Judicial Review in a Claim Defence by Third Persons Affected by Compulsory Execution*

439. Article 440(1) CCP provides that a third person whose rights have been affected by the execution is entitled to bring in a claim for having it ascertained that the item of property upon which the execution for a money receivable is directed does not belong to the debtor. The claim is brought in against the claimant and the debtor (Article 440(2) CCP).

This claim is regulated in the law as a negative ascertainment claim. In ID No. 3-10 July 2017 under interpretative decision No. 3/2015, the GMCC and the Com.C. of the SCC accepted that since in Article 440 CCP, there is no explicit prohibition, the third party may file a positive ascertainment claim to establish that he/she, and not the debtor, is the holder of the right affected by the enforcement. The acceptance of this claim will have the same legal effect as the respect of the claim under Article 440 CCP, as it will be established that the thing on which the execution is directed does not belong to the debtor.

Lodging the claim under Article 424(1) CCP, Article 124(1) CCP, respectively, does not suspend the enforcement. The debtor being a claimant to this claim having presented convincing written evidence or/and due security according to the procedure of security proceedings (Articles 389–397 CCP), can request admittance of a security of his/her claim via suspension of the enforcement (Article 397(1), item 3 CCP).

§2. Recognition and Enforcement of Foreign Judgments

I. Rules Applicable in the Absence of a Treaty

440. Where there is no regulation on the recognition and enforcement of foreign judgments and other acts in EU law (*see* item III), in an international agreement (*see* item II) or in another law (Article 3(1) PILC) the rules of the PILC are applied.

The recognition of a foreign court's decision rendered in a non-Member State is carried out by the body with which the decision is lodged (Article 118(1) PILC).[197] Thus, the possibility of direct recognition of the decision rendered in another State without carrying out exequatur proceedings was established in Bulgarian law. The matter goes about the recognition of the res judicata effect and the constitutive effect

197. The requirements of Art. 117(1) PILC (*see* para. 442) are applicable also in the direct recognition of the decision.

of the court decision. That allowed to equalize the regime of recognizing decisions rendered in the non-Member States with the one under the acting during the adoption of the PILC Regulation No. 44/2001 on decisions rendered in the EC Member States, which may be is not the most appropriate solution. The PILC was adopted during the process of Bulgaria's joining the EU in connection with the harmonization of the Bulgarian law with the European law. Preoccupied with this idea the Bulgarian legislator has adopted norms for the internal law from the EU Regulations, making them applicable regarding the non-Member States of EU.

In cases of a dispute regarding the recognition of the foreign court's decision, or the admission of the enforcement thereof, an ascertainment claim should be brought in before the Sofia City Court (Article 118(2) PILC and Article 119 PILC), carried out a special court procedure, also known in doctrine and practice as 'exequatur proceedings' (*see* paragraph 442).

441. For the recognition of a decision rendered EC Member State also – called in the Bulgarian law admission of the enforcement it is obligatory to carry out exequatur proceedings regulated in Article 119 PILC. A true copy of the decision, authenticated by the rendering court, and a certificate issued by the same court, that the said judgment has taken effect, should be attached to the application. These documents should be certified by the Ministry of Foreign Affairs of the Republic of Bulgaria (Article 119(3) PILC in connection with Article 119(2) PILC).

The decision should meet the requirements specified in Article 117 PILC so that the decision is directly recognized, as well as it being recognized following the procedure of exequatur proceedings and for the admission of its enforcement.

442. The proceedings under Article 118(2) PILC as well as those under Article 119 PILC are special adversary proceedings. However, the issue in litigation thereof is not the substantive law dispute, which is determined through the force of res judicata, but the right of having the judgment recognized, and having its recognition admitted, respectively, the literature defining this right as a procedural right aimed at granting legal effect to the foreign court's judgment that had taken effect, this granting being realized through the judgment of our court.

According to Article 117 PILC, the judgments and acts of foreign courts and those of other bodies are recognized and the enforcement thereof is admissible in those cases where:

(a) the foreign court or body was a competent one according to the provisions of Bulgarian law, with the exception of those cases in which the only grounds for the foreign court's competence in proprietary disputes consisted in the citizenship of the claimant, or in his/her registration in the court's country (Article 117, item 1 PILC).
(b) the action is not within the exclusive jurisdiction of the Bulgarian court. The Bulgarian court shall not recognize the foreign court's judgment if the latter falls within any of the hypotheses of the exclusive jurisdiction of the Bulgarian court (Article 12(1) PILC, Article 13(2) PILC and Article 19 PILC).
(c) the foreign court's judgment has taken effect in accordance with the law of the State in which it was rendered (Article 119(2) PILC).

(d) the defendant has received a copy of the statement of claim, the parties have been duly subpoenaed and there has not been any breach of the basic principles of Bulgarian law related to the parties' remedy (Article 117(2) PILC).
(e) there is no judgment of a Bulgarian court on the action on which the foreign court's judgment was rendered, the judgment of our court having taken effect, and whether there are proceedings pending before a Bulgarian court (Article 117, items 3 and 4 PILC).
(f) the recognition and the admission of the enforcement are not inconsistent with Bulgarian public peace and order (Article 117, item 5 PILC).

443. According to Article 121(1) PILC, when hearing the case, the court does not discuss the merits of the dispute that has been determined by the foreign court. According to Article 120(1) PILC, the court examines ex officio the presence of the conditions set forth in Article 117 PILC. In exequatur proceedings the Bulgarian court is not entitled to determine anew the civil law dispute, which was determined through the foreign court's judgment, the latter having taken effect. Besides, the Bulgarian court is not entitled to examine whether the said judgment is a correct one. It is inadmissible for the defendant to plead defences or make requests for evidence which are precluded by virtue of the force of res judicata of the foreign court's judgment that has taken effect, these being defences and evidence that might bring about determining anew of the civil law dispute. However, the defendant is entitled to plead defences such as the absence of conditions for the recognition of the judgment and admission of the enforcement thereof under Article 117 PILC, and he/she is also entitled to plead defence regarding the extinguishment of the receivable on the grounds of the circumstances that have occurred after the foreign court's judgment took effect (Article 121(2) PILC). Furthermore, if he/she fails to do that, these defences of his are precluded by virtue of the force of res judicata of the foreign court's judgment that has taken effect (arg. under Article 121(3) CCP).

II. International Treaties

444. International treaties that regulate the recognition and enforcement of judgments of foreign courts can be multilateral and bilateral (*see also* paragraphs 26 and 450).

Many multilateral agreements and treaties are applicable in Bulgaria.[198] Special norms were adopted in the Bulgarian legislation in order to facilitate their application.

445. There are special rules regarding the recognition and admission of enforcement of the judgments of foreign courts and other foreign bodies of the Member States in those cases which concern the exercise of parental responsibility, exercise of the parental rights, the parent-child relationship and the resumption of the exercise of parental rights in wrongful transfer of a child on the grounds of the 1980

198. Some of them are concluded by the EC, respectively EU, and are binding on Bulgaria as a Member State. In others, it is a party or has joined, respectively, it has ratified them.

European Convention on the recognition and enforcement of judgments on the exercise of parental rights (the Luxembourg Convention) and the Hague Convention of 1996 on the international protection of children concerning the competence, applicable law recognition and assistance in connection with parental responsibility and the measures for the protection of children.

The special rules easing the application of Luxemburg Convention of 1980 and the Hague Convention of 1996 are in Chapter Three-B ChPA 'Special rules for recognition and admission of judgments of foreign courts and other foreign bodies concerning the parental rights and the measures for the protection of children'.

According to Article 22h ChPA, the request for the recognition and admission of enforcement of the judgments of foreign courts and other foreign bodies in those cases which concern the exercise of parental rights and the resumption of the exercise of parental rights in wrongful transfer of a child on the grounds of the Luxembourg Convention are considered by the Sofia City Court in an open session with the participation of: the Ministry of Justice;[199] the parties to the foreign judgment; the public prosecutor. The Social Assistance Directorate of the municipality by the child's current address gives its opinion in those proceedings which are conducted under Article 22h ChPA. According to Article 15 ChPA (Article 22h(3) ChPA), the court hears out the child. It is either ex officio, or upon a request, that the court is entitled to determine an appropriate temporary measure for the protection of the child and for preventing any further danger to the child or damage to the parties (Article 22h(4) ChPA). According to Article 22h(3) ChPA, the court suspends the proceedings under Article 22g(1) ChPA in those cases where: the judgment has been appealed against; proceedings are pending before a Bulgarian court on the subject matter of the dispute, these proceedings having been commenced prior to the proceedings in the country in which the judgment has been rendered, this being the judgment the recognition and/or admission of enforcement of which is sought; another judgment on the exercise of the parental rights forms the subject matter of proceedings regarding the recognition and/or admission of enforcement of the judgment.

The court decision is subject to appeal before the Sofia appellate court. The Sofia appellate court renders its decision within one. The decision is final (Article 22i(2) ChPA).

Article 22k APC extends the range of the proceedings under Chapter Three of the APC, providing that the procedure set forth in the said chapter also applies to the requests regarding the recognition and the admission of enforcement of a judgment on the exercise of parental rights which has been rendered after the transfer of the child, if the judgment proclaims the transfer a wrongful one (Article 22k(1) ChPA). The recognition and enforcement of the judgment of a foreign country which is a party to the Luxembourg Convention is refused in the cases set forth in Article 8 and Article 9, provided that the prerequisites of Article 10(1) of the Convention are present (Article 22l(2) ChPA). The recognition and enforcement of the judgment is admissible only where and inasmuch as it is enforceable in the country in which it has been rendered (Article 22l(3) ChPA).

199. The Ministry of justice does not participate when the application has seized the court directly (Art. 22h OCA).

446. The 2007 Hague Convention on the International Recovery of Child Support and Other forms of Family Maintenance is applicable to the recognition and enforcement of decisions in cases of such maintenance when it is enacted in a country to which Regulation No. 4/2009 does not apply.

To facilitate the application of this Convention, a new Chapter 60 (SG, no. 42 of 2018). A judgment given in a State Party to the 2007 Hague Convention shall be recognized by the authority before which, on the basis of a transcript of the judgment, a certificate of its entry into force and, if necessary, the documents referred to in Article 25(1), items 'c' – 'e' of the Convention (Article 635 CCP). The interested party may request recognition of a court decision rendered in a State – party to it, following the order of Article 637 CCP by the district court at the permanent address of the debtor, at his usual place of residence or at the place of performance (Article 636 CCP).

An application for enforcement of a judgment given in a State party to the 2007 Hague Convention shall be submitted to the district court at the debtor's permanent address, at his habitual residence or at the place of enforcement. A transcript of the court decision, a document certifying that it is enforceable in the country of origin and, if necessary, the documents referred to in Article 25(1), letters 'c' – 'e' of the Convention. A copy of the application shall not be served on the debtor. The court hears it in closed session. The admission of execution may be refused only on the grounds specified in Article 22, item 'a' of the Convention within the term under Article 23(6) of the Convention. Preliminary execution of the order granting the request is not allowed. With the order, granting the request, the court shall also rule on the requested interim and seizure for security measures. It has been ruled that: the admission order has the meaning of a decision rendered in claims proceedings; subject to appellate appeal before the Sofia appellate court, which decision is subject to cassation appeal before the Supreme Court of Cassation.[200]

447. According to Article 23 Convention on the Protection of Children and Co-operation in Respect of Intercountry Adoption, for which a competent authority of the Contracting State in which it is carried out certifies that it has been carried out in accordance with the Convention shall be recognized by law of the other Contracting States. Recognition of adoption may be refused in a Contracting State only if the adoption is manifestly contrary to its public policy, taking into account the fullest protection of the best interests of the child.

448. According to Article XII Vienna Convention on Civil Responsibility for Nuclear Damage (ratified by the Republic of Bulgaria) the final judgment rendered by a court which has the jurisdiction in compliance to Article XI, is recognized on the territory of any other contracting State except in those cases where: (a) the judgment has been received through a fraud; (b) the party against which the judgment was rendered has not been given sufficient possibility to present its case; or (c) the judgment either contravenes the public laws of the contracting State on the territory of which recognition is sought, or does not comply with the basic norms of justice.

200. According to Art. 280(3) CCP however, the decisions under appellate decisions for claims for maintenance are not subject to cassation appeal.

A final decision recognized after its submission for enforcement in accordance with the formalities required by the law of the contracting party in which enforcement is sought shall be enforceable as if it had been a decision of a court of that contracting party. The substance of the claim on which a judgment has been given is not subject to further judicial review.

449. The 2007 Lugano Convention on Jurisdiction, the Recognition and Enforcement of Judgments in Civil and Commercial Matters, concluded between the European Community and Iceland, Norway, Switzerland and Denmark, has important practical applications. In Bulgaria, the Convention is applied in view of its membership in the EU.

For the same reason, the 2005 Hague Convention on Choice of Court Agreements also applies, as Chapter III of it includes rules on recognition and enforcement of a judgment given by a court of a Contracting State specified in a selection agreement, as well as the grounds for refusing to do so.

450. The Republic of Bulgaria has many bilateral agreements (*see* listed in paragraph 26) for legal aid concluded with other countries, in which the recognition and admission of execution is also regulated of court decisions rendered in the other State. Bilateral legal aid agreements with EU Member States, which were concluded before Bulgaria's accession to the EU, apply only to matters that are not regulated by an EU regulation and under the conditions provided for in the relevant act. Treaties with non-EU countries are applicable to cases in which the relevant international conventions are not applicable, as well as when states are not parties to these conventions or under the terms of the relevant international treaties, when the latter respect international agreements that have already been concluded by the parties to them (*see* paragraph 26).

III. Recognition and Admission of the Enforcement of Judgments of Other EU-Member States

451. In Bulgaria, as an EU Member State, EU Regulations are applicable in civil and commercial matters with a cross-border element within the EU. In connection with them, in 2007 a special part seven 'Special rules on civil proceedings under EU law'[201] was created in the CCP, which has many additions and amendments.

452. Regulation No. 1215/2012 for the recognition and admission of the enforcement of decisions in civil and commercial matters rendered in another Member State:

(1) A judgment given in a Member State shall be recognized in another Member State without any special procedure being required (Article 36(1) Regulation No. 1215/2012, Article 621 CCP). It shall be respected by the body before

201. *See* V. Popova, Aktualni; V. Popova in J. Stalev, A. Mingova, V.Popova, O.Stamboliev, R.Ivanova, *Balgarsko …* , *supra*, pp. 1011–1019.

which it is presented, on the basis of a copy certified by the court that issued it and the accompanying certificate. The interested party may, in accordance with the procedure provided for in Section 3, Subsection 2 of the Regulation, request that a decision be rendered that the items referred to in Article 45 grounds for refusal of recognition (Article 36(2) Regulation No. 1215/2012; Article 36(2) Regulation No. 1215/2012; Article 622(2) CCP; Article 623 CCP; *see also* item 2).

(2) In connection with the rule of Article 39 Regulation No. 1215/2012 in Article 622a(1) CCP, it was accepted that a court decision rendered in another EU Member State is enforceable in Bulgaria without the need to issue a writ of execution.[202] The bailiff proceeds to enforcement at the request of the interested party on the basis of a transcript of the court decision, certified by the court of origin and the certificate issued by this court in accordance with Article 53 Regulation No. 1215/2012 (Article 622a(1) and (2) CCP in conjunction with Article 39 and Article 42 Regulation No. 1215/2012). He hands the debtor a copy of the certificate,[203] inviting him to voluntary performance.

The debtor may, within one month from the service, submit a request for refusal to perform on the basis of Article 45 Regulation No. 1215/2012. It shall be filed at the debtor's permanent address, at its registered office or at the place of enforcement (https://e-justice.europa.eu/content_brussels_i_regulation_recast-350-bg-bg.do?member) and shall be considered immediately (Article 48 Regulation No. 121 5/2012) in a closed court hearing under Article 623 CCP (Article 622b CCP). The provisions of Articles 49, 50 Regulation No. 1215/2012 appeal is made following the order of Article 623(6) CCP.

453. Regulation (EC) No. 2201/2003 as well as Articles 621–623 CCP are applicable to the judgments in matrimonial matters, the matters of parental responsibility and matters of parent-child relationship, rendered in a Member State.

(1) The recognition of the said decisions in another Member State is directly based on a transcript certified by the court that has ruled on it and the accompanying certificate (Article 621(1) CCP in conjunction with Articles 37, 39, 41 42 Regulation No. 2201/2003) without conducting separate, special exequatur proceedings. This does not preclude the legal possibility of the person concerned, in accordance with the procedure provided for in Chapter III, Section II, to apply for the decision to be or not to be recognized (Article 22(2) Regulation No. 2201/2003). For this purpose, the procedure under Article 622 in conjunction with Article 623 CCP (*see* item 2) is established.

(2) The dropping out of the exequatur proceedings when Regulation (EC) No. 2201/2003 is applied does not eliminate the legal possibility of the interested party to apply for recognition or non-recognition of a judgment in accordance

202. Thus, the Bulgarian legislator has practically equated the certificate under Art. 53 Regulation No. 1215/2012 on legal significance with a writ of execution, issued on the basis of a decision of a Bulgarian court (*see* para. 410).

203. And a copy of the decision if it has not been served to the debtor.

with the procedure foreseen in Chapter III, section II of the Regulation (Article 22(2) of Regulation (EC) No. 2201/2003), i.e., the facultative possibility of binding the force of res judicata and/or the constitutive action. The procedure for recognition of the judgment under Article 622 CCP in connection with Article 623 CCP established in Bulgarian law is the same as the one for the application of Regulation (EC) No. 44/2001. The consolidated version of the information relating to the courts and redress procedures in the Republic of Bulgaria (http://ec.europa.eu/ justice_home/judicialatlascivil/html/pdf/vers_consolide_cr2201_bg.pdf).

The enforcement procedure is governed by the law of the Member State of enforcement. The Bulgarian means of enforcement under Article 528 CCP is enforcement of obligation to deliver a child (*see* paragraph 428).

There are special rules for admitting enforcement of the judgments on: rights of access and the return of a child entailed by a judgment given pursuant to Article 11(8) Regulation (EC) No. 2201/2003) in Chapter III, section 4 of Regulation (EC) No. 2201/2003). The exequatur proceedings are not applied to those judgments.[204] They are treated in the Member State of enforcement under the same conditions as if they have been rendered by its national courts.

454. The application for issuance of a writ of execution on the basis of EEC (Regulation No. 805/2004) or on the basis of a decision on European proceedings for claims with small material interest (Regulation No. 861/2007) is filed before the district court at the permanent address of the debtor, at his seat or at the place of execution (Article 624a(1) CCP). The scope of the inspection in this proceeding is determined by Article 20 Regulation No. 805/2004 and Article 21 Regulation No. 1861/2007. The act by which the court rules on the application for issuance of a writ of execution under Article 624a CCP, is called an order. The writ of execution is issued at the same time as it is not expected to enter into force. Thus, the Bulgarian legislator has complied with Article 20(2) Regulation No. 805/2004, and Article 20(2) Regulation No. 861/2007, according to which EEC judgments given in the State of origin and judgments in actions of small interest are enforceable in the State of enforcement under the same conditions as judgments given by its national courts. The appeal of the order,[205] by which the request is granted, does not suspend the execution (Article 624a(3) CCP). The court before which the order has been appealed may suspend or limit the enforcement under the conditions of Article 23 Regulation No. 805/2004, respectively Article 23 Regulation 1861/2007.

455. Regulation (EC) No. 1896/2006 creating a European order for payment procedure[67] is applied in Bulgaria. A European order for payment which has

204. Avoiding the necessity of exequatur proceedings is a facultative possibility and does eliminate the right of the a holder of parental responsibility from seeking recognition and enforcement of a judgment in accordance with the provisions in sections 1 and 2 of Chapter III of Regulation (EC) No. 2201/2003)
205. It is appealed following the order of Art. 623(6) (Art. 624a(2) CCP), which references the order for appeal of decisions.

become enforceable is enforced under the same conditions as an enforceable decision issued by the national courts of the Member State of enforcement (Article 21(1) Regulation (EC) No. 1896/ 2006). Article 22(1) Regulation No. 1896/2006 exhaustively provides the conditions under which, at the request of the debtor, the competent court in the Member State in which enforcement of the EOP issued in another Member State is sought, refuses such enforcement.

Article 627 CCP regulates the issuance of a writ of execution on the basis of an EOP issued by a court of another Member State. The application is submitted to the district court at the permanent address of the debtor, at his seat or at the place of execution (Article 627(1) CCP). Thus, the Bulgarian legislator treats the EOP recognized by the court of origin as enforceable in the same way as the enforcement order issued by the Bulgarian court under the order procedure under Chapter 37 CCP. This legislative permission corresponds to the requirement of Article 22(2) Regulation (EC) No. 1896/2006.

According to Article 627(2) CCP the order for issuing of a writ of execution is appealable according to the procedure established by Article 623(6) CCP (*see* paragraph 410). The appeal against the order for issuing of a writ of execution the debtor may bring in the grounds for the refusal of the execution foreseen in Article 22(1) Regulation (EC) No. 1896/2006 as well as the suspending of the enforcement under Article 23 Regulation (EC) No. 1896/2006. The procedure for appealing the order for issuing of a writ of execution established in Article 627(2) CCP in connection with Article 623(6) CCP, as well as the appeal of the judgment of the Sofia Appellate Court before the SCC is a significant deviation from the rule set in Article 21(1), sentence I of Regulation (EC) No. 1896/2006. It is not necessary the order for issuing of a writ of execution to have taken effect so that to issue a writ of execution pursuant to an EOP.

456. Council Regulation (EC) No. 4/2009 of 18 December 2008 on jurisdiction, applicable law, recognition and enforcement of decisions and cooperation in matters relating to maintenance obligations arising from a family relationship, parentage, marriage or affinity (Article 1(1) Regulation (EC) No. 4/2009).

A. The procedure of Articles 17–22 of Regulation (EC) No. 4/2009 is applicable regarding recognizing the enforcement of decisions rendered in a Member State which is a 2007 Hague Convention Contracting State. Abolition of exequatur is characteristic of the said procedure (Article 17 Regulation (EC) No. 4/2009). According to Article 627b CCP, the issuance of a writ of execution based on a decision rendered in a Member State, which is bound by the Hague Protocol of 2007, is made upon request on the basis of the documents under Article 20 Regulation (EC) No. 4/2009. It is submitted to the district court at the permanent address of the debtor or at the place of execution and is considered under the general rules (Article 406 CCP). No copy is sent to the debtor and he is not able to provide a position on it.

   The order for the issuance of a writ of execution in the hypothesis of Article 627b CCP is governed by the rules valid for appealing the order for the issuance of a writ of execution pursuant to Bulgarian enforcement grounds (*see* paragraph 410).

Refusal of enforcement or enforcement suspension in the sense of Article 21 Regulation (EC) No. 4/2009 is rendered by the district court (Article 627b(2) CCP).

B. The recognition and admission of the enforcement of a decision rendered in a Member State which is a non-contracting State to the 2007 Hague Convention is according to the rules of Chapter II, section 3 of Regulation (EC) No. 4/2009.

These decisions are recognized directly in the other Member States without any special procedure being required (Article 23 of Regulation (EC) No. 4/2009). Any interested party who raises the recognition of a decision as the principal issue in a dispute may, in accordance with the procedures provided for in sections 2 and 3 and in Chapter IV of Regulation (EC) No. 4/2009, apply for a decision that the decision be recognized. The enforcement of decisions on maintenance under Article 1(1) Regulation (EC) No. 4/2009 rendered by the courts of a Member State not bound by the 2007 Hague Protocol is admitted pursuant to Chapter IV, section 2. The procedure for admitting the enforcement of a decision or any other act rendered in a Member State not bound by the 2007 Hague Protocol is specified in Article 627c CCP. The application is submitted to the district court exercising jurisdiction over the permanent address of the debtor[206] or over the place of enforcement. The debtor is not serviced with a copy of the application. The court considers the application in a closed session (Article 627c(1) and (2) CCP).

According to Article 32(1) Regulation (EC) No. 4/2009 the decision on the application for a declaration of enforceability may be appealed against by either party under the rules for adversary proceedings. The appeal proceedings themselves are not regulated by Regulation (EC) No. 4/2009. The Bulgarian legislator has provided that order for admitting the enforcement has the meaning of a decision rendered in adversary proceedings (Article 627c(4) CCP). The order is subject to intermediate appeal before the Sofia Appellate Court under the conditions and the procedure of Article 32 of Regulation (EC) No. 4/2009 (Article 627c(5) CCP). The decision of the Sofia Appellate Court is appealable before the SCC (Article 627c(6) CCP). The scope of the verification performed by the Sofia Appellate Court and the SCC is the same. In Bulgarian law preliminary enforcement of the order with which the application is upheld is inadmissible (Article 627c(3) CCP, and Article 405(4) CCP). According to Article 36(3) Regulation (EC) No. 4/2009 during the time specified for an appeal pursuant to Article 32(5) Regulation (EC) No. 4/2009 against the declaration of enforceability and until any such appeal has been determined, no measures of enforcement may be taken other than protective measures against the property of the party against whom enforcement is sought. That is the term for the intermediate appeal. That means enforcement can be performed during the term for cassation appeal in Article 33 of Regulation (EC) No. 4/2009. Hence under the argument of Article 36(3) Regulation (EC) No. 4/2009 a writ of execution can be issued when there is a decision of the intermediate appellate court. The situation is similar

206. This text is not well coordinated with Art. 27(2) Regulation No. 4/2009, according to which territorial jurisdiction is determined according to the habitual residence of the country against which enforcement is requested or according to the place of enforcement. The usual place of residence is not necessarily related to the registered permanent address.

with the one of sentencing decisions of the intermediate appellate court that have not taken effect (Article 404(1) CCP). In the proceedings for recognizing the enforcement, the applicant can request that security measures are rendered prior to the rendering of the declaration of enforceability (Article 36(1) Regulation (EC) No. 4/2009. Pursuant to Article 36(2) Regulation (EC) No. 4/2009 the declaration of enforceability shall carry with it by operation of law the power to proceed to any security measures. However, the Bulgarian legislator has provided in Article 627c (4) CCP that court should also pronounce on the requested temporary and security measures in the order with which the application is upheld. In this case the direct effect of the regulation should be taken into account.

457. In Bulgaria, Regulation (EC) No. 650/2012 on jurisdiction, applicable law, recognition and enforcement of decisions and acceptance and enforcement of authentic instruments in matters of succession and on the creation of a European Certificate of Succession is applicable. Judgments given in a Member State shall be recognized in the other Member States without any special procedure being required. In the event of a dispute, the interested party, which indicates as a key element of the claim the recognition of a decision, may request declaratory action in accordance with the procedure provided for in Articles 45–58 to recognize the decision (Article 39 Regulation No. 650/2012). The application shall be considered under the order of Article 627e CCP by the district court at the permanent address of the opposing party, at its seat or at the place of execution.

According to Article 627e CCP, the application for admission of the execution of a court decision is submitted to the district court at the permanent address of the debtor, at his seat or at the place of execution. A copy of it is not served on the debtor. The court hears it in a closed session. Preliminary execution of the order, which respects the application, is not allowed.[207] The order on the admission is considered a decision rendered in a claim process and is subject to appellate appeal before the Supreme Administrative Court. The decision of the Supreme Administrative Court is subject to cassation appeal before the SCC.

458. In connection with Council Regulation (EU) 2016/1103 of 24 June 2016 implementing enhanced cooperation in the area of jurisdiction, applicable law and the recognition and enforcement of decisions in matters of matrimonial property regimes and Regulation (EU) 2016/1104 of the Council of 24 June 2016 implementing enhanced cooperation in the area of jurisdiction, applicable law and the recognition and enforcement of decisions in matters of the property consequences of registered partnerships in the Bulgarian CCP has not yet established special rules.

207. The court issues a ruling regarding the requested temporary and seizure for security measures.

Part X. Arbitration

Chapter 1. Arbitrability

459. According to Article 19(1) CCP, according to which the parties to a dispute over ownership are entitled to stipulate[208] that it be determined by an AC, except where the subject matter of the dispute consists in proprietary rights or possession of a real estate, or maintenance, or rights under employment relationships, or it is a dispute in which one of the parties is a consumer under (13), item 1 of AD CPA.[209] The property right must be in the power of its holder, i.e., it should be a subject of concluding a court settlement.

Arbitration is only admissible in private disputes. Arbitration for public disputes (for taxes, duties, contesting an administrative act, etc.) is inadmissible.

Arbitration decisions rendered on disputes that are non-arbitrary are null and void (Article 47(2) ICAA; *see also* paragraph 477).

460. The International Commercial Arbitration Act (ICAA) was made on the grounds of the model Act of UNCITRAL.[210] It applies to international commercial arbitration as well as to the arbitration between parties which have their residence or seat in the Republic of Bulgaria, with the exception of the cases under Articles 1(2); 10; 11(2) ICAA (§3 LFP of ICAA) when AC has a seat in RB.

The AC may have its seat abroad, if one of the parties has its habitual residence, registered office or location of its effective management abroad (Article 19(2) CCP).

208. The AC derives its jurisdiction from the will of the parties. It may be institutional or ad hoc. More well-known in the country are: AC to BCCI; ComAC of the National Legal Foundation (http://www.Tasnuf.org); AC with the Micro-Enterprise Association (http://www.bam-bg.org); AC with the Bulgarian Industrial Association (AC with BIA).

209. Any clause in a contract concluded between a trader and a consumer by which the parties assign to an arbitration court a dispute between them, outside the procedure for alternative dispute resolution of consumer disputes under the CPA, is invalid (Art. 3(4) CPA).

210. The CCP has no subsidiary application in arbitration proceedings.

Chapter 2. Arbitration Agreement and Party Autonomy

461. With the arbitration agreement the parties may assign to an arbitration court to determine property disputes that are arbitrable (*see* paragraph 459). The disputes might arise or have arisen. They are individualized in the arbitration agreement with the legal relationship they have arisen from or on the occasion of which they may arise (According to Article 7(1), sentence I ICAA). The said agreement should explicitly specify the AC to which the parties have assigned to consider and determine the dispute. The invalidity or voidance of the latter does not bring about the invalidity or voidance, respectively, of the arbitration agreement (Article 19(2) ICAA). According to Article 19 (1) ICAA, the AC rules upon its competence even where the latter is challenged because of the non-existence or invalidity of the arbitration agreement.

462. The arbitration agreement should be in writing (Article 7(2), sentence I ICAA). It is in writing in those cases where it is contained in a document signed by the parties, or in exchanged letters, telex messages, telegrams or other means of communication.

According to Article 7(3) ICAA, it is considered that an arbitration agreement is also present where, either in writing or through an application entered in the minutes of the arbitration session, the defendant accepts that the dispute be considered by an arbitration court, or he/she participates in arbitration proceedings by filing a written reply, presenting evidence, lodging a counterclaim or appearing in an arbitration hearing without challenging the competence of the arbitration court.

463. According to Article 24 ICAA the parties may agree on the procedure which AC has to observe in the proceedings.[211] They may agree on the place of arbitration (Article 25 ICAA) and the language or languages to be used in the arbitration proceedings (Article 26 ICAA). By argument of Article 24 ICAA, the parties may enter into evidence clauses. They can rule out the admissibility of testimony, can give binding proof to private documents.

464. The court before which a claim regarding an arbitration agreement has been brought in is obligated to suspend the proceedings if the defendant refers to it in the reply to the statement of claim (Article 8(1) ICAA). Where the court finds that the arbitration agreement refers to non-arbitrable dispute, is void, or is ineffective, or cannot be performed the case is not terminated.

211. When there is no agreement, the arbitral court hears the case in accordance with its rules of procedure. They are not a normative act but, by choosing arbitration, the parties agree the case to be examined in accordance with the procedure laid down in Rules of Procedure of the respective court.

Chapter 3. Composition of Arbitral Tribunal

465. The AC might consist of one or more arbitrators,[212] the number thereof being determined by the parties. In those cases where the parties have not determined the number thereof, the arbitrators should be three in number (Article 11(1) ICAA). The parties are entitled to stipulate the procedure for composition of the arbitral tribunal (Article 12(1) ICAA). Where the procedure has not been agreed on, and the AC consists of three arbitrators, each of the parties appoints one arbitrator, and the two arbitrators appoint the third one (Article 12(2), item 1 ICAA).

Each arbitrator must declare the circumstances which relate to his/her impartiality and independence. According to Article 15(1) ICAA, the parties are entitled to stipulate the procedure for recusation. However, they cannot rule out the application of Article 16 ICAA.[213]

212. Any legally competent citizen of legal age who has not been convicted of a premeditated crime of a general nature, has a university degree, at least eight years of professional experience and has high integrity, can be an Arbitrator (Art. 11(3) ICAA). A person who is not a Bulgarian citizen can also be an arbitrator.

213. If the arbitral tribunal does not uphold the challenge, the party who filed it may, within seven days of its notification, request the Sofia City Court to rule on it. The Sofia City Court hears the appeal under the order of the CCP for appealing of rulings. Its decision is final.

Chapter 4. Interim Measures and Preliminary Awards

466. According to Article 9 ICAA, either before or during the arbitration proceedings, each of the parties to an arbitration agreement is entitled to request of the court that security for the claim or the evidence be provided. Where an arbitration agreement has been concluded between the parties, regardless to whether the claim has already been brought in before the respective AC, or has not been brought in yet, the security proceedings will be judicial ones and the rules set forth in the CCP will apply.

According to Article 21 ICAA, unless the parties have agreed otherwise, upon the request of either of them, the AC is entitled to obligate the other party to introduce appropriate measures for securing the rights of the claimant. Upon admission of the said measures the AC may specify a guarantee that the claimant should submit. The arbitration proceedings allow for the enforcement of security measures which concern only the parties to the case. The AC is not entitled to impose distraint, or attachment, or suspension of compulsory execution.

Chapter 5. Conduct of Arbitral Proceedings

467. According to Article 23 ICAA, arbitration proceedings commence on the day on which the defendant receives the request that the dispute be referred to an arbitration court, unless the parties have agreed otherwise. Most of the rules of arbitration courts provide that arbitration proceedings commence with the filing of a statement of claim with the AC (Article 4(1) Rules of the AC of the BCCI; Article 15(1) Rules of the Commercial AC of the National Foundation of Lawyers (NFL); Article 16(1) Rules of the AC of the Bulgarian Industrial Association (BIA); Article 4(1) Rules of the AC of the ABME).

Most rules explicitly provide that the statement of claim is regarded as being filed on the day on which it is received in the Secretariat of the AC, and if it is sent by post – on the day marked on the stamp of the post office at the place of sending it (Article 4(2) Rules of the AC of the BCCI; Article 15(2) Rules of the Commercial AC of the NFL; Article 16(2) Rules of the AC of the BIA; Article 4(2) Rules of the AC of the ABME).

468. As for the institutional arbitration, the rules thereof set forth the requirements regarding the statement of claim. In the cases of ad hoc arbitration, if the parties have not agreed otherwise, it is Article 27(1) ICAA that applies. According thereto, the statement of claim should specify the name and address of the party, the circumstances on which the claim is grounded and what the claim consists in.

A copy of the statement of claim is sent to the defendant. He/she has to submit a written rejoinder giving his/her opinion about the statement of claim, as well as evidence in support of his/her allegations (Article 27(1) and (3) ICAA; Article 9(1) and (2) Rules of the AC of the BCCI; Article 22(1) Rules of the AC of the Bulgarian Industrial Association (BIA); Article 20(1) Rules of the Commercial AC of the National Foundation of Lawyers – NFL; Article 9 Rules of the AC of BAME). The term for submitting the rejoinder is a preclusive one. However, the failure to submit a rejoinder neither means a recognition of the claim, nor does it constitute an obstacle to having the case considered (Article 34 ICAA; Article 9(5) Rules of the AC of the BCCI; Article 22(4) Rules of the AC of the Bulgarian Industrial Association (BIA); Article 20(5) Rules of the Commercial AC of the National Foundation of Lawyers – NFL, Article 9(6) Rules of the AC of BAME). The preclusions under Article 133 CCP do not apply.

The defendant is entitled to bring in a counterclaim not later than the time of submitting the rejoinder to the statement of claim (Article 28 ICAA; Article 9(4) Rules of the AC of the BCCI; Article 20(4) Rules of the Commercial AC of the National Foundation of Lawyers (NFL); Article 22(3) AC of the Bulgarian Industrial Association – BIA; Article 9(5) Rules of the AC of BAME). This term is a preclusive one. In most rules of the arbitration courts in the country this term is the same as the term for the defence against set-off (Article 22(3) Rules of the AC of the Bulgarian Industrial Association (BIA); Article 20(4) Commercial AC of the NFL[214]). Article 9(4) Rules of the AC of the BCCI explicitly provides that the defence against

214. This provision stipulates that if the corresponding receivable is established by virtue of an award or is not contested by the plaintiff, it may be brought at a later date.

set-off may also be brought in later, i.e., after the expiry of the period for submitting the reply. It is foreseen in Article 9(5) Rules of the AC of BAME that the objection against set-off may also be brought in prior to the conclusion of the arbitration trial. It is beyond doubt that, in order for the counterclaim to be admissible, there should exist an arbitration agreement regarding it. In Article 20(4) Rules of the Commercial AC of the National Foundation of Lawyers – NFL it was accepted that this also applies to the objection for set-off, retention or unfulfilled agreement, if such disputes are within the competence of the AC. This is upheld in the permanent practice of the AC of the BCCI.[215]

469. In the course of arbitration proceedings, each one of the parties is free to change or extend its claim or objection unless the parties have agreed otherwise (Article 29 ICAA). The arbitration court may not admit the change which has been required, if it finds that the said change would bring about considerable difficulties for the other party. In exercising these powers, the AC has to take into account the fact that arbitration proceedings are one-instance proceedings and that the arbitration award will preclude the non-claimed objections and facts which the party has failed to allege in the proceedings, and at the same time the AC will have to make sure that the respective change does not constitute an abuse of the procedural law.

Different from the proceedings on alternation of the claim (Article 214 CCP, paragraphs 265–268) the grounds and the petition can be changed simultaneously in arbitration proceedings. It is not admissible to seek a change causing the lodging of a claim on a legal relationship which is not included in the arbitration agreement.

470. The AC considers the case in a session to which the parties have been summoned (arg. under Article 31(1) ICAA in connection with Article 30 ICAA). However, unlike court sessions (*see* paragraphs 27, 35, 171), arbitration sessions are not public ones.

The rules of some arbitration courts (Article 32a Rules of the Commercial AC of the National Foundation of Lawyers – *see* http://www.Tasnuf.org and Article 18 Rules of the Bulgarian Association of Microenterprises – http://www.bam-bg.org) foresee the possibility the arbitration sessions to be via an internet videoconference, if requested by the parties.

The parties have to be notified in due time of the arbitration session, or the examination of documents, goods and chattels on the part of the AC, the written evidence and opinions, as well as the conclusions of the experts have to be communicated to the parties in due time (Article 31(1) and (3) ICAA). That is necessary for the parties, so that they could prepare for the arbitration session, so that they could protect their rights, as Article 22 ICAA lays down.

In those cases where the parties have been duly notified, the AC holds the session even where a party fails to appear (or both parties fail to appear) in the session (Article 35 ICAA), except where the non-appearance is due to a reasonable excuse.

215. In my opinion, it would be right if those limitations contained in the Rules are abolished (*see* V. Popova, 'Vazrajenieto za prihvashtane s nasreshtno vzemane na otvetnika pri lipsa na arbitrajno sporazumentie', *Sp. Targovsko pravo* ('Defence against Withholding through the Defendant's Counter Receivable in the Absence of an Arbitration Agreement'), No. 3, 2000, pp. 33–37.

Under the argument of Article 24 ICAA, the parties are entitled to conclude agreements on the procedure and evidence (*see* paragraph 463).

The parties are entitled to agree that the case be determined only on the grounds of written evidence and opinions, without the parties being summoned, i.e., without accession being held with the participation thereof (Article 30, sentence I ICAA).

471. According to Article 42 ICAA, the AC terminates the proceedings by way of a ruling in those cases where: the claimant withdraws his/her claim, with the exception of those cases in which the defendant objects thereto and the AC finds that the defendant has a legal interest in having the decision rendered (item 1); the parties have agreed that the proceedings should be terminated (item 2); the AC finds that there exist other obstacles to considering the case on the merits (item 3). Where the parties conclude an arbitration bargain the proceedings are terminated. They are entitled to request the court to reproduce the arbitration reconcilement into the arbitration award under the stipulated conditions (Article 40 ICAA; *see* paragraph 473).

Chapter 6. Arbitral Award

472. Where the number of arbitrators is more than one, the award is rendered by a majority vote, unless the parties have agreed otherwise. An arbitrator who disagrees with the award is obligated to state his/her dissenting opinion. If no majority is reached, the award is rendered by the presiding arbitrator (Article 39 ICAA).

The award should be motivated unless the parties have agreed otherwise, or if the award is rendered on the grounds of an arbitration reconcilement concluded on conditions that have been stipulated (*see* paragraphs 471, 473). Where the arbitration proceedings involve more than one arbitrator, the signatures of the majority of the members of the AC are sufficient provided that the signers have stated the reason for which the third signature is missing (Article 41(2) ICAA).

The award, signed by the arbitrators is sent to the parties (Article 41(3) ICAA). It is regarded as announced upon being delivered to one of the parties. At that time it comes into force and takes effect. Pursuant to Article 404, item '1' CCP the arbitration award is recognized as grounds for execution, along with a court decision which has taken effect.

When IACs are concerned the law chosen by the parties is applied. Where the parties have not specified the governing law, the AC applies the law specified in the conflict norms which are regarded as applicable (Article 38 ICAA). According to Article 41(3) ICAA, in any event the arbitration court applies the terms and conditions of the contract and takes into account the commercial usage. The Bulgarian law is applied to DACs. §3(3) of the TCP ICAA explicitly provides that in the cases of arbitration involving parties which have their residence or seat in the Republic of Bulgaria, the provisions of Article 38(1) and (2) ICAA apply only where the disputed legal relationship has an international element which, pursuant to Bulgarian private international law, brings about the application of a foreign law.

473. The award, when the parties conclude an arbitration agreement is called 'an award under stipulated conditions' (Articles 40, 41 ICAA). The content of the arbitration bargain is reproduced in the disposition thereof. According to Article 40 ICAA that award has the force of an award on the merits of the case.

474. The correction of an obvious factual mistake in the arbitral award and the interpretation of an unclear award are conducted by the AC under the conditions, terms and procedure of Article 43 ICAA with hearing the parties. The AC may not on its own initiative interpret the award.

The AC is entitled to render an additional decision on those pretences on which it has not ruled (Article 44 ICAA). The thirty-day term under Article 44 ICAA regarding the application for an additional decision is a preclusive one. If this term is not observed, this does not bring about the preclusion of the possibility of lodging a new claim with the AC for the pretence on which the AC has not rendered a decision.

Article 45 ICAA provides that the AC may extend the term for rectifying, interpreting or supplementing the arbitration award.

Chapter 7. Recourse Against the Arbitral Award

475. Article 47 ICAA provides that the arbitration award may be reversed by the SCC in those cases where the party seeking the reversal is able to prove any of the following grounds (item 1):

(1) the said party had no legal capacity at the time the arbitration agreement was concluded;
(2) the arbitration agreement has not been concluded in accordance with the law, or is invalid under the law the parties have chosen, in case such a law has not been chosen, in accordance with the ICAA (item 2);
(3) the said party has not been duly notified of either the appointment of an arbitrator or the conduct of the arbitration proceedings, or has been unable to take part in the proceedings for reasons beyond its control (item 4);
(4) the arbitration award determines a dispute which has not been provided for in the arbitration agreement, or contains a ruling on matters which do not belong to the subject matter of the dispute (item 5);
(5) the composition of the AC, or the arbitration procedure is not in compliance with the arbitration agreement of the parties, except where the said agreement is inconsistent with the imperative norms of the ICAA, or the provisions of the ICAA have not been applied, this being valid where there exists no agreement between the parties (item 6).

According to Article 48(1) ICAA the claim for reversing the decision can be lodged within a three-month term upon its receiving by the applicant. Where the arbitration award has any of the defects specified in Article 47 ICAA, the reversal of the award is a means of protection against it. The SCC cannot verify the correctness of an arbitration award.

According to Article 48(2) ICAA, the suspension of execution of an arbitration award as a security measure in the cases of claims under Article 47 ICAA may be admitted only by the SCC upon submission of security at the amount of the interest in the reversal of the arbitration award.

476. According to Article 49 ICAA, where the State court reverses an arbitration award by way of an effective decision on any of the grounds set forth in Article 47(1), items 1 and 2 ICAA, the interested party is entitled to bring in a claim, regarding the dispute, before the competent State court, and where the arbitration award has been reversed on any of the grounds set forth in Article 47(1), items 4, 5 and 6 ICAA, the State court refers the case back to the arbitration court for being reconsidered. Each of the parties is entitled to demand that the case be considered by other arbitrators.

477. With the amendments to the ICAA from 2017 item 3 of Article 47(1) ICAA, in which two grounds for annulment of the arbitral award were established: when the subject matter of the dispute is not subject to arbitration; the arbitral award contradicts the public order of the Republic of Bulgaria, was repealed. In Article 47(2) it is ruled that the arbitral awards rendered on disputes, the subject matter of which is not subject to arbitration, are null and void (*see* paragraph 459), but nothing is mentioned about the contradiction with the foundations of the legal order, as was in the wording of Article 47(2) ICAA before its repeal in 2001.[216] In the motives of the bill for the repeal of Article 47(1), item 3 ICAA, the addition of the new (2) and the amendment of Article 19(1) CCP (*see* Chapter 1, paragraph 459) was justified by the need to protect consumers and strengthen control over arbitration. There are no motives for the repeal of item 3 regarding the contradiction with the legal order.[217] The elimination of the contradiction with the public interest contradicts Article 4(2) C, which stipulates that the Republic of Bulgaria is a State governed by the rule of law. It is also in contradiction with Article 122 C, because through it the party remains without a legal possibility to defend against such a decision. An arbitral award that contradicts the foundations of the legal order of the Republic of Bulgaria also contradicts the Constitution. It is impossible for such a decision to remain in the legal sphere.[218]

In Article 405(5) CCP, it was ruled that the court refuses to issue a writ of execution on the basis of null and void decisions within the meaning of Article 47(2) ICAA (*see* paragraph 459). The control for this nullity is assigned to the court, before which a writ of execution is issued on the basis of the arbitration decision – the district court, in the area of which is the permanent address or the seat of the debtor (Article 405(3) CCP). Its order is subject to appeal before the appellate court, which ruling is not subject to appeal before the SCC.

On the basis of item 3 of the CD No. 9 of 24 October 2002 under constitutional case No. 15/2002, in which it was accepted that the defence within the arbitration process in its entirety is carried out in two stages: the first stage are the proceedings before the arbitral tribunal; the second stage is optional and represents the protection under Article 47 ICAA, however, in the practice of the SCC (*see* Dec. No. 25 dated 23 March 2021 under comm. case 2318/2020, Com.C, II comm. department; Ruling No. 86 of 17.10.2019, comm. case No. 1579/2018, Comm. C., I comm. department) the understanding was confirmed that: a claim under Article 47(2) ICAA, which seeks to declare the arbitral award null and void; it must be filed within the term under Article 47(1) ICAA; the claims under Article 47(1) and (2) can be connected; when a claim has been filed under Article 47(1) ICAA, the court monitors ex officio the nullity under Article 47(2) ICAA.

---

216. Prior to its repeal in 2001 in Art. 47(2) ICAA it was stipulated that when during the consideration of the case the court finds that the subject of the dispute is not subject to arbitration or that the decision contradicts the public order of the Republic of Bulgaria, it declares the decision null and void on its own initiative. In addition, it was provided that a claim for annulment of an arbitration award that had entered into force on the grounds under Art. 47(2) may also be filed after the expiration of the term under (1).
217. The repeal of item 3 in this part is in complete discrepancy with the UNCITRAL model law, on the basis of which the ICAA was created and has been followed until now. It is also inconsistent with Art. V, 2, item 'B' of the New York Convention on the Recognition and Enforcement of Foreign Arbitral Awards.
218. There is still no constitutional case formed.

Chapter 8. Recognition and Enforcement of Awards

478. The sentencing arbitral awards and the arbitration agreements concluded before the arbitral tribunals shall have executive force and shall be subject to enforcement (Article 404, item 1 and item 3 CCP).

The district court, in the area of which is the permanent address or the seat of the debtor, issues at the request of the interested party a writ of execution on the basis of the entered into force arbitration decision of a Bulgarian arbitration. The arbitral award and the proof that it has been served to the debtor for execution is attached to the application (Article 405(5) CCP, Article 51(1) ICAA). The court refuses to issue a writ of execution on the basis of null and void decisions within the meaning of Article 47(2) ICAA (*see* paragraph 477).

The international agreements concluded by the Republic of Bulgaria shall apply to the recognition and enforcement of a foreign arbitral award (Article 51(2) ICAA). Bulgaria is a party to the New York Convention on the Recognition and Enforcement of Arbitral Awards. Claims for recognition and admission of the execution of the awards of the foreign arbitral tribunals and of the agreements concluded before them in arbitration cases, unless otherwise provided in an international agreement to which Bulgaria is a party, shall be brought before the Sofia City Court and Articles 118–122 PILC, with the exception of the right of the debtor to file an objection for lapse of the receivable (Article 51(3) ICAA). On the basis of the entered into force decision at the request of the creditor the court for the admission of the execution issues the writ of execution (Article 405(4) CCP in conjunction with Article 51(3) ICAA).

Part XI. Mediation

Chapter 1. Legislation: Definitions

479. The Mediation Act (MA) is the main Bulgarian law that regulates mediation[219] as an alternative dispute resolution tool (ADR). In 2006 and 2011 MA was amended to comply with Directive 2008/52/EC regarding certain aspects of mediation in civil and commercial matters. Bulgarian law transposed in a reasonable manner the Directive framework standards both for cross-border and domestic disputes.

Important law concerning mediation is Regulation No. 2/2007 of the Ministry of Justice for the terms and procedure for approving organizations that train mediators; the requirements for training mediators; on the procedure for subscribing, unsubscribing and deletion of mediators by the Unified Register of Mediators (URM) and on Procedural and Code of conduct of the Mediator (Regulation No. 2/2007 MJ). The Minister of Justice has also approved several secondary statutory acts and keeps a Unified Register of Mediators (URM).

480. Article 2 MA provides a legal definition of the mediation. It is a voluntary, confidential procedure for out-of-court dispute resolution where a third-party mediator assists the parties to reach an agreement. The goal is to reach an agreement without the formalities of the courts, resolving their disputes and keeping a good relationship. Mediation is based on the principles of voluntariness, equal participation of the parties in the procedure and informed consent of the parties. Confidentiality is another principle of mediation (Article 7 MA).

The CCP of 2007 has several provisions that encourage parties to use mediation to resolve their dispute. As per Article 140(3) and Article 374(2) after the case preparation is over the court shall schedule a hearing and instruct the parties for a mediation procedure.

According to Article 78(9) CCP, if the case is finalized by an agreement, half of the State fee that was paid shall be refunded to the claimant. The provision of Article 78(9) CCP is a good financial incentive for the use of mediation.[220]

219. *See* details on the matter in Popova, V. The Mediation in the Bulgarian and European Law, Bulgarian, European and International Civil Process, **Civil Procedure Review**, ISSN 2191-1339, 2018, n. 2 (www.civilprocedurereview.com, as well as the literature and court practice cited therein).

220. In a Resolution of the European Parliament of Sept. 9, 2011 concerning the application in the Member States of the Directive and its effect over mediation and its acceptance by courts, the EU Parliament stressed on the positive effects resulting of the financial incentives for using mediation in

In matrimonial lawsuits (Article 321 CCP), the court shall be obliged in the first hearing to instruct the parties again towards mediation or another way of amicable settlement of the dispute. If the parties achieve consent for starting this kind of procedure, the case must be suspended. Each party may request that the proceedings be resumed within six months. If such a request is not made, the case shall be terminated. Where an agreement is reached and depending on its content, the lawsuit has to be either terminated or transformed into a procedure of divorce upon mutual consent. If the parties do not achieve consent on a procedure of mediation or of another way of amicable settlement of the dispute, hearing of the case shall be continued.

Also, in the special Claim Procedure on Collective Claims the court must instruct the parties to conclude agreement and shall clarify to them the advantages of amicable settlement of the dispute. The court shall also approve the settlement agreement, if it does not contradict to the law and the common moral and if by the included in it measures the damaged interest may be defended in a sufficient degree. The settlement agreement enters into force once the court has approved it (Article 384 CCP).

481. There are specific rules concerning alternative dispute resolution in the CPA. They follow the standards approved with the Directive 2013/11/EC for alternative resolution of consumer disputes. They apply both for transborder and national disputes. Under Article 161m CPA the Consumer Protection Commission (CPrC) informs consumers for their rights and obligation in offering and concluding contracts and the possibilities for out-of-court resolution of consumer disputes including mediation.

According to Article 184 CPA the Chairman of the CPrC shall appoint – by an order, mediators who shall be employees of the commission and shall facilitate the resolution of disputes between consumers and traders. The assistance shall be rendered at the request of a consumer by filing an application with the CPrC and the mediation proceedings shall take place in a settlement, selected among the settlements where the Commission of Consumers Protection has territorial units.

The relevant rules of ChPA (Chapter IX, Section 2) do not infringe those of the MA and apply in compliance with the acts adopted by the EU Commission under Regulations 524/2013 (paragraphs 12d – 12e of the Supplementing Articles CPA).

482. The Public Procurement Act (PPA) (Appendix No. 4 to Article 23(5), item 2 'a') states that the notifications for specific procurement procedures (and *must contain* information about mediation procedures if this is provided for or if it is in accordance with the purpose of the law.

483. Article 94x CRRA regulates the possibility for the disputes under Chapter Eleven 'i' of it, related to the organization for collective management of rights, as well as other disputes for the application of this law, to be resolved through mediation. According to 94y a mediator can be only a person who meets the conditions of

---

Bulgarian law as well as on the continuing interest in Bulgarian courts which led to two-thirds of cases referred to mediation being mediated and half of them being settled via mediation.

the MA, is registered in the URM, has special knowledge in the field of copyright and related rights and is entered in the special list of mediators to the Minister of Culture.

484. As per the provision of Article 108, item 5 of the Ordinance of Council of Ministers for Inclusive Education of 2017, kindergartens, schools and the Centre for Support of Personal Development and the regional centre for support of the process for inclusive education, depending on the individual needs of children and pupils provide additional support for personal development in a case of risk – psychologist and/or pedagogic counsellor, social worker and when it is needed – an assistant to the teacher and mediator from the community of the child or the pupil.

Chapter 2. Rights That Can Be Subject to Mediation

485. Disputes that can be mediated are civil, commercial, labour, family, consumer and other disputes between individuals and/or legal entities including transborder disputes (Article 1(1) MA). Those disputes can be both legal and non-legal (Article 1(3) MA). Mediation is not held if the law requires the dispute to be resolve using another type of procedure (Article 3(3) MA).

There are special rules for mediation in family law. Mediation can be used and it is used to avoid the divorce, preserve the marriage (Article 321 CCP) and the good relations between spouses concerning children's interests, exercising parental rights and personal relations between parents and children.

A mediated settlement however is not sufficient to terminate a marriage. If such a settlement is reached the termination of marriage has to be declared by court in a procedure based on mutual consent where the motives for the termination of the marriage are irrelevant (Article 50 FC). The mediation is in practice successfully used to reach such mutual consent as well as the adjacent agreements between spouses. In case of divorce based on mutual consent, the spouses have an obligation to provide an agreement about the place of residence of the children who are below full age, on exercising their parental rights, the personal relations and the children's support, as well as about using the family home, the spouse's alimony and the family name (Article 51(1) FC). The agreement shall be confirmed by the court, after verifying if the children's interests have been protected (Article 51(2) FC). In the case of divorce in a contentious procedure (Article 321(1) CCP) the court has an obligation to refer the parties to mediation at the first court hearing (*see* paragraph 480).

Under Article 123(2) and Article 127 FC, in case there is no consent of the parents on the parental rights and obligations, the place of residence of the child, his/her personal relations and his/her subsistence, they may approach a mediator The parents can ask the regional court to approve their settlement agreement Article 127(1) FC. Matters that can be a subject to mediation are also those concerning travelling of the child abroad and receiving the documents needed for this, which shall be decided in consent by the parents (Article 127a FC and Article 3(1) MA).

Subjects of the mediation could also be disputes concerning: copyrights and related rights (*see* paragraph 483); public procurement (*see* paragraph 482); disputes over collective claims (*see* paragraph 480); consumers disputes (*see* paragraph 482).

Mediation can be used also in non-legal disputes including disputes in schools. They are important for the good relationships in school, among teachers, children and parents (*see* paragraph 484).

Chapter 3. Mediation Agreement

486. The agreement to mediate can be: in a written form, as a clause of a contract (Article 11(4) MA); in the request (submission) for mediation to the mediator or to the relevant Mediation Centre.[221] The date the parties have agreed to start mediating their dispute is the beginning of the mediation; when there is no such agreement the beginning of the mediation is the first mediation session (Article 11(2) MA).

Parties can reach agreement to mediate in a court hearing of their dispute. CCP (*see* paragraph 480) requires the court to inform the parties about the possibility of using mediation and they can agree on this during the court hearing. If such agreement is reached the court shall stop the court procedure.

221. The rules for operation of some mediation centres state that when only one of the parties of the dispute has submitted request for mediation, the centre has one day to send the request to the other party asking to respond providing suitable term (in terms of the particularities of the dispute), whether the party agrees or not to mediate the dispute. If the answer of the counterparty is positive the Mediation Centre starts preparation activities for the mediation.

Chapter 4. Persons/Institutions That Can Act as a Mediator

487. The mediator can only be a legally capable natural person[222] who: has not been convicted of crime; has successfully completed a mediation training; has not been deprived of the right to exercise a profession or an activity; has been registered at the Unified Register of Mediators (URM) to the Minister of Justice.[223] If the person is a foreigner he needs to have permission for permanent or long-term residence in Bulgaria. The latter is not applicable for citizens of EU Member States and the citizens of the states of the European Economic Area and Switzerland.

Persons that exercise functions of adjudication within the Justice System cannot mediate (Article 4 MA).

488. The mediator accepts to mediate the dispute only when he can assure his independence, impartiality and neutrality.[224] He is obliged to fulfil his duties in good faith abiding the law, good moral, procedural and ethical standards of behaviour for mediators (Article 9 MA). During mediation the mediator shall listen to both parties and consider their opinions (Article 10(2) MA). He will not impose his own opinion and decisions on the parties. The mediator is not an attorney of the parties. During mediation parties can consult attorneys or experts; mediators shall inform the parties about this right (Article 12 MA). The mediator shall not give any legal advice to the parties (Article 10(1) MA).[225]

489. Since mediation is confidential the mediator cannot share with one of the parties what the other party has confined to him/her without the consent of that other party (Article 10(4) MA). The mediator shall keep confidential all facts and documents that she has learned about through mediation. The mediator cannot be examined as a witness about facts that parties in mediation have confined to him/her unless the party who has confined the information agrees explicitly for such disclosure (Article 7 MA). Article 166(1) CCP).

490. The mediator is not liable if parties do not reach an agreement; as well as when they reach an agreement but one or both parties does not fulfil it (Article 10(5)–(6) MA). The mediators shall, however, inform the parties that they can request a court to approve their agreement which will then obtain the quality of an enforceable court settlement.

222. Mediators may cooperate in firms exercising their activities. The firms themselves however cannot be mediators (*see* also para. 491).

223. The URM is public and it is available at the web site of the Ministry of Justice at <mediator.mjs.bg/Users/OrgList.aspx>

224. The mediator signs an affidavit for impartiality and neutrality for each mediation he/she participates in, and gives them to the parties (Art. 13(3) MA).

225. This prohibition raises delicate issues in practice when the parties have approached a legal mediator in order to reach an agreement to resolve an out-of-court dispute between them. In practice, there is an understanding that in connection with the principle of informed consent, he has the right and must inform them how the law addresses these issues, as well as what is accepted in the case law.

Chapter 5. Mediation Procedure

491. Mediation procedure begins on the initiative of the parties to the dispute (Article 11(1) MA). Under Article 21 Regulation No. 2/2007 on commencing mediation both or at least one of the parties of the disputes shall submit request for mediation. The request shall contain: the names of the parties; their addresses, telephone and fax numbers; brief description of the dispute. If the party requests an association of mediators the request is filed with the association. Those associations function as coordinating centres concerning mediation. When only one of the parties has requested mediation, the associations contact the other party and help to acquire his/her consent for mediating the dispute. When both parties agree to mediate, the associations identify a mediator with the proper qualification and experience and offer him/her to the parties.

Article 11(3) MA provides that the court or another competent institution that is requested to resolve the dispute *may propose to the parties to use mediation.* This proposition has to be made by the court to the parties, via guidance and offering mediation while the proceedings are pending. However, the court cannot seize directly a mediator to resolve the dispute. It is only for the parties to decide whether to use in fact a mediator or not. *The duty of the court is imposed in* Articles *140(3), 374(2), 378 CCP which have been adopted by way of transposing* Article *5 of Directive 2008/52/EU.*[226]

The court referring the case to mediation does not himself send the case to the mediator even when parties have consented to use mediation. Approaching a mediator depends exclusively on the will of the parties. While referring the case to mediation, however, the court needs to explain to the parties what the assets of mediation are. When the parties agree in the course of a hearing to mediate their dispute and ask the court to stop the case, the court must do so (Article 15(5) MA and Article 229(1), p. 1 CCP). If none of the parties has asked the court to reopen the case within six months following the date when it was stopped, the court must terminate it.

There are often cases, when parties that have reached a mediated settlement agreement ask the court to reopen the case to approve their settlement agreement as per Article 18 MA. Thus, the parties obtain the effects of an enforceable agreement and at the same time use an informal and less stressful procedure to reach such agreement.

Parties may choose one or more mediators to conduct mediation. They participate in mediation in person or through representatives. The authorization of representatives must be expressed in writing. Attorneys and other professionals can also participate in mediation (Article 12 MA). At the beginning of mediation, the mediator informs the parties about its nature and consequences. Once the mediator is assured that the parties understand the nature of mediation and its consequences she requests parties' written consent to participate in mediation (Article 13(1) MA).

In the course of mediation, the nature of the dispute is clarified, settlement options that may be mutually beneficial are discussed, the frame of a settlement

226. In family cases the court is bound to inform the parties about mediation as a tool to resolve their dispute (Art. 321(1) CCP).

agreement is drafted. In doing so, the mediator can have meetings with each party without infringing their right to equality when participating in the mediation (Article 13(4) and (5) MA). Mediation might take one or two sessions that are scheduled after having parties consent about the time of the sessions (Article 22 Regulation No. 2/2007). The mediator shall create an atmosphere favourable for the parties to open discussions to improve their relations and reach a settlement (Article 215 Regulation No. 2/2007). He must help the parties to reach an agreement and to understand its clauses (Article 26 Regulation No. 2/2007). The mediator cannot provide legal advice and merely assists the parties to achieve a mutually acceptable agreement (Article 27 Ordinance No. 2/2017). The mediator respects the opinion of each of the parties under the dispute and requires respect from them.

The parties have equal opportunities to participate in the mediation procedure. In it, all issues are settled by mutual consent of the parties (Article 6(2) MA). The discussions on the dispute shall be confidential. The participants in the procedure are obliged to keep secret all the circumstances, facts and documents that have become known to them in the course of the procedure (*see* item 4, item 3). An exception to its confidential nature is allowed (Article 7(3) MA) only in the cases when: this is necessary for reasons for the needs of the criminal process or related to the protection of public order; the protection of the interests of children must be ensured or the physical or mental integrity of a person is prevented from being infringed, or the disclosure of the content of the agreement[227] reached as a result of mediation is necessary for the implementation and enforcement of the same agreement.

492. While mediation is pending the statute of limitations does not apply (Article 11a MA).

493. Mediation can be stopped: upon mutual agreement of the parties, death of the mediator or on the request of one of the parties and in cases described in Article 10(3) MA. If mediation is made during pending case the parties shall inform the competent authority if they have stopped the mediation procedure (Article 14 MA).

Mediation is completed when the parties reach a settlement. The mediation can be terminated: on mutual consent of the parties; when one of the parties is not willing to participate further in the mediation; when one of the parties passes away; when the legal entity party to mediation is terminated; six months upon the start of the mediation procedure. When mediation is terminated the pending cases shall be reopened if it was stopped during the mediation (Article 15 MA).

227. Under this pretext, information from the mediation itself cannot be disclosed.

Chapter 6. Settlement Agreement

494. The content and the form of the settlement agreement, through which the parties settle their dispute, reached as a result of mediation are determined by the parties. The parties may agree on liability rules in case of breach of the agreement. The form of the agreement may be oral, written, or written with notarial verification of the signatures. The written agreement shall contain the elements required under MA, Article 16. A valid settlement agreement has the legal effects of a contract and is binding only on the parties of the dispute, but not to third parties. An agreement is invalid when it violates the law or the good morals or is circumventing them (Article 17 MA).

With their agreement, the parties mutually undertake to consider that the legal relationship between them is such as agreed in the agreement. It also contains the obligation of the parties to follow it and execute it.

495. The mediation settlement agreement is neither enforceable like a judgment nor as a case settlement approved by the court. If the mediation settlement agreement is in writing and the signatures of the parties have notary verification, the non-defaulting party to the agreement can ask the court to issue an order for immediate performance along with a writ of execution concerning the obligations of the defaulting party to pay certain amount of money or to submit movables (Article 417, item 3 CCP) (*see* paragraph 498). The suspension of the enforcement proceedings can be done following the order and conditions of Article 420 CCP, as well as pursuant to Article 415(2) in connection with Article 415(1), item 2 CCP (*see* paragraphs 392--393).[228]

496. The mediation settlement agreement *on a legal dispute* in a written form with mandatory elements as per Article 16 (1) could be approved by a district court (Article 18 MA).[229] The court shall approve the agreement when it is not against the law and good morals and the parties have confirmed it.

The settlement agreement approved by the court has the force of a court settlement. As per Article 18(1) MA in relation to Article 234 CCP, the agreement approved by the court has the status of an event eligible for judicial enforcement and a writ of execution can be issued on the basis of it (Article 404, item 1 CCP) and enforcement may be carried out. As per the court practice, the content of the agreement approved by the court is reproduced in the act for its approval.

497. Under Article 18(1) MA regional courts are competent to approve mediation settlement agreements. This is so only when the mediation settlement agreement is reached when there is no case filed. In such cases the procedure is under the

228. For challenging the agreement in these circumstances *see* para. 498.

229. If the agreement is reached on a class action case the court needs to make sure that through the agreement the class interest is sufficiently well defended. When the parties reach an agreement in a divorce case the court approves it through a judgment after it has made sure that the interests of the children are well preserved. The court approval of the settlement is a prerequisite to permit a divorce by mutual consent (Art. 51(2) FC; Art. 330(3) CCP).

rules for protective procedures. Approving the mediation settlement agreement is a prerequisite for the res judicata of the mediation settlement procedure.

When the mediation settlement agreement is reach during a pending case the court that adjudicates the case must approve it – and this is to be done by the first instance, respectively second-instance court as the case may be.[230]

When the mediation settlement agreement is reached on a pending case (as per Article 234 CCP in connection with Article 18, item 1 MA) the court has to issue an order to approve the agreement where they reproduce the contents of the agreement and are terminating the case.

230. There is no obstacle for an agreement to be reached also during cassation proceedings, which is approved by the SCC.

Chapter 7. Setting Aside a Settlement Agreement

498. MA and CCP do not have rules regulating a procedure for appealing against a mediation settlement agreement. The mediation settlement agreement is equivalent to an out-of-court settlement agreement under Article 365 OCA. Bulgarian legislator has not affixed any additional power to the mediation settlement agreement. Thus, there is a possibility for a party to the mediated settlement agreement to bring an action before a court to declare the agreement void (under Article 26 OCA) or voidable (under Article 27 OCA). Any non-defaulting party to the agreement may terminate the agreement in case of a breach by the other party. These conclusions apply beyond any doubt when the parties have not asked the district court to approve the mediation settlement agreement (*see* paragraph 496).

If the mediation settlement agreement is in writing with notary verification of the signatures and on its basis the court has issued an order for immediate performance in favour of the creditor (*see* paragraph 387), the debtor may file an objection under Article 414 CCP and thus to avert the mediated settlement agreement.[231] If the creditor brings an action for declaratory judgment (Articles 422 and 415 (1), items 1, 2 and 3 CCP)[232] in his/her written answer the debtor may assert objection for invalidity, voidability or the termination of the mediation settlement agreement. If the debtor does not raise such objections the court shall evaluate the mediation valid settlement agreement as non-contested evidence and should respect its substantive legal effects.

499. The cornerstone in the options for challenging a mediation settlement agreement approved by court, is the rule in Article 18 MA whereby it is declared to have the effects of a court approved settlement. The doctrine and case law accept that the act for approval of the court settlement has the characteristic of one issued in a protective (rather than contentious) proceedings. Therefore, it cannot be appealed against (Article 537(1) CCP), but may be challenged by third parties if it violates their rights (Article 537(2) CCP), as well as by the prosecutor if it violates the law (Article 537(3) CCP). It is further settled that if the court approved settlement agreement is void or voidable, a party to it may ask the court for a declaratory judgment to declare the agreement void or voidable. If a party does not fulfil its duty under the agreement the non-defaulting party may terminate it as a contract. Along with declaring the agreement void or voidable the unlawfulness of the court order for approving the settlement agreement has to be declared. The same is accepted with respect to the settlement agreement following a mediation that was approved by court.

It seems to me that such treatment of the mediation settlement agreement when approved by a regional court is incompatible with Article 234(3) CCP and Article 18 MA, as well as with its approval by the court when the parties have confirmed it before it. This is so because under Article 234(3) CCP the court settlement

231. If the debtor does not file any objection the order would enter into force and he/she can only hypothetically bring an action under Art. 424(2) CCP. To be admissible the claim of the plaintiff must be based on newly founded facts (ID No. 4-2014-GMCC and the Com.C. of the SCC).

232. The same shall apply when the order is handed to the debtor in accordance with Art. 47(5) CCP.

approved by the court is equal to a judgment entered into force. It also does not correspond to the nature of mediation as an alternative to the court procedures for resolving disputes and the need of the need for stability and final resolution. Fortunately, following my research I was not able to find a case where the validity of a mediation settlement agreement was raised before a court. This demonstrates that mediations have been successful in resolving disputes voluntarily and preserving good relations between parties.

Chapter 8. International Mediation

§1. Cross-Border Mediation in the EU

500. Since Bulgaria is an EU Member State Directive 2008/52/EU on certain aspects of mediation in civil and commercial matters is applicable for it. The Directive is applicable (Article 1, item 2) to *cross-border disputes* (Article 2 Directive 2008/52) *on civil and commercial matters*, with an exception for rights and obligations that the parties cannot freely dispose of under the applicable law. The Directive has been successfully transposed into MA which is applicable both for local and cross-border disputes (Article 3(1) MA in relation with Article 2 Directive 2008/52). If mediation has been made in another Member State but after these court procedures are initiated in Bulgaria under, the rules of Regulation EC 1215/2012 concerning confidentiality and stop on limitations periods will be applicable to mediation. The same applies if there has been a mediation effected in Bulgaria and then, court procedures or arbitration in another Member State have commenced.

501. Directive 2013/11/EC for alternative resolution of consumer disputes amending Regulation (EU) No. 2006/2004 and Directive 2009/22/EU is applicable to Bulgaria and is transposed into the Bulgarian law. The existence of ADR possibilities before the CPC's general and sectorial committees does not exclude the possibility of resolving disputes through mediation under Article 184 CPA, as well as under the general rules of the MA.

502. In Bulgaria the Regulation No. 805/2004 for creating a European Enforcement Order (EEO) for uncontested claims is applicable. Under Article 24 a settlement concerning a claim within the meaning of Article 4(2) *which has been approved by a court* or concluded before a court in the course of proceedings and is *enforceable in the Member State by origin* shall, upon application to *the court that approved it* or before which it was concluded, be certified as an EEO using the standard form in Annex II. *A settlement which has been certified as an EEO in the Member State of origin shall be recognized and enforced in the other without the need for a declaration of enforceability and without any possibility* of opposing its recognition (Article 5).

On the basis of Article 24 and Article 3, item (a) Regulation No. 805/2004 and in relation with Article 18 MA, Article 134, Article 404 and Article 619 (1) CCP the Bulgarian court, which has approved the settlement agreement can issue a certificate for EEO in the form in Appendix II of Regulation No. 805/2004.[233]

An EEO concerning a mediation settlement agreement that has been approved in another Member State will be enforced in Bulgaria under the same conditions as a judgment of a Bulgarian court (Articles. 24 and 20(2) of Regulation No. 805/2004).

233. A mediation settlement agreement not approved by a court is not enforceable in Bulgaria. It is furthermore not public, authentic instrument under Art. 4(1), 3(d), and Art. 25 Regulation 805/2004, and a court will not issue a certificate for EEO for it.

The request to the court for issuing a writ of execution based on EEO[234] for uncontested claim certified in another Member State shall be filed with the district court where is: the permanent address of the debtor; his/her seat; or where the enforcement will take place (Article 624(1) CCO).

The writ is issued along with the order and there is no waiting period for it to enter into force (arg. from Articles. 624a(3), 404, item 2 CCP; compare with Article 407(2) CCP). *The order is appealable but, if an appeal is filed it does not stay the enforcement* (Article 624a(3) CCP).[235]

If the law of the Member State of origin recognizes the written mediation settlement agreement as an authentic instrument under Articles 25(1), Article 4(3), and Article 3(f) of Regulation No. 805/2004 and the competent court in that Member State of origin has certified an EEO under the form in Appendix III of Regulation No. 805/2004, the Bulgarian court can issue a writ of execution and the written mediation settlement agreement may be enforced in Bulgaria.

503. Regulation No. 1215/2012 is also applicable in Bulgaria. It applies to civil and commercial matters except those mentioned in Article 1(2) Regulation No. 1215/2012. The mediation settlement agreement reached in Bulgaria is not by itself enforceable. Therefore, it is not an authentic instrument under Article 2(b) Regulation No. 1215/2012. If under the law of another Member Sate (of origin) the mediation settlement agreement entered into there is an authentic instrument under Article 2(b) Regulation No. 1215/2012 and is certified under Article 53 Regulation No. 1215/2012, it will be enforceable in Bulgaria.

Under Article 2(b) and Article 59 Regulation No. 1215/2012 in relation with Article 18 MA and Article 404, item 1 CCP, the Bulgarian court which has approved the agreement concluded through mediation, is competent to issue the certificate under Article 53 Regulation 1215/2012. On the basis of Article 59 in relation with Article 39 Regulation 1215/2012, the certified mediation settlement agreement approved by the court is enforceable in the other Member States *without declaration of enforceability being required.*

If a mediation settlement agreement has been concluded in another Member State and it has been approved by a court of origin and is certified under Article 53 Regulation No. 1215/2012 the agreement will be enforceable in Bulgaria based on Articles 59 and 39 of Regulation No. 1215/2012 without declaration of enforceability being required. *Under* Article *622a CCP, a writ of execution is not needed for the enforceability of judgments rendered in another Member State.* The party may request directly the competent bailiff, who based on Article 427 CCP in relation with Article 622a CCP can enforce the authentic instrument submitting a copy of it and the certificate.

504. Regulation No. 2201/2003 concerning jurisdiction and the recognition and enforcement of judgments in matrimonial matters and the matters of parental

234. That is also required for the enforcement of a Bulgarian court decision.

235. For appealing this, *see* Chapter 2, para. 454.

responsibility, repealing Regulation (EC) No. 1347/2000 is also applicable in Bulgaria. The matters concerning parental responsibilities[236] have particular practical significance, as well as the matters around child's place of living, and personal relations between parents and children. Under Articles. 1 and 3(1) MA and Article 3, item 2 of Directive 2008/52 these disputes may be resolved through mediation in Bulgaria including when the disputes have cross-border character. Voluntary settlements provide the opportunity to agree creatively and in details all parental rights and obligations, as well as parental responsibility.[237] In cross-border disputes it is very important to be decided where the child will live, parents' rights to visits including bringing the child for a certain period to a place outside his/her normal place of living and even outside the country of its normal place of living.

Under Article 46 Regulation No. 2201/2003 the agreements between the parties that are enforceable in the Member State in which they were concluded shall be recognized and declared enforceable under the same conditions as judgments in another Member State. The mediation settlement agreement entered into in Bulgaria is not enforceable by itself. It becomes enforceable only after it has been approved by a district court (Article 18 MA). When the spouses agree to have divorce on mutual consent[238] they shall submit to the court an agreement on the children's place of living, paternal rights, usage of family home, alimony payments to children.[239] This agreement may and very often is concluded through mediation. To be legally binding and enforceable however it needs to be approved by the court. When the parties cannot agree on divorce by mutual consent the court will issue a judgment but the parties still can reach an agreement on the issues stated in Article 51(1) FC. Again, the court needs to approve this agreement (Articles. 51(10) and 49(4) FC).

When the parents do not live together through mediation they can reach an agreement about the child's place of living, exercising parental rights, personal relations with the child[240] and alimony of the child.[241] Once the regional court under whose jurisdiction is the present address of the child approves the agreement (Article 127(1) FC)[242] it becomes enforceable under Article 404, item 1 CCP (Article 127(1) FC and Article 18 MA) and under Article 46 of Regulation No. 2201/2003 may be enforced in another Member State.

If in another Member State a mediation settlement agreement has been reached concerning the issues defined in Article 46 Regulation No. 2201/2003 and it is enforceable in the State of origin without being approved by a court, under Article 46 of Regulation No. 2201/2003 this agreement will be also enforceable in Bulgaria provided that it meets the prerequisites for enforceability of judgments and if it has

236. Regulation 4/2009 is applicable with respect to maintenance.
237. The term 'parental responsibility' has an autonomous meaning under Regulation 2201/2003 in Art. 2(7) in relation to Art. 2(8), (9), (10) and (11).
238. *See* Popova, V. In: Stalev et al. Bulgarian civil procedural law. Sofia 2012, Ciela, pp. 711–716.
239. About alimony *see* note 177.
240. When the change of the place of living in relation to exercising parental rights and personal relations with the child consists in leaving the country the rules under Art. 127a FC will apply.
241. About alimony *see* note 177.
242. This agreement may be concluded within and outside pending proceedings under Art. 127a FC in a dispute between the parents.

been certified under Article 39 of Regulation No. 2201/3003. If the law of the State of origin requires the mediation settlement agreement to be approved by a court in order to be enforceable, for the purposes of its enforcement in Bulgaria the agreement should be approved by the competent court in the State of origin and certified under Article 39 of Regulation No. 2201/2003. For the enforceability of authentic instruments under Regulation No. 2201/2003 a summary procedure for recognition needs to be followed that is regulated by the law of the Member State where the instrument will be enforced (regulated in Article 623 CCP in relation with Article 30(1) Regulation No. 2201/2003) and Article 31 of Regulation No. 2201/2003.

Under Articles 41 and 46 of Regulation No. 2201/2003 an agreement that is enforceable in the State of origin concerning personal relations between a parent and child as described in the autonomous definition in Article 2(10) Regulation No. 2201/2003, including the right the child to be brought to a place different than his/her place of living for a limited period of time, may be enforced in another Member State without going through the recognition procedure if the court in the State of origin has issued a certificate according to Article 41(2) of Regulation No. 2201/2003. Concerning enforcement in the State of enforcement this agreement is equal to judgment granted by a court of the state of enforcement. Based on this certificate a Bulgarian court shall issue a writ of execution in the same way as based on a judgment of a Bulgarian court.

505. Regulation No. 4/2009 on jurisdiction, applicable law, recognition and enforcement of decisions and cooperation in matters relating to maintenance obligations is also applicable in Bulgaria. Court settlements and authentic instruments[243] which are enforceable in the Member State of origin shall be recognized in another Member State following the procedure under Chapter IV of Regulation No. 4/2009 (Article 48 Regulation No. 4/2009) [244] bearing into account whether the Member State of origin is a signatory state to the Hague Protocol. As per the Bulgarian law, the mediation settlement agreement does not have enforcement power and is neither a court settlement nor an authentic document. The written settlement agreement approved by the court has the character of a court settlement (Article 18 MA) including under the meaning of Regulation No. 4/2009 and enforcement power in Bulgaria. The court which has approved it can issue a certificate of enforceability so that it is enforced in another Member State.

Articles 17-22 of Regulation No. 4/2009 are applicable to enforcement of judgments, court settlements and authentic instruments whose origin is from a Member State that is a signatory to the Hague Protocol of 2007. It is characteristic for the latter that the exequatur proceedings are not needed (Article 17 Regulation No. 4/2009). The same rules that apply to the issuance of a writ of execution on the basis of a court decision of the Bulgarian court shall apply to the procedure for issuing the writ of execution and appealing the order for its issuance. The recognition and

243. The European legislator has given an autonomous legal definition of the concepts of court settlement and an authentic (public) document (Art. 2, Regulation 4/2009).

244. Without prejudice to the right of one or the other party to such an agreement or authentic instrument to challenge such instruments before a court of the Member State of origin.

admission of enforcement of court agreements and authentic documents of maintenance issued in a Member State which is not bound by the Hague Protocol of 2007 in another Member State is in accordance with Chapter IV, section II Regulation No. 4/2009 and Article 627c CCP. An abridged exequatur procedure has been established.

506. Regulation No. 650/2012 on jurisdiction, applicable law, recognition and enforcement of decisions and acceptance and enforcement of authentic instruments in matters of succession and on the creation of a European Certificate of Succession is also applicable in Bulgaria. Mediation settlement agreements are not mentioned explicitly in Regulation No. 650/2012. Article 3(1), items (h) and (i) of the Regulation define a 'court settlement' and 'authentic document'.

Under Article 61 Regulation No. 650/2012, Article 46, item 3 (b), Article 18 MA, Article 627f CCP the Bulgarian court that has approved the written settlement agreement shall issue (if requested by the interested party) a European Certificate of Succession. Based on the latter the party may request the court in another Member State to allow its enforcement. For this purpose, a short procedure for exequatur is being performed as per Article 45 and the following of the regulation, which is governed by the national law of the State at the place of execution. The written settlement agreement concluded between the parties in Bulgaria neither has an enforcement power locally and nor has it the nature of an authentic document under the meaning of Article 3(1), item (h) of Regulation No. 650/2012.

Based on Article 61 of Regulation No. 650/2012 when a mediation settlement agreement has been concluded in the Member State of origin that has been approved by a court in the Member State of origin it will be enforceable in Bulgaria, if in the origin State there was a European certificate for origin issued. However, a court in the Member State of enforcement needs to recognize it (Article 45 and the following Regulation No. 650/2012 and Article 627e CCP. Preliminary enforcement of the order granting recognition is not allowed[245] (Article 627e(3) CCP).

§2. International Mediation and Code of International Private Law

507. Concerning mediation settlement agreements that have been concluded not in a Member State, the PILC will apply. Under Article 122 PILC, Articles 117–121 PILC apply also to court settlements when in the State of origin, they have the same force as judgments. Consequently, when the mediation settlement agreement, similar to Article 18 MA, has been approved by a court in the State of origin and in that state it is equal to a court settlement with the force of a judgment, this settlement agreement will be recognized and enforced in Bulgaria as a judgment rendered by a foreign court. A foreign judgment must be recognized by the institution to which it has been presented. If a dispute about the recognition arises it can be resolved through a case for a declaratory judgment filed with Sofia City Court (Article 118 PILC). On the grounds of Articles 119 and 122 PILC the party seeking recognition

245. The court may, however, impose protective or temporary measures upon the request of a party Art. 627e(4) CCP.

has to file a request with Sofia City Court recognition of a mediation settlement agreement; and with that request the party has to submit a copy of the mediation settlement agreement as well as the act of the court of origin approving it; this act shall be certified by the court of origin that it has entered into force as well as that the mediation settlement agreement approved by the court of origin is equal to a court settlement with the power of a judgment and is enforceable in the State of origin. The requesting party shall submit these documents translated into Bulgarian and certified by the Ministry of Foreign Affairs of Bulgaria (Article 119 PILC). This is a classic recognition procedure. In the recognition procedure the Bulgarian court cannot adjudicate de novo the dispute that has been resolved through the settlement agreement. The debtor may raise a defence that he/she has paid the debt. A writ of execution may be issued only after the judgment has entered into force (Article 405(5) CCP).

Selected Bibliography

Mingova, A., *Otkazat ot isk, II izd.* (*Waiver of Claim*, 2nd edition), Sofia: Sofi-R, 2000, cited as: A. Mingova, cited as:*Otkazat.*

Popova, V. 'Principles of Bulgarian Civil Procedure Law'. *Civil Procedure Review* 2, no. 2: 28–73 (May–August, 2011), ISSN 2191-1339, www.civilprocedurereview.com.

Popova V., *Kasacionno obzhalvane i novija GPK (The Cassasion Appeal and the New CCP)*, Ciela. Norms (http://www.ciela.net), cited as: V. Popova, *Kasacionno.*

Popova V., *Njakoi vaprosi po obzhalvaneto na opredelenijata (Some Problems Concerning the Appeal Of rulings, Ciela. Norms* (http://www.ciela.net), cited as: V. Popova, *Njakoi.*

Popova V., *Izmenenie na iska i novija GPK (The Alternation of Claim and the New CCP)*, Ciela. Norms,http://www.ciela.net.

Popova, V., 'Otnosno razreshenieto v TP No. 1/2000 g. na BKC za predyavyavaneto na vazrajenieto za prihvashtane vav vazzivnoto proizvodstvo', sp. Targovsko pravo (*The Decision of the ID No. 1/year 2000 of the SCC on Bringing in the Defence Against Withholding in Intermediate Appellate Proceedings) Commercial Law Journal*, No. 1, 2001, 37–48.

Popova, V., *Prihvashtane. Materialnopravni problemi,* II izd. (*Withholding. Substantial Law Matters,* 2nd edition), Sofia: Feneya Publishing House, 2002, cited as: V. Popova, *Prihvashtane.*

Popova, V., Vazrajenieto kato sredstvo za zashtita na otvetnika v grajdanskiya protses, *Sp. Pravna missal* (*Objection as Defence in Civil Proceedings*), *Judicial Thought Journal*, No. 1, 1994, 56–65, cited as: V. Popova, Vazrajenieto kato sredstvo.

Popova, V., Vazrajenieto za Prihvashtane i Mejdunarodnata Podvedomstvenost, *Sbornik Pravni Izsledvania v Pamet na Prof. Ivan Apostolov* (*Defence against Withholding and International Subservience, Collection of Legal Research Works in Memory of Prof. Ivan Apostolov*), Sofia: 2001, cited as: V. Popova, *Vazrajenieto za prihvashtane.*

Popova, V., *Vazrajenieto za prihvashtane s nasreshtno vzemane na otvetnika pri lipsa na arbitrajno sporazumentie', Sp. Targovsko pravo* (Defence against Withholding through the Defendant's Counter Receivable in the Absence of an Arbitration Agreement), *Commercial Law Journal*), No. 3, 2000, 33–37, cited as: V. Popova, *Vazrajenieto za prihvashtane s nasreshtno vzemane.*

Selected Bibliography

Popova, V., '*Die internationale Zustaendigkeit und die Aufrechnungseinrede im bulgarischen gerichterliche Erkentisverfahren*', *Zeitschrift fuer Zivilprozess International. Jahrbuch des Internationalen Zivilprozess,* 6. Band 2001, 265–275.

Popova, V., *Aktualni problemi na evropejskija grazhdanski protses i chast VII na GPP (Actual Problems of the European Civil Procedure),* Sofia: Publishing House Ciela, 2011, cited as V. Popova, *Aktualni.*

Popova V., *Problemi na zashtiata na otvetnika sreshtu iska i novija GPP (Problems of the Defendant's Defence against the Claim and the New CCP),* Published in: Popova V., *Izbrani sachineija t. III (Selected works, volume III),* Sofia: Publishing House Ciela, 2011, pp. 9–54.

Popova, V. 'Order for Payment Proceedings in Bulgarian Civil Procedure Law'. *Civil Procedure Review* 2, no. 3: 17–97 (Sep–December, 2011), ISSN 2191-1339, www.civilprocedurereview.com.

Stalev, J., A. Mingova, V. Popova, R. Ivanova, *Balgarsko grajdansko protsessualno pravo, VIII izd. (Bulgarian Civil Procedure Law, 8th edition),* Sofia: Ciela, 2004, cited as: J. Stalev, A. Mingova, V. Popova, R. Ivanova, *Balgarsko.*

Index

The numbers here refer to paragraph numbers.

Index

Index

www.ingramcontent.com/pod-product-compliance
Lightning Source LLC
Chambersburg PA
CBHW072243240926
51846CB00012B/152
* 9 7 8 9 4 0 3 5 4 9 2 5 5 *